ANN BELFORD ULANOV

SPIRITUAL ASPECTS OF CLINICAL WORK

we fall into identification with powerful spiritual images and forces (Chapter 12). Clinical work has its own particular ways of addressing and grounding spiritual experience (which subject I take up in Section IV). Spiritual longings turn up in transference; clinical methods of active imagination (from Jung) give first-hand experience of transcendence operating in us as well as addressing us (Chapter 13). The analyst must become conscious of her/his longings for transcendent spiritual contact in countertransference to analysands' material, to the emotional field with the analysand, and to the analyst's own experience of things spiritual (Chapter 14). The dogged complex that entraps us round and round so that we succumb to repetition compulsion only breaks open into creative repetition of ritual when we at last find the deep meaning trying to reach us through the chronic vexing symptom. Here, psychic reality and spiritual fact come close together (Chapter 15). Once again, the question regarding where to put the 'bad' must be taken up, now in terms of how the analyst's own hate impacts clinical work. This focus raises spiritual as well as technical clinical issues (Chapter 16).

After decades working as an analyst, the question must be posed for the analyst: 'Then what?' How does what we glean from depth analysis go on living in us, transforming us? What ways does that work bear on the meaning we find and create in life, our picture of the whole, our version of the spiritual universe? That question comprises the Coda (Chapter 17).

I express warm thanks to those persons who generously gave permission to cite their experiences with psyche and spirit that feed the rest of us.

Ann Belford Ulanov
Woodbury, Connecticut
2004

I. Conversations Between Psyche and Soul

do mind and soul go together and how does the space between them hold hope for recovery and regeneration (Chapters 2, 3, 4)?

Such questions usher us into intimate experiences that comprise Section II. How do we relate to this Other that speaks in and through our psyche (Chapter 5)? Trying to be really married to another person, with all the aggression and sheer fun of that daring, pulls on spirit as much as psyche (Chapter 6). Suffering the fear and distress of physical illness can reveal psyche and spirit reaching for us through the very disease (Chapter 7). The gift of consciousness itself, so precious and yet not ultimate, requires us to fathom pivotal dreams and moments of spiritual clarity, and respond to such questions as: 'To whom, then, do we, with our consciousness, belong? To whom do we give it back?' These questions change our ethics (Chapter 8).

Section III takes up spiritual issues directly, to name what we find the source of spirituality to be, lest, clinically, we become conscripted into dilemmas about money, suicide, sexual acting- out. The spiritual question arises about what we believe the source of transformation in clinical work to be (Chapter 9). More searing questions press in on us when we try to find our place in the universe, such as: 'Where do we situate the negative or the 'bad'? What do we do with violence? What dangers threaten when we consecrate our energies towards non-violence (Chapter 10)? Dreams bring us bulletins from the psyche to our awakening consciousness. The psyche is also the flesh through which God incarnates. Dreams connect us both to our animal root impulse and to the Spirit that wants to step over into our daily concrete life, generating in us a new consciousness and sense of ethical relationship to others (Chapter 11). Yet spiritual inclinations can contribute directly to terrorism, inflating to gigantic acts of violence. The psychic routes to such catastrophe can be charted in terms of how

Introduction

In this twenty-first century, the beginning of a new millennium, we can look back on the twentieth century in which depth work with the psyche, as a distinct discipline, was born. What an extraordinary venture this is – that we can find in the most personal details of our memories, wishes, hopes, problems, even madnesses, recurring patterns of imagery and behavior that bespeak the psyche in us. Like the body we all share, where each of us has her or his own experience of her/his body, different from others yet joined in being roughly the same kind of body, so it is with the psyche. We all deal with the facts of sexuality, aggression, dreams, symbol-making, conscious and unconscious, yet for each of us our experience of this psychic life is uniquely our own. What an astounding discipline this is, whatever our school of psychoanalysis. We have the means to study psyche, and empirically, to document its life in us.

Precisely in clinical work and more astounding still, is the return of keen interest in the life of the soul, or what is generally called "spirituality." We seek to study the spiritual aspects of what we do clinically, to study spirit moving within us. Why should clinicians be asking about spiritual matters at all? And why now?

Section I takes up these questions from different angles, conditioned by the people I am speaking to and what emerges between us. Of particular significance are the different views spirituality and psychotherapy offer regarding dependence, ruthlessness, breakdown and breakthrough (Chapter 1). How

Contents

For Barry

in memoriam

1918 – 2000

ISBN 3-85630-634-X

Copyright © 2004 Daimon Verlag, Einsiedeln

Cover design from a drawing by Barry Ulanov

Spiritual Aspects
of
Clinical Work

Ann Belford Ulanov

DAIMON
VERLAG

Chapter I

Clinical Work and the Transcendent

Clinicians also trained in religion engage in a hybrid profession. Still more complicated is the fact that we represent among ourselves diverse religious traditions and diverse psychoanalytic schools. This puts us in the hot seat. People want to know, how do psychotherapy and spirituality go together, even speak together?

We represent concretely in our lives and work two rivers that once were one, called the cure of souls, and that now at the end of our century and millennium, begin to flow toward each other again, evidenced in this conference on clinical work and the life of the spirit, and in the increasing interest on the part of all schools of psychoanalysis in spirituality.

We must remember that religions are centuries old and their counsels timeless, expressing sighs of our souls too deep for words. In contrast, depth psychology is barely a century old. That it exists at all as a sturdy route to the depth of human action shows its remarkable strengths of insight. Hence we must pause momentarily to reflect on the function of depth psychology for spiritual life as a people of God, as Yahweh's spouse, as Sufi lovers of the divine Absolute called Allah, as beggars Jesus invites to the feast.

The function of depth psychology for spiritual life is to pull us down into matter and into what matters. We need spiritual life in the body of everyday life which is limited, beginning and ending, connected to sex and aggression, hence the importance of Freud and drive theory. Without this instinctive connection, spiritual life wafts upwards into an airy-fairy thing, without tonus, without tissue aliveness, without guts.

We need to include in spirituality our life in relationship and our dependence on each other to repair the deep hurts we inflict on each other, hence the importance of object relations theory and the intersubjective school of depth psychology. Without this relational connection, spiritual life amounts to defensive armour for our isolated, hurting, split-off selves gone into hiding.

We need to include in spirituality self experience in which the All and Vast and Holy get housed, out of which we reach each other in interdependence, hence the importance of self psychology theory. Without this self connection, spirituality becomes a wordy thing, chatter, not tough loving out of selves with deeply forged loyalties to the transcendent.

The All and Vast and Holy live in our world, our social tribes and practices. Hence we need to include in our spirituality the insights of systems theory, genograms, family and group therapy. Otherwise we miss the fabric of the whole and settle for separate scraps, precious as they are, but not woven into what carries us all together. Spiritual life becomes numinous moments but does not change our everyday striving for better patterns of justice.

We need to see that whatever the transcendent is, it *is*, and can speak to us, break in upon us whenever it chooses – in our dreams, our symptoms, our sexual experience, our money, our body. Hence we need Jung's idea of the ego opening onto a bigger, different center he calls the Self, right there inside us, that gives us back pictures of ourselves that confront and correct the daily living of our lives. Otherwise spirituality gets segregated to special times of day or week, to special postures marked off as sacred, forgetting that the sacred, as Ricoeur says, is an ever-present presence, everywhere, a zone of combat.

Spirit aims to set up another locale in our body, in our consciousness, another lens for what matters. It breaks into what we take as customary. It deconstructs the ego down into the endless flow of unconscious processes. Spirit exerts its effects in place of our great foolishness, our unhealing wound, our stable full of muck, but also delivers us into a larval level of life, the slime from which we emerge. Spirit puts us back into the bath, in alchemical terms, into a psychic space where we dissolve the fictions of our ego, both individually and collectively, to impose frames of meaning on life situations as if these were the ultimate frames of reference. Spirit makes us see this other unconscious level of living going on all the time, building up and tearing down so that nothing results unless the ego intervenes and catches the fish tossed up by the wave, catches in a net of image the incoherence of tumultuous emotions on which we ride.

We need Spirit and we need human consciousness; we need both or we get neither. We need ego to be deposed, not center stage, but there, engaged, on stage. We need the current of unconscious life and we need the Spirit that speaks to and through both conscious and unconscious. Depth psychology and spirituality meet in their intent to gather up all the parts of us individually and in community to live together a whole life, anchored in the here and now and open to the transcendent.

When we are working with people in our clinics, hospitals, offices, prisons, mosques, temples, churches, I see us as if in one of the novelist Trollope's books. He always begins his chronicles in this fashion: "... five miles from the nearest railroad station.... whether it should be called a small town or a large village I cannot say. It has no mayor, and no market, but it has a fair.... situated on a little river ... and has a quiet, slow, dreamy prettiness of its own.... Mr. Gilmore's character must be made to develop itself in these pages ... He is to be our hero" (Trollope 1924, 1-2, 4). Trollope's genius portrays the gripping seriousness, the compelling narrative of the Vast and the All through the most particular and peculiar. No fame, no outsized talent or riches. Ordinary people through whom the wonder of life shines forth so clearly that we stay up late at night to finish the story we already know, indeed have known from the beginning pages, how it will turn out. But it is the coming that grips us. For in this person's story is all our stories, of seeking love, wanting health and goodness, falling instead into madness, sometimes rallying, sometimes rescued, sometimes sinking into sorrow and lostness.

Jung describes coming upon spirit in a similar manner: "this door, a highly inconspicuous side-door on an unsuspicious looking and easily overlooked foot path ... leads to the secret of transformation and renewal" (Jung 1973, January 30 1934). Similarly in our work, with one individual, or only small groups, or with one family at a time, so tiny, all of life shines through, gathers the primordial into lived presence. We look for the true way of each person, hearken to what makes them thrive fully, what commands their allegiance to the ultimate, what makes them part of the whole.

What do we believe about the connection between the clinical and spiritual? What end do we have in view when we begin a new 'case'? What is our spiritual perspective and how is it expressed in our clinical work? For make no mistake about it: the angle of vision from which we do clinical work affects and effects our technique. We need to know what we know about our own spiritual standpoint, I believe. We need to bring it into articulate conversation with ourselves and each other, for these resources make possible our going on doing this work long after our own analysis ends, decades beyond the completion of our training.

I am not talking about using religious language with clients. I am not talking about imposing personal God-images on clients, bullying them into some prescribed theological form. I am talking about risk, venture, seeing the wind blow through the interpretation about to be made, the geyser that wells up in the transference-countertransference field that makes both clinician and client know in the intimacy of what they feel for and with each other that they are parts of a large whole. All the divisions, hierarchies, fall away in the presence of this presence.

Wholeness

What is the end in view for depth work with the psyche and for long work in spiritual practice? Wholeness is a word often given in answer to this question, that somehow the bits and pieces will collect into an unbroken assemblage. In moments of clarity and fulfillment, we receive the impression that something is being unified, redeemed from fragments, being returned to its primary source, returned from exile, in the language of Jewish mysticism (Neumann 1989, 88).

Wholeness is a word become sullied in pop psychology – you too can achieve it, buy this tape and acquire more joy, etc. Any of us who labor year in and year out, decade in and decade out doing psychotherapeutic work know such cheery ads are nonsense. The more conscious we become, the more we see how unconscious we are. The more parts we gather, the more their multiple roots and interconnectedness become visible, as if we belong to a giant jigsaw puzzle whose pieces, missing and found, seem innumerable.

It is precisely here, I believe, that clinicians also trained in religion have something special to contribute to psychotherapeutic work. We know from our religious training that wholeness is a fugitive concept, a myth the ego makes up to bolster its courage, or to aggrandize its puny size. When we fall for this ruse, we become consciously or unconsciously contemptuous of those we serve. We see them as less developed, less conscious, as ill, as resistant, as borderline. Each psychological fashion manufactures its own swear words. Less developed than whom? Than us, of course, who know the theory and the goal of attainable wholeness that we reify into a brass ring to be grabbed as we whiz by on life's merry-go-round. This is just ego posturing, whistling in the dark that we fear, rather than the dark as embracing the true well of the infinite.

Spiritual traditions instruct us that we are never whole. We are the sinners, the ones living in bondage in Egypt, disobedient to Allah's will, mixed up in the ten-thousand things. But even in that condition we are loved while yet sinners, Yahweh calls us into an exodus from oppression, Allah calls us to daily prayer, and the Bodhisattva refrains from bliss until each of us can attain it too. Even in our broken and lost condition, we know we are found by something bigger, more complete, whole. *It is the whole and we are the parts.* That is what the life of the spirit tells us: not that we become whole, but that the whole that is calls us to construct whole living on earth, gathering the parts within us and among us so that in our mortal bodies, our bodies politic, the bodies of the laity, the mystical body where the eternal takes up residence in the temporal, wholeness will reside and "in the full range of its significance ... embraces nothing less than the unitary reality" of all of life (Neumann 1989, 88). Spiritual life challenges us in our clinical work to know this fact and to name it "to venture out beyond the presumptive security of our psychological knowledge and to risk encounter with the unknown." (ibid.) We venture into clinical theology.

To go on doing this work week after week, year after year, decade after decade, and feel alive, excited, grateful for the doing of it, we need this view of the whole enterprise, or we do not last. We get infected, and to protect ourselves, we grab our theory as if we know what each client must be achieving and moving toward. We close up against surprise, against the living reality of life coursing right there in our office that makes each analysis an adventure, an advance of the new into visibility.

Naming

Spirituality points to this All, this presence, and goes further: it names it. We must do the same or it is not real in the body of our work. We are not then in relation to it; we do not converse with it in our self-state. We do not look straight at who makes itself known through a client's symptom, who names itself through a client coming upon a creative solution in a new symbol that astonishes as much as it heals what was broken and bleeding.

If we do not name for ourselves what this it is, we relate to it anonymously, collectively, in language of inherited tradition without rescuing it into our own personal words. Is this Jesus? Jung had his own vision of a green Christ that proved so palpable he kept the picture of Christ's face on the Turin shroud in his office covered. Is this energy? Is it abstract symbol? Primordial animal-god? (see Ulanov 1986/2002, 164). Our consulting room blazes up into emotional intensity. Closeness to this emotional fire makes us into a sublimated and subtle body, a different form, as wood becomes smoke and heat, and as iron is cooked and made glowing. Spirituality in the consulting room can also possess us, burn us up, destroy us. Thus spirituality is needed to instruct how to proceed, how not to fall into the fire, into identification with this transcendent power that seems to come from we know not where.

If one function of depth psychology for spiritual life is to bring Spirit down into the matter of our daily living, then we need to look at the practical effect of consciously claiming our spiritual stance as part of our psychological training and work. Awareness of spiritual presence and of our peculiar image and names for conversing with its presence affect our methods of doing psychotherapeutic work.

History Taking

Consider, for example, history taking, common to any treatment method regardless of school. Hans Loewald, indebted to Freud, influenced by Heidegger, and developing his own ego psychology emphasis, writes imaginatively of recovering the past as present, not as facts repressed and remembered, trauma buried and reconstructed, but as conversion and reorganization of what was into what is now (Loewald 1980). This approach changes what was and what is by their mixture. Loewald emphasises the admixture of the analyst's ego with the client's to make up a bigger view of the client's experience, additional possibilities of apprehending what is true. Loewald's description of these currents in the transference-countertransference relation are moving, yet do not go far enough. I think the reason lies in Loewald's heartsickness over Heidegger's betrayal to Nazism that caused an irreparable breach for Loewald between himself and the philosopher who functioned for Loewald as a link to the Source.

If we pursue this image of constant interpenetration and reorganization of the past into the present so the mixture of parts makes moments of wholeness, we gain eyes to see the Spirit breaking through into the material of the analytical work. The linear view of past proceeding as the crow flies straight into the present yields the wrong notion that past progresses into a more developed present. Loewald's writing gives this evolutionary view that later is better and earlier more primitive.

The spiritual view realigns us as circling always around the same center spiraling down to its origin point. The past we now include is no better and no worse than what we are now including it in this swing around the circle. Now is more in that we have lived longer, and less in that we may have strayed farther from the center. Circling around the point, is the point, rather than ascending stages where we look down on preceding ones as inferior, and which can translate into a hierarchical transference-countertransference model of the therapeutic couple. The spiral model evinces our mutuality because what we are doing together is circling around the same center, a surround that holds both our egos and simultaneously dissolves their ascendancy. Rilke's words come to mind: "I am circling around God, around the ancient tower, and I have been circling for a thousand years, and I still don't know if I am a falcon, or a storm, or a great song" (Rilke 1981, 13).

For example, listening to a woman consumed by obsessive compulsive doubts, repeating over and over again – should I exercise but will I become too ill, but if I don't then I will feel bad, but if I do will I overtire myself worse – this questioning was like a buzzsaw or the grind of a lawn mower in the office. I could hear no psyche, only this constant grind, yet I felt pain like blood seeping all over the floor. The agony of it took my breath away. I felt completely useless; no way into the conversation, and no way out. Nothing I said dented the buzzing or sopped up the blood or lessened any of the pain that flooded into the room.

Here is a situation we might easily describe as a person not yet reaching a firm ego; the obsessive questioning made a hedge against fear of chaos, deprivation, rage. In a colleague's lecture an idea arrived to listen to this client in a different way – that she did not need to progress to a more advanced stage of ego consolidation in order to be in dialogue with the bad her obsessive thoughts kept at bay and with what the psyche addressed to her from a larger transcendent world. Instead, I heard her already in conversation with the bad and with this larger world the transcendent conveyed. Her conversation was carried on in terms of these questions, albeit repeated and compulsive, but a conversation nonetheless. The reality of the psyche and the reality conveyed through the psyche were already addressing her and she was replying through her obsessive compulsive disorder. To my utter surprise, the buzzsaw questions shifted from her own body to her husband's attitude toward her. Still the complaints came round and round, but now between her and this other who was closest to her. The circle enlarged and her panic ebbed to consider his responses. The only change was the shift in my attitude of listening, to hear that this woman was already in dialogue with the transcendent through her symptomatology.

Another example concerns the integrating of what Jung calls the brother animal, the sister animal part of us. Remember that game we played as kids: what animal would you be? It is a game now played under more exalted names of shamanistic soul retrieval, seeking one's power animal who will return to us a lost bit of soul. In this heartwrenching example, a girl of six was faced with fraught life in the body and at a scarce distance from her own birth. She spent more than half her life battling leukemia to which she eventually succumbed, affecting not only

24

her parents who spent alternate nights in hospital with her for three of her six years, but also her older sister who, for a third of her nine years, was shadowed by a dying sibling. With such sorrow that plunges a whole family into the semidark of grieving, it makes a big difference to know that at any time in life we are always doing the same thing: circling round its center, in orbit. This perspective shifts the sadness of a lost future, of a life not lived longer, into the present. It is not how long but how close she, the child and bringing her whole family, is to the center.

Take another example, less tragic but no less heartwrenching, of a woman now in her sixties putting anguished questions to herself about her deep ambivalence in sexually loving another woman. She says, I know I would prefer otherwise, that it be a man, and I feel bad toward my partner because it is different for her. We look into the long river of her sexuality, where it went underground and where it now bubbles forth in sustained relationship where she risks bodily intimacy. She knows her preferred option foreclosed because of the continuing sexual invasion by her oldest brother, happening because he, too, was a loveless child, unheld in a family container where neither child's unique authority of being was welcomed and fed. At thirteen he grabs closeness through sexually invading his six year old sister, who also suffers unmet dependency needs. She responds to tactile pleasure at the same time feeling so burdened with his theft that it becomes an isolating secret, so desperate she soils her underwear and continually hides it. No one ever asks, where are your underpants! This lack bespeaks the lack in the household.

Conversing with these painful facts, she reorganises them in relation to her present question of ambivalence toward her female partner. She sees the insistence of the sexual in her body – that it will be lived, it will bubble forth in one form or another.

This angle of vision yields a gratitude, even in ambivalence, that she and this lively, durable current of being was not buried alive. Difference can be accepted, even difference from her partner whose history leads her to single choice, unconflicted.

Dependence

Our view of dependence shifts when we consciously use both clinical and spiritual perspectives in therapeutic work. When we see psychic growth less in terms of stages and more in terms of spiraling around the center, it introduces a radical equalising of the inequity of power between therapist and client. Some differential remains but it contributes to building a safe container for the client who pays us and comes to our offices to see us and therefore hires us as employees. Both parties are realigned around the center which relativises the ego of each. The client can lean her whole weight on the therapist because the space is contained and the time lasts just so long, and because both are leaning and looking to the center that supports all of us.

Most analytical theories say that the new comes in as a result of the client introjecting the new object of the clinician, that this is the source of transformation (see also chapters 9, 11, 14, 16). The spiritual view extends further into unknowing about the origin of the new, the mutative agent. The personal dependency on the therapist is unavoidable but not sufficient. For who is to say the therapist is such a better object than former objects? That view shadows our clinical profession. We need each other to mediate the transpersonal but we are no substitute for its reality. With the spiritual perspective, we see this more clearly because we see through the visible to the invisible; we see through psychic reality to reality of the whole. Dependency on our therapist delivers us into seeing our dependency on psychic reality which delivers us into seeing our dependency on transcendent reality, and further into the unknown. These successive dependencies are like those pictures that gave us our first taste of infinity. For me, it was through comic books. On the cover was a picture of a child reading a comic book, and on and on in infinite regression. For one of my teachers, infinity broke in upon him through a series of Russian dolls, one contained in the other.

Here is an example of multiple dependencies. The client herself is an analyst and says to me, you succeeded in evading my efforts to trap you, to pin you down to what that small room in my dream meant, to defining what it was. She had dreamt twice of that room recently. In the first dream, she began in art class, painting a beautiful scene. Suddenly she was hurled out of that space into a too small room, desolate and trapped. Several weeks later, she dreamt of a gigantic snake trapped in a too small room, flinging itself against the walls to get out. In the dream she is standing there trying to come up with a way to let the snake out.

I reply with a question: what urges this hastening toward definition? She says she wants to help her own patients connect to healing images the psyche offers in dreams. I say, helpfulness can be a form of the ego wanting to do it and this is not needed. The analyst does not have to do it all. The psyche does it, or something through the psyche does it. The psyche gives this image; staying with the image in unknowing will sustain the connection. Trust the psyche in your patient to feel connected to by this big snake.

Dependence on me gives way to dependence on the psyche for giving her a view of herself seeing this big snake energy and wanting to liberate it, the snake that came into the desolate too small room of the previous dream. Dependence on the psyche giving this picture leads to a spiritual question of the origin of this picture. Who is sending or giving the snake image? Without transferring to me the knowing, the connecting to truth – e.g., tell me what the dream room means that traps the snake – she would not have seen through to her dependence on the psyche already addressing her through this arresting image of the snake in the too small room. Receiving dependence on me leads her to depend on the psyche, and that leads her to depend on something coming through the psyche, something that she does not know, feels she may never know, a new kind of unknowing that she and I work on together. Circulation of different dependencies mix and separate from each other, as a sequence and a simultaneity.

Affect

I interrupted this woman's knowing because the image inter-rupted my knowing. The huge snake flailing about impressed me, pressed in on me. I knew that nothing I knew was any match for that big serpent. No words I had could contain its otherness. Besides that, it frightened me! And left me in awe. My affect, my fear in this case, brought to the psychic image a human feeling response and thus rectified what the early Christian theologian Origen calls "the chilling loss of the divine 'warmth' of love" (Drewery 1975, 33-62). We lost that in the fall from living with God. In making our way back through God's grace, warm love is given to us. Warmth is restored to psyche. In clinical terms, this means our affective response, our immediate human reactions of fear, sweat, attraction, anger, desire, not a head trip, not the deadness of a schizoid scanning-ray consciousness, bring us near to the living image. "The image may in fact be a projection, but the dynamic order that is perceived by means of the image is not" (Neumann 1989, 435).

For us to respond to an image is to become involved not only in our own conversation with psyche, but with the reality it conveys to us. We are led to perceive a chain of dependency: on each other, on psychic reality, on the author of psychic reality. The snake image caught in too small a room compensates a onesided consciousness in the dreamer, involving her in making a bigger space. She does not live in a vacuum but also within a collective consciousness. The huge snake may also compensate for insufficient appreciation in our culture of energy coming through the female and for the power of the transpersonal. Will she receive it? Will she make a space for what comes through her female person, through her artistic imagination (of the first dream)? Whichever way she responds affects her neighbor, bringing the serpent power, its primordial presence to the rest of us through her life, or foisting it off onto us by her refusal.

What will happen to the snake energy if the dreamer does not receive it? Here clinicians are pressed by varieties of faith. Do we believe in psychic reality, that this huge snake is a real image that is saying something to the dreamer with its distress of hurling itself against the walls of the too small room? What happens to the energy pictured in this real image, energy that transcends the dreamer and us too? At the very least, we can say the energy depicted here gets blocked and turns frantic, like living in a tenement and hearing a violent fight going on in the next room.

Psychic reality is real; it exists within us and between us. We exist in it. What each of us does or does not do in relation to this reality shoves others or makes open a way for them. Think of our life together in institutions, businesses, schools. We create a psychic atmosphere. If it is narcissistic, our creativity together is blighted. If we do our best to depend on each other and on the psychic atmosphere we share, and on the reality that bids us through psychic affect and image, then we know something of heaven on earth. The wholeness of each of us depends on our wholeness together. Jung sums it up: "The images of the unconscious place a great responsibility upon [us]. Failure to understand them, or a shirking of ethical responsibility, deprives [us] of [our] wholeness and imposes a painful fragmentariness of [our] life (Jung 1963b, 193; see also chapters 8, 11).

Madness

Such efforts to respond to the whole mean inclusion of all different parts, even ones we shun. Our experience of dependence in analysis brings threat, because its major form comes through accepting our transference of all sorts of things to the therapist. I remember in my first visit to the doctor after foot surgery; it was as if my foot was her foot, it belonged to her. Would she give it back to me whole? Could I destroy the operation? I was so overtaken by my foot belonging to her, that I failed to ask any of the questions I needed answered, and this after a hundred years of analysis! The suspicions, manipulations, the power, the omniscience we ascribe to the therapist shocks us. Do we consent and let all this flood out? Or do we refuse? If so, we too can get a too big snake trapped in a too small room.

Even admitting shameful parts, we can refuse them by not taking the arrow all the way into our heart and what our heart opens to. We get stuck halfway and repeat over and over again the same blow. We may repeat the humiliation endlessly because we refuse to give way to the rage it evokes. Or we can just fall into the rage and identify with it and get caught round and round, projecting it into objects of self-destruction, like drugs, or into our relatives, persecuting them because we feel they persecuted us. Jung says, "every individual who wishes even to approach his own wholeness knows very well that this means bearing his own cross" (Jung 1948/1958 cited in Jung 1953, 325).

Worst of all, the feeling of madness attends our hard efforts to differentiate ourselves from powerful primordial images. Any effort to gather parts of ourselves into some sort of unity, makes us differentiate ourselves from prevailing collective psychology. We expose ourselves to madness prevalent in our times, just as Buddha under the Bodhi tree had to process all the misery of existence, or Moses had to wrestle with Yahweh because of the sins of the Golden Calf, or Milarepa had to build singlehandedly one house after the other on the mountainside and then tear them all down without explanation from his teacher Marpa, or the individual Muslim must respond to the call of the minaret to the obligation of witness, awareness of Allah (Chang 1962, v 1, 680; Cragg 1956, viii-ix).

In our time, we are exposed to violent oppositions of riches and poverty, tinsel and rags, surfeit and deficit, hyperactivity and inertia, compulsive control and addiction, liberations and genocides. We can get caught up in what Jean-Luc Marion calls the logic of evil. Evil above all else makes evil. First it imposes sorrow and suffering. Then it builds a desire to do evil. We build an irremediable logic that protests our innocence and our refusal to suffer without passing it on to others, accusing them, transmitting it to them. In this logic, the only good God is a dead God, to satisfy the hate exercised by vengeance (Marion 1991, 23). The logic of evil triumphs and accuses us all, and thus guards evil like a unique horizon (ibid., 17). Evil plunges us into a sadness so dense that we despair of ever escaping or even wishing to escape (ibid., 41).

What then rescues us from this plight? Only, says Marion, the One who says, evil stops here. It stops with me. I refuse to

31

transmit it. I endure it without rendering it. I suffer it without making suffering; I suffer it as if I were guilty. Bion says of Christ on the cross that he is both a criminal and a deification.

Paradox

The impact of such spiritual assertion creates paradox. What tradition do we draw upon in our clinical work that asserts the power and presence that meets and transcends evil? To what vision do we refer the evil, large and small, that we meet in the consulting room? We meet such objective power and presence in the face of evil in our subjectivity. We must respond for any tradition to become real and potent to us. Hence we live in paradox. Without the subjective, the objective does not exist; yet our subjective capacity to endure and go on existing, doing clinical work, depends on some objective reality sustaining it. Large and small inhere. One is not real without the other. Our ego is relativised and remains essential.

One critical way we live paradox in the clinical setting is when the psychological and spiritual perspectives at first seem to collide, but in fact conjoin in mutual enhancement. It may be necessary in treatment to regress to the place where madness began to accumulate, where we "lost our soul" (see Milner 1969), "went up into a space over my head," as one woman put it, "gave up on myself," as one man put it. Here the wound was dealt, the rupture from "true self" living occurred, the breaking of what Jung sees as the ego-Self axis (See Winnicott 1971, Jung 1963a, 494f, 545ff, pars. 704f, 778ff; see also chapter 11). Such regression feels to us like the loss of our ego stability, and worse, a loss of the whole notion of ego – our accustomed ways of thinking and imagining, of fitting into the culture around us, our sense of structure and language. In this pre-ego place, we often fall mute, fill up with unnameable sadness, abandon hope. In clinical work, this regression feels dangerous, because our tie to self and reality rests on our dependence on the therapist. When we are children in such a state of dependence, we are graced with a lavish loving, an ability just to depend, lean on, trust and entrust. But as adults, we know the other person is not a god-like parent, but a mere fallible mortal like anyone else. How can we lean our whole weight on him or her? We are understandably ambivalent. And not all analysts take on this responsibility, and not all patients can financially afford such intense and protracted clinical work.

Just at this place of rupture, spirituality contributes something unique. For what manifests as a fearful regression looked at psychologically, from a spiritual perspective is an arrival, a finally coming to our senses. Traditions speak of it as breakthrough to the zero point (Zen Buddhism), as becoming like a little child (New Testament). We advance to the true sense of dependency on the transcendent, having lost our old mind based on ego, and entered a new knowing where ego is offered, and we are supported in a community of believers. The mending of wound, the regrowing of connection to the root stem of our being must still occur, but the starting point is radically different. People speak of it as having been dead and now they are alive, having been lost and now they are found. The spiritual perspective supports, indeed infuses with energy, the psychological task. The psychological task fleshes out the spiritual perception of our true way of being.

Another principal way we experience paradox in the clinical setting has to do with the goal of wholeness that we aim toward and know is unattainable. We can never make ourselves whole; we can never perfect our society no matter how hard we work nor how good our intentions. Our psyche includes the unconscious that is always unfolding inside us and between us, like a revisionist who speaks out of turn, interrupting, tossing a live snake into the pot, and, if idealised as a superior truth-teller, retreating into mundane dreams about laundry (See Phillips 1995, 7). We can never solve our incompleteness of knowledge. Our lifelong dependency on each other to evoke and celebrate the life in us, its uniqueness and that it matters, leaves us always with a door open to the unexpected, never entire. Through the unconscious and through others, the growing sense dawns on us that something in us and beyond our control, acting through the one who interrupts and the one who depends, brings into view something that unfolds itself. Any theory we devise, any social project, any religious doctrine, all fall short of the whole. We cannot achieve wholeness; we cannot make it right, whether it is our child's problem, our own compulsion, our society's wound.

What clinical work teaches us is that we are the unfinished parts of the wholeness of reality in which we live. To see that the very solving of the problem that took us into analysis embarks us on a new path and a new dependency unseats our ego. Though essential, our ego is not ultimately in charge; we know in our bones we do not author our life, but receive it. We move into a different kind of knowing and depending. Vigorously holding to theories about the psyche, to beliefs about the author of the psyche, we see now they do not sum up the reality of psyche nor the transcendent it discloses. We do not close the gap between the finite and the infinite. We cannot cross it from our side. Instead, our theories empty out before the living person of the client. Our images of God empty out before the unknown as it intimately touches us through dreams, symptoms, dependency on others, insights. Our ego knowing seems to empty out into what Jung calls becoming a Self that is a greater surround and cannot be grasped in its totality: "This experience is charisma, for it is not vouchsafed to us *nisi Deo concedente* … but only if we give up the ego as the supreme authority and put ourselves wholly under the will of God" (Jung 1975, 28 March 1955, 235).

Out of this space of emptiness the new arises, a presence that resists definitions and reifications and makes itself known. Like the popular movie, "Raiders of the Lost Ark," when the Ark is opened, it appears that nothing lies within. Nothing. Empty. Emptiness. But as the thieves who steal it look into this emptiness, to grab it for their own aggrandizement, its power swirls into terrifying force that withers the flesh on their bones. The only appropriate response, as the hero instructs the heroine, is to close your eyes, bow your head, tie yourself to the ground, so the nearness of this force does not sweep you into dust. We need emptiness to respond to this fullness. The power of the formless creative force destroys all forms we achieve for it, as well as spurs us on to make them.

To meditate on this paradox convicts us of the bankruptcy of our formulas and definitions. The tiger jumps out of the cage, because the tiger is alive and will retain its liveliness, will not give it up to our nets of meaning. It will give us itself, even submit to our killing it, but it will not be dead. It will break through with its everliving presence, even after we do to it our worst.

Devotion and Energy

To see through emptiness to presence takes devotion. One of the ways spirituality impacts on clinical work is this reminder that we need steadiness of attention to do the work with the living psyche and the liveliness it reveals. We need a devotion that goes on week after week, decade after decade, to tolerate the relativisation of our ego-knowing and the acceptance that it also is essential. To make clinical work transparent to the spiritual presence takes time and practice to go on witnessing to it, to bring the warmth of affect back to the chilling abstractions of psychological jargon and theological formulas. Warmth brings reconnection. We need concentration, meditation, to keep the fire going, to fan the spark sent out from the unknown that falls in our lap. We must translate this spark, this glimpse of another presence into continuing contemplation in the here and now daily work. Otherwise, that spiritual glimpse remains a darting glance, not the meeting, mixing, conjoining of the eternal in time, the wordless in words, the Vast in the space of this relationship, the peculiar idiom of this person with whom we are working. Our devotion must build up durability to see through to what St. Francis de Sales calls "la fine pointe de l'âme" – the point of unity between our spirit and the spirit of God (Frank 1965, 143).

This presence, this fine point of soul, however, also means brute energy that may push and shove us out of the way – through illness, symptoms, even breakdowns. Such force may be required to subdue our inertia, our round of habits in relationship, patterns of work, what we are convinced we must do (or have) in order to survive. This force may yank us out of our homegrown security, or out of our habit of drifting and just reacting to whatever comes along, summoning us to focus and engage. We are manoeuvred to renounce goals for our gain, to be the burning flame for others, in order to see that we are not the flame but it is, to open the heart in devotion to this presence that engenders all things.

The result of this spiritual and psychological apperception is liveliness, livingness. It communicates itself to us and we live it, in it, out of it. The result is not products, valuable as they are, like babies, books, money, contracts, health, peace. It is, itself, and hence available to us in many forms and in all our conditions of life. Even in poverty, illness, we can feel the breath of the infinite on our face. Wholeness means seeing we are part of a whole reality, circling round it with our clients in each session. Wholeness means the dignity of each part, not just the good ones, but all of them fitting and necessary. Wholeness means infinite variety that mirrors the creative multiplicity of this presence. It lives us, as Yahweh hovering over the mercy seat in the Holy of Holies, as Christ giving the eternal God in the bread and wine, as Sufi mystic seeing "that nameless Glory which the mind acknowledges as ever-undefined. Silently, their Lord replies: I am the Mirror set before your eyes and All who come before my splendour see themselves: their own reality" (Ryce-Menuhin 1991, 195).

This form-creating energy creates order out of the jumble of facts. It deconstructs any fixity of stance or theory we would substitute for itself, pulling us into the depths which author us. We can appreciate our theories and formulations as stammerings to speak of the whole as images for it that we must keep making, with joy and pleasure to make and play with. We are relocated to live on that frontier where the it that lives us and the us that lives it dwell. Then we feel in a clinical session that the psyche is doing the work, and our egos do not have to do it all. Instead, we feel with our client that something is doing both of us simultaneously. This energy resides in the psyche of each of us as well as at the center of reality, so that contact with it urges images, ideas, projects, projections, impulses and creations that flow through us into the world and flow back from the world to us.

The woman who dreamt of being hurled into the too small room, and then of the snake trapped in the too small room, dreamt again of the art class and not knowing what to draw, "having nothing of my own." The teacher comes and squashes her drawing. Then she begins in the dream to draw a tree, its top, and its roots, but the middle is a big gap. Some hand, she says, comes out of the drawing with a photo of a little girl with a big scar in the shape of a cross on her stomach. Have her vital organs been taken out? Her sexuality? the dreamer asks in the dream. But I see, she says, this girl completes the picture. In her next dream, the woman says, I am drawing a tree now and I know what I am doing. I am in it now. The picture is alive and evolves and I put animals in the middle to connect the top and the roots. Listening to her, I see that the lost maimed part brings her back to the animal root impulse (see also chapter 11).

This woman's dream sequence illustrates how we are driven to make pictures of the ineffable, invisible presence at the same time we are working on our psychological problems. The difference between us and the it that our images point to but never grasp convinces us that truly all flesh is as the grass, we move from dust to dust. Yet, at the same time we participate in the thrumming of being itself. Its presence goes into our bodies as energy, as stillness; into our minds as ideas, insights, hunches; into our hearts as love. This true, spontaneous gift can only be carried by our free creativeness, a willingness to live the life given us. When we receive it, we can join in this passage from I Chronicles 29:9, 14-15a, 22: "Then the people rejoiced, because they had given willingly, with a whole heart.... for all things come of thee and of thine own have we given thee. For we are strangers ... and sojourners.... and they ate and drank before the Lord on that day with great gladness."

Address given to Blanton/Peale Graduate Institute of Religion and Health, May 1997.

References

Chang, G. C. C. 1962. *The 100,000 Songs of Milarepa*. 2 vols. New Hyde Park, N. Y. : University Books.

Cragg, K. 1956. *The Call of the Minaret*. New York: Oxford.

Drewery, B. 1975. Deification. *Christian Spirituality, Essays in Honour of George Rupp*. ed. Peter Brooks. London: SCM Press.

Frank, S. L. 1965. *Reality and Man*. trans. Natalie Duddington. New York: Taplinger.

Jung, C. G. 1948/1958. On the Psychology of Eastern Meditation. *Collected Works* 11, *Psychology and Religion: West and East*. trans. R. F. C. Hull. New York: Pantheon; cited in Jacobi, J. 1953. *C. G. Jung: Psychological Reflections*. New York: Harper Brothers.

Jung, C. G. 1963a. *Mysterium Coniunctionis. Collected Works* 14. trans. R. F. C. Hull. New York: Pantheon.

Jung, C. G. 1963b. *Memories, Dreams Reflections*. ed. Aniela Jaffé. trans. Richard and Clara Winston. New York: Knopf.

Jung, C. G. 1973 and 1975. *Letters*. eds. Aniela Jaffé, Gerhard Adler. Princeton, N. J. : Princeton University Press.

Loewald, H. W. 1980. *Papers on Psychoanalysis*. New Haven, Ct. : Yale University Press.

Marion, J. L. 1991. *Prolégomène à la Charité*. Szikra à Giromagny: Mobile Matiere.

Milner, M. 1969. *The Hands of the Living God*. New York: International Universities Press.

Neumann, E. 1989. *The Place of Creation*. trans. Hildegaard Nagel, Eugene Rolfe, Jan van Heurck, Krishna Wilson. Princeton, N. J. : Princeton University Press.

Phillips, A. 1996. *Terrors and Experts*. Cambridge: Harvard University Press.

Rilke, R. M. 1981. *Selected Poems of Rainer Maria Rilke*. trans. Robert Bly. New York: Harper & Row.

Ryce-Menuhin, J. 1994. *Jung and the Monotheisms*. London: Routledge.

Trollope, A. 1924. *The Vicar of Bullhampton*. London: Oxford University Press.

Ulanov, A. B. 1986/2002. *Picturing God*. Einsiedeln, Switzerland: Daimon.

Winnicott, D. W. 1971. *Playing and Reality*. London: Tavistock.

Chapter 2

Mending the Mind and Minding the Soul:
Explorations Towards the Care of the Whole Person

Conversation

The two worlds of psychiatry and religion have not always been on the most cordial terms – there has been much mutual accusation and much mutual suspicion. From the psychiatric, and even the depth psychological perspective, religion has been seen as a delusion, a product of infantile wishes projected onto the cosmos. It has been thought to keep us childish, looking for a divine mommy or daddy, and to leave us unable or unwilling to face the harshness of reality and the reality of the unconscious. In addition, religion has been seen as a short-circuiting of ego-functioning. Instead of growing our way to an attitude or a position, religion has been viewed as a ready-made formula picked from a religious tradition. Religion has been seen as augmenting psychotic processes, as tempting the ego to fall into identification with archetypal energies, as offering an eternal mother's lap with instant gratification for pregenital strivings, or as offering ammunition for a punitive super-ego. Religion has been perceived as the weapon of repression, authoritarianism, even of theological sadism, not to mention a great deal of fuzzy thinking.

The religious perspective is not much better. Psychiatry and depth psychology have been viewed with fear and disapproval. I have called this the "Christian fear of the psyche" (Ulanov, 1986/2002). Psychiatry and related disciplines are accused of promoting a pseudo-religion of their own in which we no longer think seriously about wickedness or evil, but rather we think about what we are projecting. We no longer think seriously about achieving a life of faith, but instead about achieving a "mature identity." Worse yet, we don't think about making the world a better place, but instead think about how to "get in touch with our feelings."

Much conflict has existed between psychiatry and religion. Hence, it is a momentous effort that is being made here to inaugurate a vigorous, active, ongoing dialogue between the two disciplines. They are not the same, and they should not be collapsed into one another. A gap persists between them which we need to respect and value, for it preserves the space between the disciplines that makes their engagement and conversation possible. The conversation between the two disciplines of psychiatry and religion (which is the name of the Program at Union Theological Seminary) mirrors the conversation that goes on in each one of us between the psyche and the soul, a conversation that is going on all the time, if you will, in Being itself. We can understand, then, why so much resistance to this conversation is exerted from both sides! The conversation between psychiatry and religion echoes something mysterious that goes on inside each of us and at the center of Being.

Theology has known about this conversation at the heart of Being for a long time. There are doctrines that deal with it. For example, in Christian theology there is the doctrine of the Trinity, hammered out through the vigorous controversies in the third and fourth centuries about the nature of God. Christians made the audacious effort to describe what goes on within God when God isn't doing anything, but is just sort of sitting around being. The Trinity is an effort to describe God's inner object-relations, or what happens between God's id, ego and super-ego, or the congress between God's ego and Self. Despite the numerous arguments, all agreed that the inner life of Being is a vigorous, active, spirited conversation between different persons, i.e., different aspects of Being. Engagement and exchange go on all the time at the heart of Being. We are attempting in this symposium to listen in on this conversation.

The chaos theory is very much on my mind. The chaos theory states that when a butterfly lifts its wing in Chicago, the atmosphere changes in China. Who knows, maybe we are a butterfly wing. Our talking about these matters of psychiatry and religion may make accessible deep resources of Being for people in this hospital complex and people outside of it, too. We live in a unitary world, where body and spirit cohere, inner and outer life meet, individual and community join. What we do with these two disciplines of psychiatry and religion bolsters our inner conversation between psyche and soul and enables us to perceive it going on around us all the time.

When I speak of psyche, I mean the conscious and unconscious processes that enable us or disable us to be a person in the world, in relation to others and to life. When I speak of soul, I mean the willingness to be such a person in relation to self, other, and God. In old-fashioned terms, soul is a place in us that is like the doorway always open, through which God can barge at any moment. It is an unlockable door. From the psyche's point of view, when we take an interest in religious experience, we want to ask how it functions in ourselves, in our group, in our world. Does it breed illness, or does it promote health? From the point of view of the soul, we ask a different question of religious experience. We want to know, "Is it true?" From the psyche's point of view, when we feel summoned or called by God we ask, "What was this experience like? How do we accommodate it?" But the soul question is, "Who is calling, and what is to become of Thee and me?" In actual life, of course, psyche and soul are intertwined. Oversimplifications are only of limited use, and then only in symposiums, not in living. But it helps to have these two angles of vision in mind when confronted with tough clinical problems.

For example, a man sought treatment because he was compulsively attracted to teenage girls. With a great deal of labor, it was discovered that he had lost his own adolescence. He said, "I put behind me my dreamy, poetic, idealistic yearnings. I put behind me my soul life." He did this to achieve a solid ego as a barrier against the pull of addiction to drug or drink that had afflicted every member of his family. He succeeded. He got a solid ego, a place in the world, a profession, a marriage, and a standing in his community. But the compulsive attraction to teenage girls overcame him. He was amazed to discover that the girls were the age he was when he had cut off his soul life. In this fearful compulsion that made him feel suicidal, a piece of unlived soul was hiding that now came knocking at his door. It was as if he now could afford to deal with the split-off soul-part because he had built up enough ego strength to do so. And now he must include this soul life or it would destroy him through public scandal and scathing self-judgment. He took up again the conversation with the missing part that was interrupted in his teenage years and it benefitted not only himself, but others in the world as well. His treatment took place some fifteen years ago. You will remember that at that time a great rash of teenage suicides occurred on the east coast. By odd coincidence, or Jung would say synchronicity where an outer, non-causally related event meaningfully intersects with our achievement of inner insight, this man was asked through his profession to speak to an auditorium of teenagers about suicide (Jung 1952). His ability to connect with their soul-life was so great that for several years he gave a number of these speeches. His inner conversation helped others in their conversations.

In a more dramatic example, a man suffered spontaneous ejaculations whenever he was confronted by a woman holding a baby or a small child. This occurred in the supermarket, on the bus, in social gatherings, wherever. This man was not at all religious, but in the midst of this vexing body symptom, hid an unadmitted, unacknowledged payment of respect to the power of the feminine, and particularly to its Madonna or Holy Mother aspect. It was as if his unacknowledged religious instinct to venerate a power beyond himself expressed itself through this symptom. If he was not going to pay respect consciously, his body was going to act it out in a literal pouring out of his life fluid.

This religious dimension must be recognized one way or another. It wants to penetrate concrete life, achieve some visible form. This means that in training mental health professionals to help people who are mentally distressed or emotionally disturbed, the training must take account of one's own religious life or non-religious life, one's own God-images, one's own complexes around religion. If we fail to do this, this unexamined religious life will adversely affect our countertransference reactions as easily as do unexamined sexual complexes, images, or drives. In training, we must do the hard reading in spiritual and religious texts that we do in psychological texts to construct a bigger territory to draw upon in our work. It also means we must make the spiritual dimension a part of the whole treatment. It is not something tacked onto the end of treatment like a pretty scarf to embellish a psychological outfit we have worked hard to put together.

The spiritual dimension is to be taken into account in the initial phases of treatment, where we know it proves a very useful part of the diagnostic procedure. Does this person's religious life promote their craziness, or does it promote their health? That is important, but it is not enough. We need conversation with the spiritual dimension all the way through treatment. Remembering that the two disciplines must not be collapsed into one another, that we need exchange between psyche and soul, we realize it is not enough to alleviate symptoms and recover ego functioning: we also need meaning. Religious experiences, like sexual ones, do not always lie on the surface of the conscious mind. They are often hidden in the unconscious, and we feel great resistance to digging them up. It is an essential part of our training first to find this dimension in ourselves before we can reach to it in our clients. When any of us falls ill or subject to troubles of the heart, mind, or soul, we have lost more than our ego functioning; we suffer more than these distressing, vexing symptoms. We have lost our way; we are living in exile. Conversation between parts of ourselves has been blocked or interrupted.

One suicidal woman said, "I feel like a dried up lake, exhausted." After many months of treatment, she finally confided a dream she dreamt before coming to treatment. I am not allowed to quote the dream because she said it was too precious. In general, I can say that the dream represented a picture of how her soul had been murdered. On the plus side, the dream picture gave her the container, the image, to deal with the agony of annihilation. But, on the minus side, she felt her soul had been made extinct. Although she was not a religious person, this dream was a spiritual event to her. To miss that dimension is to confine ourselves to efforts of recovering ego-functioning which is of priceless value but which will not endure if the spiritual aspect is omitted. If we do not already know this, our patients will tell us by their fierce resistance to recovery when the soul is left out.

I am reminded of Winnicott's words about his psychotic patients. He said, "You may cure your patient and not know what it is that makes him or her go on living. It is of the first importance for us to acknowledge openly, that absence of psychoneurotic illness may be health, but it is not life. Psychotic patients, who are all the time hovering between living and not living, force us to look at this problem, one that really belongs not to psychoneurotics but to all human beings" (Winnicott 1971, 100). When any of us seek help from a counselor, psychiatrist, therapist, or analyst, we feel a blow to our souls. We feel we are living in such danger that we have to seek out an office or a hospital which will give us a space safe enough to recover. As many of us know, the person who is in the role of helper must temporarily hold the hope for the person who has lost it. Holding the hope means listening in on the person's inner conversation with a center deep inside and a transcendent center far outside. That listening creates a space for the conversation to be resumed.

This spiritual dimension of clinical work is real and cannot be faked. It is not mumbo-jumbo; it is not pious phrases. To speak of it in religious vocabulary is the exception rather than the rule. Many psychoanalysts approach this spiritual dimension, but they talk about it in their own psychological vocabularies so that we do not always recognize it as spiritual. Such Freudians as Hans Loewald talk about the space between the archaic primary-process thinking of the unconscious that unifies and the secondary-process thinking of consciousness that differentiates, and how the conversation between them makes us feel alive and real. Winnicott talks about the space of illusion, the transitional space, where we not only find the self we create and create the self we find, but it is also where culture grows, including religion. Kohut talks about the elusive self that cannot be defined, that inheres in and transcends the structures of the psyche, and without which we do not feel alive. Klein talks about the space between recognizing our aggression and the springing up spontaneously of our instinct to make reparation for destructiveness. Jung talks about the space between the ego as the center of consciousness and the Self as the center of the whole conscious and unconscious psyche. This space that many analysts recognize is where the conversation occurs between psychiatry and religion, between psyche and soul, between us and the transcendent.

Ruthlessness

If we acknowledge the spiritual dimension in the mending of the mind and the minding of the soul, what do we talk about? What do we speak of concretely? First of all, this conversation has no ulterior motive; it makes no converts and takes no hostages. There is no sign-up sheet; no new committees. There are two disciplines here and a space of exchange. In the exchange we are all trying to listen in, to align ourselves to that mysterious center we experience as transcendent. We may experience transcendence as being outside ourselves, our social events, our world, beyond our finite dimension.

We may experience transcendence as something deep inside ourselves, beyond our ego processes, and in those sacred moments of communication when the transcendent enters ego-consciousness. Or it may be all three meanings of transcendence (see also chapter 5). But in this conversation, we are concrete. We are not talking about talking to each other. We are not talking about trusting each other. Trust, when it is real, does not come by our putting it on the agenda. If the toilet is backing up, it furthers nothing to discuss with the plumber how we want to trust each other while the toilet overflows. Trust comes in this conversation between two disciplines as it does with the plumber. It comes as a gift, a by-product of working together on the concrete problem at hand, clearing the blockage, opening a space for free flow. So what are concrete meeting points in this conversation between psychiatry and religion, between mental health and the life of the soul?

The first is the fact of ruthlessness. We all know the devastation wreaked by mental illness and emotional distress. Minds break up into little pieces and no glue can stick them together again. People turn to stone, inert, dense to any breath of feeling. People are invaded by archetypal energies and feel compelled to act with violence toward self or others. To address such illness we need brute, ruthless strength. I don't mean ruthless in the technical sense of lack of regard to consequences for self and other. I do mean ruthless in the colloquial sense of primordial aggression and the capacity to use it to sustain a long treatment, to yank somebody back from the precipice of suicide, to remain intact before the blast of a negative transference, to risk taking somebody off medication, to persist in concentrated focus on the best self of the other person. We need ruthless strength to pull, push, woo, receive and support that best-self in our analysands which always returns us to our best-self.

I think, for example, of the work of Marion Milner. In her book *The Hands of the Living God,* she reports her experiences of 22 years of treating "Susan." Susan presented herself at the first session saying that she had lost her soul and that the world was no longer outside her and that all of this had happened since she had received ETC (Milner, 1969, xix). Milner hung on and very slowly Susan grew a unit-self. But it would not have happened if Milner has not processed her own unit-self right there during all those years. For Milner to do this, she needed to know all about what she described in a later book called *On Not Being Able to Paint*. There she explored "the angry attacking impulses" that are an essential part of a person, "the monstrous creatures" that represent parts of ourselves, the desires "to attack and destroy frustrating authorities," "the wolfish appetites" that cannibalistically devour the other (Milner, 1979, 41, 45, 46, 63). This is ruthlessness.

Closer to home, consider the writings of the Medical Director of this hospital, Otto Kernberg, who reminds us to see others as other, neither merging with them as in the borderline conditions nor treating them as a gas tank to fill up our needs as in the narcissistic disorder. A narcissistic disorder will not be healed by empathy alone. We must use aggressive energy actively to dismantle the pathological grandiose self, and with the borderline condition, we must actively and aggressively limit the patient's acting-out in the world and his acting-in the transference. I see love in this work, but it is love with teeth.

Religion knows all about such ruthlessness and who calls us into it. This is the Christ who comes with a sword as well as peace. This is the Christ who says leave your father and mother, leave your fields and houses to follow me, who calls us to differentiate from our parental images, from our cultural values and find our own way to the center. This means knowing that we are known, and using our aggression to gather all the bits of ourselves so that when the Lord calls we can answer with Samuel, "Here am I." Without reaching this level of aggression, religion degenerates into Mary, meek, mild and powder blue, and Jesus who is pink. In the Hebrew Bible a ruthless Yahweh says, "Come, I am going to make you a people, and I am going to mark out the territory with the law, with the commandments. Take it or put yourself outside this alliance." In Buddhist meditation a Roshi comes to whack between our shoulder blades to make sure we are not just drifting and dreaming, but instead making our way in a precise spiritual direction to the All. This journey directs us to the center. It is not just cozy chats with the Holy.

Ruthlessness also figures at the other end of the health spectrum: we need brute strength to survive integration. Winnicott points out the terrific anxiety that accompanies integration. We define who we are as self, distinct from all those persons and forces now defined as not-self. Unconsciously we expect attack from them (Winnicott, 1988, 117, 119, 121). To be healthy means we are slightly depressed because we are aware of the inevitable mixtures of bad and good in ourselves as well as others. It takes aggression to be responsible for all our feelings, the bad as well as the good, and to hold these opposites together (Klein, 1975, Jung 1959, para. 70-77). Religion knows about this struggle, and knows that integration is not perfection. There is no perfection here below. There is no utopia. That only leads to splitting and violence, where all the good guys are in the corral and all the bad guys are outside to be persecuted, like a borderline condition writ large. Integration means bringing all the bits together, whether in a social community or in a psychic economy. It is a process of struggle and it always lands us in ambiguity, and in surprise.

Remember the parable of the sheep and the goats. Jesus describes how the sheep get saved and the goats damned. The big surprise is that those who thought they were goats turn out to be sheep. They ask, how can this be? Jesus explains that in as much as we visit those in prison, clothe the naked and feed the hungry we have done it for him. In this huge hospital complex and in all the different kinds of work that are represented at this symposium, there are goats who will turn out to be sheep. In this work, you are visiting people imprisoned in their obsessions. You are helping to clothe those naked of defenses. You bring food from the center to those starved for love. But the outcome is never perfect. It is always ambiguous because the transcendent is too big for our finite containers. Religion recognizes with tough-mindedness that ambiguity is the inevitable state of symbols and events where the infinite manifests in the finite. This is not fuzzy thinking or sentimental feeling. When the transcendent takes a small bit of the here and now to show itself, it is always capable of being seen as madness or as stunning revelation. This ambiguity is fact, and it requires ruthless strength to tolerate it.

Fate-Destiny-Providence

Another topic for our conversation is fate, destiny and providence. The suffering of persons who seek psychiatric confinement, or the suffering of those who seek psychoanalysis, psychotherapy or pastoral counseling, is not just discomfort, nor even just dysfunction. Most often it is agony. In places of agony, we lose the thread of our inner conversation. It is interrupted. Sometimes it is made mute. That is why in every city of our country you will find people yelling on the street corner, having imaginary conversations with God or their enemies or you, a perfect stranger walking by. The conversation between ego and deeper Self is so basic to living that when it is interrupted, it will be displaced and transferred into a fantastic dimension. Sometimes it is transferred into the body.

Joyce McDougall writes of psychic deprivation that manifests in severe psychosomatic disorders. Our earliest anxieties and the deepest psychotic layer of our anxieties do not reach words to contain them, nor dream images to express them. They do not even achieve psychoneurotic symptoms to release them. Our missing conversation with this level of our anxiety falls onto organs of the body, and the body must express it in myriad, chronic, obstinate psychosomatic sufferings (McDougall, 1989, 53). It is especially poignant when this conversation through body symptoms falls not into our body, but the body of our child.

Many years ago, I treated a woman who after many months of work slowly confided secrets she had held for years. What brought her to treatment was not her secrets, but her youngest child who had been suffering chronic constipation from birth for which no organic cause could be found. The child was four years old when the woman sought treatment. His body carried on the stopped-up conversation of his mother. Gradually, as she let go of her secrets, about prostitution to pay off debts to loan-sharks and gangsters, incurred by her husband's compulsive gambling, and about the paternity of this youngest son, her son's constipation disappeared. He said to his mother, "Don't worry, Mommy. I'm going to be all right. I can let go now." As she began conversation with these mute anxieties, bringing them into words, the little boy's body was released.

People who suffer agony, people who suffer deprivation of soul, who suffer obstinate body symptoms, feel fated. When we feel fated, we feel caught. We need to find places like this hospital, or any resource to recover a sense of destiny as opposed to fate. Christopher Bollas talks about our destiny drive, which he defines as a capacity to generate a future (Bollas, 1991, 47-48). We see from the rioting in Los Angeles in 1992 what bursts into society when people feel they have no future. Wild anger, protest, destruction burst out when we feel fated, when that inner conversation has been foreshortened.

Religion knows about this loss of hope. It knows about our need for a neighbor listening, so that we can find our conversation again. It knows about our need for God as the silent witness to our truest self. Religion knows about the God who is with us in all our hells, in all our cesspools of conflict. Sometimes it is religious experience itself that restarts our conversation. For example, a student took clinical pastoral education (CPE) in a big, crowded city hospital (see also chapter 10). Mentally ill people were brought in off the street; violence frequently occurred in the emergency room, and there were rows and rows of crack babies lying in their tiny cots looking like little old men and women, shaking, not making a sound. Their parents did not want to see them or to pick them up, but just left them there. One morning, halfway through her course, she got up to go to work and found herself crying and unable to stop. She had the wit to call a friend. Her friend had the wit to hear what was going on and found her a refuge by arranging admission to a private hospital. In a psychodrama session, a profound experience happened to her. The leader suggested, "Now talk to God. Imagine you're talking to God, and tell God what's up, why you're here." She began by describing the crazy people, the violence, the crack babies and how, as a chaplain, she wanted to help and love the poor. Suddenly it poured out of her mouth, "I hate the poor! I hate their indifference, their cruelty! I'm in a rage about it!"

From the psychological perspective, she uncovered the pent-up aggression she had outlawed and made homeless by putting a religious maxim over it that demanded she "love" the poor. Separated from her aggression, she felt helpless and exhausted. Reconnecting with her aggression initiated a theological conversation in her about the necessity of aggression if we are to do any loving at all. The psychodrama leader went further, suggesting, "Okay, now you be God and answer what you yelled." The student was astonished when she heard herself speaking as if she were Christ: "You don't have to sacrifice your life, for I have already made the sacrifice, the last sacrifice. I weep if people don't take this love. But, I have made the last sacrifice." The student felt she found not only her own aggression, but also toughness in God's love. After taking a day or two to digest this, she checked herself out of the hospital, returned to her CPE placement, and finished her work.

Religion reminds us that the sacred is a structure of the psyche. Religion is not an add-on, and not just a helper in making initial diagnoses, but is going on all the time, from beginning to end. Religion takes further the sequence of moving from fate to destiny. The CPE student felt caught in a fate and felt the fatedness of people in the hospital. What she recovered was a sense of her own destiny, and a capacity to listen for its thread in the life of the people whom she confronted in the hospital.

Religion takes us even further in recognizing that we cannot live from the ego-world alone. Even in the most dire straits we must recognize the transcendent element. We discover that even though we seem to be going only back and forth between our problems, actually, like a sailboat tacking across a waterway, we are creating a path. Discovering this line of destiny opens us to see how the transcendent is touching us, now through a problem, now through a symbol, now through an outer event. Religion tells us how the line from fate to a sense of destiny goes on unfolding into a sense of Providence: that we make a difference, that we matter to what matters. This is not a childish wish, but a theological fact.

Jung describes how we experience the transcendent as an element outside us working in us. In its transcendent function the psyche spontaneously goes back and forth between opposing points of view. We can augment this process by consciously entering it and imagining conversation between our ego perspective – what we want or wish or need – and the perspective of the unconscious that threatens to overwhelm us through a depressive or anxious mood, through a fit of anger or grandiosity, or through a burst of energy or inspiration. As the two sides converse and confront each other, gradually (and with much effort to sustain the dialogue) a third point of view arises spontaneously that includes and surpasses the two opposing ones. It may come as a new image or attitude or insight. Whatever form it takes, it impresses us profoundly. It feels like a solution or a path marked out "in accord with the deepest foundations of the personality, as well as its wholeness; it embraces conscious and unconscious and therefore transcends the ego" (Jung, 1964, para. 856; Jung, 1960, para. 131-193; Jung, 1963, para. 753-756). I would add that through this building up of a third point of view that transcends the ego, we feel the Transcendent touching us, and maybe even guiding us (Ulanov, 1992, Ulanov, 1975, Ulanov, 1982). That which seems far outside us seems to touch, through this process, deep inside us.

When we take seriously the sacred as a structure of the psyche, it introduces a different kind of knowing, one that realizes the limits of ego. It does not replace consciousness. We are driven to use paradoxical language. We move into a knowing that is an unknowing. It is a knowing about deep levels of experiencing that makes our defenses more porous, that softens the lines of separation between subject and object, self and other. It makes our ego more transparent. Some of us call this a feminine mode of knowing, but whatever we call it, this knowing-unknowing paradox introduces us to conversation between ego and archaic mind, between psyche and soul, bringing us to a new level of discourse with our neighbor, including our neighbor God (Ulanov, 1971, 168-193). This is not regression to a pre-oedipal state; it is reaching forward to perception of the unity of Being and Word. It feels free, creative, generative. This is what persons come looking for. If we know it, they will know that we know it, and feel *found*. Fate unfolds into destiny – a line, a path – and we feel breaking in on us a bigger reality, that makes us now see that all along we have not just been unfolding; we have been led. Religion calls this Providence.

So What?

At this point we might ask, "So What?" And we have all had people in treatment who ask, "So what if I get better? Then what?" Only the determined conversation of psychiatry and religion is tough enough to give the answer: this is the way it is. Like Yahweh told Moses, "I Am Who Is With You." This God is with us in all our hells and all our happiness. This God, not stuck to one place or to one graven image, is a portable God, traveling above the mysterious mercy seat in the Holy of the Holies within the tabernacle of the Ark.

In the Christian tradition, the answer to, "So what?" comes in person, in the presence of Him Who Is. It does not come in a political program, or in a mental health plan or philosophical concept. The answer comes in person, as presence. And the presence feels big, abundant, like suddenly discovering new budget resources. This abundance feels good. And it is good because it is, as the philosopher Iris Murdoch reminds us when asked what goodness is good for. She replies, "Nothing. Goodness is good for Nothing" (Murdoch, 1969, 254).

It usually falls to the lot of those in the conversation between psychiatry and religion to carry this yoke of feeling good for nothing and useless. Despite treatment plans and theories, what are we really doing anyway? Are we doing anything? We often feel foolish, as if we are just sort of hanging out with our patients in the locked ward or in the privacy of our offices. It is not always clear who is the doctor and who is the patient.

What are we doing when we enter this conversation of psyche and soul, of us and God? We are being; we are present. This is not just nodding to being. We are affirming it. We are not, as a patient once yelled at me "here to get mental health!" What we are doing is getting at the source and giving back to it. This sort of work is unlike any other because it benefits from what does not work. The world of the human psyche and soul is like nothing else because failure is as important as success. We need ruthless energy to see this because this makes fate which strikes us down transform into destiny which leads us to see providence which shelters us. We meditate in this conversation on our failures as opportunities for a success to come. Everybody in this room knows the surprise of finding that it is the wounded place in ourselves that makes the link to the patient, not the developed part of ourselves. Ruthlessly, we meditate on our antipathy, our resistances, our failures, and we do not allow ourselves to be impeded by them. We face the hate and bring it next to the love. A religious realism permits us to do that. We do not lose our compassion when we recognize our hate. We find a basis for it. In this odd work nothing is wasted. We need ruthless energy to go on seeing that nothing is wasted. Everything in our lives is gathered up into the conversation and gives a chance to see God made manifest.

So we who work with the psyche are making an act of faith whether we are religious or not. Our work is not pure science. Its technique is the technique of faith. We work with somebody in ourselves in order to work with somebody in our neighbor. What is given us to live allows us to reclaim all our resources, even our earliest perceptions of the transcendent. This is not regression but a gathering of all our responses. So if we once thought of God as a loving mother who goes on loving us and does not stop just because we got a C – or failed to make the team, we may be able to see now that God does not stop loving us just because we are looters, or crack addicts, or people who put themselves forward as helpers in the mental health profession.

In this profession we have the opportunity to go on with all our resources, both bad and good. And this is where ruthlessness pays off. We are ruthless with our doubts, with our incomplete performances because we know they too have a purpose. A woman recently brought this home to me in a fresh way. She brought to her session two or three poems of Rilke's soon after she was released from a hospital in which I had placed her because of a suicidal risk. She was able to gather up this trauma into the thread of her life. She was not religious, but she had a profound conviction that what she had gone through not only was gathered into her own destiny, but contributed to Being itself, and was in an odd way, then, providential. One poem she brought illustrates this (Rilke 1981, 175):

> To work with things is not hubris
> when building the association beyond words;
> denser and denser the pattern becomes –
> being carried along is not enough.
> Take your well-disciplined strengths
> and stretch them between two
> opposing poles. Because inside human beings
> is where God learns.

Are we relieved then, of feeling foolish and good for nothing? I'm afraid not. This work pulls us into the center. The ruthless energy it requires can build in us a durability so we can enter into what lasts – like the permanence of a stone, or the redness of red. This ongoing conversation between the disciplines of psychiatry and religion, between psyche and soul within us, that mirrors the conversation going on in Being itself, brings us to the mysterious and inexhaustible joy which is always associated with the transcendent. We are not just getting mental health. We are claiming ecstasy, that which builds upon and glows with mental health, that which sometimes has been called spiritual health.

Plenary Address New York Hospital Cornell Medical Center Westchester N.Y. 1992

2. Mending the Mind and Minding the Soul

[Haworth co-indexing entry note]: "Mending the Mind and Minding the Soul: Explorations Towards the Care of the Whole Person." Ulanov, Ann Belford. Co-published simultaneously in the *Journal of Religion in Disability & Rehabilitation* (The Haworth Press, Inc.) Vol. 1, No. 2, 1994, pp. 85-101; and: *Pastoral Care of the Mentally Disabled: Advancing Care of the Whole Person* (ed: Sally K. Severino, and The Reverend Richard Liew) The Haworth Press, Inc., 1994, pp. 85-101. Multiple copies of this article/chapter may be purchased from The Haworth Document Delivery Center [1-800-3-HAWORTH; 9:00 a.m. – 5:00 p.m. (EST)].

References

Bollas, C. *Focus of Destiny, Psychoanalysis and Human Idiom.* London: Free Association Books, 1991.

Jung, C. G. Synchronicity: an acausal connecting principle; in *The Collected Works 8. The Structure and Dynamics of the Psyche.* New York: Pantheon, 1960.

Jung, C. G. Archetypes of collective unconscious; in *The Collected Works 9:1.* New York: Pantheon, 1959.

Jung, C. G. The transcendent function; in *The Collected Works 8. The Structure and Dynamics of the Psyche.* New York: Pantheon, 1960.

Jung, C. G. *Mysterium conjunctionis*; in *The Collected Works 14.* New York: Pantheon, 1963.

Jung, C. G. A psychological view of conscience; in *The Collected Works 10. Civilization in Transition.* New York: Pantheon, 1964.

Klein, M. On loneliness; in *Envy and Gratitude and Other Works 1946-1963.* New York: Delacorte Press/Seymour Lawrence, 1975.

McDougall, J. *Theaters of the Body, a Psychoanalytic Approach to Psychosomatic Illness.* London: Free Association Press, 1989.

Milner, M. *The Hands of the Living God.* New York: International Universities Press, 1969.

Milner, M. *On Not Being Able To Paint.* New York: International Universities Press, 1979.

Murdoch, I. On "God" and "Good"; in *The Anatomy of Knowledge.* ed. by Grene M. Amherst, University of Massachusetts Press, 1969.

Rilke, M. Just as the winged energy of delight; in *Selected Poems of Rainer Maria Rilke,* trans. Robert Bly. San Francisco: Harper, 1981.

Ulanov, A. B. *The Feminine in Jungian Psychology and in Christian Theology.* Evanston, Illinois: Northwestern University, 1971.

Ulanov, A. B. *Picturing God.* Einsiedeln, Switzerland: Daimon Verlag 1986/ 2002.

Ulanov, A. B. 1992/1996. The Perverse and the Transcendent, *The Transcendent Function: Individual and Collective Aspects. Proceedings from the Twelfth International Congress for Analytical Psychology.* Chicago 1992. ed. Mary Ann Matoon 1993. Daimon Verlag, Einsiedeln, Switzerland; and in Ulanov, A. B. 1996. *The Functioning Transcendent*, chapter 3. Wilmette, Ill.: Chiron.

Ulanov, A. and B. *Religion and the Unconscious.* Louisville: Westminster, 1975.

Ulanov, A. and B. *Primary Speech: A Psychology of Prayer.* Louisville: Westminster, 1982.

Winnicott, D. W. *Playing and Reality.* London: Tavistock Publications, 1971.

Winnicott, D. W. *Human Nature.* London: Free Association Books, 1988.

Chapter 3

Psychoanalysis and the Spiritual Quest: Exploring the Cross Roads

Why Now?

There is a tremendous increase of interest in the resources of spirituality for depth psychology in all its schools. We must ask, why now? The first reason is it is harder and harder to deny the reality of the psyche and the role it plays in social action. More crucial still is the potentially lethal effect of religious ideology in combination with mental illness. Such a mix-up destroys not only the individual but many others as well. We have only to remember the massacres at Columbine High School in Colorado, and before that the rash of children killing children across the country, the lone gunman invading the Fort Worth Baptist church to murder many and the man killing children in the Los Angeles Jewish center. Add to this the religious fervor of the genocide campaigns waged in Serbia, Croatia, Kosovo, and the millions massacred in East Timor and the violent burnings and trappings of victims in the religious wars of India.

Mental illness is not isolated. It spreads out to the whole of us. If one of us goes missing, the rest of us cannot function. We cannot ignore this fact by invoking prejudice, saying such crimes and madness happen only in inner city neighborhoods or poor sections of the world. Misuse of religious belief to justify hate crimes happens in every section of society, making it urgent that we investigate the relation of spirit and psyche.

A second reason that spirituality becomes more crucial to psychoanalysts springs from clinical work itself. Psychoanalytical theories have extended further and further back in chronological time of persons' lives to locate decisive events leading to pathology, to the point where theory tries to describe what it is to be at all and what is required for us to become a person. Winnicott emphasises holding and the facilitating environment, Kohut stresses mirroring, the idealised object and the function of the selfobject, Bollas the transformational object, intersubjectivists the witnessing other, let alone Klein finding oedipal conflicts in the one-and-a-half-year-old.

This type of theorising amounts to psychological metaphysics; we are studying being, what it is to be, how to recover it if it is lost, what originates it. As clinicians, we study being not abstractly but in personal and social terms. We need the resources of spirituality with its long tradition of metaphysical speculation to be in conversation with this clinical exploration of being itself. Further still, types of experience occur in the work of deep analysis that exceed psychoanalytical theory and require a personal answer. These experiences have to do with the source of transformation, the sense of finding one's path, the struggle to articulate felt meaning that links us with the center of reality.

A third reason for this interest in spiritual quest comes from the fact that psychoanalysis is one hundred years old and the question arises, after analysis what? (see also chapter 16). Enough patients have been treated and ended treatment and yet there are others who are never done with it. Some people stay in analysis forever because they find in the relationship to the analyst a kind of regard, an emotional field in which they can speak their deepest thoughts and dare all their feelings, and voice spiritual yearnings for meaning, for devotion to something transcendent. They do not find this quality of communication outside analysis. It may depend on the person of the analyst specifically; it may depend on what is transferred to the analyst and not reclaimed by the client to be lived in her or his life. But the analytical couple is not a substitute for actual relationship in life, whether with a spouse, a lover, friends, devotion to work, or soul connection to the transcendent.

What makes it hard to build this depth of relationship to self and other outside of analysis? We discuss this theoretically as the exchange between self-object and objective-object relations that analyst and analysand learn to negotiate. The analyst mirrors the patient and evokes deep experiences hard to grasp in words, and the analyst exists objectively as a center of agency and affiliation too. In spiritual terms, attention is paid to naming the reality that comes through transference and what the transference symbolises. These intangible facts, both psychic and spiritual, add zest to living, a willingness to thrive and reach for the ultimate.

The theoretical question arises whether analysis breeds a new kind of consciousness not inaugurated elsewhere. I question this claim as our hubris. Analysis does engender a precious kind of consciousness, one imbued with unconsciousness, that mixes knowing with unknowing, conceptualisation with openness to pre- and trans-conceptual perception. But artists, poets, children, mystics, and crazy people in short spurts, know this kind of consciousness too.

Finally, a last reason for an increase of psychoanalytic interest in things spiritual comes from awareness of how much fear and ignorance of traditional religion exist among clinicians.

Spirituality is claimed; religion is eschewed as moralistic, coercive, dogmatistic, narrow-minded, with punitive superego rules that squelch emotion, sexuality, aggression. This split of spirituality from religion poses a problem, but one that invites inquiry. To include in our idea of psychic reality the freedom with which the divine approaches us opens for discussion both psychological and theological categories.

Mutual Contributions

What do psychoanalytic and spiritual traditions offer to each other? Spirituality possesses its own line of development; it is not derivative, but it interacts with other lines of development, for example, of the ego, of our defenses. The spirit often uses psychological complexes to speak its own purposes, using what is at hand. Hence it is difficult to separate psyche and spirit because in life they are intertwined. Sometimes pathology is the stable in which Christ is born, the only door the spirit can gain entrance. We are capable of both pathology and spirit, but that does not mean they are identical. Sometimes spirit uses physical illness to bring about an opening of the heart, for example, and the dropping of false-self living. For instance, one woman who found it very hard to receive from others, though she herself often gave generously, found when she was ill and her ungiving neurotic friend embraced her and said it was an honor to have her as a friend, that she burst into tears. She took in fully what her friend said and felt grace happened to them both, the friend to give, and she to receive.

The point here is that the spiritual develops alongside other lines of development and exists from the beginning of psychic and physical growth. We do not grow up and then add on spirit. The Christian terms of the New Testament puts it beautifully: God loves us while we are yet sinners. It can be redemptive to see spirit working in the most awful of our complexes.

Spirituality in relation to the transference-countertransference field of analysand and analyst increases equality between the two. Both are beggars before the transcendent. The projection of authority onto the analyst is reduced as is any evasion of authority by the analysand. We are all refugees and all of us are children of God.

Psychoanalysis helps fortify us against coopting spiritual needs and insights for defensive purposes. For example, highly spiritually developed persons may assume, because of their spiritual worldview, that work on the wounds of childhood and from bad marriages is all done with, when in fact, it has not yet begun. To reach those wounds may require the dismantling of the worldview, not because it is wrong, but because it is employed as a rigid, defensive shield. Or spiritual gifts may not be sufficiently integrated with the rest of the personality which may be underdeveloped emotionally or sexually. Then the person is at risk of inflation, falling into identification with the role of guru, and in danger of becoming assimilated to the projective identifications the followers would lavish onto him or her. More serious still is the danger of becoming assimilated to the archetypal energies that collect around a spiritual leader that can overwhelm one's ego and initiate psychosis.

Psychoanalysis offers insight into short-circuiting ego development by too much projection of our own authority onto religious teachings or figures, thus encouraging our own masochistic attitudes. Psychoanalysis reminds us we cannot offer an ego to something beyond us until we have one, and one that is sturdy, functional, grounded in everyday reality. Psychoanalysis can also alert us to the danger of spiritual practice being misused to augment a punitive superego with excessive penances, prescriptions, proscriptions.

Both psychoanalysis and spirituality underline how dependent we are upon each other. We need an other who sees and takes interest in what they see in us in order for us to come into our own personality. Without personal connection, it is hard to relate securely to the transpersonal, though it is not impossible. We need personal mediators of spirit who transmit its reality in manageable bits.

Psychoanalysis recognises this dependency in the emphasis most theories give to the analyst as a new introjected object in the analysand's psyche, claiming this as the mutative agent in treatment. Spirituality has a different view, one more accurate, I believe. It agrees with how dependent we are on an actual other person, but it sees through that person, so to speak, to the transcendent on which all of us depend. The new introject does not invent the relation to the It of the transcendent. The philosopher-theologian Jean-Luc Marion says we need distance in order to see this It. Jesus had to ascend to be seen and received by everyone, freed from one location in time and place to be for all. Also the transcendent can swamp us and suitable distance makes experience of it bearable. This spiritual perspective protects the analyst from hubris and becoming assimilated to the archetypal role of healer, which is disastrous for the analyst. It also allows the patient to do the work and be done with analysis because the mutative agent is not the analyst as miracle worker (see also chapters 1, 11, 14).

Spirituality contributes to psychoanalysis another point of view about problems, pain and wounds which bring us to treatment in the first place and which we want fixed, or taken away, or just make us oblivious of them! It is important to find images the analysand uses. It helps in treatment to surround an analysand with as much mythic material we can find and they can bear, to accompany their suffering with the company of other humans who also felt the world was about to be destroyed, or who felt all the light had vanished, abandoning them to the dark of depression, or a fearful journey had to be undertaken, a descent to the underworld, or a river to be crossed, or a rescue of the maiden. These mythic traditions encircle the patient and break the isolation of illness, providing a community and also giving a map of the territory of suffering. Technically this is not necessarily a spiritual perspective but rather symbolic thinking, but the spiritual endorses it as a route to spiritual presence.

Symbolic thinking keeps the patient's ego from rigid defensive thinking, from a kind of literalism and malignant regression to symbolic equations (Klein) instead of symbolic amplification. When we are developing, we fasten onto symbolic equations first and that is healthy. For example a man in his eighties remembers his first radio that he earned by winning a current events contest for all the New York boroughs. It was a treasure, a numinous object. It conferred honor on him and linked him to the wide world of news and of imagination. He invested libido in the world and in imaginative heros like the Lone Ranger, Tom Mix, Green Hornet. But if we regress to symbolic equation or remain fixated there, then the radio no longer symbolises relation to the wider world but becomes a literal end in itself, and usually a malevolent one. We fear the radio listens in on our thoughts, broadcasting them to the world.

Spirituality supports mythic and symbolic thinking because it recognises the reality to which they point. Many religious stories accompany us into the hell of feeling punished, or dead, or being parched in the wilderness, or attacked by demons. The stories coax us out from literalisms back to symbols through which our ego can begin to converse with illness happening to us. We must converse with the illness, with its arrival, and what it means, but we cannot do this alone nor with a brittle ego. We need the support of other sufferers to bathe in the psyche, to get wetter, more pliable, less rigid.

Psychoanalysis helps us see that being enlightened does not

mean we are problem-free. Furthermore, problems may be another entrance into transcendent reality. In the mathematics of the spirit, we may even compute our suffering as offering for another's relief, and discover that nothing, no principalities or powers can separate us from the love of God. In illness too, we can love and serve God.

Spirituality suggests a different relation to psychological regression (see also chapters I and II). Regression in aid of reaching the critical hurt, the basic fault, the initial rupture from the center, is hard to do in analysis because we go back to pre-ego states, or at least to where our ego feels like a wobbly egg yolk, barely formed and very vulnerable. We feel frightened of releasing the usual thought forms and imaginative containers that hold our ego consciousness. Our sanity feels threatened. We feel hugely dependent on the analyst whose faults we perceive and who we see can fail us, probably must fail us. It feels as if we become again like a child to an adult, but when we were actually a child, we lavishly loved our parents and endowed them with magnificent powers and forgave them with the generosity of a child's loving. Now we are an adult resting our confidence on another adult who, like us, is all too human. Maybe we cannot even find or afford such an analyst willing and able to do this regressive work with us.

Spiritual traditions know a lot about this movement of soul and reframe it not as regression but arrival, and offer the full support of tradition and community in undergoing such a journey. Spiritual traditions aim at reaching for the zero-point, the shedding of ego through forms and habits, the stripping of the dark night of the soul, the childlike entry into the eternal now. Here we enter a different relation to ego. No longer identified with it, now with more space around it, we use our ego but also experience nonattachment to it.

Does this arrival, whether we call it regression or release, introduce a new kind of consciousness? I believe it does and psychoanalysis helps us map its territory. This new consciousness lies between primary process, nondirected thinking of the unconscious and secondary process, the directed thinking of consciousness. It combines the two kinds of consciousness to make a third that is spiritually attuned. This kind of consciousness is needed for the multicultural reality of the twenty-first century, a kind of ego at home in cultural, spiritual and psychological diversity, including that of gender. Here we identify and are committed to our own point of view, our own sorts of faith in the psyche and spirit. We are not saying just anything goes, or drifting on the trends, eschewing having to vote for one candidate or position, or avoiding passionate choice for a partner, or devotion to one religious faith. If we cannot project libido into things in the world, it becomes dead to us. We are as if depressed; this is not nonattachment.

In this new consciousness we are rooted in this world, this body, this end of the century and also disidentified with our way. We embrace it as one way, and see it is not the only way. If we go deep enough into depths of psyche and love of God, we meet our neighbors of other traditions. As the Dalai Lama says, my enemy wants the same things I do: to be secure and satisfied and not to suffer. And we are finite. We cannot do a hundred spiritual traditions, not even five! Faith is not exclusive, but particular.

We see our ego point of view, honor it and engage it, yet it is not ultimate. We live the paradox of being there and being free from there. We live in the space between opposites. This is the kind of consciousness where lion lies down with lamb, where the table is spread before us in the shadow of death, where our cup runs over. Here the psyche is objective, and the ego is relativised. Yet our ego response is essential to see all these things.

We clinicians are an odd breed, many of us after decades of analysis with one, two or more analysts, and different modalities of group, marriage, child work, let alone years of self-analysis. Does it ever end? Why does it take so long? Spirituality has much to contribute here. In the new kind of consciousness we see through to the point of it all. If we see that, we can be done with analysis. If we do not, we usually persist in analysis because that is the place we glimpse this other reality. We need to see through the psyche, through unconscious and conscious, through dream and symptom, to reality speaking to us. Spirituality insists on naming this reality; otherwise we carry on an anonymous relationship with it, too generic, not specific and personal, and one in which we deny our dependence and need to be seen and recognised (see also chapters 1, 5, 11).

In analysis we can achieve symbolic thinking, but that does not hold up in the emergency that takes us to the hospital, or against great pain, or the arrival of dying. Then we just want someone to take away this awful state, to let us disappear into a novel like *War and Peace* or the plays of Shakespeare. Or we seek just to lose consciousness, to be knocked out. We need connection to It, to what we mean when we use the word Spirit, to the reality the icon witnesses, a reality for whom and with whom we suffer. This reality must be personal in some way and accept our dependency. We may have visions of far mountains, or hard rock, or fiery suns, but we cannot talk to them in a way that confides our fears and hopes.

Spiritual Practices

How do patients' spiritual practices influence their analyses and how does therapy influence spiritual practice? Here attention must be paid to patients' personal God-images, images of the transcendent operating in the patient's practice (Ulanov

2001, chapter 1). These will be idiosyncratic, numinous, varied, life-giving, sometimes life-threatening. We need to attend also to group God-images of an analysand's particular tribe, be it gender, race, denomination, or ex-denomination. From what ethnic roots does this person spring? Is class, politics, heritage, cultural forms like literature, painting, dance, important to this person's sense of location spiritually? Attention must also be paid to official God-images that impact the patient. What images of the transcendent have come their way from Scripture, worship services, teachings, practices of meditation, or the absence of same? In all of these images (or textures, sounds, scents, tastes), we find examples of the spiritual and psychic meeting, intertwining. The point in psychoanalysis is to see what the psyche has created and how to accommodate it and whether it works for health or illness. The point in spiritual practice is to be responsive to what shines through such images, to correspond to the One who bids us through the image of imagelessness, who moves us to gratitude for the tribe we belong to, for the gifts of sacred texts, or for people like the Dalai Lama or Julian of Norwich.

Any spiritual practice that endures eventually comes to the end of all these kinds of images. Becoming conscious of them also means becoming conscious of the gap between them and the ultimate to which they point. We reach the end of our Jacob's ladder of images. It does not span to the infinite. All our images are finite and fall short. Arriving there causes a crisis in spiritual practice. The dark night of the senses and of the spirit descends. We cannot reach the other side from our side. Earning merit by achievement is transcended by grace where judgment has perished, a grace that includes all of us in our need, oppression, desolation. Something crosses from the other side that liberates us from repeating patterns (repetition compulsion), from operating according to *quid pro quo*, you do for me and I will do for you. The new crosses over to us from its side; a new thing happens in this fearful night, this gap. The new is not a product of the past, but includes it; it is not an invention of the ego, but needs the ego's response. It is like the bones of Ezekiel resurrected into livingness, new life.

How does the spiritual practice of clinicians influence their work? This question has been neglected, primarily out of fear of unconscious imposition of the analyst's worldview on the analysand, or, worse, a kind of proselytizing. But remaining unconscious of our spiritual stance does not protect our clients. Only consciousness does. Consciousness of our political stance, our sexual life, our theoretical position protects us from imposing our views on our patients. The same consciousness applies to our spirituality.

The three levels of countertransference in clinical work also address spiritual matters (see also chapter 14 and Ulanov 1996, chapters 1, 6 and 7). Have we worked through our own complexes around spirit (abnormal countertransference), or do we need to do more work on them? What is our idiosyncratic response to spiritual issues (normal countertransference)? Our sense of placement in the universe, from what roots we live our life, gets into the room with our clients. How does what the client's unconscious induces in our reactions meet with our spiritual experience (objective countertransference) to create a unique mixture in the transference-countertransference field between us?

The emotional field between analyst and analysand proves crucial for this spiritual issue, as it does for any other issue. What the analyst believes influences the angle of vision to perceive psychic processes and glimpses of spirit. For example, I believe that we do not invent the new, nor does it totally depend on us as a new introject. Something constellates between analyst and analysand that we cannot create alone.

3. Psychoanalysis and the Spiritual Quest

Something arrives through us that addresses both of us, though not necessarily in identical ways. Or, for example, a certain quality of sacrifice occurs on the part of the analyst, to carry the projections of the analysand, especially if they are negative, and not retaliate, explain away, but to accept them for a time and even acknowledge that they wound. As analysts we also sacrifice the living out of the relationship with a client in a "real" way, especially if an erotic tinge or spiritual magnetism occurs that promises that a relationship would be possible. We process the urge to act out into deeper psychological meaning (Ulanov 1996, chapter 8). Or, for example, how we view the outcome of analysis reflects our own spiritual standpoint. For me, it is livingness that is the goal, not products, even wonderful products we value highly like effective work evidenced in salary, books, fame, or effective relationships with a mate, a spouse, a child.

Livingness comes from connecting to the center of reality, however we name it; it pours through us regardless of our degree, great or small, of health, wealth, wisdom; it makes us glad, filled with gratitude to be alive.

Address given to The National Psychological Association for Psychoanalysis, the 8th Annual Annette Overby Conference November 1999.

References

Klein, M. 1930-1975. The importance of symbol-formation in the development of the ego. Klein, M. *Love, Guilt and Reparation & Other Works, 1921-1945.* New York: Seymour Lawrence/Delacorte Press.
Marion, J.-L. 1977. *L'Idole et la Distance.* Paris: Éditions Grasset & Fasquelle.
Ulanov, A. B. 1996. *The Functioning Transcendent.* Wilmette, Ill.: Chiron.
Ulanov, A. B. 2001. *Finding Space: Winnicott, God, and Psychic Reality.* Louisville, Ky.: John Knox/Westminster.

Chapter 4

Psychotherapy and Spirituality

"The wind blows where it will; you hear the sound of it,
but you do not know where it comes from or where it is
going. So it is with everyone who is born of the Spirit."

(John 3:8)

These words from the Gospel of John capture the terror we
feel when we address the topic of the Spirit. The living reality
of Spirit is always implied in any discussion of spirituality, and
particularly so when we link it with psychotherapeutic work in
our own offices, for there, if healing occurs it always brings with
it a sense of mystery. Something bigger carries both analyst and
analysand in its current and our psychodynamic theories as well
as our theologies cannot grasp it.

Spirit

A certain autonomy associates with Spirit. Like the wind,
it will blow or cease, come and go, according to its own law.
We might hear it but we cannot control it, or even direct it. It
moves us, but we do not invent it. When we invoke Spirit, we

are calling on powers beyond the human ego to aid in the work of healing, and we are turning straight into its path.

That is no small turning. Traditionally, Spirit brings an order of being which is suprahuman, not limited to time and space, nor even bodily frame. (Cross 1958, 1281-83, 649) Spirit is breath, movement, energy, a vital power, warm intense life force. Who knows what it will do? It spades up accepted opinions and casts them into the wind; it might overshadow us like Mary, making us pregnant with a life so new it changes our life forever. It might drop us into a depth where we totally communicate with each other even though we speak different languages, uniting us all together in a modern Pentecost. It might summon us as Jesus called out the fisherman to follow him, so that we must leave our known fathers and mothers of inherited psychoanalytic theories to follow an unknown new thought.

Spirit gives us gifts, all different kinds, but we do not always take them, or are unable to. Then we put ourselves outside the overflowing fountain of water; we do not go down to the pool which the healing Spirit stirs up to release us from our crippling; we will not brood on the formless void, the dark deep waters over whose face the Spirit moves just before the act of creation. Is this reluctance, this refusal, this removing of ourselves the dreaded blasphemy against Spirit, the one sin that will not be forgiven?

Yet Spirit also moves us to connect with parts of ourselves, with each other, and to link us with the very inner life of God. For the Spirit moves us to pray, makes us utter sighs too deep for words, intercedes for us with the transcendent abyss we have not yet learned to call by name. The Spirit brings to our tiny particular reality the love dwelling at the Source of reality. Spirit makes a bridge to the Source, proceeding as it does in western theology from the Father and the Son. Augustine writes of the Spirit as the bond of union in the Holy Trinity, thus describing what we might call the energy circulating between God's inner object relations. (Augustine 1935)

The Spirit is thought to search even the depths of God, thus manifesting the absolute freedom within the Godhead itself. We can readily understand the fear that gripped the early church when it outlawed as heresy Montanus's insight that the Spirit operates in each of us. What an outpouring of revelations – new, different, ever-changing – might result! How could we hold on to any consistent doctrine if we accepted that the Spirit spoke to each of us at any time?

With a force like this, you can see I mean what I say when I use the word "terror." This breath that we call Spirit can disrupt traditions, drive us into the desert of temptation, descend on us in a baptism of blessing, bestow upon us deeds of valor or words of prophesy, comfort us in our mourning, prepare a place for us after death, and so break up accustomed patterns of thought that we can only describe what just took place as a miracle. Spirit means the freedom of God, the utter, absolute freedom that convinces us of the gap between us and the infinite. Any image, idea, symbol, or program that we cherish as our best human values – whether of health or politics – can never be identified with the transcendent.

Psyche

What of psyche, that other reality we are addressing? It inhabits a realm very close to Spirit as both are etymologically associated with spirit as breath, *spirare* in Latin and *psukhe* in Greek. Linked with the root word *therapeutikos* and *therapeuein* denoting to attend to, take care of, to hold and to support, we arrive at the meaning of psychotherapy as the practice of attending to, caring for the animating breath or spirit present in our clients and between us.

Depth psychology as a discipline, now a century old, has introduced us to new perceptions of reality. First and foremost we recognize the reality of the psyche, psychic reality, as something as objectively there as a table-leg that barks our shins, even though we cannot see the psyche or touch it. Psychic reality is as objective as the fragrance of baking bread even though we cannot smell it. We do not hear or taste psyche. Its reality is not conveyed through sensuous experience or rational sequence of thought. Hence Bion tells us our proper attitude as therapists is to eschew memory and desire for they take us back to the visible conveyed through our senses, and to the rational conveyed through our logical ideas. (Bion 1970) The psyche is the invisible yet present reality of, for example, an anxiety that heaves up our stomachs or makes our bowels loosen or our palms sweat. Psychic reality also exists among us and through us as those "river-beds into which the water of life has dug deep ..." what Jung called archetypes, those primordial patterns of response which we flesh out afresh through the contents of our cultures and personal histories (Jacobi 1959, 53 cited in Wyss 1966, 342; see also Jung 1948, paras 277ff.; Jung 1953, para 329).

Both psyche and Spirit have reintroduced for our attention the reality of our body. Psyche moved through two teenage boys' bodies to make them take aim and shoot their classmates in Columbine high school in Colorado to revenge lethal wounds to self-esteem. These boys were called the "discards," the "scum" of the school. Anytime we doubt the invisible reality of the psyche, we need only look to the violence in our society that moves us to terrible acts. Psychic fantasies of revenge or greed or power are one thing; but when they inhabit our bodies and we move to act them out, no one can doubt the reality of such psychic facts. We discover nightly in our dreams what the psyche says are facts for us, in contrast to what we wish or feel should be.

Spirit too must inhabit a body to become real in time and space. Otherwise it just wafts upwards into ethereal realms, the stuff of dreams or inflations or superstitions. To be real, Spirit must step over into concrete reality, into time and space, the limited dimensions of you and me, of this community and that group. The body, whether it is our own or the body politic or the mystical body of Christ, is the only way Spirit can be seen – in the flesh, in definite form and shape, limited, but real. Thus it is that simple acts of kindness bring us the breath of Spirit, of some bigger goodness, here for a moment through another's gesture or word, given simply, generously, without asking anything in return.

This leads us to a third perception of depth psychology. In our time, the beginning of this new millennium, Spirit is down. In contrast to earlier centuries when Spirit was experienced by people as going up above the riot of instincts, abstracting a calm steadiness from the turmoil of emotions, bidding us rise up over the turbulence of social and national strife, into an unchanging eternal truth, for us the opposite direction indicates our path. For us Spirit is down into the midst of life, into the psyche in our bodies which stirs up gender disputes, into social and political issues that move collectivities of people into war, into national conflicts, into mass marches or demonstrations. (See also chapters 7 and 11.)

Depth psychology shifts the location of the conflict and con-versation of Spirit and flesh down into our own concrete ordi-nary selves, no longer found in a metaphysics above the world's life. The horrendous conflict in eastern Europe, for instance, is matched by theophanies of the Virgin Mary at Medjugorge before the Slavic eruptions. Or, in our work as psychotherapists we are searching out the ways of Spirit through the psyche of actual persons in the midst of repressions, dissociations, displacements, flashes of hope and new possibility. We are not rising above psychic distress to find a way out, but going down into it to find a way through. We go down into matter to find greeting us what matters. In the symbolism of masculine and feminine, this new way of the downward going road is definitely a feminine mode of inquiry. (Ulanov 1971, 169-192) Or, using the Christian narrative, our work takes place in the midst of the muck of the stable, with those parts that do not get housed in the civilised Inn. We await the new to be revealed where the poor, outcast parts of ourselves get lodged, where our nearest neighbors are the beasts in the manger, those "animal root-impulses" that are the first to recognise that the new is born. (Ulanov 1998)

By directing us down into the thick of our experience, we learn from depth psychology a fourth perception of real-ity. It adds a new line of interpretation to our hermeneutic disciplines. It adds psychic meaning – that we must inquire into psychic factors of, for example, those Columbine shootings, or the Kosovo rape camps, or the Truth and Justice meetings in South Africa. In reading a religious text, we must add to the literary-form criticism and the socio-political interpretation, the line of psychic interpretation: what is the history of this particular image, where has it been used as a symbol before in this and other traditions? What is the psychic effect, both good and bad, of this language on contemporary readers? We cannot reduce all levels of interpretation only to the psychological, but neither can we any longer omit it. (Ulanov 1986/1999, chapter 5) Theology now is not done in the abstract, but down in the midst of the embodied realities of color, political location, sexual identity, social class. What needs to be augmented is the psychic meaning of different images of God, inquiry into what psychological reality they reflect, what spiritual origins and paths they denote.

A specific hermeneutic issue, of interest to only a few of us, but, surprisingly, of significance to every clinician because it bears directly on how we do our work, is the relation of psyche and Spirit. Are they the same, psyche now just being the modern word for an ancient reality? Are they different, and if so how, and how are they related? Are they completely separate so that we need not concern ourselves with these questions in our clinical work? That used to be the dominant position in clinical practice: work with the psyche, leave all that spiritual stuff to religious people. Religious experience was seen as manifestation of disorder, illness. Not until a psychiatrist himself had a profound spiritual experience did "religious ideation," as it was called, get removed from the diagnostic manuals as a symptom of pathology.

How we each answer the question how psyche and Spirit are related greatly influences how we work clinically in the transference-countertransference field (see Ulanov 1996, chapters 1, 7). For myself, I see Spirit working through psyche just as it works through any other form of life – politics, history, music, painting, other people, the living planet, even books! I see psyche as a necessary ground of experience both within and far outside us, both in our own interior and between us. Psyche is another kind of flesh through which the Almighty can put a paw on us at any time. It is a most immediate and intimate flesh – our dreams at night, our daytime fantasizing, our conflicts repeated over and over again with different people. Those repetition compulsions, for example, tell us in no uncertain terms about original sin – that we cannot start over from scratch but instead always find ourselves embedded in generational and social conflicts that have impacted us. And we may also see that hiding in our despised fetish, for example, dwells the rejected stone that proves to become the cornerstone. (See Ulanov 1992/1996, chapter 3)

Mythology

To be interested in working with psychic reality takes us to a depth level in our daily consultations with clients. More than ego-solutions and ego-mastery, we are seeking how to live from the depths. To be interested in spirituality means we are alert to signals of transcendent reality that exceeds not just ego-mastery but the whole human psyche, the whole realm of culture and society. We are looking to that reality in which we all dwell, a reality that breaks open the parochialism of all religions. We need to discuss with ourselves what horizon contains us, what we believe about what we are doing clinically.

Freud speaks of his own horizon as his mythology, which for him was his theory of the instincts: "Instincts are mythical entities, magnificent in their indefiniteness. In our work we cannot for a moment disregard them, yet we are never sure that we are seeing them clearly." (Freud 1995, cited in Wyss 1966, 165) Or, if we adhere to Object-Relations theory, what reality do we believe those objects attest to? What subject originated them? What kind of ontological premise is revealed when we see that our client's "bad mother" was herself a victim of her own "bad-mother," and so on, like a genealogy, all the way back to Eve? If we subscribe to the more recent Relational Psychology, that recognizes the subjectivity of the analyst as well as of the analysand playing a crucial part in constructing an intersubjective reality between them, what status does that reality hold? Did the two just create it? Was it there to become manifest before the two built it? Is intersubjectivity a symbol of the nature of reality, that always includes relation to someone else just as Husserl says, that to be conscious is to be a subject aware of an object, for there is no isolated single consciousness? Bion tells us we want to obscure our belief systems by calling them theories. (Bion 1965/1991) I am calling us back to the unspoken reality those theories attest to, to see if we can tease it into words and share discussion about it.

To recognize spiritual aspects of clinical work is to set the clinical enterprise in a bigger bowl, with more elbow room to do the work. We believe in our theory but we also see that it can be blasted by something new coming into the work. We need to muse on what that something is, for it is the reality to which our symbols and theories point. Neither theory nor symbol will be effective if we neglect our relationship with what we believe that "it" to be. This means we engage that reality, with all four feet jumped in, with heart and soul, mind and strength, not staying outside looking at it aesthetically as if we could take it or leave it. That careless attitude is a kind of mental prostitution where we shun loyalty to what claimed us, acting as if we can flirt with all kinds of ideas or events and not ever be bound to them. If we recognize where, or to whom, we belong, we can risk encounter with Spirit that may break open the theory that has contained our work.

Does such passionate engagement mean we become fanatics? That is the great fear – that we become not wed to the reality that touched us, but stuck there, falling into identification with our theory and foisting it onto everyone else, including our clients, as "the" truth which they too should embrace. Religions have a lot to answer for here – what with their crusades, inquisitions, holy wars and purges of anyone who does not identify with the official doctrine. Theological sadism joins with the psychological variety to bully people into conformity with threats of excommunication, damnation, or labeling them mentally ill. But the opposite of a schizoid knowing-about ultimate reality while staying safely out of reach of a heart's commitment is no better. There we float above engagement with the very reality we speak about, afraid to risk giving ourselves wholeheartedly. Anyone with the slightest experience of a spiritual path knows how defensively self-deluding that position is. God offers to be the center of our life, or if rejected to be outside our life, but God will not be just a part of our life.

A Clinical Example

Sometimes a client speaks a narrative suggestive of transcendent reference. For example, a middle-aged white woman who does not identify herself in specific religious categories but would see herself in the bigger bowl, so to speak, of Judeo-Christian tradition, spoke of how "Providence intervened" in the beginning of her new job.

The woman had originally sought therapy because of anxiety so great and frequent, we could say she suffered panic attacks to an alarming degree. In this new and desired job, closer to her own creative talents and ambitions, she could feel the threat of her old panic in the face of her colleague's criticism of her first piece of work which revived the relentlessly critical imago of her mother. She said, this woman has "that voice that threatens to annihilate creativity – mine and everyone else's. Like Mom she takes away any creative impulse, stultifies it and I feel worthless, hopeless." But another colleague asked her if that first woman had, as she put it, "acted crazy" yet, and when my client said yes, this colleague arranged with their higher-up boss that my client's work need not be reviewed by this overly critical woman.

What felt to my client like Providence intervening was this other person's kind act and also the intervening insight my client achieved. She saw her own temptation to slip right back into panicked helpless hopelessness in the face of critical attack. But this time she saw that the source of criticism did not originate in her own worthlessness but arose in this other woman whom everyone recognised as objectively difficult. In a previous job, and in her childhood, my client could not see the difference between outer and inner attacks because the outer attack converged with her conviction that her deficits caused the onslaught. If she would just work harder, be better, do more, then no one would attack her. Now she could see the difference between herself and the outer woman, and grapple afresh with her temptation to take the problem on herself as of her own making in a self-defeating effort to control a threatened annihilation.

She felt the new arrived in this present job – a new object of a helpful co-worker and a new ability in herself to see the critical colleague as a subject in her own right. She gained new clarity into how she hogged the stage with her own low self-esteem to fend off a feared obliteration. She said, "How thin the veil is," between going along pretty well and falling into the abyss, and between this world and the next. She said she saw how she displaced the contingency of life onto her mother. During this stress at the job she forgot to bring to her mother on a visit some dresses, so then she had to mail them. Her mother was frantically critical lest the dresses be lost by the Post Office. My client said, "If I lose Mother's dresses and she never speaks to me again then I will die, and be in a horrible darkness and isolation." But it was immediately clear to both of us from the work we had done that the feared death was one she had already suffered in the past, and more than once. Her biological mother kept her briefly and then she was fostered out, living until she was three with a woman she came to feel was her "real" mother. The foster mother was prevented from adopting her even though she fought in court to do so, because she was deemed too old. While the court battle raged between this woman and my client's adopting parents, the client was placed for months with a third "mother." In our therapy work we hazarded how a child under three would blame herself as having done something horribly wrong and was sent away from her loved mother as a result.

When finally she was adopted by the people who became her parents, she had suffered three ruptures – from the biological mother, the loved mother, the second foster mother. Her adopting mother suffered great anxiety which she dealt with by chronic fault-finding and explosive temper. My client felt she had to swallow her own hate in response to these ruptures of connection, and toward her adopting mother's constant criticisms. That buried anger made her feel chronically guilty and inadequate and chained my client to a sense of her own worthlessness. In fearing her mother's anger if the dresses were lost, my client once again repeated the cycle of abandonment, rage, feared annihilation as fitting punishment for her rage. In the new job, she nearly repeated in the present what she actually had endured in the past: losing her mother(s), blaming herself, and trying to secure her foothold in the universe by pledging to work hard, to "be better."

When in her early forties, my client suffered the threat of annihilation again in a dramatic way at the birth of her child. Securing a committed intimate relationship with a partner had unfolded as she worked through her anxiety in therapy. After the successful birth of her daughter, my client, when returned to her room and without any nurse present, suddenly suffered three rapid strokes. Fortunately she was able to cry out and another patient came in, sounded the alarm and my client pulled through with no long-term damage. No medical condition explained why the strokes happened.

In working over the psychic meaning of this trauma, we hazarded that the three seizures were, on a psychic level, the three ruptures from the holding container of reality that happened right after her own birth and in the first three years of her life, in the successive loss of three mothers before her adoption which brought her an outward container of a family she dearly prized, but not the inner security of a mother on whose love one can depend. Those were the deaths that her panic attacks displayed, attempted to fend off, and summoned her to integrate. Then she was a daughter to her mothers. Now she was a mother to a daughter and the trauma resounded once again. On the surface of her analysis the problem was anxiety and buried aggression. In the depth of her analysis was the work of integrating her experience of living on the borders of psychic life and death by developing her own articulated relation to reality itself.

During the treatment years, my client often spoke about the "little green men" who could appear at any time and whisk your life away. By this she meant the fragility of life and the nearness of death. Her anxiety attacks only yielded when she embraced her own standpoint toward reality, the bigger bowl in which we sit. She felt this standpoint allowed her to direct her aggression and anxious energy to the actual tasks of her job. But, in the opposite direction, as she saw a bigger reality, she felt what can be called dread of the good. (Ulanov and Ulanov 1983/1998, chapter 5) She was touched, even overwhelmed, that "Providence intervened" in the form of the co-worker who rescued her from the captious colleague, and in the form of her own capacity to see the new situation with new eyes, that she did not cause the supervisor's criticism, that it was not a repetition of her old complex, that she had worked through her anxiety and aggression and need not succumb to an orgy of self-doubt, but could creatively direct her aggression and anxious energy to the actual tasks of her job. "It was so good I was afraid I was going to die!" she exclaimed. "It is brighter than what I live in; it is red, scary. Is this pointing to where I came from, started, to be grounded in?" Meditating on these thoughts she said she found herself curling up in a ball and rocking back and forth, "as if I might cry and have a person put arms around me. I sobbed."

Hearing this I felt the body knew what her ego had not known, her body-consciousness knew both the loss and finding of being a self held by a greater reality which broke in upon her ego awareness. This was more than therapy; it was Spirit touching her, giving her a sense of being held in the universe, granting her not just a foothold but a lap, a protected space to feel cherished. The therapeutic task shifted into a new zone: how to focus on the good, to withstand it, eat it, chew it, digest it, celebrate it with all her heart, mind, spirit and strength.

Did I use religious language with this client? No, not especially. But I was musing and thinking in terms of the good, the abysmal pit, the birth of the new. Elsewhere (Ulanov 1999a; Ulanov 1999b) I have taken up how the spiritual comes into therapy through the countertransference of the clinician. Here, the bigger bowl I was sitting in allowed me to imagine and construct with my client the psychic reality of her life journey and where she had felt menaced and blessed by a bigger spiritual reality. One could talk about this example of panic attacks without mentioning the spiritual dimension. It is there whether we notice it or not, as Bion says of truth in his characteristically obscure way: "... O ... is an absolute, inhering in ('incarnate in') everything and unknowable by man.... Nobody need think the true thought. It awaits the advent of the thinker." (Bion 1970, 101, 103)

Acknowledging this larger reality sustains our work. It is always there. But we do not recognise or name it. When we do, we see more. If we are discouraged about the value to the world of our work, or when we are tired, it makes a difference to remember, in the vocabulary of the Christian story, that Christ died for this particular individual in our office. That perception links our work with the inestimable value conferred on each person by the center of reality. Work with this person thus confirms the whole human family, much as Døgen, the thirteenth century Buddhist, meant when he said if one person tries to realize Buddha-nature, it benefits all of creation.

A Different Consciousness and Another Clinical Example

Where do we come out as a result of this twin focus on the resources of Spirit and psyche in clinical work? We grow into a different kind of consciousness, one in process, emerging. We might call it simultaneous consciousness because we are at once aware of the here and now and the beyond, of this moment and the eternal. We are mindful of being limited in and simultaneously transcending space and time, of being very tiny and linked to the All and Vast. Because of this link, spiritual traditions tell us this consciousness is full of praise, of joy, and at the same time beholds abyss and void. Describing this living state, this state of livingness, is like catching running water in your hand. Clinical examples will help.

One is taken from a decisive phase of a long analysis, twice a week sessions, with a white woman in her forties, a medically trained mental health professional, married, mother of two children. The example illustrates how this new consciousness breaks in upon us, usually at first with a sense of dis-ease, dis-orientation and it is sometimes, as it was here, the job of the therapist to carry awareness of this wider consciousness at first. As the one girl in a family of four brothers, daughter of a famous successful father and a mother of poised persona and social activity, she grew up sustaining a big gap in mothering care and paternal intimacy. A wild child who bonded with her brothers but who also had to fight off their stronger, older intellectual and bodily power, she got by by what she called "passing." "I lied, pretended I knew what I didn't, acted as if I didn't care, floated from group to group, took drugs from the age of nine and never learned how to do things." When she came to herself, she got admitted to educational institutions and trained for a profession, but she felt she had to memorize much of her work and did not trust her intelligence. At the time of this example, we had arrived at a number of clear insights – that she sought treatment because she was living over a gap in her upbringing where she did not learn how to learn from experience, but developed a hyper-vigilance and list-making to accomplish the chores of child-rearing and housekeeping, living. This kept her on a short leash of chronic anxious tension in the face of feeling overwhelmed.

Two traumatic physical events also dented her confidence in her capacity to sustain herself intellectually and emotionally, one the result of a car accident which left her unconscious for seventeen hours, and the other a sudden period of panicked depression two weeks after the birth of her second child, precipitated physically by total loss of estrogen. In both events, she felt not only panic and despair, but fright that her cognitive capacities were impaired, that she could not remember what she was told about the safety of her husband and first child in the case of the accident, or comprehend directions about feeding her baby. She also projected her panic into a dreaded future of Alzheimer's disease which her mother was now suffering, fearing either as her mother's daughter she was genetically programmed to inherit it, or that she had "fried her brain" in her drug-taking years and would thus succumb.

A measure of relief from dread of losing her faculties was gained when we traced the psychic meaning of the physical trauma – that she had fallen into the gap of her childhood where she had not been held and mothered into life, neither taught things nor grasped them because father and mother were not providing an emotional container that held her as she grew into her own skills for living and relating. When her second child was born, a girl, she fell into the gap between daughter and mother that she herself had experienced. The psyche was pressing her to relate to the gap consciously and integrate it, not, as she put it, just endure and "move on."

Resentment and rage had also been a theme in our work. Her valiant efforts to cope and manage daily living, her determination to expose her children to the many opportunities that a big city affords, and her spiritual stance that what she could contribute to the world was simple acts of kindness, frequently left her depleted. She got caught overdoing the giving role. Emotionally exhausted, she then attacked herself for feeling resentment and rage: "What is the matter with me! Other people give and survive. Why can't I do it better?"

The new event she introduced was a golden retriever puppy as a pet and good presence for the family, though we had questioned beforehand whether it would amount to overload and resentment. For it was she on whom the care and training of the dog fell, as one child was away at camp, the other too young, and the husband out of town on business. Her anxiety rocketed; her dread of losing her faculties, that she could not do what all the books told her one did with puppies, threatened to overwhelm her. Her vigilant list-making, her efforts to push herself just to do more and it would come right finally met their match in the fuzzy face and rambunctious sweetness of this little beast who chewed and vomited, got diarrhea, barked incessantly and also wowed and wooed everyone who saw her on the street when taken for a walk. My client's pattern of pushing for mastery, and just doing more broke down and she felt despair as well as shame that she went into free-fall anxiety over, of all things, a puppy!

We scheduled additional sessions. It was clear this was a momentous time. She had fallen into the gap between what ought to be and what was, but this time someone was there with her; she was not alone in a hospital ICU nor in her apartment with a new baby, nor a lonely little girl with four bigger brothers. The field between us offered a container which helped her let go of the skills of mastery, vigilant list-making and perseverance. In Buddhist language, the dog was like an insoluble koan in the face of which her accustomed ways of thinking and perceiving broke down. She could not do what she always did. My mind, and gradually hers too, broke open to perceive a bigger reality that activated another kind of consciousness than that of the usual achieving and suffering ego.

Identification and Disidentification

This new kind of consciousness often begins by disorientation. The distinction between the breakdown of ego defenses and the person breaking down introduces its main feature: we are both identified with and disidentified from our accustomed ego-stance. We know how we usually approach reality; we see our own mode of awareness, the ego we are usually identified with, but we are also pushed out of it; it does not work; we get disidentified with what we used to take for granted. Now we see it, instead of just being it. My client longed to be able to master this dog, or, to decide to give it away. She could do neither. Stymied, acutely suffering, weeping, her old "body and mind" dropped away.

It took me awhile to see that through this problem-to-be-solved the psyche was engineering something radically new. Her old approach had used up its brownie points, so to speak, and was not going to work. Now she could not overgive and leave out her own needs and feelings; they had to be included. And she could see the necessity of including her own self-care more easily in relation to a dog than she had been able to in relation to her children or husband or the suffering neighbor she helped on the street. (In Jungian vocabulary, she had fallen into identification with the opposites of the mother archetype, either all-giving, or all-consumed with fury and resentment.) She could not exhaust and deplete herself for a dog, nor did she want to. She got help from a trainer, a dog-walker, and even considered giving the dog to a good home (which she located). She saw her usual way of coping and that it was not working. She held in her consciousness the tension of losing her old way and not yet having found a new way to proceed.

Identifying and disidentifying from our usual ego stance gives an added dimension to clinical work (Ulanov and Ulanov 1975, 188-190, 218-219, 231-232). Usually we adopt a causal approach, looking for the cause of the present problem in the past object relations and cultural conditioning. In addition, we might adopt a teleological approach that inquires into what new attitude the present symptom is leading us, what final cause beckons us to develop a new openness to a part of ourselves or other people. Simultaneous consciousness looks to the whole surround, not just the past cause or the future result. In this approach we sit in the middle of the bowl, so to speak, allowing all sides of the conflict to speak of its entire reality without being overly restricted to the lines of our own questions and needs for meaning (Bright 1997). Instead, we are open to the whole reality out of which the conflict arose. Here psyche and Spirit seem to intertwine because we recognize a reality that is objectively there, not reducible to our causal or teleological constructions. We look to see and hear what different things come in all at once.

Knowing/Not-knowing

This shift in consciousness accompanies the shift in clinical theory from seeing repression as the problem and knowing as the cure, to seeing dissociation as the problem and inclusion as the cure (Stern 1983/1997). Inclusion means beginning in a muddle rather than with a clear goal. All parts being included means affect, thought, image, unconscious unformed tendings, impulse, dream, fantasy, need, confusion, determination, and lassitude, dis-ease and ease as well as a destruction of any former clarity we knew. All the lost sheep come in and all at once, so that this new consciousness means knowing and not-knowing simultaneously.

I sensed something was afoot with my client and her puppy long before I knew about it. I felt pulled into some bigger view without at all understanding it. I knew the dog-walker and the other ego strategies would help, but more was looming here. A kind of formless energy amasses in this kind of awareness, something luminous hovers on the horizon that does not yield to an inquiring reasoning ego, but only hints to us of its presence through sources of consciousness outside the ego.

Theorists from different depth psychological schools converge on their descriptions of what this knowing/not-knowing is like. Jung talks about consciousness emanating from the whole conscious and unconscious psyche, a bigger center he calls the Self, which addresses the ego. Bion talks about being-at-one-with versus knowing-about, even using the religious word atonement. Winnicott talks about the being element

93

out of which all doing arises, a theory Guntrip elaborates upon as a true being-knowing versus a false doing-knowing. Philip Bromberg writes of health consisting of our ability to stand in spaces between realities without losing any one of them (Bromberg 1993, 401). Thomas Ogden writes of the "analytic third" where patient and analyst are permeable to each other and a third intersubjectivity grows between them which differs from each of their single subjectivity (Ogden 1994). Spiritual traditions talk about the cataphatic and apophatic ways of advancing spiritual life. The cataphatic approach uses the things of this world to perceive God's presence. The perfection of our baby's ear at birth bespeaks the existence of a Creator. Thus our images and thought-forms, the beauty of nature, the goodness of people, the help given in suffering, all testify to the grander order of God. The apophatic approach emphasizes the gap between this finite world and the transcendent. No thing can serve to convey God who breaks all our thought forms, smashes our images, exceeds the natural beauties. We mount to God by discarding, shedding all our definitions and pictures of the transcendent.

This simultaneous consciousness includes all these opposite ways of knowing about and being one with; it stands between the cataphatic and apophatic spiritual practices and sees both as contained in a large reality. We cannot grasp this reality through sensate experience nor through reasoning about it, but nonetheless it is objectively there, holding all our ways of knowing and being. We know it and cannot know it simultaneously. Instead, we live in a place of paradox, not unlike Winnicott's transitional space, with its excitement and creativeness, for that reality is there to be found as we are creating it. By not totally identifying with any one way to perceive or know, we imaginatively destroy all inherited versions of truth or the path to it, including our own, as we imaginatively find the true way in this moment. One is keenly aware of the tremendous vitality of this larger reality, its rhythm, its beat. A woman's dream captures it. She dreamt she saw Fred Astaire dancing, and saw him as a genius of grace. He called out to her, "Where is God?" And she yelled back, "In your feet!"

On a personal level, we can feel the shift into this simultaneous consciousness by the mark of an identifying and disidentified ego. We know our accustomed stance and still could take it up, because like riding a bicycle, once learned, we can always do it. But we no longer see our ego stance as the only approach, but can walk around it, sympathizing with its origins in our early object relations, good and bad, in our cultural location and the constructions that issue from it. The ego position we identify as our own now exists like a free-standing statue. We see it from all angles and are not stuck in it. We accept it and let go of it simultaneously.

This new consciousness is characterised by opposites held simultaneously in awareness. We engage in a third kind of thinking, neither just the directed thinking of consciousness according to logic, based on sense experience and communicable in language to others, what Freud called secondary process thinking; nor only nondirected thinking of fantasy where image piles on image, expressing instinctive desires and private experiences, which Freud called primary process thinking. This third kind of simultaneous thinking combines image and thought, impulse and pause; we are in it and talking back to it at the same time (see Edinger 1994, 4; Ulanov and Ulanov 1994, 366-382).

Some other center takes precedence over our usual ego way of proceeding. And it communicates indirectly. We get hints, not explanations; we get body feelings not logical proofs. In New Testament terms, these hints are called "signs and wonders," inexplicable noncausally related phenomena that coincide, and convict us with a profound meaning even though we cannot explain them causally. The coincidences transgress inner and outer boundaries, physical and psychic parameters, so that we feel amazed and impressed, by a deeply stirring sense of meaning (see Ulanov 1997/1999, 137). The meaning marks us even though we cannot explain its happening; we never forget it. The meaning originates outside our invention and we are shifted from understanding it to receive it, from explaining it to witness it.

With my client, the body tone of her crying signaled another source than just her ego's inability to cope with the dog. We knew, of course, that this little female puppy symbolically carried her to the lost little girl she had been who did not know how to cope and no one taught her so she was afraid all the time. She built defenses of pretending she did know or did not care or she just buzzed on drugs floating above the scary situations. But that insight did not exhaust her weeping. If she had not, with her usual courage, stuck with the nameless dread engulfing her I would never have received the hint of another order of being going on.

I asked her what did *she* want – to keep or give up the dog, thus underscoring the need to include her feelings, not just giving to the family. We saw she could not repeat trying to be the omnipotent mother of all to make up for not being mothered herself. But, she wailed, "That's just it! I don't know!" She had fallen into non-knowing. She had been dumped into the gap which she suffered as a child but never lived in relation to. She survived being identified with the not-knowing after her accident and in her depression, but she never lived it consciously related to it. Now she was in the gap with all four feet, looking around to see what this space was like. She could not "move-on" ignoring her feelings; she could not make lists of what to do to get out of it. She fell between the abstract ideals of how to raise a dog and the reality of this wiggly, barking, jumping, curious, wooly animal. She felt unsupported, unheld, uninspired by her own ideals. Instead she felt inadequate before them to the alarming degree of wondering if her mind was intact and could she go on functioning. She felt contemptible, not measuring up, as if "something is *wrong* with me!"

Her not-knowing tipped my own. A low-key chronic countertransference, resistant to analysis with her or by myself, fell into place. We had worked on various negative aspects of her feelings toward me, criticisms of what I said or how I said it, or how I failed to get what she meant, but my feeling of never measuring up, of being an incompetent dope never went away. I had felt dumb in her presence, somehow always disappointing her expectations, not measuring up to her image of what she needed, as if she held me in contempt. I saw now an objective piece of my countertransference, that I was getting what she got: contempt for not reaching the ideal. The new event of her being with the dog and falling into the gap of learning to learn herself, illuminated the origin of my suffering. I suffered what she did; I too fell in the gap between expected ideals and human reality. I laughed to discover that both of us were in training, not just the puppy.

From an ego point of view my client adding the dog to her overburdened schedule was a disaster, a repetition of omnipotent giving to those she loved to compensate for not being given to, and then feeling depleted, resentful and angry. But from a depth level, the psyche was engineering a course entirely different, not to learn more about the gap in her past and her defenses against it, but to live in it, through it in the present, including all her negative affects toward the dog, not just positive feelings. *She* was learning how to play and to discover what was play to her, along with the dog. She could not know the answers because she had to live her way toward them. I could not give her the answers because she was creating and finding them as she went along, sorting them out in and outside of our sessions. With the female puppy she was connecting to the wild, lonely child she had been and learning how to integrate her, learning how to learn in contrast to measuring up to the abstract principles advised in the books she read. The dissociated part was returning to the fold with all the uncertainty of an untamed lively young puppy. She was feeling along how to build a bigger container to make room for all the parts.

I was aware of a bigger reality opening to her; my client was aware of losing her former stance, feeling her usual ego mode collapse, and if she did not disidentify from it, she would collapse too. The field between us held the energy of the new, which she had still to find her way of living.

Spiritual Location

Jung uses the word synchronicity to refer to coincidences of inner and outer events which are clearly not causally related, yet make a powerful impact of meaning on the person experiencing the coincidence. Through such events, we perceive that we dwell in a larger dimension which Jung calls acausal orderedness which we perceive as a unitary reality. When such a connection to the larger reality occurs, we experience what Jung calls absolute knowledge, a sense of coming upon something that just is, that we know through different routes than our usual ego knowing (Jung 1952; von Franz 1992). I want to expand on this insight with an example of a woman experiencing this larger containing reality. In the practical work of therapy, it is in such experience that the Spirit and psyche are in close conversation and each has something to offer the other from which our patients benefit.

98

In this new simultaneous consciousness, wherein synchronistic events are familiar happenings, our ego is moved into a different location. Our sense of I-ness no longer lodges only in the ego but increasingly in relation to the ever-present reality of a larger whole which we inhabit, again like sitting in a bigger bowl. St. Paul's words, "not I but Christ lives in me" aptly describe this dislocating of the ego by the arrival in consciousness of a central presence. Yet our ego is relocated, "found," not knocked out. The ego circles around a deeper center that communicates through body, through intuitive hints, through synchronistic happenings, as well as through the images and ideas the ego formulates.

In Christian tradition, the ego plays a crucial role. Without ego, our little "I" does not know it inhabits a larger bowl of reality; it does not receive nor transmit that message. A clinical vignette from the analytical work of a professional woman who was on a much needed vacation illustrates how dramatic this coinciding of ego-collapse and ego relocation can be. This happened to her before she returned to analytical work, reporting who she had gained access to, which is what therapy with a spiritual component can lead to, namely, a different relation to reality, embodying this new consciousness in living. Then we do not have to be in therapy forever. How we live in relation to this larger reality is the crucial thing.

Before this woman had left the country she met with her assistant several times to go over the work-plan to be completed upon her return, especially in light of ferocious office politics. They agreed on future actions to secure the direction they both believed in in their non-profit organization. She had even asked him if there was anything she should be aware of in his plans that would affect the future work. No, he said; *Bonnes vacances*.

But two days after she arrived abroad, he telephoned with his news that he was resigning and taking another job. This announcement, like a blow, nearly knocked her out. She felt betrayed. Stunned, conflicting emotions stirred her up. She said she felt threatened on her job, even desperate without his help to get all the work done. Why hadn't he told her he was considering another job? What happened to the trust she thought they shared? Was their relationship so much smaller than she had believed? Did he not realize how much work he was leaving her with, into what jeopardy he plunged her? She felt let down, deceived, full of self-doubt, and her old complex that she had worked on in therapy reasserted itself: once again her dependence had not been met. She was left alone, disregarded. At the same time she was trying to contain all these emotions and not let them flood into her family's vacation and ruin everyone's trip. In this highly charged situation she dreamt the following:

> I am to speak in some educational or worship setting and am afraid.
> I must climb up high into a sort of pulpit. In my hands I am clutching all my notes and papers, but when I get up there, I drop them all, making a big mess. I just totally collapse, not just the papers, but I fall to the floor too. I can find nothing or get anything together. I just collapse.
> Then a priest appears, a stranger. He picks up the papers which become a bunch of sticks, like the childhood game I loved called Pick Up Sticks, or like a bunch of stalks. We are now on an open high hill at night. I can feel the wind blowing. He throws the sticks into the air and the wind catches them and they become scintillating lights in the dark heavens.

She said she felt blessed, made calm by this dream. The problem of all the tumultuous emotions was still there, as would be all the work waiting for her upon her return. The old problem of feeling let down was still there. Yet something shifted. Working it over, she said, I did collapse. The dream shows me that after I collapse some larger perspective comes into view. And the sticks of the childhood game which required concentration was linked to moving into this new zone and the sticks also reminded her of stalks used in a diviniatory procedure. The sticks tossed up into the night sky become lights in the dark bowl of the heavens. She said, I perceived something bigger which held me, and I would not have seen it if I had not collapsed.

This woman's experience was not so much a coincidence of inner and outer events as it was what such coincidence leads to – perception of a larger wholeness to which we belong, which just is, absolutely, there. In the language of symbols the unconscious shows that the collapse of our small ego stance is linked to perception of the Vast lit by the stars that confers a sense of being received. The priest figure here lends a religious significance to this realization, as well as the wind blowing like the mysterious Spirit. To see oneself placed in this larger whole brings a healing effect because one's personal problem and collapse is linked to the numinous – the blowing spirit, the stars as lights in the dark.

The dreaming ego was put in its proper place and the dreamer felt a sense of meaning holding her, surrounding her, which helped her accept completely human failure and the opposites she felt in her relation to her assistant. She had counted on him and he had let her down, but that did not mean their relationship had to be destroyed. Maybe, she said, he was afraid to tell her, afraid to leave their relationship and go out on his own. Her dependency was met by reality itself.

Healing consists in living our own connection to the meaning (von Franz 1992, 257). The larger heavens showed themselves through her here-and-now problem and her childhood game of Pick Up Sticks. To the dreamer, and to me listening to her working over the images, this feels like an act of creation going on right now – the whole manifests through her personal little part. Her new perception arrives not through the ego but, in this example, through unconscious dream symbols. The dream offers to consciousness, both the dreamer's and now the rest of us too, a sense of the simultaneity of the immediate and eternal. The question then is how to house this knowing, and to go on living with it.

This dream-knowing comes to the ego like a cloud of knowledge, full of emotion, conveyed in an image. Like the anonymous fourteenth century mystic (1924) who wrote that we recognize God's drawing near only through a Cloud of Unknowing, we eschew the precise knowing of the ego through rational reflection on sense experience. What we know comes from another place in another language. Therapy now must address new clinical tasks which will involve whatever a person comes to claim as his or her spiritual practice.

New Tasks, Both Psychological and Spiritual

From a psychodynamic view this new spiritual location changes our relation to our projections. And especially those onto the ultimate, namely, our God-images. We usually work in therapy to become conscious of our projections in order to withdraw them from other people or outer situations. For in projection we expel from ego consciousness parts of our emotions or actions or fears or power motives that we cannot accept as our own but instead want to blame on our neighbors. We try to find where those contents belong to us and own them. In Jesus' parable, this is the sheep that got lost from the fold that we must go out looking for and return to the rest of the personality because we cannot function properly as long as this part is missing.

In this new ego location we face a different task. Now we must work to include in awareness what we might call our projective integrations. Our projections signal what is approaching. For the dreamer it was the experience of blessing, being held in a larger circumference. We notice through our projections what we must integrate, enlarge our self to include. This is not so much the sheep in the Jesus parable that got lost, as it is a new sheep that arrives out of the wilderness to surprise us. Here we are not defending against something that we must claim so much as we are expanding to own something new. How will we live it?

For my patient of the first example, it was living with Providence that intervened, bringing goodness. For the patient of the second example, it was the livingness granted her through the lively puppy whose arrival said a new way must be found – no longer measuring yourself against abstract ideals, but rather, like a puppy, groping along to learn what guides you, what you depend on, how you are supported by life's rhythm. In this last woman's example, it was how to combine opposites of betrayal and blessing in relation to the assistant and to a large reality that met her dependence. Projective integrations are not contents we expel but rather contents newly appearing on the horizon from deep inside us and from outside us in the world, the new calling out to us to link up and live more.

The spiritual task then facing us is how much reality can we stand? How much can we integrate to incarnate into livingness? How much can we participate in continuing acts of creation? The result of this relocation of consciousness toward the whole surround is not products – not more money, status, wealth, books, babies, political programs, nor even new health plans. The result is not products, however valuable they might be, but livingness, an alive gladness in being which can be felt even in our dying. We can feel the breath of the infinite on our faces even if poor or mentally deranged. It is there for our taking, there in its endless giving out of itself. Christian theology talks about this fact as the self-communicating love of God, that the Spirit reveals itself through its own activity and ways. We do not earn it, or receive it according to our merit, but rather according to its gift.

To catch the rhythm of livingness expands the ego to perceive diverse points of view. With the ego being dis-located as the center of consciousness, we are more sensitive inwardly to hints from body, intuition, and outwardly from others, from seemingly the air around us. We can entertain more easily the opposites of different theories, traditions, beliefs. Open to coincidences that prove so meaningful, we still retain an inquiring critical ego to evaluate them. This is not a mindless position; it is an ego congruent with the multicultural patterns emerging around us in this new century. Knowing in our bones that we do not originate truth, our ability to hear truths that others discover expands. We learn instead of defend, and feel grateful.

A silent kind of intercession may develop with our neighbors both near and far, even with people who come before and after us in history (see Ulanov and Ulanov 1982, chapter 9). In spiritual time and space no barrier of past, present, future, or of nearness and distance exists. We can pray for people in the past and make a difference; we can pray for people in Somalia, Kosovo, Korea. Open to the One approaching us in the many, our projections onto them snag the new approaching us, announcing itself for our integration. This noticing calls out the best in the other, and intercedes between us and them, guiding us through prejudgements to new perceptions of who the other is.

The danger for such an ego is how much lightning it can stand. For fear of burning up we may numb out, cut off, dissociate from the plenum all around. We refuse, for example, by not hearing Jesus say, Come eat, live abundantly, enter the bridal chamber, collect the little bits and pieces you have because then you can feed five-thousand. Or the danger is to lose our little ego-receiver by falling into the plenum, once again identifying now not with the small rules and regulations that hound us but with the All and the Vast. Then we become fanatics.

Our best protection from these twin dangers, surprisingly, comes from a spiritual rather than from a psychological source, and constitutes, I believe, one of the principal ways religion contributes to depth psychology. Religion teaches that we must name this transcendent presence breaking in on us, and that it names us. In Christian tradition, for example, it is not enough to come upon the All and the Vast. We must enter an ongoing relationship between a me and a Thee. We cannot address the transcendent in general, or anonymously as, Hey You. It is not sufficient to dream a numinous experience. We must live in relation to this other who arrives.

Personified God-images further this conversation. We are to call God by name, to have a name for the transcendent in our prayers. Though our images for God fall far short of reaching across the gap between infinite and finite, we still need them to make the going into spiritual practice. Though finally, in Christian tradition, the gap is bridged by God coming to us in person, as a living name, a word made flesh, we still need personal ways to register the astonishing fact that we are noticed, held, cared about by the Vast and the All. We must live the livingness of the interchange, the conversation God initiates. Otherwise it is just a momentous event we remember but do not incarnate (see also chapters 13, 14, 15).

Having names for God makes the interchange alive and real. We must have our personal names for God – what I call our subjective God-images – and we must register our official names for God (objective God-images), taken from the religious tradition in which we find our spiritual home (Ulanov 2001, chapter 1). And we must receive God's self-naming which bursts apart all our titles for God. For Christians, for example, the transcendent reveals itself in the living word of Christ.

But the conversation goes further. Trying to converse with this living word in the person of Christ, Christian Scripture (Revelations 2:17) speaks of God giving each of us a new name, known only to God and us. Van Ruysbroek, the 14th century mystic, writes about Christ as the sparkling stone of God, the evident, manifest presence of the fecund abyss through which we each receive our personal name (1965, 95). In psychodynamic terms, we might say this is the name of our true self (Winnicott), the name of the Self in us that knows God (Jung). Living that name, making it real, here and now, is the gift of the Spirit that blows where it will, planting us, blessing us, expanding us, making us glad.

Address, National Institutes of Psychotherapy, New York City 2000.

References

Augustine. 1935. *De Trinitate. The Library of Christian Classics, Augustine: Later Works*. trans. John Burnaby. Philadelphia: Westminster.

Bion, W. R. 1965/1991. *Transformations*. London: Karnac.

Bion, W. R. 1970. *Attention and Interpretation*. London: Tavistock.

Bright, G. 1997. Synchronicity as a basic analytic attitude. *Journal of Analytical Psychology* 42, 4, 613-639.

Bromberg, P. M. 1993/1998. Shadow and substance: a relational perspective on clinical process. eds. Stephen A. Mitchell and Lewis Aron.

Relational Psychoanalysis. The Emergence of a Tradition. Hilldale, N.J.: The Analytic Press, 1999.

The Cloud of Unknowing. 1924. ed. Dom Justin McCann. London: Burns, Oates & Washbourne.

Cross, F. L. ed. 1958. *Oxford Dictionary of the Christian Church.* London: Oxford University Press.

Edinger, E. F. 1994. *Transformation of Libido.* ed. Dianne D. Cordic. Los Angeles: C. G. Jung Bookstore.

Freud, S. 1964/1973. *Standard Edition* XXII. *New Introductory Lectures on Psycho-Analysis and Other Works.* trans. James Strachey. London: Hogarth Press.

Jacobi, J. 1959. *Complex, Archetype and Symbol in the Psychology of C. G. Jung.* London: Routledge & Kegan Paul.

Jung, C. G. 1948. Instinct and the unconscious. *The Structure and the Dynamics of the Psyche. Collected Works* 8. trans. R. F. C. Hull. New York: Pantheon, 1960.

Jung, C. G. 1952. Synchronicity: an acausal connecting principle. *Collected Works* 8. trans. R. F. C. Hull. New York: Pantheon, 1960.

Jung, C. G. 1953. *Psychology and Alchemy. Collected Works* 12. trans. R. F. C. Hull. New York: Pantheon.

Jung, C. G. 1963. *Mysterium Coniunctionis. Collected Works* 14. trans. R. F. C. Hull. New York: Pantheon.

Ogden, T. H. 1994. The analytic third: working with intersubjective clinical facts. eds. Stephen A. Mitchell and Lewis Aron. *Relational Psychoanalysis, the Emergence of a Tradition.* Hillsdale, N.J.: The Analytic Press, 1999.

Ruysbroek, J. V. *The Book of the Sparkling Stone.* in *Medieval Netherlands Religious Literature.* trans. E. Colledge. New York: London House & Maxwell, 1965.

Stern, D. B. 1983/1997. Unformulated experience: from familiar chaos to creative disoder. eds. Stephen A. Mitchell and Lewis Aron. *Relational Psychoanalysis, the Emergence of a Tradition.* Hillsdale, N.J.: The Analytic Press, 1999.

Ulanov, A. B. 1971. *The Feminine in Jungian Psychology and in Christian Theology.* Evanston, Ill.: Northwestern University Press.

Ulanov, A. B. 1986/1999. Image and Imago: Jung and the study of religion. *Religion and Spirituality in Carl Jung.* Mahwah, N.J.: Paulist Press, chapter 5.

Ulanov, A. B. 1995. Spiritual aspects of clinical work. *The Functioning Transcendent.* Wilmette, Ill.: Chiron, chapter 1.

Ulanov, A. B. 1992/1996. The Perverse and the Transcendent, *The Transcendent Function: Individual and Collective Aspects. Proceedings from the Twelfth International Congress for Analytical Psychology.* Chicago 1992. ed. Mary Ann Matoon 1993. Daimon Verlag, Einsiedeln, Switzerland; and in Ulanov, A. B. 1996. *The Functioning Transcendent,* chapter 3. Wilmette, Ill.: Chiron.

Ulanov, A. B. 1997/1999. The opposing Self: Jung and religion. *Religion and Spirituality in Carl Jung.* Mahwah, N.J.: Paulist Press, chapter 7.

Ulanov, A. B. 1998. Dreams: passages to a new spirituality. National Conference of Jungian Analysts. Chicago 1998. See chapter 10.

Ulanov, A. B. 1999a. Countertransference and the Self. *Journal of Jungian Theory and Practice.* Fall 1999, 1, 5-26. See chapter 13.

Ulanov, A. B. 1999b. Psyche and spirituality. Jamaica Hospital, Department of psychiatry. 10/22. unpublished.

Ulanov, A. B. 2001. *Finding Space: Winnicott, God, and Psychic Reality.* Louisville, Ky.: John Knox/Westminster Press.

Ulanov, A. and B. Ulanov. 1975. *Religion and the Unconscious.* Philadelphia: Westminster.

Ulanov, A. and B. Ulanov. 1983/1998. *Cinderella and Her Sisters: The Envied and the Envying.* Philadelphia: Westminster; new edition Einsiedeln, Switzerland: Daimon.

Ulanov, A. and B. Ulanov. 1982. *Primary Speech: A Psychology of Prayer.* Louisville, Ky. John Knox/Westminster.

Ulanov, A. and B. Ulanov. 1994. *Transforming Sexuality, The Archetypal Worlds of Anima and Animus.* Boston: Shambhala.

von Franz, M.-L. 1992. *Psyche and Matter.* Boston: Shambhala.

Wyss, D. 1966. *Depth Psychology, A Critical History.* trans. Gerald Onn. New York: Norton.

II. Intimacy

Chapter 5

Otherwise

Otherwise always means more and more of what is different, not more of the same. It is more because it is different from the same. The Other is what gives us being and supports our being, but not by surrounding us with endless ditto marks, duplicating our point of view. The Other is not a yes by ditto, but a yes more, much more than meets the eye, more than we thought possible, more than we hoped; other is a different way, wise to the more, different from current trends of opinions.

The Other is something separate in identity, distinct in kind. In order to see the Other, I must be myself and all of me. To be two, or more, we each must be one. In order for the Other to be more, we must hold our own views, hopes, reality. Otherwise, we become other-dumb. No conversation exists, no discourse back and forth.

This conversation goes on in many unexpected places, making them spaces of excitement, creativity, imagination. In the archeology of the soul, we must reach the "new foundations" Jung urges we are in need of: "... We must dig down to the primitive in us ... we need a new experience of God" (Jung 1973, 5/26/23, 40). We must dig to find that which is Other, the more that adds itself to us each day as something to be learned, to be lived.

At a previous Trinity Institute conference I spoke about digging down to our mysterious and ever present pictures for God that bring us the radically Other in the familiarity of our personal and cultural life. We must reckon with how our God-image, for example, one woman's sense of blessing issuing from a dream of a singing painting, confirms or conflicts with a traditional picture of Yahweh as the God who speaks words. Our subjective God-images picture how God is to us, mirroring us. We all have such pictures. We are created to be picture-making creatures. Our objective God-images picture the official God of religious traditions, whose scripture, revelation, believing communities tell us God is (1986/2002, 165-185).

I want to stress again how crucial it is to bring our pictures of God together with what our traditions image as God, and how we live in that gap between them. If we do not notice our God-images, then we can fly off into a religion of words, a schizoid religion, and never know the living Word. Or the opposite threatens. We can fall into unconscious identification with our God-image and turn into theological bullies, coercing everyone else to identify with our pictures of God (see also chapter 12).

Our task, I believe, and especially for clergy who are God's housekeepers, is to live with this gap, always attentive to its opposite sides: to look for the pet Gods people bring to their spiritual life, and the ones put forward, like the toys of tradition, the God-images of scripture and of believing communities crafted over history. With all these pictures we can then ascend and descend on our Jacob's ladder toward the Holy One who creates us as image-making creatures, and who breaks all our images with its own mysterious presence.

One of the major contributions depth psychology makes to religious life and spiritual traditions is to keep them open from the bottom up, offering openness to the unknown, to what may come up from deep foundations and surprise us, answer us in terms we do not know, have been unconscious of, in terms of the Other, of the otherwise. For example, in the crisis of a father dying, his son prays fervently for guidance. Shall all life-support be withdrawn as the father had stated years ago in a living will instructing no extraordinary measures to be taken to prolong life? He will surely die if such is done, though slowly and painstakingly. Or should the son as the only family member who believes in God and the afterlife, not decide how and when his father should die by withdrawing food and water, but leave it between his father and God?

He prays. No answer comes. That night he dreams: he is making a film in Russia which is the Ur spiritual place for the dreamer, the place of foundations, the authentic. A woman in traditional Russian dress is being filmed standing before a church. At her feet stands a brightly colored male pheasant which, in the dream, is like a "fantastical bird, a fire-bird" (shades of Stravinsky?). The bird flies straight at the camera, "straight at me," the dreamer says. Then it flies out of the picture only to reenter again at a deeper point, and then if flies off.

The dream answers the prayer, but what does it say? It speaks other-wise, not in words of direction, or even feelings of guidance. Instead, a bird flies in the face of the dreamer. Who is this bird, so brightly colored, so fantastical? Here, I burst out laughing at what the dreamer has told me. I was so struck by the specificity of the psyche, the concreteness with which it addresses us from its other side of consciousness. This particular dream pheasant, for all its fantastical otherness, was exactly the stuffed pheasant his father had played with as a boy with his sister. It was the only thing the sister's family had offered the dreamer as a memento of her life when she died. The father had grumbled over their stinginess, but laughed to find his old plaything again now in his own family.

The dream does not answer yes or no to the son's urgent question, but digs down to the foundations from which a yes or a no arises. The dream gives a hint: the pheasant flies up on its own wing, finding its own way right to the dreamer, and out again, then flies in once more and then is gone. The dreamer's ego does not have to do it all, does not have to make the bird fly or decide when it should stop. Something else, something other that possesses its own instinct, volition, momentum and direction does it. To see it, to get an image of it on film, indicating it registers consciously, the dreamer must place himself in the intense authentic spiritual country. The bird takes wing from the woman in front of the church. For this particular dreamer, the Holy often approaches him through the image of female presence.

The dream gives an example of how depth psychology contributes to religion by suggesting three meanings of transcendence that happen in clinical situations. The transcendent alive deep in the psyche, perhaps in those soul foundations we dig down to, is, first, that which transcends the ego. The dream issues from another deep down place inside us addressing our life and death question from its other-wise to our consciousness. This sort of experience stops us cold. We realise we have forgotten that God can speak to us through the flesh of our psyche too.

But the transcendent is also something well outside us, beyond our little psyche and soul. For where does the dream come from? Where does the unconscious come from? This is a second sense of the transcendent originating beyond the human, coming to the human, supporting it by always giving it the wisdom of the Other in terms of the different and the more. We are not cast adrift in such searing moments of death of our parent. It answers us by its presence.

How then do we respond? What does my dreamer do? Here is the transcendent in a third way, the way of our ego trying to align itself with the unconscious and what speaks through the unconscious, the way of our digging down – as we imagined as children, digging all the way down to China – to affiliate ourselves with the other we unearth. The third meaning of transcendent comes through our trying to live in relation to it, in our familiar bodies, together in social life, in our politics and jobs, on the subways, in our cars, with our friends, and our enemies. The third meaning of transcendent is the Other, wise, here and now which we reach for, receive.

Others in Self

We are all familiar with what depth psychology has amassed as evidence for the astounding fact that we cannot even be a self without an other. Many of us are familiar with the shocking experience in our dreams or our problems of coming upon bits and pieces of others looking at us in the deepest depths of ourselves. We discover other-wise; if we knew all in advance that according to our theory that this and this will happen, then we show ourselves simply other-dumb, imposing a know-it-all theory on land yet to be mapped, let alone on a person yet to be believed.

Take a not unusual example that took a client and me to the edge of the new. Born into generations of family and into a culture in our country that prizes appearance above all – what Jung calls persona, how we appear to others and how we see ourselves appearing to them – this woman suffered the smashing of her persona life through no fault of her own. At four, when family fortunes changed, they moved to a small town her mother hated. So her mother went daily to the big city of appearances nearby, leaving my client alone from four years old on. Her child's mind made sense out of this abandonment by saying she was no longer cute enough to hold her mother's attention. As she grew up, both parents fell into alcoholism, with public behavior still deeply humiliating to my client, now a middle-aged woman. Her first marriage suffered a catastrophe before it ended, brought on by her husband doing illegal things in his work that led to being arrested, exposure in the press, imprisonment. What she calls "the theft of my privacy," the breakdown of appearances, even though now having raised her children alone and married for a second time, has left her demoralised and fearful. Much ego work was to be done, which she did well.

But the deeper question still rose up: what possible point dwells in all these accumulated exposures to the public gaze with no protective shield? What meaning comes to her in this ripping away of the persona time and time again through no fault of her own? The meaning slowly gathers as she gathers herself to ask these questions. A conversation begins between her self and the other, which would not begin if she was not seeking it. It transcends her accustomed ego frame of reference; it is other-wise, coming from beyond her ego commitment to persona values. Her subjective God-image broke down and other values broke through. This woman was put in the position of breaking the allegiance of generations of her family and her culture to persona values. It falls on her head to break through the conditioning of this emphasis on good name, good blood, good manners, good breeding, good appearance. She broke through to what was other-wise and brought to her consciousness the wisdom of other values by which to live. What were these values to be? That was the adventure.

We may say, especially for New Yorkers where you can run down the street naked and people barely notice, that this is not anything. Believe me, it is. Take your dearest value and have it torn from your hands; feel yourself treated with disdain, feel yourself helpless, hapless, and you will feel the impact of her suffering. It falls to this woman to dislocate the values centered on surface and relocate them in the deeps, not on what you look like (and she is beautiful and very stylish), but who you are, not on your apparent life, but on the real. This is the wisdom of the other point of view.

Take the typical example of facing in ourselves what we would rather blame on our neighbor, saying it is her fault, his doing, not our own. This theory of projecting onto others, what Jung calls our shadow, comprises a great contribution of depth psychology to ethics and to concerns of justice. In every situation of social oppression hides the personal projection of hated traits in ourselves. We segregate them and cast them out of ourselves. Because the psyche is alive, it must go somewhere. It parks on our neighbor's lawn, makes a mess there. Our inner repression translates into outer prejudice. We say he or she is not like us, but a them, an other to be put in a ghetto. We red-line the district and refuse to lend money to anyone in it, just as we refuse to invest any libido, any energy, into that part of ourselves that lives in shadow. We outlaw it, put it outside the accepted bounds of consciousness and then feel we must defend ourselves against it and therefore must take arms to shoot, to bomb, to annihilate this other. By this route we all build up the possibility of injustice, war, and death of neighbor.

Knowing about the shadow does not make it go away. These are living parts of our psyches, both individually and collectively and they want living relationship to us as other than themselves, so to speak. A very strong example comes from a woman of sixty-odd years very developed religiously (see also chapters

6 and 8). She is someone, I suspect, who is the real thing, a genuine religious, rare in my experience. Why does she bother to come see me? Because dreams that leave no trace of themselves hurl her out of bed screaming. She awakes pounding her head against the wall, or a bed post. The dreams bring something so other, it communicates only in compelled behavior, not in language or picture. But the extraordinary thing about the wisdom of the psyche is that if we pay it attention and respect, the psyche responds by working around the trauma to make something of it.

For my patient, the psyche gave fearful images. Our only consolation was that they were now dreamed instead of enacted. The one I call to your attention is this: the dreamer is seized by the back of her neck, dragged by another woman into a classroom and about to be bludgeoned to death. She dreams she is being murdered. No discussion; just, I am going to kill you. What had been so left out and pushed beyond a point of no return that it relates only by annihilating? What is so alien to human consciousness that it breaks in with such violent intent, bent on murder? To a person so far on the path of spiritual development, why has such an extreme opposite appeared? She is not one to project and push her faults onto others, nor is she meek and mild. Rather, she is a tigress. But who is this other about to hit her in the face?

Much work was done before she arrived at this insight: I don't acknowledge the reality of the shadow, she said. I see goodness in people and expect them to bring it out. I say in effect (in her spiritual direction work), o.k. that is the past, now shape up and bring out this treasure that you have. The reality of the shadow is what I do not acknowledge, that it has its own other point of view, its aim to thwart.

She thus enters a new depth of relation to all that skirts the good, says no to it, wants to kill it. She is forced to go there by the others who attack her in her dreams. I even wondered if she was entering the dark night of the soul, that because of her remarkable spiritual development, she is being asked to face archetypal evil while learning to hold onto the good and defend her own life. This is not a naive woman. She knows first hand poverty, suffering, violence in others she has worked with in her convent life and her mission of spiritual direction with others in the world. But the stubborn reality of evil, that it does not easily yield, is what she had not acknowledged. The psychological problem opens onto the theological problem.

Dramatic as this example is, this is familiar territory. Less familiar is confronting the other within us who approaches life from a departure point opposite to our conscious gender stance. Human like us, but as if from another body, this other brings us wisdom from the other side, acting like a threshold into our deepest places of fervor, conviction, about the center. A dramatic example concerns our first dreamer with the dying father. When his father was just sick and not yet dying, this man dreamt he was with his father in Jerusalem, explaining all the religious paraphernalia, which the dreamer likes and his father does not. Before they leave, they must pray. They kneel in the chapel. The dreamer finds himself naked, stripped of defenses, he says. A candle is on the altar with the wound of Christ carved into it. The dreamer asks for the blood of Christ; the candle oozes blood which the priest catches in a glass. The priest turns to the dreamer who must drink it. Is it Christ's blood? he asks. No, the priest says; it is the housekeeper's who is probably a saint. The dreamer drinks the blood and there is more of it than he thought.

For the dreamer, the mediator who gives access to the mystery of Christ's blood is the female. This housekeeper type keeps showing up in pivotal dreams and always brings more than he expects. We can feel how other-wise this dream is

– bringing something precious from an other place to confront and orient the dreamer in relation to his father, both literally and symbolically. Perhaps the dreamer's subsequent agony of deciding whether or not to remove life support for his father is the sequence of drinking the blood of Christ mediated through the housekeeper's blood, a human being and a saint, both closer to the dreamer's humanity than is Christ, and yet other because female to his maleness.

All these examples are normal facings of the plurality of others in the self and help us understand our pathology in terms of how we treat the other in our midst. Pathology means not unfolding into the new, into living, but rather getting stuck in repetition, or dislocated, or fragmented, or falling into the void instead. Repetition means a complex grabs us and we go round and round, maybe with different people but always with the same ending. We repeat instead of create. There is no other, only the same, again and again, like the sad plight of our being caught in an addiction or perversion, or the sense of illness in our social life, where we elect different leaders or parties and the same crime, negligence and bad education afflicts the country.

To be dislocated is to be other-directed but not other-wise; we suffer dissociation. We are not where living is, as one patient said: "We are not where I am and I do not know how to get there from here, so I give up." To suffer dissociation is to have part of us living as if in another room. Sometimes that room is locked up tight, with a No Admittance sign on the door. We split up our inner population, like Polish Jews in Nazi times forced to survive by living in sewers, or citizens of Bosnia who need food but cannot connect up to its source because of war.

Fragmentation is loss of glue that binds us within a shared container. Instead, we feel like confetti, like random bits that do not hold together, just as many of our young in urban and rural ghettos feel at the mercy of randomness with no social fabric protecting them. At any moment they can be shot in the streets, or even through windows of their own apartments. Life does not cohere, but flies apart and is lost.

Falling into a void is like dropping into nothingness. Where there should be an other or a structure or a shared net of meaning, nothing looms instead, as if we could fall endlessly. As a result, we may desperately grab at others to stuff them into the hole, just as we throw money at social problems as if that will make a ground to stand on, but fails to do so.

The Other Who Comes To Us

If we do not fall into pathology but keep facing the others inside us, where do we end up? In an amazing space, offered to each one of us every day. You will remember our subjective-object gods – our pictures of God which mirror and empower us, God on our side of justice, or like the woman's numinous dream of the singing painting. You will remember our objective-object God – pictures of God given in scripture and tradition, God as law-giver, as Creator. Where we arrive now is facing the Other who comes toward us out of the gap between these two kinds of pictures. We can call it the objective-subject God, who treats us like a subject. Here is the breaking through of the other-wise; it is so different, so more, we can only call it the wise Other. Like Teresa of Avila reaching the innermost room of her Interior Castle, to find waiting for her, looking right back at her, the One she called His Majesty, so we find right there, this Holy One who crosses the gap to us. The transcendent here and now is not to be systematized nor made into a mental health or political program. It is to be lived.

Depth psychology knows about this realm of the other-wise, and the great contribution it makes to religion is to help us live aligned to it. For from this level of living comes the healing we seek in clinical work. All the schools of depth psychology know about this realm and write about it in their different vocabularies and jargon, though they avoid naming it in itself. It is important to name it, so that when we come to die and our pheasant bird takes wing, we can know whom we have loved. For that is what carries us to the other side.

People know this area of living, this space dug up at the foundations. In clinical situations they describe it in terms that are so concrete, they reach to all the rest of us. Patients say, it is where lightning strikes the ground; it is a white flaming flower at the bottom of the well; it is the garden that blooms behind my back when I wasn't looking or working on it; it is the huge elephant seal that emerges from the sea and asks me: when are you going to be you? All these people say these images from dream or imagination convey the sense there is something they can rely upon, a reality that transcends their ego that can be trusted, that seems to care if we betray it by not living our truest selves.

To these dreamers or imaginers, these images point to a source place that is generative, originating. It is the core place, yet oddly Other, in us, not of us, like an objective subject right there in the midst of us, at the root of our subjectivity. Is it a That? an Isness? Is it the authoritative one who says in a man's dream: The answer to all your questions is Yes? Is it glowing energy, an unspeakable state of consciousness? Let us call it presence.

Although depth psychology has its theories for this originating place, it shies away from speaking about where it comes from or why it is. Some authors even use religious language – words like sacred or transcendent or faith – but always add, this is not meant in a religious way. But they are talking about religious matters, just as my analysands are sharing what matters. What are we to do here, and especially you officials of the church, the keepers of religious matters, and on your twenty-fifth anniversary?

The Church has a name for this Other who crosses the gap into our lives and there is nothing more other, more other-wise than the name of this Institute whose birthday we celebrate. Trinity is the name, the picture, of what Simone Weil calls the friendship occurring in God, what I call the humming, buzzing and also silent, but ceaseless conversation going on all the time in reality's heart. Trinity is a name for what God is being when God is not doing anything, but just sitting around being. Trinity is a conversation that catches us up in a life of love and communion with God and with each other to lead to glory glowing forth. God's inner object relations are also God's relation to us.

For many of us, nothing can be more other than this name and doctrine of the Trinity. I am one of those who had no instruction in theology of the Trinity. I used to think it was because I was expelled from Sunday School, but now I think not. My best friend went all the way through and she remembers even less than I do of any instruction on this subject. Clearly the dread preachers feel when Trinity Sunday approaches and the flurry of invitations go out to guest preachers to cover this event, suggests that many of us would prefer to pass by this doctrine on the other side, despite the fact that the Trinitarian formula is used in every prayer and blessing. Its otherness is other-wise and depth psychology which builds up religion from below, from unconscious to conscious, of body in spirit, helps us speak of the experience of Trinity. Depth psychology helps us live in relation to what the doctrine symbolises, not to argue about it, or endorse or revise it, but to penetrate to the experience of the secret life humming there. We meet in ourselves this Other who crosses to us and lives in us.

The area of Father is deeply mysterious. It feels like truth at the center. To live from there makes us deeply happy, a simple happiness in being. We cannot control or cause this central life, nor even destroy it, though we come close to doing so, or at least of our access to it. It is from this place that people find the ability to rescue others from holocausts. From here people find the guts to stand up to totalitarian governments, to survive prison sentences, to see illness through to its end. From this originating source come the seeds of the original poems of a Rilke, a Gertrude Kolmar, the novels of a Patrick White. From this place comes the desire to pray, and go on praying.

Psychoanalysts call this self-experience and recognise that its mysterious core is not to be penetrated. Hence the trauma of crimes of rape or child molestation or driving another crazy prove so heinous. They breach a level of being that should always be revered. This self-experience mirrors the transcendent unfathomable abyss of being, the presence of God for whom we can find no word except in the living of it. This presence partakes of the silence behind the godhead in Eckhart's thinking. This is the God whose face we cannot see but only live in relation to, who can only be grasped in the living word coming to us. This Holy of Holies shows us in our own deepest experience that there are no graven images for God, only living presence that mirrors the living God.

Self-experience in humans is made in the image of the unfathomable, inexhaustible, ungrudging source of life who gives in an unending generosity. As Lady Julian of the fourteenth century writes, God dwells in our soul. Our soul is created to be God's dwelling place and the dwelling of our soul is God who is uncreated (Lady Julian 1978, 285). Living from our true self is to live in this God who mysteriously dwells in us. A clinical proof of God is the joy we feel when we live our true self. This plenitude of life and love, says Lady Julian, this Ur-source is God's motherhood in wisdom and lovingness and is God's fatherhood in power and goodness (ibid.). We are contained, enclosed, held, joined in this mysterious Trinity, our created nature to our uncreated nature at the core, which is God. As a result, at the soul level, there is nothing between us and God. In endless love, our soul is kept whole there and we shall never be lost. We are treasured, known, hidden in God and loved without beginning.

It is this loving, this ungrudging giving, this exchange and indwelling, that forms the basis of our loving each other. All effective social action springs from this core and is effective because the first commandment is kept first. The second commandment, loving self and neighbor, never replaces the first. Generous love flows into us and out from us to and from each other.

To know and live self-experience, we must be in life, in the world, dependent and interdependent with others. We need to know, to participate in what is given us to be with others. A contemporary man's dream illustrates this well. His task was to read a book with thin pages behind which dwelt lions. He needed to read it the right way, otherwise the lions would eat him. The lions were his devouring depression that ate him up, making his life bleak and joyless. The book was an old book of common prayer he bought that had beautiful pages and that symbolised the transcendent to him. He had to get his ego attitude in right relation to the transcendent, to what is beyond his psyche that the book points to. This knowing as aligning differs from our usual kind of consciousness to master and control the objects known.

This can be called the realm of the Son – a consciousness that knows that the incomprehensible will always exceed our grasp and we accept that. This consciousness proceeds from the source place and stays connected in it, a living knowing because living from this place. This consciousness includes how to master things and cope, enabling us to survive. But then something other, too, something altogether otherwise is here: a knowing that wants life to thrive, a reaching toward the unfathomable core that shows us the secret of life.

To get something conscious is to become less afraid of it. To get it known is to be able to contain it in word or image, to make something of it, to share it, unfold it, hide it, dig it up, plant it, sell it, treasure it, give it away. This consciousness lives in the body and lends our seeing a wide-eyed contemplative gaze. We can then imaginatively perceive the world and create it afresh. We know in our egos as the center of consciousness and we know the others in us outside the realm of ego, and we know the presence of something more, the other-wise, different, more, Buber's Thou.

This kind of consciousness forges a space in the world – even in the subway or supermarket – for an alert kind of seeing. We see what is and what transcends. We gain double vision. We must be up to this kind of double vision which means life in the body and the body politic, the mystical body of Christ planted on earth. Otherwise it blazes and burns us right down. I have seen clients fall ill, have their sight afflicted or their heart or their brain when peering into the mysterious Other, especially in its appearance as void. Although we cannot in any way reduce physical afflictions to psychogenic causes, nonetheless, the psyche is in it too. At the very least, the dreamer is being put on notice to get the right way to read this book or the lions will eat him! That is why, I believe, someone as tough as Hadewijch of the thirteenth century will write, "Love thus bursts our dikes ... she ravishes us out of ourselves" (Hadewijch 1980, 63; see also chapter 8). To live this love we must grow all parts of our humanity, with nothing left out. She says of her own humanity, "I have integrated all my diversity and I have individualized all my wholeness" (ibid.).

This double vision means living from this core of us as well as knowing about it. It means witnessing it to others, recognizing it, and holding their being with this same core in our attention. The root of all social action for Simone Weil consists in the ability to give such attention to each other, to ask: What are you going through? (Weil 1951, 115). Thus this consciousness with its double vision welcomes the other who is more, different from the same. We facilitate the otherness of the other, which is the secret of psychotherapeutic work when it works. Something new releases in us and between us, not authored by either of us, only facilitated or thwarted. What comes forth is intimately personal and spreads hope in being to all of us.

This double vision consciousness generates the new, comes forth into the world, makes space for being to manifest here and now, calling us to witness it between us, in the body of our daily living. This experience is what Trinitarian language means when it asserts the incarnation makes actual, visible, knowable the otherness of God. The Son never divorces from the Father who declares, Behold, I make all things new.

What helps us live this way? And go on living this way despite blows of fate, meanness, unkindness, the fraying of hope, despite war, poverty, illness? Here we enter the realm of the Spirit in Trinitarian language. S. L. Frank, the Russian philosopher and theologian helps us grasp this Spirit. The light that shines in darkness, what I call the ego level of consciousness, has only the same valence of power as does darkness. It does not overcome darkness in unambiguous fashion. Or, we could reverse the metaphor and say the gleaming darkness does not dispel the scorching, glaring light in the world. At the level of the world, the ego level of both individual and collective consciousness, light and dark compete, do not understand each other, do not conquer each other. We never exist, then, in an unshadowed world, in a world free of pitiless glare.

At the depth level, the soul level, "the spiritual sun that shines on the world does not know eclipse and cannot go out; it shines eternally" (Frank 1946). At that level, we arrive home. The gleaming blackness that Gregory of Nyssa and Gregory the Great see as the apex of spiritual life that houses God's presence, has come. We are no longer left in the glaring desert. We are brought home.

We live, then, in double consciousness of ego and depth levels, feeling energy circulate between them. One woman said, there is this energy that will kill me if I cannot find a way to house it. It never goes out, but I do. The energy is Christ going on praying at Gethsemane even while being forsaken, going on aligning himself with the Father, even though the Father is silent and does not answer Jesus' prayers. The disciples go to sleep, cannot stay awake; they represent us in our humanness. We fall away from aligning ourselves with the transcendent while this Other in us goes on doing that aligning. The disciples sprawled in sleep are our poor human frame, and Christ praying into the dark is the energy that never goes out.

This energy, the Spirit, is always circulating – going out from the source, coming to us, through us to others, through others to us, back to the source and out again, never needing to sleep. Our job is to get with it, go with it, willingly allying with its currents like a good swimmer, or, as in many spiritual exercises, like a good breather. This energy comes to most people who stick at analysis or at spiritual direction. It weaves among us as well as within us. It is as if a conversation gathers strength. We can almost hear a buzzing in our neighbor between the parts of her being, in all the bits he gathers.

5. Otherwise

Such a buzzing, humming conversation is the exchange going from the source to the visible and back again. It makes palpable the webbing that connects us all to each other and to the source. It is community in the making. On the ego level our task is to attend to the kind of community in which we already live. At the depth level, our task is to affiliate to the communion that our community mirrors. As we align ourselves to this communion, community blossoms among us.

Depth psychology is concerned with experiences of reality, with the link between persons and symbol and the reality the symbol points to, not with making new symbols, but with connecting to what is given. This humming, buzzing, even silent circulation of energy among the levels of life, the neighbors of life, the Ur-source and the incarnate life that moves us into its currents of communication, is a conversation going on all the time. We just come to listen in on it, and then to correspond with it.

If we do not call this reality Trinity, we must call it something because we cannot gather all the bits of ourselves and our world into conversation with this Wise Other unless we go on trying to name it. We do not conduct human conversations with people without ever addressing them by name. The surprise is that as we gather the bits of ourselves in conversation and discover that we are in fact part of a larger, continuing conversation, this Other seems to gather itself into relation with us. This relation is as passionate as Hadewijch's phrase, we "abide ... mouth in mouth, heart in heart, body in body, and soul in soul, while one sweet *divine nature* flows through [us] both ..." (Hadewijch 1980, 66), and as other-wise as Simone Weil's description of it loving us: God "loves not as I love but as an emerald is green" (Weil, First and Last Notebooks, 129, cited in McLellan 1990, 192).

Address 25th Anniversary Trinity Institute, New York City, 1994.

References

Frank, S. L. 1946. *God With Us*. trans. Natalie Duddington. New Haven, Ct.: Yale University Press.

Hadewijch. 1980. *The Complete Works*. trans. Mother Columba Hart O.S.B. New York: Paulist.

Julian of Norwich. 1978. *Showings*. trans. James Walsh S.J. New York: Paulist.

Jung, C. G. 1973. *Letters*. vol. I, eds. G. Adler, A. Jaffé, Princeton, N.J.: Princeton University Press.

McLellan, D. 1990. *Simone Weil, Utopian Pessimist*. New York: Poseidon Press.

Ulanov, A. B. 1986/2002. *Picturing God*. Einsiedeln: Daimon.

Weil, S. 1951. *Waiting on God*. trans. Emma Craufurd. New York: Capricorn Books.

Chapter 6

Coniunctio and Marriage

We can look at marriage in terms of which archetypes it constellates and what sorts of living experiences unfold in it. We find ourselves living with and towards our partners in patterns that arrange life's problems with unmistakable emphases. We discover that certain imaginings, somewhere in the background of our lives, have had a strong hand in shaping what we do and say. The archetypes show themselves in our ordinary behavior. For example, a patriarchal and matriarchal image of married union reveals itself in the habit of each mate addressing the other in parental language, as mother or father, or as Mom and Pop (Jung 1927, para 260; Ulanov 1971, 257). Another strong archetypal image that hovers over some marriages is one of friendship, a Hansel and Gretel connection. (See also Kast 1986 for further illustrations.)

I want to explore very different patterns of living that may unfold in marriage, when the coniunctio archetype, the union of opposites, is dominant. When this archetype comes into play in the life of a couple it carves out a space for the marriage that differs fundamentally in source and goal from a marriage undertaken for collective reasons, such as belonging to a social institution, entering a contract, providing a frame for reproduction, or dutifully conforming to convention. The space this archetype constellates differs just as much from marriages undertaken for personal reasons, such as to please our parents, to become pregnant, to find preferment in society. In this archetypal space we do not aim to get a parent for our inner child, and yet remarkable repair may be occasioned for the child parts in us. We do not aim to get the other to change the environment for us, to raise our economic class, for example, and yet remarkable transformation occurs inside and outside us. We do not seek a guarantee of happiness ever after, yet we may live joyously together.

When the coniunctio archetype is active and concretely experienced by a couple, it creates a zest in the air, an excitement about being alive, real. One feels uniquely oneself yet engaged in one of the central mysteries of life that touch the whole family, both the present-day and the intergenerational one.

What is the Coniunctio?

The coniunctio archetype is associated with the image of a mating in the *vas*, the alchemical vessel, in which base elements are mixed up, added to, and worked over to transform into a stone-hard new center of being (Jung 1953, para 218-219; von Franz 1980, 159-160). In such a marriage the cooking would be operating in each partner, in between them and in both together. The interpenetration, differentiation, and integration of elements in each person's psyche would be worked on, as well as the meeting and matching and mating of all these elements between them. Such a joining is intimate at a very deep level, causing radical intrapsychic changes as well as changes in the most habitual behavior. One man, for example, expressed outright astonishment to learn that a female friend changed her sleeping patterns upon marrying. He could not imagine giving up his single large bed, as she had done, to sleep with her partner in an ordinary double bed. "But why didn't you at least get a big queen or king-sized bed!" he exclaimed. "Because I did not get married to go on as I had, but to sleep *with* this one I love," she answered.

Such a marrying is accepted by each person deep down, not as dogma, not as driven by shoulds and oughts, not as imprisoning, not maintained to satisfy functions. Rather, it is entering through a door that opens onto constantly changing patterns, so that at any time anything may happen. It is at once secure and absolutely open for the new to come in. The archetype is by definition indeterminate, so there is no one model or stereotype of how to be married (Ulanovs 1994, chapter 1). This is especially true when a marriage finds its dominant archetype in coniunctio images, for they speak of an ongoing process, joining disparate elements in many different stages and ways.

For example, the coniunctio image operating in a marriage helps us perceive problems and opportunities between the two people in the light of a strong question: What is the Self engineering? (Ulanov 1994) I am using the concept of the Self here to denote the whole psyche in each partner, unconscious as well as conscious, and something more as well that gives us access to a sense of absolute reality, or of God, or of what Jung calls the *unus mundus*, the whole of existence beyond us, both material and psychical. When, perhaps, we face a problem of communication, where one partner assumes the other knows what is meant without actually verbalizing it and feels cruelly abandoned when the other fails to understand, we can see it as an issue of the necessary death (*mortificatio*) that must follow upon a lesser coniunctio.

The partner who expects to be understood without having to make the effort to communicate is caught in a fusion of ego and unconscious content. This is a "lesser" coniunctio because the ego is contaminated with unconscious contents that need to be differentiated (Edinger 1985, 215). Nonetheless the fused state remains a coniunctio because it has come about through trust. Heretofore this partner had remained mute, filled with a noxious suspicion of rejection. To assume, now, that the other follows along with one implicitly is an achievement. Some bit of ego trusts that it is held in attention by an unconscious inner matrix and by the receptive listening of the other person. A joining, a coniunctio, has mended some splits in each self and in the relationship. Now much gets said, even if some sentences begin in the middle of a paragraph and meaning is left tacit.

To ask what the Self is engineering in such an impasse allows each person to acknowledge gains that have been clearly made and permits growth in this argument to keep growing. When a speaker says (or shouts) "I'm mad at you! You should understand me without my explaining everything!", both partners can stop and ask what happens when we are not understood. They can unearth the threat of the old disintegration when one feels dropped by the other. They can join in supporting the fledgling trust that has been moving between them, but also see that something more is called for. The impasse tells them how to go further: "Speak!" it says, "speak more! Get a hold of what you want to express; I want to hear it!" The outrage on both parts signals that something bigger is trying to establish itself by busting through a joining that had already taken place. That joining is now too small. It is not content to remain at a "lesser" stage.

In the vocabulary of alchemical symbolism, this joining is too impure, the elements need to be better differentiated. As with all psychic events, so with this impasse: we find its meaning by looking back to its cause and forward to its purpose. Looking backwards, a couple can see that the lesser coniunctio, where each trusts the other will understand and offer a warm welcome, is not invalidated by some present difficulty. The past stands. It just is not enough. A further joining is needed, no more the old one of unconscious merger or fusion of elements in each separately, but now something new crafted out of precise choice and with passion. Each partner wants more, not less, much more clarity about what the other wants to give, to share, which means that each must become better at finding what it is on offer and in discovering ways to receive it. The person is pulled into growth. It is work, but work with a glad ending of feeling more, not less, of oneself. The other person, the hearer, the receiver, wants to develop better hearing, stronger reception, but without being manipulated into a parental role, or, out of a misguided defensiveness, violently repudiating that role as insulting. Now, the incomplete elements of the former conjunction can be allowed to perish as both persons get to work building bigger meetings, more spacious joinings, that allow for differences between the two.

This is not to say that arguments and impasses are jolly occasions. They always bring suffering. But if we feel our suffering has purpose, that like a bulb breaking through a sidewalk, new life and beauty and possibility are being engineered, then we can endure the suffering and have faith in its hidden meaning.

This example illustrates a major theme in the coniunctio archetypal image. It joins opposites in three ways: the *complexio oppositorum*, the *coincidentia oppositorum*, and the *coniunctio oppositorum* (Jung 1959, para 355, 423; Jung 1963, para 176, 541-542, 662). The complexity of opposites we experience when a lot of ambivalent emotions come upon us, in opposite impulses, such as to speak, to shut up, to get mad or to accept, to repudiate or to welcome, and so on. All these parts are real enough. They fall upon us and whiz between us in great turmoil. Like Cinderella, we need to sort our seeds.

The coincidence of opposites feels more familiar: the same pairs of reactions keep turning up. We have been here before in this same impasse; I wait to hear what you mean and you wait for me to guess it, to know it intuitively. The opposites still crowd in, but now we discern some order, recall how it was before, and compare it comfortably with the present siege. We have more of our own feet.

This sense of recognition is immensely reassuring to arguing couples. Instead of feeling hopeless, stuck again in the same old impasse, they can see that they are engineered to arrive at this place. In fact, I might say to new couples that the first year of marriage is inevitably a time of laying out what they will be fighting about for the next decade. In any relationship worth its salt, the two will find themselves pushed to work on their most basic personality problems and the most deep issues between them, which, because they live in the world, in history, must mirror the major issues that bedevil civilization now.

The work of love is to link, to connect up, to make whole, to make gracious, to make glad. Love makes space for its own flowing from surface to depths, from each to other and back again, planting the world, making it bloom, building a bridge that extends beyond the grave. Anneliese Aumüller, the late Jungian analyst, quotes from Jean Gebser: "People who believe that there is pure coincidence lose their lives to meaninglessness. Each so-called coincidence adds to the exhilarating meaningfulness and inexhaustible richness of our lives, by making it more obvious that we are participants in the whole." (Anneliese Aumüller 1963, 190)

The conjunction of opposites arrives at a union of the different elements within each person as well as a union between them that supports each in being entirely his or her own true self. In some miraculous way, enough room exists for every element within each person to be included and none to be compromised. This comes about by a mysterious alchemy: we hold our own ground, but also differentiate it from contaminating elements and find ways to relate even to them, instead of either repressing them or falling into identification with them.

In the example above, the partner who expected to be understood without fully saying what was intended, was still living in what for an adult is a contaminated state, reduced to the role of child relying on its mother. The other partner might in fact have a mother complex and slip only too easily into that role, or feel indignant that any mothering is demanded. Each person, then, must differentiate ego from threatening complex – the one to be child, the other to be mother. If they play out those roles of mother-child, either through endorsement or repudiation, they remain contaminated, in themselves and in relation to each other. Sometimes the complex of the one partner can tell when the other is slipping into the child role again. How? Because, one can say, I feel the compulsion to be motherly. To see one's complex and hold it, rather than falling into identification with it, is to decontaminate it. It is now only a part of me; it does not rule me or my relationship.

This intercession of consciousness, curiously, makes space both for the complex and for transcending it (Ulanovs 1975, chapter 11). It is part of the "me" I bring to union with the other, but I bring it now; it does not bring me. Thus, the coniunctio stage does not mean each partner is perfect. But now we bring ourselves to each other instead of being driven against each other by compulsive behavior. And we find we can do paradoxical things. Our ego exerts itself to the fullest to work through problems with our partner and yet we know that the ego is not going to fix things. In the spirit of I Ching's *Wu Wei*, we know a "Doing nothing, but also a not doing nothing" (Aumüller 1963, 192).

The complexity, coincidence and conjunction of opposites occurs over and over again in a lively marriage. It is the process by which persons go on becoming their truest selves, responding to what is fished up from the unconscious in each separately, and to what gets dredged up between them. They see all of this, sort it out, work with their own and each other's projections and introjections, and learn to unfold in relation to the objects that thus come more clearly into view. Slowly, egos become purged of possessive and power motives, what Augustine called *cupiditas*, an inordinate self seeking, aggrandizing compulsion to get, get, get, an unchecked appetitiveness gone wild. Paradoxically, our ego becomes increasingly disidentified but also fat and full, living a full life. Because our ego is empty, life can gush through it with all its juices.

This process of dealing with opposites over and over again in many different patterns forms a marriage very different from the one Jung described – and Bion after him – between one partner who acts as the container of the relationship and the other partner who is contained in it (Jung 1931, para 331-334; Bion 1970, chapter 7). Winnicott sums up the problem of the patterns of container and contained when he says, "*not all married couples feel they can be creative as well as married. One or the other of the two finds himself or herself involved in a process which could end in one living in a world which is really created by the other ... The whole problem may, for instance, be hidden under a couple of decades of child-rearing and emerge as a mid-life crisis*" (Winnicott 1970, 44).

In the coniunctio image of marriage each person is both container and contained, both for themselves and for each other, now in one, now in the other, sometimes both in both. This makes for fission, not fusion, for fire, not boredom. In the coniunctio arrangement neither is allowed to clamp down on personal impulse for the sake of compromise with reality demands to the point where they lose access to the creative imagination in their marriage. Both seek the alive and real in themselves and in each other. This takes time, much conversation and work. Yet it produces in each the feeling that they are contributing to the world a small example of how to be passionate and alive in a permanent relationship, imaginatively making the world. I have known such couples and their contribution is a true one. People say about being around them that it gives them hope, that it shows them an example of love in action, an incarnation of intimacy that does not cramp but expands relationship. In one case, a woman said that because of friendship with such a couple, she dared to marry again, after an unsatisfactory marriage that had ended years ago. I saw it could be done, she said. That is the point: the coniunctio archetype must be *lived* and lived in the world; otherwise it is "hanging in the air" (Jung 1953, para 559). Marriage is one way to do it.

In the coniunctio arrangement, the focus is on content, on the tiger, not its cage. The tiger is what is going on in each person. What is each one's life project? What news does each bring from Self country? What do they experience together pushing and pulling them toward a greater center? This is the focus of conversation, the angle from which the problems in and between them are addressed. In Jung's language, we could say marriage can be a means of individuation for each partner (Heisler 1970; Guggenbühl-Craig 1977).

Aggression and Repair

How then do we live in a marriage that constellates the coniunctio archetype? What happens? I have some examples. The first concerns what happens to aggression and the need for repair. Aggression is used in the service of love to scour away all that is not love. Each person learns to renounce fighting dirty.

Both give up going after the painful spot in the other that in more tender moments had been entrusted in great confidence. Each learns to sacrifice sadistic gratification not because "the health of the marriage requires it" or to be "mature." I have never found that such good motives meant much at a time of intense in-fighting.

The persons give up sadism the better to get hold of its tremendous energy, to use it for purposes of pushing through to the real and the true. The grandiose motives of winning the fight or defending oneself give way to what really matters, to find the underlying issue. One partner may say, "I'm not sure I want to be in this relationship at all" and the other might hear that, hold onto the hurt, and bring its energy to explore the feeling moving round it. Such pushing takes stamina. One wants the truth, even if the truth at any given moment may be confusion and fear.

The real and the true are the best in each, and what the Self moves into place. The best self does not mean a perfect self but just including all the parts, negative and doubting, angry and forlorn, as well as hopeful and enthusiastic. How to see that? How to discern the right direction? How to see where one may be caught in an old complex and where one might slip loose from it? How to know when to be silent and when to persist? These questions too, take great energy, especially if we seek our answers in a rhythm of living rather than adherence to rules. We need aggression to focus on the true worth of the other, to dig it out, and to work to restore it, and to differentiate that effort from trying to impose our image on the other.

Why should we go to all this trouble, all this work of love? Simple: Because this other, both so dear to us and so maddening at times, is made in the image of God. A transcendent presence lives in him or her. We dig down to it and excavate it. As a couple we give radical support to each other, but avoid falling into the role of therapist or parent. We each support the other's inner growth to become all the person he or she is. This includes the inner child and all the wounded and undeveloped parts as we look to repair them. But that is still not the main focus or aim. The aim is to discover what the Self is engineering. Are you listening? Will you go for it, live it, do it, love it? The support must be vigorous, summoning, lavish, and aimed right at the center of the other person's existence the way the other is connected to all existence. Betrayals in marriage usually issue from betrayal of this deeper center.

Each partner fights to strip the other of false living, or pretense and half-truths, of posings and mopings. Each fights for the full being of the other, which includes the full contra-sexuality of the other. We assert this sexual polarity in the other and fight against the symbiosis that occurs when each unloads the opposite sexual pole onto the partner (Ulanov 1971, 259, 296-302). How then can each of us accommodate the mixture of perceiving masculine and feminine ways of doing things, perceiving the world and acting in it, of knowing about it in ourselves? By reaching to the archetypal level of anima and animus, to see how the marriage between them opens to the indeterminancy of the archetype and steers us clear of the entrapping security of the stereotype. There is no premium put on the husband doing the so-called masculine things, or the wife enacting all the feminine roles. Nor do we follow, with a legalistic precision, a marriage contract which allots so much of each kind of task to each partner as guarantor of equality of chores and responsibilities. Both of us must reckon with two modes of being human in ourselves and find ways to live with a partner who is struggling to do the same. The carrying of tasks can then be decided on the basis of personal aptitudes and preferences. Where both hate the same task, they do the wretched thing together, as for example one couple did the laundry at ten o'clock at night. Both hated it and put it off until they could finally face it together.

Once we understand that aggression is the means through which we secure the energy of living support, we can dig into each other, salute each other, witness each other's conversation with the Self, and fight through to the truth of each other. Aggression is repaired. No longer is the goal to see who wins or loses, who struck the keenest blow, whose defenses were the best. We aim to use our aggression to explore, unearth, pursue, receive, sustain, and support the best in each other. Our aggression works to clear away impediments, tangles and snarls, interfering blows that obstruct, block, bury, and divert us from our main concern, from the sources of our loving strengths.

This does not mean we are not wounded. Of course we are. Of course we hate fighting. But we begin now, separately and together, to see that our fighting can lead somewhere. We have excavated some old hurts and healed them – together. We have finished with some vexing issues. We have opened up new channels. This brings hope and an end to our fearful despair that aggression can only be destructive. We know now that aggression can serve love as well as destroy it.

Ruthlessness and Creativity

Ruthlessness is something most of us fear as grossly self-indulgent and abusive. It feels irrational. It is too easily confused with the violence of spouse-beating. Nonetheless, ruthlessness as I use the word here is a fine, strong, positive part of a marriage arranged along the patterns of the coniunctio archetype. Ruthlessness, in this sense, belongs to a person with a developed ego that is not drawn into and lost in the unconscious, as would be the case with a spouse-beater for example. It belongs to an adult who has not given away too much of primordial aggression and sexuality. Such a person retains the capacity we see in children of going right at an object, in moves backed by instinct. For instance, a child opening a present and discovering a stuffed bear hiding in the tissue paper does not refuse the bear by doubting that this really is a gift: "Really for me? No, no; I had better not take it." The child does not reason this way, but goes right at it, picks up the bear, nuzzles its nose, fingers its fur, loves it, eats it, chews it. We think a child is being its own true healthy self when it behaves this way. We applaud it and feel glad for it. We delight to find just the right bear for the child to unfold his or her self in such lavish use.

This ruthless love of a bear is what Winnicott calls using an object instead of merely relating to it. A child is moved by its own instinct toward an object and in unfolding itself in relation to the object (Winnicott 1968, 233-235; Winnicott 1971, 89-90; see also Bollas 1991, 26). The child is not at this moment concerned with protecting the object from instinctual assault or with the consequences to the object or even to its own self. The child is not trying to harm or destroy the object, but rather to use it for instinctual gratification. If the consequences turn out to be dire – if, for example, a nursing mother bursts into tears when her child bites her breast and communicates that she has been destroyed by this attack, then the child may out of love for the mother withhold such impulses toward lusty eating. On the other hand, a mother might yell "Ouch!" and remove the offending teeth momentarily, but at the same time convey recognition, and even pleasure that the child's teeth have arrived and that such excited eating can occur because she, the mother, knows how to protect her breast. A baby can then hold onto the pleasure of instinct without diverting energy to control it by repression or dissociation because the mother knows how to survive out of herself, not because the child has spared her. Winnicott calls this primitive display love admixed with aggression (Winnicott 1958, 22). I call it love with teeth.

A marriage patterned after a coniunctio image is one where love has teeth with profound impact for a couple's imagination and creativity. It connects with a pair's aggression given over to the service of love. For when we allow ourselves and our partners moments of ruthless interaction, we are no longer concerned to protect them from the full force of our being all of who we are, or the full force of our energy. We do not whittle ourselves down to what we think are appropriate proportions so that we will not threaten, intimidate, overwhelm or hurt each other. We just are ourselves and trust the other to be in the same way. As a result there are joyous interchanges and noisy ones and some of profound stillness where two – each of whom is other to the other – really meet. As if we were animals, we see stepping into the forest's clearing another animal of the same stripe and fur (Ulanov 1986). We meet our mate.

This psychic move changes our fantasy and deepens our creativity. When each of us risks being other to our partner, in such moments of ruthless expression, we take risks. On an unconscious level, we destroy our projected image of the other. We let each other fend for him or herself. We do not seek control through projected images of who we want the other to be, or fear the other might be, or need the other to be, or think the other needs us to be. We let be. And we discover, uncover, greet the one who is left after our projections have been destroyed. The other is more than we thought, still standing there after we have given up on getting our way. We greet the freshness in otherness. Still on an unconscious level, we renounce omnipotent fantasy that would style reality according to our wishes, and discover what Winnicott calls the real externality of the other, who lives from an independent subjectivity

DAIMON VERLAG

To learn about our latest publications, visit our website at
www.daimon.ch or, if you would like to receive a free copy
of our latest catalog, please return this card with
your address:

Name: _____

Address: _____

_____

ZIP code, city , country : _____

_____

(Winnicott 1971, 88-90). This may happen when the other disappoints us: he or she fails to live up to our idealized image and the image is destroyed. Thereby we release ourselves and the other to find out who is actually there. If we are using our aggression to reach the best self of the other, this is all gain, no loss; it is a scouring away to reveal the real. We may have lost a fantasy but we have gained a reality with which to interact and in which to unfold our own self. The fantasy that went into trying omnipotently to control the world, is released now to perceive the world imaginatively.

We see this clearly in the sexual arena. There, the more "teeth" our loving has, the more vigorous, variable, and pleasurable sexual congress will be. While engaging and attending to each other's needs, the two may also move into mixtures of the conscious and unconscious that allow each the freedom to drive toward climax. This is not neglect of the partner but joining on a level of ruthlessness that increases erotic intensity (Bollas 1991, 27). If too much of the ruthless element is split off, the couple may fall into a mere helping mode with each other, a sort of Hansel and Gretel cuddling and soothing that lacks sexual tonus, or one person may simply service the other, who will then feel guilty for taking satisfaction at the expense of the partner, who in turn may be tempted into feelings of martyrdom. In extreme instances, ruthlessness may become dissociated and acted out in scenarios of perpetrator and accomplice (See Khan 1979, 22-23).

When we let ourselves go with all that we feel and meet up against the other doing the same, a sense of immediacy develops. We see the other with a startling freshness. We feel amazement before that familiar partner of so many years: Who is this? Who is this other coming toward us? This is how I understand the shift from omnipotent fantasy to creative imagination. The plans and preconceptions about who I am and who the other is and who we are together as a couple are momentarily wiped out in my amazement before the otherness of this one who stands before me. Like Heidegger's notion of being thrown into *dasein*, into being human — something that at any moment may go out of existence — all that I have known and been is destroyed, even if only unconsciously. This moment now is all there is and all there is to live confronts me now, in this moment. Such immediacy brings a tremendous creative freshness to living. One is called into presence, to be all there, right now, for there may be nothing else. Right here and now, one seizes, receives, takes, and yields. Life becomes exciting and new. We are never sure about exactly what will happen.

This destroying in unconscious fantasy is like the cleansing in alchemical operations, where over and over again elements are submitted to fire, to water, to separation, to calcification, to washing and purifying. This renews us in the midst of the familiar and makes us cherish the familiar instead of treating it with contempt. For passion to persist within a permanent relationship, boredom must be destroyed. It is automatically purged when in unconscious fantasy we dissolve the projections upon our relationship to discover its external reality afresh. Unburdened by stultifying knowledge, we come to each meeting with a sense of expectation. Newness, excitement, surprise come into the diurnity of our days. We claim both our imaginings and the actual reality of the other. To newness is added moreness.

Joy and the World

The newness and moreness bring joy, even in the midst of toil and stress. Stress and joy are simply two more opposites to get mixed, coincide, and unite. The hardships of living join the sense of fun that arises from keen interest in what the Self has been working in us. The goal is no longer linear, looking to arrive at a certain point and then to lie back forever after. The journey is circular, in alchemical terms, circumambulating around a center, so that the center glows and radiates its presence and energy into every little cranny, into each little misery and wounded place until every part of us individually and together is caught up in its energy and presence.

This sense of presence and liveliness creates an atmosphere of serious play, as with children. A marriage patterned around the coniunctio archetype provides a space with firm boundaries and enough room for real play. The two persons are really in it, not threatening divorce all the time, or collapsing the space of exploration by citing rules that require them always to stay together. That is looking to the cage, instead of to the tiger. The tiger is always circling around the crucial question: what is the Self engineering?

The engineering becomes complex, then, for each partner brings both a conscious ego part of themselves and an unconscious contrasexual part to the other. There are at least four presences to deal with now, and the four may at any time multiply into further relationships: ego to ego, animus to anima, then one person's ego to the other's anima or animus, and within each person, ego to contrasexual part. Crowds! Conversation whizzes along among these parts in every sexual meeting, in every fight, in every encounter. A couple aware of all these participants has much more elbow room in a fight and much more possibility of play in times of calm. For example, a woman can recognize that familiar screech of animus pitch in an argument, and may even take time out to put herself in better touch with this other force in herself in order to place the animus energy behind, not in front of her ego, so that she can better say what lies heavily on her heart. Or she may actively call on this animus energy to help her patiently penetrate the fog surrounding her mate, holding to her determination to reach him and not be put off by his mopings and sulks.

In sexual encounters, when the anima and animus as unconscious elements mix with the conscious tenderness of two people seeking comfort and pleasure with each other, their sexual meetings make space for impersonal sexual elements, even a touch of the ruthlessness discussed above, to ignite and be housed by a personal caring, each for the other. This imbues sexuality with freshness and opens it to a long range growing around a center that mysteriously combines spiritual and sensual elements. Familiarity with these mixtures of the conscious and unconscious, and personal and impersonal sexual energies, allows for much more play. The two come to know multiple exchanges of roles relating ego to ego, animus to anima, ego to anima or animus, and even transferrals person to person of egos and contrasexual parts. She may become the beast and he the beauty; she, the hero and he the trapped royalty, and just as quickly he the nurturing earth and she the lightning sky; he the disseminating energy and she the enfolding dark. The complexity of opposite parts is welcomed, their coincidence applauded, the conjunction understood always as a mysterious, powerful, joyous event.

Living a marriage in relation to the coniunctio archetype works remarkable changes in our experience of suffering too. The marriage becomes an entry point for all or any of the sufferings and the blessings of the world. Mutual penetration on conscious and unconscious levels reaches back into generations of a family and effects changes in its legacy of complexes. For example, the contamination of unconscious animus opinions about men – they are just "like that," meaning they are drinkers, or live unexamined lives, or are full of temper, whatever the accumulated ancestral experience has been – may come to a full stop with this daughter in her marriage because her man penetrates that set of assumptions and fills the space left in their wake with different living patterns. Or, on the other side, the anima premise that women properly belong in secondary roles may be upset and then discarded by the full ego life of a woman caught up in the excitement of her own projects, enlarged by her love of her mate. Not only are the ancient prejudices shaken up and made more fluid in the living experience of this couple, but something sharply different comes to replace the stereotypes which the inherited prejudices mirrored. The two persons feel they are building a new space, a new shared reality, where roles are more comfortably exchangeable because loving is more intense.

In terms of their own personal suffering, the two partners may be surprised to learn how closely their wounds match, forming still another coniunctio pattern. For example, a woman plagued with anxiety who needed more aggression to throw off some of the self-blame to see where faults might be located outside herself, discovered that under her mate's opposing tendency to cast blame upon others, and always aggressively assert his own stance, was a man as anxious as she! He dealt with anxiety with anger; she, with self-doubt. This insight cleared away a lot of the brush when they fought with each other, but it also brought them closer as fellow-sufferers who could learn something from each other about how to deal with the anxieties that afflicted them both.

In all these examples, the common thread is the building up of new spaces, and new realities. In alchemical terms, this is the lapis, the city, the mandala, the gold of everyday life. Oriented to what the Self is engineering, the two persons rescue and promote what is original in each other, develop faith in the unique presence of the other, both supporting it and unfolding their own uniqueness in relation to it. Thus is the new brought about; we do not "settle into the married years," but instead feel our time together is too short! One woman reported she was astonished to hear her answer shot back from inside her to a man asking how long she had been married: "Not long enough!" And this was after twenty years.

The reason for this joyous excitement, I believe, is that the goal pictured in coniunctio symbolism is to reach an incomprehensible core and to live it, not to "know about it." A couple plays with the combinations of opposites flowing between them, and within each in the presence of the gravitational pulls of the Self, to assemble being around the center it provides and thus to build a new psychic structure which can promulgate new contents into consciousness. This coniunctio is what distinguishes creative work, where we discover with creative insight into ourselves or the world around us. Here the world is our marriage. The play of masculine and feminine opposites between two of us makes a universe for true relationship.

It cannot be a relationship apart from the world. It must pull the world in and pull the two persons into the world. Why this is so has to do with the center that goes on being constructed. That core of freedom keeps producing new forms of itself that insist on going out to others and pulling others into it. In alchemical terms, the conjunction of opposites produces the lapis stone. Flowers spring up around it (Edinger 1985, 220). The mysterious center that the lapis symbolizes has a contagious effect. It gives life to all. It multiples itself in others. It lends zest to the air. This is the greater coniunctio, that does not break down but breaks through the bounds of our ordinary perceiving in time and space to the presence of the beyond.

The cause and effect of the conjunction of opposites is love, a love in time and outside time. Behind the concreteness of the marriage of two people in the twentieth century stand the ancient symbols of the mystical marriage of a royal king and queen, of Sol and Luna, of Yahweh and Israel, of Christ and

Church. To be aware of this dimension is directly to participate in mystery: this is a coniunctio in everyday life. As Jung says, "Whatever the learned interpretation may be of the sentence 'God is love,' the words affirm the *complexio oppositorum* of the Godhead." In his medical experience, he says, he has never been able to explain the mystery of love. "Being a part, man cannot grasp the whole. He is at its mercy. He may assent to it, or rebel against it; but he is always caught up by it and enclosed within it. He is dependent upon it and sustained by it. Love is his light and his darkness, whose end he cannot see … If he possesses a grain of wisdom, he will lay down his arms and name the unknown by the more unknown, *ignotum per ignotius* – that is, by the name of God" (Jung 1963a, 353-354).

Published in Psyche and Family: Jungian Applications to Family Therapy. *1996. eds. Laura Dodson and Terrill Gibson. Wilmette, Ill.: Chiron, 113-129.*

References

Aumüller, A. 1963. Personal Stimulus of Jung. *Contact with Jung.* ed. M. Fordham. Philadelphia: J. B. Lippincott Co.

Bion, W. R. 1970. *Attention and Interpretation.* London: Tavistock.

Bollas, C. 1991. *Forces of Destiny, Psychoanalysis and the Human Idiom.* London: Free Association Press.

Edinger, E. F. 1985. *Anatomy of the Psyche.* La Salle, Ill: Open Court, 1985.

Guggenbühl-Craig, A. 1977. *Marriage: Dead or Alive.* trans. Murray Stein. Zürich: Spring.

Heisler, V. 1970. Individuation Through Marriage. *Psychological Perspectives* 1.

Jung, C. G. 1927. Woman in Europe. *CW 10 Civilisation in Transition.* New York: Pantheon, 1964.

Jung, C. G. 1931. Marriage as a Psychological Relationship. *CW 17. The Development of the Personality.* New York: Pantheon, 1954.

Jung, C. G. 1953. *Psychology and Alchemy. CW 12.* New York: Pantheon.

Jung, C. G. 1959. *Aion. CW* 9:2. New York: Pantheon.

Jung, C. G. 1963. *Mysterium Coniunctionis. CW* 14. New York: Pantheon.

Jung, C. G. 1963a. *Memories, Dreams, Reflections.* New York: Pantheon.

Kast, V. 1986. *The Nature of Loving.* trans. Boris Matthews. Wilmette, Ill.: Chiron.

Khan, M., Masud R. 1979. *Alienation in Perversions.* New York: International Universities Press.

Ulanov, A. B. 1971. *The Feminine in Jungian Psychology and in Christian Theology.* Evanston, Ill.:L Northwestern University Press.

Ulanov, A. B. 1986. For Better and for Worse. *The Psychoanalytic Review* 73, 4.

Ulanov, A. B. 1994. Self-Service. *Cast the First Stone.* ed. L. Ross and M. Roy. Wilmette, Ill.: Chiron.

Ulanov, A. and B. 1975. *Religion and the Unconscious.* Louisville, Ky.: Westminster.

Ulanov, A. and B. 1994. *Transforming Sexuality, The Archetypal Worlds of Anima and Animus.* Boston: Shambhala.

von Franz, M. L. 1980. *Alchemy, An Introduction to the Symbolism and the Psychology.* Toronto: Inner City Books.

Winnicott, D. W. 1958. Psycho-analysis and the Sense of Guilt. *The Maturational Processes and the Facilitating Environment.* New York: International Universities Press, 1958.

Winnicott, D. W. 1968. The Use of the Word "Use." *Psychoanalytic Explorations.* ed C. Winnicott, R. Shepherd, M. Davis. London: Karnac, 1989.

Winnicott, D. W. 1970. Living Creatively. *Home Is Where We Start From.* ed. C. Winnicott, R. Shepherd, M. Davis. New York: Norton, 1986.

Chapter 7

Embodied Spirit, Inspirited Body

How to bridge spirit and mind in relation to the body? This precarious position means the bridge can break from either side, as we have seen in history – those who claim the spirit alone will heal us, those who claim illness can be reduced to wrong mental attitudes, and both denying the facticity of the body that connects us – through blood, tissue, instinctive energy – to our brother and sister animals.

Many of us are professionals caring for others. All of us are or have been patients – some in the past, some right now, and all of us, probably, patients-to-be in future. So what we discover and discuss about mind, body, and spirit, means *our* bodies, *our* minds, *our* spirits. I would add a fourth distinct category, the psyche which means the unconscious, not the psyche we know, which is more or less the realm of conscious mind, but "the unknown as it intimately touches us" (Jung 1916). The amazing fact about the unconscious is that it exists, it *is*, and is *un*conscious. My questions are, What does the unconscious contribute to healing? What do body, mind and spirit look like from the point of view of the unconscious which is the territory of psychoanalysis?

Psyche

Psyche refers to an objective reality, as real as a table that bumps our shins, as real as the power of a myth that makes a country's political leader decide to massacre an entire race, as real as a delusion that makes a man shoot strangers on a Long Island train or a school campus. Psychic distress can suppress our immune system and increase our risk of physical illness (Hill and Mullen 1996, 241). Psyche may make us believe we do not live in our bodies but in a box fixed over our heads. Psyche can present its demands through the body, through that psychosomatic ulcer that pokes holes in our stomach, or through that anxiety that is so great that it induces angina attacks and even cardiac arrest. Psyche can present its demands through the mind, filling us with paranoid thoughts or voices that make us torture our children or assault strangers. But it is not only negative. Our psyche manufactures dreams and seminal thoughts which lead to new poems, new loves, new inventions, new breakthroughs in science. Enlarging our psychic consciousness can often prevent bodily illness because we are now able to suffer consciously what was earlier loaded into our sinus infection, or our throat reflux, or our hypertension.

Accepting our unconscious psyche ushers us to a place both beyond and before our ego, before all the egos of all of us, a place where we dwell together, not an abyss but a plenum, a fullness of interconnections and complex communities where we dwell as members of the human species on this earth. Here we live in sympathy with one another, freed for the moment from the tyrannies of developing, progressing, achieving. Here we recognize a diversity of ways of being amongst us, but a certain objective way to be for each one of us. Finding this way is what Jung means when he says that in addition to analyzing our unconscious, our unconscious analyzes us (Jung 1973, 2

May 1947, 460). The psyche does not reduce us to catchy formulas of our early past, summing up a whole life's struggle as a conflict from our toilet training. That thinking comes from our egos and is helpful in its own small terms. Psyche speaks to us in a language other than words and conscious logic; it speaks in terms of affect, impulse, image, to take us down beneath words and concepts to primordial experiences that can only be expressed symbolically.

Symbolic thinking and speaking make up the riverbed of psyche, from which scientific experiments emerge, rational thinking develops, and art, music, theology and medicine are crafted. But psyche itself, moving along like a river at the base of each of our lives, a river that flows unceasingly among and beneath all of us, speaks in its own terms, its own kind of flesh or matter in which the transcendent spirit incarnates. If living too close to the river we fall in, we go mad, or merely neurotic; we force psychic issues into our bodies which make them ill. If we live too far away from the river, we live dried up, parched, forcing our bodies to suffer beneath the surface what should be carried consciously.

What we mean by psyche is both our conscious and our unconscious mental processes that enable or disable us to become persons in touch with ourselves, with others, with the transcendent. Psyche, fueled by the energy of our bodily instinctual life, acts in us as an interrupter, introducing those odd blank spaces – like the dead air space of radio or T.V. – where repressed content makes its way from unconscious to conscious awareness. We know that person's name! What happened to it? Where did it go? We just killed the person off is what happened to it! The unconscious is the improviser, ever revising our point of view, never concluding once and for all, but speaking out of turn, giving us pause, keeping us open minded (see Phillips 1995, 3, 7ff; see also Lear 1998, chapter 3). Even when we are ill, in the hospital or in the hospice, the unconscious goes on, having opinions about what is happening to us, making something out of this experience of sickness or even of death. To know this, to see this in our patients, is to allow them and ourselves to go on living right up until the moment we die.

The fact of the unconscious brings what we say here today very close to home, touching our fears and denied terrors about dying, raising our blood pressure as we listen to techniques directed to lower it, arousing our longing for spiritual meaning that makes our hearts race while we learn techniques to steady its pace. Healing includes both ends – connection to our animal root-impulse and our longing for what makes our life hold meaning. One of my analysands who was completing her analysis when a terminal brain tumor struck her down, said in the year of her long day's dying – after she had managed to face into the dark and see what or who awaited her – that finding and creating what was given made it "worth it: It is *all* worth it," she said. Her spirit quickened as the tumor hastened her toward death (Ulanov 1994).

Illness

We know from ourselves, and from the people with whom we work, that illness, physical or psychological, breaks through the conventions of our lives, plucks us out of ordinary time into no-time – as in a feverish state where we hover above our beds in and out of consciousness, or in those dread moments when nausea reverses gravity to pour our body upward and out. Pain pushes us into different spaces and pulls us away from familiar ones. The husband of my patient with the cancerous brain tumor put it succinctly after his wife's first seizure: "Hospitals, MRI's, Cat scans, brain surgeries – this is her life now." And his, too – to follow along. For we can only bear the colossal loneliness we are plunged into by physical or mental illness if others stand with us, loving us, asking the pivotal question of us, more important than any other, the central spiritual question: "What are you going through?" And then waiting to hear our answer.

Our ordinary life is deconstructed by illness, of whatever kind. We are pressed against the seams of our life to the breaking point, breaking through to the no-time and no-space, which with luck and with grace becomes a liminal time of transition where we may find and create new depths of self and symbol. The seams mark our points of distress, often conveyed to us through a mysterious shadow on our lung that does not yield to biopsy but leaves the pathologists puzzled. We cling to technical explanations in order to throw a net over this no-place we have landed in, bereft of linear time, not knowing at all whether we have a future. We want the doctor to explain it, tell us the cause, tell us the cure and how to move in the shortest possible straight line from one to the other. We capture our terror in a concrete action we know we can perform. But often illness escapes our nets of technical explanation. The cause of physical pain remains indeterminate. For all we know medically, we still do not know very much, as one psychiatrist dedicated to helping lifelong sufferers of schizophrenia put it: We know in this disease there is a screw loose in the mind; we just don't know which one (Wyden 1997).

Illness, whether it is psychic or physical, brings vulnerability, both psychic and physical. Vulnerability may be one of the gifts illness offers us. For this pressing on the seams of our lives, deconstructing our presence in the world by moving us to see we could just as easily not be here, introduces us to the full sorrow of life, the pain and suffering that threaten to exile us from simple happiness in being, not to speak of the moral distress we suffer at another's pain and death. At any moment our utter contingency can jump up in us, lifting us from the here-and-now into touch with the beyond.

For many of us, the onslaught of physical illness makes us lose the psyche altogether, and feel spiritless. We are reduced to what afflicts our bodies or minds and cannot get ourselves above the water. We forget the crucial role the psyche plays in illness and in its healing. Jung says it well: "… it is advisable to approach every illness from the psychological side as well, because this may be extraordinarily important for the healing process. When these two aspects [psyche and physis] work together, it may easily happen that the cure takes place in the intermediate realm…." (Jung 1973, 10 July 1946, 428-429).

It is precisely that realm in-between, the space of that bridge between body, mind and spirit which is our concern right now. For illness pushes us into that space, and healing occurs there, I believe, in that intermediate zone somewhere between body and mind, spirit and psyche, in the complexity of relationships among all these human faculties. Think of a wheel with its different spokes, any one of which can lead us to the center around which the whole turns. At that center exists free space, allowing the whole wheel to turn. My focus is on what is revealed about body, mind, and spirit from the psyche's perspective. No matter where we start, however, we are always led to that free space of the center on which everything depends. It is from that space that the transcendent addresses us and brings healing.

Healing may mean the cessation of illness and return to ordinary life, even if we are changed forever by the illness. Healing may mean the sense of healing illness inaugurates, even when we are not cured physically. Like my patient who felt, even in dying, it was all "worth it," healing may bring a fullness, a bliss, an arrival into a thrumming peace that really passes all understanding. For to feel our lives deconstructed, revealed as contingent, not permanent, fragile, not durable, we suffer the uncovering of the stress points we cover over in our daily rounds and see how partial and relative our constructions of meaning may be, yet none of this means *no meaning.* Meaning exists. An objective way – a way full of meaning – exists for each of us. The life of the Spirit is the journey to find the way to live it. That way is what religion honors and speaks about. Healing means we have found it and accepted the fact that it has found us.

In the last years of this century, we have divorced or sharply differentiated spirituality from religion. Still, spiritual hunger exists strongly across all the world's populations. Many prefer the word "spiritual" to the word "religious," feeling that religion means coercion into set beliefs to which we cannot easily find connection. For many, religion suffers from reification – it has become the thing it should be pointing to, and hence it must be deconstructed. Those of us who have worked as chaplains in hospitals know how thoroughly physical illness, swift or lingering, smashes our God-images, exposing us to what lives behind them. Mental illness does the same, and also demands that we face into the threatening nothingness behind those broken God-images in order to receive the energy to get well. Glimpses of the transcendent beckon, and central to the treatment is to find the eyes to see it and the ears to hear it.

Such a smashing deconstruction does not mean nothing is true, but that all our images of the transcendent ground of life are only of parts, limited by our particular time and place. Illness brings us to see that and to be faced with the presence of the transcendent beyond our images of it. Reality exists. Illness thrusts us to the head of the line to face there ultimate questions of the meaning of life and death, to face that presence and see if we can relate to it. That relating must be conjugated in the grammar of the body, mind, spirit – and psyche.

Body

What does the body look like from the point of view of the depth psyche? Body looked at from the point of view of the unconscious means animal root-impulses that energize our whole person. Body means definite forms, individual and specific, in time and space. This is the earthly hut we inhabit. This is the abode in which the spirit incarnates which we strive in a spiritual life to make into a small temple for God, or whatever name we use for transcendent reality. Body is limit, boundary, individuality. We do not live in relation to the transcendent in an abstract way, but in the dimensions of our exact size in inches, our weight of however many pounds, our genetic inheritance, our time and its years, our skin that is soft or rough and eventually wrinkles, our hair that turns grey, our bones that may come to ache. Body is a gathering sexual desire that opens onto deep inner humming satisfaction in orgastic pleasure; body is exploding laughter that raises our temperature and pulse, contracting our thoracic muscles, setting our vocal chords and lower jaw aquiver, expelling breath at so many miles per hour (Maitland 1995, 72). Body is muscle and blood, a heart pumping, a stomach secreting, a mysterious and lavish assembly of organs and structure, surface and depth, full of instinctual energy as mysterious as the spirit in its clamorings to live and live well. Body from the point of view of psyche means animal root-impulse – and many psychic disorders stem from being cut off from that root impulse, from instinctive energy (Ulanov 1998). Jung speaks of our brother and sister animals as "actually holier than us since [they] cannot deviate from the divine will implanted in [them]...." They are the most pious servants of God: guided by instinct, they do God's will (Jung 1975, 28 March 1955, 235).

Body means neighbors. Through our bodies we touch each other, see, smell, and hear each other. Body means history, context defining qualities that gender, class, race, historical era, educational level, cultural location, economic status confer. For Lacan, the path of healing means to put aside our ego based on our legal identity – the group, the family, the country we are born into – in order to claim the identity we create from our own desire (Clément 1993, 91). Our body is social, partaking of environmental provision (or its lack) in the ongoing process of forming our self in relation to others. Just as the body sheds its skin and replaces its cells regularly, so the self is a work in progress (Kristeva 1995, 6-7), a process with continuity, in community.

When we look at the body from the point of view of the unconscious, we see how body can be used to hide and display a person's suffering. Psychosomatic illness occurs in the intermediate realm shared by mind, body, and spirit. The psyche turns that troubled space into a gap of madness, which when healed becomes precisely the opposite, a space of healing. Chronic eczema attacks the skin, for example, allowing a child to display and disguise erupting rage in bodily form. Asthma that steals one's breath permits physical display of the unconscious belief that someone is suffocating one's very existence. Colitis explodes the bowels to express the murderous intent to bury one's enemy in filth. With Winnicott we can see that psychosomatic disorders insist on a split between mind and body in order to speak from the soul and tell its story. Healing comes when the psyche's integrative forces grow the split together, allowing us to abandon defense in favor of whole living (Winnicott 1964 and 1969, 106).

Looking at the body from the perspective of the psyche can also give us insight into a psychic factor in physical disease. It is unequivocally wrong, I believe, to reduce bodily illness to psychic causes. That reduction adds the insult of blaming the patient to the injury of the sickness that has already reduced his or her bodily integrity. This sadistic performance dresses itself up in a know-it-all costume, a good example of where we choose the tree of good and evil over the tree of life.

Noticing what factors may be working in an illness does help us deal with its effects and find a cure. When I think of clinical examples I am overwhelmed with material. I select here only analysands who suffered major physical illness, and for whom bodily illness was mixed up with psyche and spirit. A striking example is offered by a woman in her early twenties. She was suffering from myocarditis, an infection of the heart so severe that she had to stay in bed for a year, get used to bedpans, submit to a powerful drug, rawufia. She was finally, remarkably enough, cured of this life-threatening disease. In her late twenties she began analysis for depression, in the course of which we discovered an unguessed component of her heartsickness. Her father had died suddenly of a heart attack when she was sixteen, just after telling her to get rid of the toilet paper that boyfriends had tossed in a Halloween escapade into the trees on their front lawn. She had never mourned her father's death, but had rather succumbed to all the excitement caused by the radical change in her family's life. Looking back, she saw her disease of the heart included a total collapse at the loss of her father. She took to her bed for a year (see Ulanov 1996, chapter 10 for fuller discussion).

In her fifties this woman was diagnosed with ovarian cancer and endured the inevitable and frightful side-effects of heavy doses of chemotherapy – "lava stomach," nausea, constipation, loss of hair and eyebrows, fatigue. Calling for help the summer this harsh treatment was occurring, she said the issue was not so much the cancer. She was a "tough turkey," she said, in coping with chemotherapy. Rather she feared she might collapse emotionally and slide into depression once again, not from physical but from psychic causes. An unusual friendship with a man from another country, younger than herself, had recently ripened into a passionate love and sexuality between them. That, too, frightened her and she realized she was using her surgery and chemotherapy as an excuse to back off from intimacy, even though her doctors assured her that was not at all necessary. She feared how much she loved this man; feared the emotional dependency her feelings opened her to, not the physical dependency the illness occasioned which her lover had met splendidly, helping her shop and cook the right meals for her condition, understanding her fatigue, and all that went with her illness. Having done much psychological work, she knew the cancer was not her leading problem. The emotional vulnerability and dependence brought by surrendering to her feelings were. The imagined emotional death was worse than the threatened physical death. By telling me this, even though our work together had long since finished, she held herself to her own truth and did not let herself hide in her illness. That takes pluck, courage. That spared her the grievous aggravation of her physical symptoms for unconscious reasons.

No space exists where we can stand, or kneel, outside of time, place, and our bodily existence and simply observe. We are matter and we matter. We are, through our bodies, ever in the midst of the boundaries, limits, and cross-currents of others' influence, dependent on each other to come into existence at all, to sustain the traumas that tear us out of our belief systems, and to help us toward death with a cool drink of water, a soft hand on our forehead, a bed remade with fresh linen, and finally an accompanying presence sitting with us as we face into the dark.

In psychoanalytic work we bring into open awareness what goes on all the time, if somewhat secretly, in the company of others. We listen to our analysand as a bodily presence, not just as words and emotional responses. What is the rhythm of breathing? Is the voice raised to a shout, or hard to hear? Does smell communicate? (I once treated a woman whose cologne was so fragrant I could scent her arrival from my closed office when she seated herself in the waiting room. I once had to analyze a man's repelling body odor as his consciously denied but acted-out hostility to others.) Experiencing a person in the body does not allow for neutral or abstract responses but imposes on us an ethical demand to respond immediately in our body, to commit ourselves to the other's journey, or to refuse to do so (Khan 1971, 246, 250).

No spiritual life can be sustained if it does not include the body. Breathing exercises, meditational postures, images, alpha rhythms, holding yoga positions, whatever one's chosen path – spirit lives in body. It is embodied or it is not. Remember, in the simplest terms, healing means doing what the body itself wants – to be touched, to be held, to be stroked, to be entered, to pour itself out, above all to be supported. We want to be recognized in our bodily presence. Whether in illness or health, the body possesses a language of its own. Our organ dialect shows itself most poignantly in hypochondriacal symptoms where the body's speech is made to substitute for words. Even in healthy times, somatic language undergirds and surpasses words, conducting us to a zone of communication that transcends ordinary limits.

Mind

Mind contains much of our capacity to reflect on experience, to reason about it, to make maps and diagrams and to plot courses. Mind introduces a space between us and our experience. It opens an interval to us of freedom from instinct and introduces choice. Freud calls it the procrastinating function of thought. We see how much healing the ability to think can bring when we look at social ills spawned by too hasty action. "If I had only held my temper and thought out the consequences I would not have hit my spouse, or attacked my neighbor. But I was just carried away." The illness of addictions of body and spirit – to drink, to do cocaine, to overwork, to rigid counting, to obsessions about what I should have said, or about why they do not like me – all these detour the body's instinctive energy down dead-end roads. Conscious thought introduces bigger spaces where we can choose instead of being compelled to do something.

Mind calms our fears with explanations of what is happening to us. It was not really an act of God we experienced, but hormones out of balance. It was not the world coming to an end, but a fainting fit because of too low blood pressure. We can understand our complete surrender to panic when we learn our erratic heartbeat had accelerated wildly. Mind explains. It can also exhort and enlist animal root-impulses and direct them to goals. Mind can create systems of meaning to communicate with others and join them in comparing and contrasting the best procedures to follow.

Psyche shows us that mind can be misused – especially if it is a good mind – to substitute for body functions or shared existence with neighbors (see Corrigan and Gordon 1995). Then the mind deadens or covers up dead places inside us. In psychoanalysis we speak, for example, of the schizoid condition where the mind forms a shield against others around us, and keeps our own feelings locked up, isolated, and hence keeps them too young, never developing in the natural congress with others (see Guntrip 1969). We see the consequence of this plight in many popular films where there is no story anymore. Pyrotechnics substitute for plot unfolding out of character.

Sensationalism replaces mounting drama. The literal acting-out of anger and fear, of phobias, crowds out any reflective contemplation and differentiation among emotions. In such films imagination no longer exists; it has been abandoned.

Loss of imagination means loss of reality. Frightening consequences of this double loss are the rash of real-life actings-out of children murdering children. A child uninstructed by stories, fantasy games, fairy tales that teach indirectly how to turn over in imagination gigantic feelings of rage, revenge, ambition, fear, gobbling hunger, impulses to shoot, chew up, burn, and yell at others has, in our culture, only the literal models of television scenarios or movies with little story-line. There, emotion is literalized into action. But such action is no more real than fantasy feelings. The reality of what was just done does not register. One of the little boys who killed his teacher and some of his classmates in Arkansas did not grasp that he could not just go home after his arrest. He was reported as saying, "I'm going home now." When detained, he said, "Well I'll have pizza and a soda for dinner." When it was finally borne in upon him that he must stay in jail and live under its rules, a guard heard him crying for his mother. Here is a child whose imagination we have failed to instruct, a child who acts out instead of using mind to contain, metabolize, and learn to humanize the primitive human emotions with which we are all assailed.

Our mind can also dissociate from our physical existence and load suffering onto the body, that wordless animal self, the beast that must carry our amassed hostilities like a stockpiling of weapons in the world, only here it is clotted around the heart, filling up the arteries. For our minds can cut off what we fear and do not understand or cannot process. I have even seen cases of chronic allergy of the skin turn out to be the site of unprocessed sorrow, conserved there on the body until the person could afford to face it and feel it. The body instead of the fullness of the conscious person wept annually with skin eruptions. We can see the mind coping in the hospital where medical procedures so often breed this kind of dissociation. We put up with them, like bad airplane seats, in order to get somewhere else. Much patient care could be improved and healing promoted if we remember what it means to us when the technician cheerily says, "Oh this test is not so bad." One of my patients challenged that remark by asking, "Have you ever had this test?" "Well no," was the reply. The woman then described what it was like to be locked alone into an X-ray chamber at 10:30 at night, the only available time, to see blue flames shoot through her head, as part of her treatment for a malignant tumor.

Our mind brings inspection, invention, application, but not formulas. We want to be understood, not robbed of our experience, even of a terminal illness, by being probed, questioned, and talked about as if we were not actually there, but only an object to be studied, fixed, or, barring that, to be discarded, no longer seen or heard or worth attention. We deeply resent other minds seeing us as a specimen. One of my patients suffered from the rare Kreuzfeld Jacob brain disease. He made medical history by not going psychotic before he died, as had happened in all other recorded cases, because, I believe, of a great act of spirit he was able to make because of the psychic work he had done in analysis (Ulanov 1996, chapter 9). He had agreed to go to one of the best New York hospitals so doctors and residents could study this scarcely seen, fast-moving disease; he knew it would kill him. But after a few days there he called his sons to get their van and take him out because he felt reduced to bug status, treated as an object, not as a person to be studied, but a specimen that happened to drag along with it a human personality.

We cannot use our mind to separate people from their bodies. Mind contains bodily components – the brain, the central
nervous system. Mind is precious. When some of us lose it in
handfuls, as in the affliction of Alzheimer's disease, we treasure
all the more its value where it allows us to reflect, consider,
hold, remember, and create continuity that accords us a sense
of ongoing identity. Mind weaves continuity through the self in
process.

Healing sometimes comes through mind opening to a reality
that the body already knows but so often suffers alone without
the help of compassion from others. One man sought therapy
because of massive anxiety, because of a diagnosis some six
months before of chronic lymphocytic leukemia that at his age,
in the late thirties, could soon prove fatal. Had he been in his
late sixties, it would have progressed so slowly that he probably
would die in good time from something else. Leukemia at his age
demanded regimens of severe doses of chemotherapy and finally
an extremely strong bout of chemotherapy to prepare him for
the harvesting of his own bone marrow, to be preserved for a
future autologous transplant. In addition, the so-called "tumor
burden" in the marrow of his bones – the excess of white in
relation to red blood cells – had to be monitored constantly
and his general health kept under steady supervision.

He could hardly deny the truth: he was seriously ill. But his
mind did somehow act to deny it. The affect of his anxiety did
not include that of being ill. He knew "about" it and talked
"about" it, but no emotion pumped through it. The red blood
cells of felt illness drained away. A major part of our work
together amounted to arriving at the truth, the fact that he
really was sick. Only by our seeing the symbolic value of his
illness did the illness become true to him. Accepting actual
sickness came about only after searching ferociously into the
symbolic use to which he had put his illness. I would find myself

saying, for example, that his performance to meet others' expectations "bled him white," as did his perfectionism: he still obsessed that years before when taking Graduate Record Exams he made a perfect 800 on all tests except one where he "only" scored 780. This was a brilliant exceptional man, recognized by others, sent to this country to do advanced scholarly work by the religious order to which he belonged.

This was also a compassionate man who had worked around the world – in leper colonies, in poor countries, in refugee camps. But now he showed little awareness of, or mercy for his suffering body. Much of the analysis aimed to permit us to arrive where he could feel what it meant to be ill with such a real physical illness. We discovered that his illness functioned to supply him a space of refuge from demands he felt forced to meet, overriding his animal root-impulses to say no, or to exercise his own aggression in making choices, or to register his own desire for what he loved. Instead he came laden with the burdens of a lifetime of energy sapped by the need he felt to comply with others' expectations which then deadened whatever he did. Illness granted him a free space, a respectable excuse for not doing what others wanted or what his over-active ego-ideal demanded. He projected expectations onto others, and divined what expectations they brought, and then could only unfold himself in relation to others in terms of obligation. Feeling duty-bound nullified his vitality. Life lost its redness. The marrow of his bones was crowded out by the burden of deadening obligation. He said, "When I feel others' expectations, I feel trapped, deadened ... and leukemia is a prized possession; it got me out of things."

In the treatment, I could feel in my own countertransference the smothering of red blood cells which should bring oxygen. He would be talking along, giving information but not really connecting; the effect was stifling. It felt weird. Though he was visibly present, it was as if there was little emotional reality to what he said. Finally, I voiced my need for more red-blooded reaction, which brought the relief of his sobs. He eventually found words for what his bodily presence had acted out: "Where we are now is not where I am alive, and I don't see how we are going to get from here to there." We had to go on catching ourselves to be sure we were not merely going through the right motions, looking as if we were doing analysis but actually the real life was all split off. I would ask, for example, if we were in the dead place, the "where we are not alive place." It was as if his body was communicating its pain to my body by making my own potential for pain act up in his session. Not in the sessions before and not in the sessions after his appointment, but only in his session would my hip start to hurt, there in my own weak place. Then I would know we were veering off course again into fine sounding words, but without red blood cells. I would squawk, and he would repeat the mantra "we are not in the alive place" and we would reconnect ourselves.

We discovered together a whole piece of himself hiding in the illness space. Here lurked a very different kind of "guy," whom he himself described as "gluttonous, ravenous, grasping." Here there lived a big chunk of his primitive aggression and ruthless desire. This part of him could find no place to live in his conscious adaptation as a genuine religious dedicated to his vows, dedicated to serving others. Here was hidden his split-off sexuality, which insisted on being lived, one way or another; otherwise, the vow of chastity was a mockery, a mere subtraction, not an offering or act of love. This hidden piece of himself taught him that in order to serve God he had to accept all that God had given him to be. Any of us who deny a big chunk of ourselves shuts off access to others and to the center of reality. He said with his usual wit that the vow of chastity has a lot in common with sex, because it is about extravagance, about squandering, about making lavish, ultimate, dramatic gestures. This part of him that had been hiding out in his illness stepped forward now to be included in his conscious life and thought. His illness would then be just illness, and his conflict between his vows and this aggressive, desirous, virile assertion could be suffered consciously. He wanted all of him to be seen, and to be accepted as a man, a whole man, neither "side-lined" into a make-believe job because of his illness, nor in denial of his animal root-impulses. He wanted to be an embodied spirit.

Once this split-off part was seen and his mind no longer denied it, the whole mix changed. Disease, he said, was no longer "a magic place," and he was no longer disappointed that he was not more ill. Sickness was just that, a bother, a suffering, a procedure that would have to be faced and lived with, but not a refuge from the world. Taking with him into the world the ravenous, aggressive, ruthlessly desiring part of himself changed the whole mix of his body-mind-spirit. He described it sometimes in terms of the priestly function – his function – of administering the Eucharist – the giving of bread and wine. The Eucharist, he said, is a banquet that is always messy, for we couldn't be addressing all these different kinds of people at once unless we were right in the midst of things. His desire was to be drawn into that "midst" and to feel fed with – and to feed – all of the body. "The Eucharist is the dream for the world" he said "how we might all be, how the world might be, different, diverse, all people coming together to celebrate life."

Psyche and Spirit

I put these two together because they are so often mixed up and used interchangeably, and because they cannot be reduced to tangible parts as mind and body can so much more easily.

Philosophically, mind and body are first and second orders of being, with material parts, located in tangible sections of body, distinct areas that can be studied empirically and experimentally, in more identifiable places than psyche and spirit. Spirit and psyche are what the philosopher Charles Pierce calls thirds – intangible, not found in identifiable places, but nonetheless *there*, existing, mediational and unitive, containing in their processes the *un*knowable, the *un*analyzable, the *un*speakable no matter how many mental concepts and bodily gestures we possess (see Knight, 80). Psyche connects us to the *un*conscious part of human spirit; spirit connects us to the *un*fathomable spirit of the divine. With both we enter the world of symbol that points to, but cannot capture; that represents, but cannot equate with; that, in the words of Emily Dickinson, tells the truth but tells it slant. There is no other way to tell the truth. It cannot be accessed immediately, but only met in terms of "as if," by analogy, by image or affect presenting to us the unknowable as it immediately touches us (Dickinson 1960, 506-507, #1129).

All helping professionals need to ask of themselves as well as those they care for, What are the major symbols in this person's life? What acts as a bridge to their unvoiced worries, their unspeakable fears, their undared hopes? By what truth have they been living until now? What truth is breaking in upon them in this crisis of illness? We cannot bring in the spiritual aspect of healing if we ignore the spiritual objects of our patients. And those objects tell it slant: they speak in symbols.

Sometimes, to see what the psyche is making of our illness is the shortest route to healing. Jung says, for example, "If the *archetypal situation underlying the illness* can be expressed in the right way the patient is cured." Or, even more strongly, if we can see that our ailment is not ours alone, but "a general ailment – even a god's ailment – then ... [we are] in the company

172

of men and gods, and this knowledge produces a healing effect" (Jung 1976, para 231). Illness which usually makes us feel so terribly alone can also be understood as our participation in a human problem that all of us share, and that we can each contribute to its solution. Then we may feel our suffering is not wasted, and that brings some healing. Even more mysterious is the release, sometimes even the cure, that comes when in a lavish spiritual gesture we offer our bodily suffering in intercession for someone else. Here psyche in its reality enters the zone of the objective reality of spirit.

The psyche can use disorders of the body, or of the mind, or even of the spirit, to bring to conscious awareness an unlived hope, a split-off trauma, a chronic fear. The healing questions we must ask are, "What is the psyche engineering in this illness?" "What meaning is being made of this illness?" "What meaning is assembling now in our own or in our patient's mind, body, spirit, coming toward us through this illness?" We must keep open to the answers, for each of us as a patient contributes something to the world around us, to the whole human family, really through what we learn in being sick and getting well, what each of us discovers and achieves in the dying process.

We all know stories of people who influence others through their ways of dying. My patient who died of Kreuzfeld Jacob brain disease had what in religious terms is called a "blessed death." All who come in contact with the dying person in such an event receive a blessing specific to themselves. The one who is dying gives, without planning to or doing anything consciously about it, a life-giving insight, a spiritual boon or healing moment to all who come in contact with him.

This man several years before had been a long standing member of my therapy group. When he was diagnosed as having just three months to live, some of the group members journeyed to see him. All of them, to their surprise, reported

173

receiving a concrete life-changing gift from their dying colleague. This bestowal of blessing happened because he in his
death experience was so firmly anchored in the source. It was
not something he did or set out to do. A mark of the center of
life is that it moves outward, enlarging itself as it communicates
itself to those who can receive it. This communication did not
just happen to group members. He was famous enough to be
written about in his way of dying in magazines and newspapers
and there too it was reported that those of his friends, past and
present, who came to bid him farewell in his early death, felt
they had received a blessing for their ongoing lives.

We might ask today what the psyche is making of the upheaval
in our national health plans. I see a radical shift of transference
between patient and doctor and surprising alliances of opposites. With HMO plans assigning groups of doctors to patients
instead of each selecting the other and building up a life-long
relationship, and insurance companies interposing themselves
between doctors and patients to decide who gets what and
how much treatment, transference of authority for health by
patient to doctor is loosening and disappearing. Energy that we
used to project outside ourselves and locate in the doctor to
take charge of our bodies now reverts back to each one of us.
This influx of energy causes anxiety, a feeling of not being safe.
But it also moves us to take command and find ways to house
this energy and use it. At the same time traditional enemies
that Western medicine has long opposed and even viewed as
crackpot – homeopaths, herbalists, acupuncturists, practitioners of complementary medicine – are now allies of all who tell
us to take into our own hands the governance of our mental
and bodily health. Such authority transfers back to each of us
responsibility for our own health and permits us to become
together a community of active agents in our suffering and our
healing. In this conference we are such a community.

If psyche means all those conscious and unconscious processes that either enable or disable us to live as persons in relation to self, to others, to God, *Spirit* means our willingness to do so. Deep down in each of us dwells an indefinable and unfathomable presence which we experience as the urge to pray, an impulse to do a simple act of kindness, a movement of heart to go the extra mile without the reward of extra pay or praise, movements of mind to concentrate on the essential, cutting away all mere verbiage and empty nattering. We want to bring something to birth. We are moved by something moving us that brings deep satisfaction when we consent.

Spiritual life requires such consent, such a willingness to respond, being neither lukewarm nor fanatical but just listening to the still small voice, receiving the commandments of our religious traditions, hearing the word spoken directly in our own hearts, knowing we have been summoned. People describe the experience as a penetration through the heart, like an electric current; they feel lightness; they feel fire; a blessed blue flame fills them. Whatever the specific experience, all feel moved to gratitude to something outside themselves that surpasses understanding but seems nonetheless very clear and closer than breath. It is, some say, as if something else were breathing our breath through us (see Ulanov and Ulanov 1975, 248; see also Ulanov and Ulanov 1982). Trying to grasp this ungraspable moment, people speak of prison bars breaking open, of walking on fluid water as if on solid ground, of mind and body dropping away, of being raised to life again. The desert blooms.

Spirit requires symbolic speech to describe its presence. It will not be captured in rigid form or logical argument. It will not wed itself to metaphor. It dances out. It is a fountain, life overflowing, life-energy, wind blowing where it will, a vital power. People forget that the very nature of symbol is to represent the unknown or unknowable, to capture the infinite in finite form.

Thus the ambiguity and ambivalence of symbols for spirit are inevitable, for the part can never speak the whole.

Spirit always surprises us because it brings the new, and brings it often right there in the old, and in everyday terms. So it is that even our aged body and psyche can surprise us in embodying a new thought, in seeing a way through an old problem. We are not just waiting for death, but glad until we die. Little epiphanies accompany spirit: something holy shows itself in human form, new images arrive, we wake up to correspond to what addresses us. A moment of total meaning is then created, one that promotes healing of mind, body and psyche (Hill and Mullen 1996, 244).

But we can exploit spirit too, just as we can misuse mind, body and psyche. We might even look at pathology here as impoverishment of spirit. Typical spiritual disorders stem from diluting the spirit, reducing it to some simplistic formula as, If I do this then that will happen. We reduce spirit to a coping strategy to help in illness – a cheaper way to regulate blood pressure or steady heart rates. We forget that we cannot just raid spiritual vocabulary or practices while denying their referent. Spiritual *means* Spirit, relation to something transcending human categories. We cannot just *use* spirit however worthy the use. That is like saying, Yes, I'll marry you because you will make me rich, not because I want to be with you. Spiritual development takes us from loving God for our sake to loving God for God's sake. And it is the open-ended prayer that God's will be done, that God's goodness be shown even in this most desperate illness that brings the fullest healing (Dossey 1998). For then we do not treat the transcendent like a deal-maker sending in prescriptions in exchange for certain promised behavior.

Another related spiritual disorder casts God as working along a reward-punishment axis. Many patients must battle an attacking voice that says they received this dread sickness as punishment for betrayals committed, for shirkings, for mean-spiritedness. The more sophisticated version of this attacking voice is not much better; it says we are punished with this illness because we failed to eat right, or exercise enough. Moralism knows no bounds and if we neglect to recognize the irrepressible energy of spirit it does indeed sneak into our lives negatively, shaking a finger at us like an oversized nanny scolding our faults.

Spirit can be latched onto in a conscious or unconscious orgy of omnipotence. We act as if the body does not exist at all, as if a history of atrocious food and climate, of breathing polluted air, count for nothing. Spirit, we say, makes us historical beings angels, not affected by physical surroundings. Evil can be bypassed in the new age dawning if we just take the right vitamin supplements and practice the right spiritual disciplines. This sort of omnipotence flees from the hard facts of genetic constitution, environmental depredation, the physical effects of rage, indifference, ignorance, lust, cruelty, all hiding in the outblown notion that if we have the right belief system nothing can touch us. Phooey. The body is the designated house for spirit, the proud one. It will not bear such insults lightly.

We can also indulge in spiritual greed, hunting up the next new high, the next heady insight, without ever knitting into the flesh of our daily life the insights we have already been given that tell us to change our behavior. Here we treat spirit like a honey-pot into which we can dip for new sensations and possibilities without ever making them flesh, that is, incarnate in our politics, our family life, our workplace. The body wants to be inspirited, not hopped over.

Spirit is our capacity to experience the transcendent in ordinary life, conscious that we are related to transcendent reality. We feel spirit in the gift of forgiveness. We know it as freeing inspiration. It brings its peace to us. It lifts us into bliss. It also descends on us its great weight, pushing us to an action we know we must do, such as saying we are sorry to someone we have wronged, or signing up for a dangerous duty to defend what is right. Spirit can be felt as gladness, as joy bubbling over, as gratitude for beauty. It brings us to see the goodness that is just there, good for nothing; just being, radiating to all. Spirit will not be captured in a tight fist or a special possession we think is ours alone. It is free, in itself and us, wanting to be lived by us.

Something in us corresponds to this fiery determined freeness that invades us not to conquer but to liberate, to lift us from depression, to rouse our sympathy, to enable us to stand in our neighbor's shoes. People show this indefinable spirit when they risk their lives to hide Jews hunted down by Nazis; when a chaplain can speak the prayers of God on the death march to Butan; when a student chaplain all alone with a deformed baby baptizes it before it dies, the only one to welcome its presence and name it as part of God's family and bid it farewell. In caring for the ill, in myriad ways we show spirit to give to and to receive from our patients.

Spirit pushes hard to step over into concrete life. It insists on being lived by us. It wants to know us joining up with its germ inside us. For that we must consent, must willingly go with it, be glad in it, find practices that secure relation to it. For that we need mind's reflection and language to name what we seek. This is where spirit returns to religious precincts, no matter the tradition. For we cannot go on relating to the transcendent in some anonymous way, never calling it by name, never building a specific history of relation with it. We surely do not expect to relate to our life partner by never calling him or her anything, or just calling out "hey you." We do not relate to our children that way, never marking them by name or building with them a history of places, meals, activities, but calling them "child." Why do we think we can do this with God?

God wants to live with us and be known by us and have us know that we are known. So a mind-body-spirit-psyche conference means developing and paying attention to our own history with spiritual objects. How have we lived with this free dancing-out spirit? What did we call it? When did we know it best? Where did we lose it? What happened to the names we used to call it? How long has it been since we talked or imagined or dreamed of this God? Have the animals left our religion, taking with them our own animal impulses? Is that why we do not cry out in fear, hide under Holy wings, get mad, seek solace, find food in God? What is our spiritual history? Caring for the ill and dying, researching how to make life more liveable and possible is hard labor, in the trenches. We need resources of mind-body-spirit and psyche to survive and thrive in it.

A most pressing question for spirit is what happens to it when we are gravely ill. Our connection to it often crumbles then; spiritual life and religious belief can seem useless in the face of mortal sickness. Yet the presence of chaplains in mental and general hospitals witnesses to the theological fact of spirit, that its resources may be the most comforting, enabling, fortifying when we come to the head of the line to face death in life. The chaplain asks the essential question of the person: What are you going through? And asks it of the whole mind-body-spirit-psyche person. This attitude carves a bigger space for our answer – what we make of the illness in our body, what meaning assembles as it advances toward us? What glimpses of the transcendent bestow themselves in this experience? What spirit builds up as we make our way toward our end? I offer the following example of this kind of conversation a woman in her sixties conducted with her body and mind and spirit in the context of her psychoanalysis as she confronted an obscure, lethal illness, hard even to diagnose, and without, as yet, any known cure.

An Example

Our sessions are at my office, though at times she may be away for six weeks in a rehabilitation center to improve her fuzzy speech, or steady her wobbly gait. We must work on the phone if she cannot be brought to the office by her closest friend who is beset by a demanding schedule. She can no longer leave the house alone.

Originally she sought therapy because of violent night-time episodes that inhabited her body but had not yet reached her mind or psyche. She found no words to capture her agitation, nor any dream images. Instead, she found herself picked up and hurled out of her bed, or awakened by her own growling, cursing, and screaming. She would wake up banging her head against the wall, the bureau, or the bedpost. Black and blue and sometimes cut, deeply frightened, she entered therapy after seeking – as she continued to do while in therapy – every kind of medical and neurological consultation. None of it yielded anything clear or trustworthy. It was an alarming situation. Had she not been a woman of psychological discernment and great spiritual maturity (a vowed religious of extraordinary quality), she and I could not have faced together what unraveled before us. By listening hard to the screaming, which she began to tape, and paying close attention to every bodily symptom in the night-time escapades, we rescued from pummeling anonymity the acting-out of the body and brought it into dream images.

The first dreams showed her yelling to a girl to get away or she would kill her, a man behind bars grabbing her from behind, a foreign object coming at her from somewhere in the universe, to save herself from which she must hurl herself into that universe. We spent a lot of time on one of these dreams. It featured a man determined to murder her. He hunted her down on a long steel contraption that looked like a tower on its side. There was no escaping. I've thought of this dream many times since the medical diagnosis which finally came three years later. By then she had seen many different doctors, all sorts of specialists, because her whole body had begun to act up.

Once the night-time terrors were captured into dreams, the rest of her body broke out in new symptoms – dehydration and blood problems, for which she underwent long treatment, bad bronchitis, a vestibular ear disorder which also required long treatment. She suffered from great fatigue, had difficulty writing clearly. Her speech was slurred. Above all she suffered increasing dizziness and with a dangerous tendency to lurch suddenly. Problems retaining urine required bladder surgery, an operation that failed, the doctor said, and he offered to do it again for no fee. He referred her to still another neurologist, who finally made a diagnosis that was successively confirmed by subsequent doctors. What she had was multisystem cerebrum atrophy. The cells at the base of her cerebellum were shrinking and first one body-system and then another would fail. Once her mind had a map of what was wrong with her, however, her sense of disorientation and overwhelming fears of any number of diseases that her condition might evidence, relaxed somewhat. She could now focus on how to go on living with her great affliction. Looking back at the growling repudiation in those early night terrors, and the psychic meaning we made of those dreams, we now could see their simple bodily meaning. With all her animal root-impulse she was attempting to hurl out of her system her debilitating disease. She was right to curse and scream "Get out of here or I'll kill you!" because the animal in her knew this murdering disease was sending her on a long, slow, crippling journey to death.

The psyche's dream-speech directed us to two critical lifelong areas of neglect: her body and her aggression. These neglects were not the consequence of her own choosing or her choice to enter a religious order. She was not a namby-pamby nun hiding out from the world, nor a rule-keeping obsessive one. She is, I believe, the real thing: a person in love with God, a woman of advanced spiritual development, with all the flexibility and freedom that it brings. She entered her order after college and after deciding carefully between marrying the man she was going with and her call to God. Sought out as a particularly discerning and able spiritual director, her spiritual attitude might be summed up in one sentence: "God does not care about our rules, but only that we let God love us," and her ability to say and mean, "What God wants of me is that I want for myself; I want to be at the river and God is the river."

What was neglected throughout her life, as a child, in her training as a nun, in her work in the world as teacher, director of a center for spiritual life, and a noted spiritual director, were the limits of her body and the conscious use of her aggression not only for others but for herself. Now in her illness, she was being forced to live in her body, as gradually she was forced to relinquish work. Allopathic medicine offered her no treatment, but her neurologist did encourage her to seek out complementary medicine, comparing her in her sixties fighting with all her strength to stay well to another patient, only twenty-four years old, with the same condition and already in a wheelchair. Her average week was taken up with many appointments to stabilize her balance through the Alexander method, with acupuncture, which could not regenerate cells but could strengthen the lateral cells, increase her energy, and improve circulation to her numbingly cold feet and hands. She took herbs to calm her night-time screaming, therapy for her voice, and massage for her cerebellum.

In our analytical work she uncovered early trauma around aggression whose effects she gradually traced through her whole life. As the youngest of five in a poor rural family, she was particularly sensitive to the atmosphere of her parents' deteriorating marriage. Her father loved her as his favorite and was, she said, a wonderful playmate, but never a providing or protecting father. No sense of masculine energy at its best came from him, she said; he survived, but never thrived. She linked that undelivered energy to her early superiors in her Order too, who did not know how to provide or protect but could only demand, censure, and use you for extra chores and errands, especially if you were the only one with a driver's license. Teachers in her rural school used aggression to shame and humiliate instead of to enliven, challenge, or encourage. She remembered one particular teacher who made her doubt her own intellect.

Her father's temper was gigantic and swift and petrified her with fear, not for herself but for her mother. She took on herself the role of her mother's protector, positioning herself every day after school at the dining-room table to do her homework where she could keep one eye on her mother in the kitchen and the other on her father in the living room, alert to any eruption of anger between them. She remembered one dreadful fight when she was ten. Her father was about to smash her mother's head with a platter. She put herself between them, crying, screaming, "Stop! No! Don't!" and trembling so violently her body went on shuddering after the moment passed. Her mother was deeply shaken by her daughter's bodily fear and promised she would never see them fighting again. But my patient felt that afterwards her mother turned all her fighting spirit inward upon herself, grew sick from cancer and died. If only she could have defended her! A victory in our work came when she arrived at the statement, "I no longer feel responsible for my mother's death. She made her own decision."

Still more potent in its effects was a related trauma centered around aggression. After this dreadful fight between her parents, who slept in different bedrooms at her father's instigation, she had consciously decided that if her father attacked her mother in the night, she would murder him. With all the energy of the animal root-impulse and the psychic determination of a child of ten, she screwed herself up to the sticking point – alert, ready, intentional – to kill the father she loved if he threatened to harm the mother she loved even more. She secured a knife from somewhere and kept it in her hand while pretending sleep in her bed. When she saw her father's shadow in the hall, she woke to quivering alertness, ready to spring up, to stab him, to kill him, if he went toward her mother's room. When he went only to the bathroom and then returned to his bed, she quieted down, but her whole body-mind-spirit self was still ready to murder. A link could be made here to the dream murderer hunting her.

This formative experience, I believe, shocked her whole psychosomatic organism, with lifelong consequences. This was not oedipal sexual jealousy, for she liked to see her mother go to her father's room for sexual congress. It was her father – moody, irascible, possessive – who would sexually reject her mother because he could not control her. My patient felt when her parents were together sexually and affectionately, that two warring halves of the world were united in peace. She felt safe – but never for long, because tension would soon break out again. What she feared was violent, unleashed, out-of-bounds aggression. In this night-time intention of hers, she willed herself to be the author of such violence if necessary.

She controlled her chronic fear of aggression by becoming counter-phobic – using aggression to override her fear which she somatized into bodily forms. She became the school and family daredevil who would speed her bike down the steepest hill without holding the handlebars, or ski down the straightest mountainside because she was afraid of falling. She counter-acted her body's pressures by overriding its fear that no ground existed to support her securely. Now in her late adult years, it was precisely her body that could not support itself steadily on the ground!

We learned that her body had had to carry all the fear, and had paid for it. For example, she became conscious of the fact she had always held her breath when frightened, never breathing freely, all these years. She began to see that in walking her head greatly preceded her body, as if looking around corners to see what could happen, thus tipping her off balance toward a later disorder. Her immense gifts of intuition and her rich permeable medial nature also contributed to her bodily life, carrying not only her own unconscious issues, but flooding in with everyone else's problems and possibilities, which made her greatly attractive as a guide for others. She did not know how to say No; she did not know how to limit herself. She said she took in the environment and felt responsible for it; no matter that it was too much for her limited strengths.

A pivotal dream in the second year of her five-year therapy kept returning to her with new layers of meaning. In this dream three women question a fourth who looks blind but may not be. My patient, the dreamer, the fifth woman, wants to answer for this apparently blind woman but the others tell her that this is not allowed – the woman must answer for herself. She does not do so. She remains silent. Then the other three put her alone in a dark room and shut the door. The dreamer hears the door click shut, leaving the woman in the dark, alone; it is terrible. My patient came to feel this shut-up woman was herself – the part of her that never stood up for herself. "She disgusts me," my patient would say, "I did not speak my own truth." "No one stuck up for me and I did not stick up for myself." "My mother was my father's prisoner. She could never walk out [because of the children and their poverty]." My patient felt she had betrayed this part of herself and that she was blind in the sense of closing off what she had clearly seen as her teacher's sadism or the Order's rigid way of training novices, taking it on herself, instead, to adapt, to make it work.

Two years later she returned to this dream and imaginatively met and spoke to the betrayed woman. She apologized to her for never visiting her, for feeling disgust for her. The figure answered that she had gained wisdom being alone and now was ready to step out. She said to my patient, "You lurch because you accommodate too much to others at the expense of being aware of your own opinions." My patient called this woman "Dear One." The woman replied, "It is time to come out and go just step by step," which made my patient see that time is not an essence but a process. Now her body enforced limits through its own needs for care. Eventually she found this advice very freeing, even in the midst of her terrible illness. "I feel liberated!" she said, "I have limits; I can listen just so long to others and then that's it. I am more factual. I no longer insist on bringing out the other person's good. I respect their choice. I leave you free. In that old dream, I tried to answer for that fourth woman and that was not allowed. I can spot the evil now. I used only to see the good and urge the other to realise it. Now it is up to them."

Her psyche opened at both ends – to the body and to the spirit. The body, despite her daily suffering of disability, also returned in an instinctive determination to do everything she could to regain her health, or at least to maintain herself independently. She lived in an apartment with another nun and made regular visits to the Order's institution when her house-mate was away due to her own work. The institution, which included an infirmary, became a target of her rage, now freely felt and expressed and processed instead of closed off in body. She got mad at the nuns for wanting "to get into my sickness because they won't get into theirs. They are excessively nice and will kill me with kindness. I could kill them. I'm so mad. They would make me a prisoner with their kindness and ideas how my sickness should be changed, instead of respecting my being in charge of my illness and knowing what is good for me."

Her dreams gave her much animal support for her physical efforts, and also made a bridge to the spirit connecting her to a reality beyond herself. She dreamt over the years of a series of animals landing, speaking, or visiting – one dream brought just the sound of a cougar's paws as it jumped into her awareness, hitting the ground strongly. A camel, capable of the long haul across deserts, a caribou tumbling out of a cone, an Irish setter "licking me and making me laugh," a strong healthy bumblebee with four strong legs appeared. And birds, especially birds. One climactic dream shows a green dove after having come through an ordeal, ruffled from its suffering. In the dream she looks at the bird and has the sense she is beholding her own suffering looking back at her (see also chapter 7). She makes a sound to communicate with the green dove, to connect with it, and just at that moment of her chirping a green shoot emerges from the dry stick the bird stands on. Working on what this green shoot symbolized, she said that this green was an adult color, and that resurrection meant a new attitude in the old body. People are annoyed, she said, because they want a whole new body, but Christ in his resurrected state bore the wounds of this body, the crucified body. It is the new spirit which is the seed of everything.

Over the years, a few dreams piled up spiritual meanings that changed her consciousness, despite increasing physical deterioration. She felt very much alone, tearful, discouraged, overwhelmed by her dizziness, the nausea it brought, the cold inflicted on her limbs, her inability to walk steadily. The manger dream came first, simply showing her "trying on" the walls of the manger for the holy family, choosing the brown color, not the extremes of black or white. Brown was earth to her, the color of the ground, altogether pleasing. She was to carry on her body the walls of the manger, in effect to be the stable, thus the steady container, for the coming of Christ into the world. She felt the walls of this portable manger marked limits for her medial nature. Limits make incarnation possible, she said. She said she no longer prayed the old way, which she called symbolic, where she meditated on levels of meaning in the text. Now, she said, there is just presence, and she uses her energy not to figure out various meanings, but to surrender, to receive. The symbolic method used to work, but no longer does, she said, because now the symbol is not God; it is simpler, more stable-like. The stable in which the Christ is born is now her body.

Almost a year later, she referred again to this manger dream, saying, in place of her old fears the animals of the manger were building up a container. Two years later she again came back to the dream, saying her body was a fragile container for the energy of God, and that the world was no longer black and white to her, but now a natural color, brown. She said that in the spiritual direction she was still able to give to a few people, now she just goes in "at the zero point, and little things appear," with God working through them. "I go where the hot spot is, the energy, which is the body way of doing things." She felt she now had the gift to let people be as good or bad as they were. She felt, for herself, that "God was working through my illness and that I am in the resurrection of my life, that the crucifixion *is* the resurrection. Illness led me into this dark night. God does not design it for you, but just uses whatever is in your life. I am looking for healing. If God wants to give it to me, God can. I am doing everything I can as if it all depended on me and praying as if it all depended on God. My mind, body, heart – all are merging toward oneness, freer, and it could be done any way; it matters what God wants, which is what I want."

Another powerful image came a year after the manger dream. She was lying in a hospital and calling for the nurse, who comes and puts a light white blanket over her body. This "god-nurse" says she is making a new formula, but it will take time. My analysand linked this image to the manger dream, saying, "What God wants is in my heart." Several months later she dreams she stands in a big room that is being renovated, with three of the walls complete and the fourth not yet finished. Three combined with the fourth is an ancient motif. It addresses the task of how to integrate into what is already completed and in place in our lives (the three), the additional new thing (the fourth). I wondered if this dream spoke of tasks for her to do before death could come. Right after this came the green-dove dream, where she said she felt compassion for her suffering body; "I feel so sorry for my body. It's been through a lot."

Some months after that, a dream showed her taking a small piece of brown felt cloth to the altar. Of it, she said, "I gave what was ready, and you can only give felt material, what you feel, what matters." Right after that dream came another with three and four, reminiscent of the dream several years before of locking the silent woman up alone in a dark room. Here a group of three are hiring a fourth, and want the dreamer to interview this fourth person because the dreamer would not be fooled: she could spot the evil, and the good.

You will note that the unconscious seems unconcerned in her dreams with her physical disability. Its focus is elsewhere, seemingly intent on integrating the left-out body parts and the aggression, and on conjugating the effect of this integration in her daily life. The major change seemed to be the conversion of her energy to endure a taxing disease. I was amazed at her endurance and courage, her cheerfulness and humor, while not denying her grief at her lost health and her anger at people trying to tell her she was only sick and nothing more.

She is extraordinarily edifying to work with. The effect of the analysis seemed to make more sturdy the bridge to spirit, which she experienced in clear Christian terms. Psyche also opened an additional way through which spirit could come in. Her most recent dream suggests that she is almost home. It came to her when, with a sister nun, she gave a small retreat on dreams and the spiritual life. This dream so struck into her, afterwards she had to rest two days:

I walked into a square and at each corner there was another square. I walked into the center – it was a holistic center and I said to the person with me, "Is this what it is all about?!" At one side of the wall there were bleachers facing front and the woman present-ing spoke from there. She had paper dolls of things to present and a book kept them straight. People were all around.

I went out to the middle of the square and stood there with a white feather with black on top. I went around and around, having dipped the tip of the feather in red and made a perfect circle, but touched only the center of each wall of the square with red. I made a circle within the square. Nothing smeared nor smudged. I think, Oh, I have to make it bigger and get the four corners in too. I went over to the bleachers and said, suddenly realizing it, "Oh my God I did all that walking!" I said to the woman, "I can walk! I can walk!"

When I heard this dream, I wondered if it presaged death, or healing, or both. The dream shows she combines the circle and the square, a variation of the mystery of three and four. The dream shows that she is utterly relieved of her physical disability. Is healing to be in this life or the next? It is important to note that spirit does not replace body; rather psyche makes images which allow us to see spirit coming in. She still suffers her physical condition, still knows the effects of the shock of intending to murder someone she loves, she still possesses her history of neglecting her body limits in favor of her remarkable gifts of intuition. This history lives as part of her even though she has radically changed her behavior, lives as part of her but does not reduce her to its determination. For psyche makes a bridge to the spirit, and spirit always ushers in the new. Spirit does not replace body and psyche nor substitute for them. It includes them but is never determined by them.

This woman has been granted powerful religious experiences in her illness, not only in her dreams, but in her waking life. She felt, for example, in her dizzy spells as if she had suddenly become aware of the infinite right there, next to her, and she lurched away in amazement. Sometimes she felt the presence of the holy shoved her. Did this make her treasure her dizziness? By no means. She would love to be healed of it. But she also would not want to deny what came through it. So often we discount the importance of such experiences if they do not bring physical cure with them or at least some tangible healing. We even doubt their veracity, suspecting that our psyche is compensating for our physical decline by pretending a flamboyant spiritual experience. But this attitude betrays a reduction of ourselves to body alone. Only physical cure matters. Those of us who have been seriously ill know that this is not the whole truth, that these odd, ineffable experiences matter a great deal and we must speak of them to others.

A serious problem for this woman was the way her head preceded her body as she walked. With it, she tended to look down and that further increased her imbalance, making as if to tip her forward and over. She found herself staring as in a trance, and was extremely annoyed if her housemate, for example, called on her to stand up straight, look up, look ahead. She felt interrupted in contemplating something beyond the immediate visible world, and could only be recalled by the clear calling of her name.

We sometimes tend to doubt the veracity of such experiences accompanying illness because they do not make the illness go away. We suspect the psyche of making all this up in an orgy of wish-fulfillment or as compensation for our physical decline. But this woman's experience reminds us that the meaning of incarnation is to live in the flesh, not to take the flesh away. The flesh means the mind and psyche and spirit too, not just the body. These powerful numinous experiences at the ego-level vie with the forces of body illness, of our history, of our doubting mind. Spiritual experience does not whisk all that away. Nor is spirit defeated by these earthly factors. At the ego-level the forces of health vie with the forces of illness. Spirit, mind, body, psyche all compete and conflict with each other. At a deeper level, beneath the ego and beyond it, where the germ of the transcendent is to be found, such epiphanies witness to what has already happened, which religion firmly annunciates. Spirit has come into the world, is present right next to us, between us, among us, having already claimed us.

Here, then, body, mind, spirit and psyche converge at the center of a wheel which turns around the free space without which no turning can happen. Healing occurs here in this zone, intermediate and central to all the spokes. Truth speaks to us indirectly. For body's somatic knowing is nonrepresentational. It is a lived knowledge, like the animal-root impulse. It connects with the wordless space out of which mind's reflections emerge. At the foot of psychic consciousness dwells the unconscious, before words or even the representations of images. Here we are joined through a sympathetic nervous system which exists beneath our cerebrospinal system, which in turn supports our individualizing intellect. At this depth-level we are all parts of a larger whole, joined in a great range of emotions about the whole shared life with creatures and things.

Perceiving life from this perspective, even in our death-dealing illnesses, we see that we never suddenly become whole, but are in fact already parts of wholeness which is our end as it was our beginning. We emerge from slime; we become dependent on each other, individuals sharing existence and learning to look in the same direction – to our point of origin and our end and purpose for being. Then we perceive that we do not become whole in ourselves but recognize we share as parts of a larger reality. This breeds communion among us, a sense of fellow feeling, animal neighborliness, creaturely sympathy. Finding our way to that perception and integrating it into our daily lives – the three with the fourth again, mind, body, psyche, spirit – unfolds our own particular spiritual path that is objectively offered and made available to us if we subjectively find, create, and enlarge it.

That is why to tell the truth, we must tell it slant. How else to enter that zone of *unknowing* where healing takes place? There even our symbols falter, stammer in their effort to speak of what inhabits each of us down deep inside us and also lives far outside us.

Our conference was advertised as offering a new paradigm. There can be no new paradigm in the sense of a formula with answers to all our health problems, individual and cultural. There is, however, material with ancient roots and old perceptions with clinical evidence for their continued truth and relevance. What is new is what the psyche tells us about spirit at the end of this first century of depth psychology. It tells us

that spirit is down, not up above the instincts, not a renunciation of the body, not a repudiation of the body of politics, of
experience in society, of the mystical body (see also chapters
6 and 10). Spirit lives amidst our psychic images which arise
spontaneously from the deep unconscious. Spirit lives amidst
matter and all that matters to us, whether that is how to pay
our mortgage or how to secure a kidney transplant, or how we
may live together in peace when our ideals and aims conflict
with and seem to cancel each other. Psyche, too, is flesh in
which spirit incarnates. Through psyche, we discover a door
opening to the power of spirit and the capacity it gives us to
transform death-dealing events – illness, every sort of disability,
trauma, murderous violence – into life-giving access to the center of reality. Spirit teaches us that health is living connected to
the reality that waits for us, seeks us, pours itself upon us, loves
us. Then, whatever way we come to this truth told always on
the slant, we can say with my dying patient, "It is worth it; it is
all worth it."

That illness, psychic or physical, which takes us out of time,
can deliver us into timelessness, the eternal now, where *because*
of the suffering it has brought, we become old-fashioned psy-
chopomps. We dwell now among those who move between
worlds, this one and the next, between our own lives and the
lives of our neighbors everywhere in the world. We move into
the free spaces of mind, body, psyche, and spirit. In this intermediate zone we become mediators of the *un*analyzable gift of
life that is ours even in the shadow of death.

This is spirit. Spirit wants to be lived by us, with a vitality that faces cheerfully toward the new. Spirit wants to be
witnessed, whatever our situation, however dire our illness.
What story, we must ask, is unfolding between our patient and
the transcendent, between us and our patient? What do dying

persons show us, how do they contribute to us? Spirit asks to
be honored, be respected, be loved.

*Plenary address Conference on Mind, Body, Spirit, Morristown
Memorial Hospital, Morristown, N.J. 1999.*

References

Clément, C. 1993. *The Lives and Legends of Jacques Lacan.* trans. A. Goldham-
mer. New York: Columbia University Press.
Corrigan, E. and Gordon, P.-E. eds. 1995. *The Mind Object, Precocity and
Pathology of Self-Sufficiency.* Northvale, N.J.: Jason Aronson.
Dickinson, E. 1960. *The Complete Poems of Emily Dickinson.* ed. Thomas H.
Johnson. Boston: Little Brown & Co.
Dossey, L. 1998. Prayer, medicine, and science: the new dialogue. Vande
Creek, ed. *Scientific and Pastoral Perspectives on Intercessory Prayer,
An Exchange Between Larry Dossey, M.D. and Health Care Chaplains.*
Binghamton, N.Y.: Haworth Press 1998, 7-38.
Guntrip, H. 1969. *Schizoid Phenomena, Object Relations, and the Self.* New York:
International Universities Press.
Hill, E. W. and Mullen, P. M. 1996. An overview of psychoneuroimmunology:
implications for pastoral care. *Journal of Pastoral Care* 50, 3, Fall,
239-249.
Jung, C. G. 1916. The transcendent function. *The Structure and Dynamics of
the Psyche. Collected Works,* vol. 8. trans. R. F. C. Hull. New York:
Pantheon, 1960, 67-91.
Jung, C. G. 1973 and 1975. *Letters.* 2 vols. Eds. G. Adler, A. Jaffé. Trans. R. F.
C. Hull. Princeton, N.J.: Princeton University Press.
Khan, M. M. R. 1971. To hear with the eyes. *The Privacy of the Self.* New York:
International Universities Press, 1974, 234-251.
Knight, T. S. 1965. *Charles Pierce.* New York: Washington Square Press.
Kristeva, J. 1995. *New Maladies of the Soul.* trans. R. Guberman. New York:
Columbia University Press.
Lear, J. 1998. *Open Minded, Working Out the Logic of Soul.* Cambridge: Harvard
University Press.
Maitland, S. 1995. *A Big Enough God.* New York: Henry Holt and Co.

Phillips, A. 1995. *Terrors and Experts*. Cambridge, Mass.: Harvard University Press.

Ulanov, A. and B. 1975. *Religion and the Unconscious*. Louisville, Ky.: Westminster/John Knox Press.

Ulanov, A. and B. 1982. *Primary Speech: A Psychology of Prayer.* Louisville, Ky.: Westminster/ John Knox Press.

Ulanov, A. B. 1994. *The Wizards' Gate*. Einsiedeln, Switzerland: Daimon.

Ulanov, A. B. 1996. *The Functioning Transcendent*. Wilmette, Ill.: Chiron.

Ulanov, A. B. 1998. Dreams: passage to new spirituality. Paper delivered at the Chicago C. G. Jung Institute. See chapter 11.

Winnicott, D. W. 1964 and 1969. Psycho-somatic disorder. *Psycho-Analytic Explorations*. 1989. eds. C. Winnicott, R. Shepherd, M. Davis. London: Karnac, 103-118.

Wyden, p. 1998. *A Medical Breakthrough*. New York: Knopf.

Chapter 8

The Gift of Consciousness

Consciousness

We do not need psychoanalysis to convince us of the necessity and value of consciousness. It is a gift we soon see in our newborn children – a spark, a scintilla, a waking up to the world that allows us to inhabit the world with our own creations through introjection and projection, through our receptions of and responses to what is given us. We see this spark with excitement when our baby first recognises us, when a student suddenly gets a Greek verb structure, when our scientists crack a problem in space. In New York City we all yelled out to each other, stranger to stranger, on the street that day when we first put a man in space: "We did it! We sent a man to the moon!" We know right away if that spark dwells in another person, or fails to. One of our children would say when very young, "There's no one home inside him," or, "Someone is home in him, he is busy inside." In the sudden recent death of a close friend, his three-year-old grandson said at the funeral, which in Greek Orthodox tradition is an open casket, "He is there but not in."

Such language reminds us of the soul, and consciousness is not the soul and they cannot, I believe, be equated, thank God. For if our soul were limited to our little blip of consciousness, that blinks off and on and frequently gets invaded by compulsions and obsessions, or blotted out by panic or lethargy, we would all be in a very bad state! Soul is bigger, wider, deeper than consciousness, and may include conscious consent, indeed requires it for a steady spiritual life, but cannot be reduced to it. Soul as the thirteenth century mystic Hadewijch says, is the abyss where God meets us (Hadewijch 1980, 86). Soul, I would say, is the unlockable door in us through which God can at any moment put a paw on us, claiming us, quieting us, summoning us. Psyche includes those conscious and unconscious processes that enable or disable us to be persons in touch with ourselves, with others, with God. Soul is our willingness to be a person in touch with others, our selves and with God (Ulanov, A. and B. 1975, 91-92).

Consciousness develops not only spontaneously when basic needs are met – for food, shelter, rest, cleanliness and exercise – but also and principally from someone else holding us, handling us in our bodies, and presenting to us bits and pieces of the world (Winnicott 1960). We get an ego – the center of consciousness – by someone else lending us theirs. To gain this precious sense of I-ness, we need an other on whom to depend. We need support and response and presence to become conscious. We depend on someone to evoke our self in order to gain a self. That someone is often a woman, and always includes women, and a womanly part of men. This puts the feminine mode of being both at the start and finish of life and at the heart of the gift of consciousness.

All schools of psychoanalysis chart the growth of conscious-ness and the dependence on which it rests. Indeed, no matter which school of depth psychology we consult, they all reach further and further back in their theories to discover the origin of being at all, the ontological premises of becoming a person. Here we find the familiar developmental stages of Margaret Mahler of symbiosis, separation, rapprochement, or of Melanie Klein, the paranoid-schizoid and the depressive positions which round out, fatten up the traditional oral, anal, phallic, genital stages of Freud, and deepen the psychosocial stages of Erikson's trust, autonomy, industry, identity, generativity and so on. In the last decades analysts even use religious language, such words as sacred, prayer, faith, gratitude, mystery, but almost always in setting forth their theories (with the exceptions of Freud and Jung) deny the referent.

Regardless of which theory we follow, consciousness is recognised as supported and promoted by some mysterious force including instinctual body energy, which we call the unconscious. We recognise this energy in our animal friends, guided by their instinct. We who have instinct also have this mysterious consciousness which allows us to choose against instinct, even to choose against God, and thus lose our animal eye.

Consciousness figures centrally in human life. We mourn its loss as an immense catastrophe if our children get trapped in autism, if poverty and illness blight its imaginative flower-ing. War reduces us to crude instincts where we abandon sympathetic consciousness of others in the pursuit of survival. Pain can knock out consciousness altogether. From scripture, revelation, the evidence of mystics' experience, we learn that our small consciousness, this immense yet fragile gift, seems to figure centrally in our response to God. We register from all these sources that God summons our free response, requires our mindful obedience, desires our desire to answer back, to contribute. We who are given the gift of consciousness are faced with its Giver asking for the gift back as our free, intentional, glad offering. Somehow our knowing, our imagining, our answering God's presence is cherished by God.

The great commandment sums up God's insistence on desire, telling us how we should love: all-out, lavishly, first God, then self, then neighbor. One love pours into the next, overflowing, like the great streams of heaven cascading down upon us. Ethics changes from a duty to an overflow, pouring out unceasingly from the source of reality itself, running into our heart, soul, mind and strength, into and over, under and around our neighbor and from our neighbor to ourselves and back again to God in abundant life.

Hadewijch's vision arrests us just here, reaching all the way from her thirteenth century right into our hearts now at the end of our twentieth. Her vision displays a tree whose roots begin in heaven, growing downward to earth. The branches nearest us are faith and hope. An Angel says to her, "You climb this tree from the beginning to the end, all the way to the profound roots of the incomprehensible God!" (Hadewijch 1980, xi). In this vision of the spiritual life, which forms a major part of the love mysticism in the Flemish Beguine tradition, we climb up to love which is God's mysterious center. Our soul, which is a bottomless abyss, forms a passageway to the depths of God, just as God is a passageway for liberty of our soul. In the abyss, consumed in the flame of love, God beholds us, and we God. But only through conquering love – that is loving God, the first thing first, with the whole heart, mind and strength – can we be conquered by Love – that is, ushered into living in God. We must conquer love, she says, so Love can conquer us.

Our desire to love God thus wounds us. It dislocates all our other loves, even our desire for a complete religious life, a finished spiritual journey, a successful ministry. All these loves burn up, are set aside, dislocated like Jacob's hip, when Love that is God conquers us. If we are not so wounded but go on walking upright on two feet instead of with a limp like the "flame of Jacob," then we do not become flame, we do not give way to love. "For Love is that burning fire which devours everything" (ibid., 60). "Love shows herself unreservedly to the [one] who loves...." (ibid., 63). "But before Love thus bursts her dikes, and ... ravishes [us] out of [ourself] ..." we must be "one spirit and one being with her and in her ..." and "offer her noble service and the life of exile ... in all obedience" (ibid., 63).

Exile and obedience for Hadewijch mean removing all obstacles in the way of loving full out, aggressively conquering all that stands in the way of putting the first thing first. From a psychoanalytic point of view, Hadewijch is a woman who uses all her strength and all her eros; no repression of sex and aggression here! She actually hears a voice that salutes her as the "strongest of all warrioresses" the one who "conquered everything and opened the closed totality ..." to know "how I am God and man!" (ibid., xxiv). And her image of how God comes into us is saturated with erotic intensity: "the two so dwell and penetrate each other that they abide in fruition, mouth in mouth, heart in heart, body in body, and soul in soul, both one thing through each other, but at the same time remain two different selves" (ibid., 66).

The result of Hadewijch's conquering love and being con-quered by Love is that she lives in the Trinity. She does not become unconscious but her consciousness is relocated, given back to its deepest foundation in the "fruition of love ... with an equal eye for justice" (ibid., 84). She says of this new life "I have integrated all my diversity, and I have individualized all my wholeness" (ibid., 113). Thus she does not become whole in herself, but lives with her whole heart mind and soul as part of a greater wholeness.

In psychoanalytical language, in this achievement God is no longer only a subjective object – alive and real to us but marked as our own idiosyncratic image of God but not shared in community with scripture and congregation. Nor is God any longer only an objective object – a figure of tradition and scripture that we know about but with which we do not feel personal intimacy in lively connection. God surpasses our categories of subjective and objective, and descends beneath our categories of immanent and transcendent to blaze forth as objective subject – living, breathing, close, and yet beyond all. Hadewijch and those like her inhabit and transform Winnicott's transitional play space into living not only from the center of the self, but more: from the center of reality which she inhabits and which inhabits her. As she puts it "I have stayed to play in the Lord's place" (ibid., 113).

We are faced then in religious tradition with paradox. The precious gift of consciousness, the ego life which the unconscious seems to promote as much as it interrupts and revises, builds up only to be offered beyond itself, back to the Giver. Hadewijch's tree, whose roots grow down from heaven to earth, meets the other tree pointed out by the serpent in the Eden garden. Adam and Eve are addressed first by God and then by the serpent, told opposite things – not to eat of the tree lest you die and why not eat for you will not die. Right there, in the moment of choice, consciousness flexes its freedom (what Tillich calls dizziness and Kierkegaard calls dread). We took the route of the serpent, choosing the know-it-all-tree, not the tree of life, thus perverting the serpent power to uses of our ego, instead of using our ego to relate to that serpent and to develop the wiliness and cunning in order to do so. As a result we are exiled from the tree of life.

We whine about the consequences of this exile, reasoning that God created us this way, and even created the serpent, so why are we to blame? The fault is not really ours so someone else should pay, thus manifesting the Adam in all of us – that masculinized protesting logic, what Jean-Luc Marion calls the logic of evil (Marion 1986, 17-18). First we protest our innocence; then we reason, well if we did do it, you made us do it. Then we conclude with revenge against an innocent bystander because someone must pay for what we suffered (see also chapter 10).

Adam here represents in us that process that turns against the other in blaming, that denies and projects, fingering Eve as the culprit. Eve in us speaks our curiosity and active interest that can be beguiled and that needs the cunning of doves and the wisdom of that very serpent to see and behold, and not be beguiled. In any case, God answers our whining in person, saying in effect, Yes I did create you this way and I will pay the cost, I will pay the debt, and evil stops here. God's advent in Jesus means God comes personally to take the blame we avoid. Though innocent Jesus suffers as if guilty, accepting the exile of the cross, not protesting but consenting to take on and into himself all the pettiness, raping, pillaging, mean-spiritedness, the torturing and grudge-holding, the ignorance and denials that we commit and suffer every day. He mounts the cross, which in a recent show of Byzantine Art at the Metropolitan Museum in New York City, depicts the serpent again, now as vine winding around the tree, now as cross.

In Hadewijch's vision the roots of the vine, of the living tree grow down from heaven and we climb up into the fathomless love of God. Yet the serpent so often depicted in primordial symbols and in contemporary people's dreams grows up from below. In psychoanalytical work we climb down to the source beneath and before the ego, to the unconscious roots of the ego's problems and potentialities. If we could look behind the tree above and the serpent below, we would find the paradox of religious experience: the roots in heaven and the roots in the depths join. What looks opposite is united. God the Creator puts the serpent in the garden. The roots of God's living tree meet the roots of the serpent tree of life. They are all one, beckoning us to become one, one in heart, mind, soul, and strength, loving all-out, lavishly, as one people of God, all of us made visible in communion with each other here in this garden on earth. The story that begins in the garden ends up in the city where we no longer need separate sacred from profane; we no longer need special temples (Rev. 21:22). God breathes everywhere; all of human consciousness permeated, saturated, rooted and blooming in the living God.

Fear of the Psyche

With such good news, why do we suffer so, and drive each other crazy? We fear the gift given us and still make the choice for the know-it-all tree instead of the living one. What is it we fear? I have found within our religious tradition a tremendous fear of the psyche. Years ago I wrote about it as 'the Christian Fear of the Psyche' (Ulanov 1986/2002, 5-23). Yet I know in my bones, my old bones at this point having taught and practised clinically for thirty-one years, that there is no future for the church without including, consciously including, the psyche. We fear the flame right there inside us, between us and among us. Even when it is offered us!

A contemporary woman dreamt of being smacked hard on the back of her head and spine, like the blow that wakes up all the energy symbolised as the Kundalini Serpent rising through the bodily chakras to blossom into communion with the divine.

Then, in the dream, the woman fell down backwards into a well, hanging upside down by her left foot. Looking down she saw blooming at the bottom of the well a flaming flower shaped like the fleur de lis. The smack and the falling symbolized to her her tremendous effort to wake up and get unstuck from a lifelong anxiety and get connected to life-giving energy. The flaming flower astonished her, stopped her, felt like a living thing to her, given as gift symbolising the presence of the holy even in a dark pit of the well, burgeoning life there in the depths, delicate and feminine as a flower, yet sturdy, indestructible. To fear the psyche through which such intimations of the transcendent are bequeathed to us every day, is as if this dreamer shunned the gift, refused the flower, reduced it to fancy interpretation or psychic complex. And did not take it.

We fear the spontaneity, the livingness offered us every day. Somehow we worry that if we accept that the psyche too is part of the flesh that incarnates God, it means we are replacing God with the psyche, that we are replacing scripture with dreams, that revelation has slipped from the roots in heaven to the roots in the unconscious. Among professional learned Christians a deep suspicion is leveled against the psyche as purportedly replacing God. I like Jung's answer to that accusation, saying, I can't even replace a lost button with my imagination or ideas. How could I ever replace God?

I have thought a lot about this fear of the psyche and our defenses against it, defenses that play out in ignoring the tremendous impact of this discipline on interpretation of scripture, the doing of ethics, the understanding of doctrine and symbol, let alone the practical work of ministry. It is not easy to admit we could act out our aggression in a preaching style that bores our congregations to death, or that hectors our flock to think a certain way and makes them feel guilty if they think another way. There is Freud's death instinct at work! Freud's own wry remark calls us up short. He said he never found a large amount of sadism in his makeup, so he did not have to devote himself to serving humanity. This certainly puts a new light on our wish to serve others! We indulge a kind of omnipotence of benevolence, as if somehow, we, not God, had, like Diana of Ephesus, a multitude of breasts that never ran dry of milk.

The psyche can no better rival God than can politics, or our reason, or our ethical maxims or science. The psyche adds a new hermeneutic to the theological enterprise as also the flesh through which God makes manifest the mysterious doings of the good news, of love in action, of the blooming tree of life. We are as vulnerable with the psyche as we are with any other human enterprise – of taking the part for the whole. Thus we have had the political God, the psychological God, the jot and tittle God, the God of rules, the God of formulas, the sexually defined God, the racially defined God, God as dead, red, black, gay, female, male, psychological force, revolutionary activism. But, as Jung says, God never defends himself against our names for him (Jung 1988, 39). God is merciful, always forgiving us taking the part for the whole, our God-image for the living God. God is ruthless, breaking through those images, scattering the imaginations of our hearts, to address us with immediate holy presence.

The psyche then, brings us to the frontier with the holy, as every other human endeavor does. The psyche feels more momentous because it is nearer to us, and utterly democratic, addressing each and everyone of us, cutting across divisions of education, class, sexual stance, health (both mental and physical), country, historical epoch and culture. We share the same kind of mental life, but not the same mental life. Hence Hadewijch's remarkable statement from the thirteenth century is apt now: "I have integrated all my diversity and individualised all my wholeness" (Hadewijch 1980, 113). To recognise the reality of psyche is to enter into an additional level of community, where, like fellow-refugees, we all face sex and aggression, dreams and symptoms, anxieties and potentialities, needs and contributions. We all face the marvel of consciousness and the impulse to give it back to its mysterious Giver.

Religion, and particularly the spiritual life, focus on who the Giver is, who it is that knocks at our door, who has been hunting us down the years, saving the best place for us at the feast. Religion speaks of this other source as the source above and beneath us, between and before us, a surround that brings the vast eternal into the tiny precious now. Religion salutes what stands forth from the center of reality as its author and goal, addressing us, calling us into communion with itself. Our task is how to live ever aware of this as the fundamental point of life, not to turn away, not to perjure and pretend we do not know it. And not to pretend our pictures of it and our theories about it can substitute for our living there.

Meaning

Ricoeur reminds us that we constantly and inevitably collapse the horizon of the infinite into only one finite part that has mediated the infinite to us. The better the meaning we fashion and fasten on, the more it mediates to us the reality of the divine, the more our temptation to reify it, capture it, possess the truth through it. Thus we come back, again and again, to the know-it-all tree. We know the difference between good and evil! We succumb to our knowledge of the good, the lure of its perfume and heady power. We take what mediates the divine presence to us in place of the divine. We read the map of the territory of the holy instead of going there, or acknowledging it is already here. Jean-Luc Marion says that is why Jesus ascends to heaven (Marion 1986, 163ff). He must leave us so we can find him finding us everywhere. If he stays here in specific form, we substitute that for the substance of his total presence.

We are thus returned to the paradox of consciousness. How do we find and create meaning without explaining it away or reducing it to our invention? How do we recognize objective meaning, that we did not originate, without excluding as frivolous (if not blasphemous) our subjective meanings that feel so real to us? How do we get free of meanings that have trapped us, so that we find it sinful to change them even though they no longer transmit to us the presence and power to which they point? Even our very own dreams which arise spontaneously in our sleep can fall prey to a fetishism of the text – as if they do not mean anything nor make any difference until we interpret them! And what of lost meaning, those of us who know despair, who can find no way through but only round and round in repeated compulsions, suicidal depressions, anti-social behavior?

The clinical enterprise offers a good laboratory for these large human issues. All of them come up in the work of depth analysis. That is not the only place they turn up, but it is a good place to look at the issues of subjective and objective meaning and the paradox of building up consciousness only to find it relativised. In the clinical encounter, we face the problems of finding a meaning which supports and builds up our consciousness, one which we know is objectively there and we can count on, and which is also alive and real to us, quickening our spirit and feeding out blood. Meaning eludes us, nothing feeds us. We know all about meanings that religion speaks of, and that inhabit our culture. But they are dead to us. We cannot connect. And we feel impotent to create any new meaning. And even if we could, such meaning feels like will-of-the-wisp, a cotton-candy variety, ready to vaporize the moment we taste it, a false bottom that drops us back into the void the moment we lean our full weight upon it.

Most of us who seek out analysis feel similarly troubled. Trauma has trapped us, one missing part makes the whole unviable. Either feeling suicidal or homicidal, out of control in eating or anxiety, or overcontrolled so that the suffering besetting us can only be referred to in the vaguest of terms – something does not feel right, we say, or I can't connect. We feel blocked, caught in repetitious plots with the same old ending, unable to break through to new meaning even if we are breaking down. Hence the meanings that we inherit from culture and from religion do not hold. The net frays, breaks; we fear to plunge endlessly, without rescue or resource.

We know the existence of meaning only negatively – it has abandoned us, delivered us into feeling that we live in a random world, with no foothold, no support for the person we want to become, with no one touching us with love, wanting us to see something wonderful, desiring with us intense conversation, no one wanting to hear from us our news from the frontier with the transcendent. No one wants to find out what we feel, or say in the face of death; we no longer can laugh full out. We feel bereft, drifting, or falling.

We settle into routines but get caught in repetitions which at once try to solve the problem we suffer, both to express it and to hide it, to liberate us at last while barring our way. Like a fairy-tale witch, we gnash our teeth, live in isolation where no-thing grows, a victim of unlived life (Ulanov, A. and B. 1987, chapter 2). What troubles us individually, troubles our community too. For the one lost sheep, that one of us, or that part in each of us – our secret shame, our unguessed violence – that sheep remains lost unless we go out looking for it, and we cannot join with others until we find it, and others cannot be a whole community as long as this one is missing.

An example will help — stark and startling to me, as in all my years I had not seen such a cutting off of every aspect of life in mid-life as this man faced. His job had let him go which dissolved his research team, the space he did it and its funding. So he could not just take up a similar job somewhere else. His marriage wavered and entered a space of separation. The woman who tempted him into new life had left him and refused to acknowledge that anything earthshaking had happened between them. His creativity abandoned him. No job, no mate, no friend, no funds, no new on the horizon to beckon him. Stalled in the water. No dreams even. And the very few that appeared over months showed characters who could not have cared less about getting conscious, growing, facing up to trouble, etc. He would dream of people who did not want to go on the trip; who rejected the conversation; who refused to go outside when someone was caught in a crime. Consciously, he was eager, even desperate to engage the psyche, to delve into the whys and wherefores. Unconsciously, nothing, and what little appeared put "cancelled" across his plans. After six months of work, a dream arrived that announced a new level. In the dream, set in time of monarchy and carriages, he anxiously tries to reach the queen through the crowds to get something from her as she sits in her carriage. The queen puts three large coins in his hand and he rushes through the crowds to complete his mission: to give the coins to the executioner — a large fat woman — to chop off his head. They discuss the best way to do it clean and quick and the dream ends with the shwoosh sound of the blade severing his head from his body.

What are we to make of this — to cut off his consciousness, to sever the intellect from the body? Whatever meaning was to arrive, it would arrive by another route, not his brain. Images did come which described this letting go activity. He felt himself to be "a piece of seaweed drifting on the ocean." In a dream a dog barked as he entered an apartment but he could make no headway understanding what the dog meant because, "I don't speak bark," he said. "I'm dying," he said; "The core is melting;" "I can't be a hyphen anymore for anyone else's life. I must be my own verb."

The point was this: we constructed meanings which were subjectively real, of causes that led to his present affliction. We also investigated possibilities of where the present troubles were leading, that their meaning was also to be found in what they assembled to come toward him as his future. His consciousness grew more sturdy which helped him endure not-knowing how his marriage would come out, his unemployment, his sense of being totally cut off from any sure direction, indeed, the whole hiatus that now defined his life. He felt stronger, less panicked, more open to what might be addressing him in this dramatic halt to his life. Plucked out of ordinary time of the daily routine and eager to connect to eternal time of the meaning of life, his consciousness of the whys and wherefores, and of the tendings towards sustained our analytical work. But. Neither construction of meaning through creating the causality from his past nor the assembling of a future was enough.

To find the root causes in his ghetto upbringing where nihilism threatened every day in terms of random violence in his Projects building elevator, or from retaliation on the streets if even accidentally one bumped some tough guy, helped him face the nihilism now invading him. Before, he had always been able to surmount it through his brilliance and his unending hard work – he had gotten out of the ghetto and into a stimulating life that brought him meaning by a sense of contributing to the greater good. But now, in mid-life, he found himself back in a timeless zone like the ghetto, where nothing matters, and anything could happen. He could disappear under the waves and the world would not care; he would make no difference.

Nihilism coupled with relentless violence was, for him, the one lost sheep that needed to be found consciously so the whole rest of him could again function. We had to go back in the past to go forward into the future that was beckoning. He needed now not to surmount the nihilism, but to see where it led him when it was included. It led to chopping off his head – at first. Another approach, another vision, was needed.

He and I could create, formulate, devise meanings and respond to the weavings of meaning that generated the analysis, that came toward us, so to speak. We could ask, why did all this happen now? What was being constructed, what plan set up for the future? Why did events come in this form and not some other? But were all these subjectively real constructions any more than just that? Too flimsy to withstand reality outside the office, outside the sessions we shared? Was there nothing objective here? No solid durable meaning that we did not devise, on which he could rely? Some objective path intended for him that he was groping to find which would convict him with its authority and purpose because he and I knew that this path did not originate with us and that we did not invent it? Or, to speak from a spiritual perspective, is there no enduring objective given meaning that exists outside our subjective ones that cannot be turned into an idol? This objective meaning is what religion stands for, and work with the psyche, I believe, demands from its practitioners acknowledgment of the ontological premises of their clinical methods. All language of the psyche springs from language of the spirit and the psychological work functions at its best in collaboration with spirit.

To entertain in clinical work that objective meaning exists for each of us, given to us outside our own invention and construction, while at the same time receiving the task, taking on the making of meaning, constructing lines of causality from our past relationships with others (the object relations school) and from the history of our defenses against instinctual conflict (the drive theory) and to map how our ego has built up consciousness using the images provided by our cultural historical context (ego psychology and theories of cultural conditioning), means living in the paradox with which religious experience is so familiar. We must really become conscious and do our ego work to make sense of the insensible, and unbearable. And we must at the same time know that all our conscious constructions of meaning are relative – to our object relations, to our experience of instinctual drives, to our cultural context, to our ego functions. We need all these and we can see through them.

If we can tolerate this relativity of consciousness, its necessity and preciousness and its ephemeral nature, we can be freed from consciousness, and freed for consciousness of our ego as looked at by some other presence that makes itself known to us when we are sufficiently empty to make room for it. We see our consciousness, no longer identify with it. We feel the roots that grow down from heaven and up from the serpent tree below. We look at our consciousness instead of only through it.

From the point of view of consciousness, this dislocation, this wounding as with Jacob's limping, feels like a breakdown, a cutting off of our head, decreed by the queen. From the point of view of the large psyche and reality beyond the psyche this breakdown breaks through. We empty of consciousness which makes space to behold spontaneous life given us, through the graciousness of our Creator, the blooming flower surprising us at the bottom of the well. But we must be turned on our head to find it. In religious language, this emptiness is submission, humble letting go of ourself, a losing of our life to find that we are found by the consciousness of a greater Subject. Sometimes we experience this being looked at by another presence very

213

forcefully in dreams. Dreams give us immediate experience of paradox: where we are both subject and object, subjects but also objects of attention of a greater consciousness that both includes and transcends us.

A woman in her sixties dreamt, "A dove all green in color had just come through some ordeal and stood and looked at me. I made an impromptu sound to call to the bird, and when I did, a little twig pushed out budding green, the same color as the bird." The dreamer suffered an enormous ordeal of physical illness that stole her balance and slurred her voice. The bird looking at her also embodied her ordeal; it had come through something hard. Thus in the dream she was seen and her suffering recognized; spontaneously she responded, trying to make a sound to speak to the bird. When she did, a twig barren of leaves sent out a green shoot. The object of another subject, her suffering looked at her through the animal eye of the dove. Being religious, she associated the dove to God's spirit. Beheld, she wanted to behold, to reach out in sound, in animal noise to acknowledge the suffering of the creature that acknowledged her suffering. When she did, from the barren twig a shoot of the new came into being.

Such a dream brings news of what lives in us beyond our egos and points to what spontaneously creates the psyche and holds it (see also chapter 7). So do other human events. Not just dreams. And not just psychic examples. Falling in love brings news from the frontier with the transcendent – archetypal moments that break in upon us at funerals, at births, at moments of loss, and moments of forgiveness where the old that had died and was gone returns in new form – and we are given the power to recognize its gathering up of the blighted old suffering and delivering of it into new living. We climb up to the roots of the It that lives me, not the I, but the Christ thrumming through our veins. We climb down to the It that lives me, not the ego but the primordial unconscious, with its deep structures of the timeless that give us archetypal pictures which Jung calls "the tools of God" (Jung 1975, 130).

We can talk about psychic structures and how they impact upon ego-consciousness to break it down to emptiness so that we can receive the spontaneous gestures of a life living deeper in us. We can talk about trauma breaking up our trappedness in fruitless repetitions, breaking us down to this empty place. We reach an emptiness which allows awareness of the other to come in, an other that steadfastly makes and remakes us, breaks us apart to break through to us with its larger life, its eloquent presence that comes through word, through image, through fur, through music, through utter silence, through a crowded emotion, through play, through the offering at a worship service, and the high stepping of a rock concert. But the willingness to respond, spontaneously to choose the tree of life, the effort, despite losing our balance and our voice, to chirp out at the bird who sees us, that response is asked of us and given to us to give back.

Living

To see this relocation of consciousness and give way to it, we need a different kind of consciousness. At the end of the twentieth century, this kind of consciousness partakes of a feminine mode of being, a process living in all of us, male and female. We need to consent, to go down, to fall apart, to be in the midst of, not to know with the clarity of logical progression and summary conclusion, not to abstract and generalize but to cherish the particular as a mother cherishes the particular child in her womb. We need to ponder in the heart, not the head, and like Mary take the sword-piercing into our soul and consent to be the mother of revolution, the bringer of the One who ends all religion, all reifications of infinite into finite. She delivers into the world the One who presides over and obviates all divisions of gender and class, of education and beauty, of wealth and intellect, of creed and ideology. This One brings the news that each of us is pondered as a special child of God, carried and delivered into the world. This kind of consciousness ushers us to the foot of the cross where, with that gaggle of Marys, we too are tough enough to survive the stripping of all our projections onto God, of all our God-images, and idols of the holy, to behold the God who comes and makes all things new. This God calls us by our name as the risen Jesus called the Magdalene, thus allowing us to knit up the continuity of the One who was, whom we lost, with the One now before us as the One who is, the isness of life itself. This unknown we receive in the flesh, in the small, inhabiting us and changing all our values.

For the unfolding of this arrival is not a series of products, like books, babies, jobs, or even mental health. The dreamer of the green dove and twig discovers through her own ordeal of illness that the resurrected body still bears its wounds. We live in history and history shapes us in this life. The new pushes out our boundaries and endows us with life, but does not magically whisk away all the costs of mortality. Depth psychological treatment is not magic. It digs out and digs down to this dimension other than the ego from which life springs. It dislocates and rearranges the ego to accommodate this life if the soul is willing. It flows through us then, not from our ideas of the good, but with its own. It brings news from the frontier. It brings life.

The result of contacting this dimension, and opening to what speaks through it, is living, not products, but new living, living in the new. Analysts know about this and describe it in their own vocabularies. Winnicott talks about living creatively where we see everything afresh with enjoyable wonder. Bion reaches toward the unnameable O that we hope for as the truth of every session. Freud's goal of love and work breathes the All into the mundane everyday. Jung writes of seeing through the eyes not of the ego but of the Self, that mid-way region between psyche and what transcends it. The ego serves the Self and the Self serves the transcendent. Hadewijch speaks of living all the concrete humanity of God in Christ, which means the debt-paying, offered for all others.

Many, if not most, clinical encounters do not open into specific religious vocabulary. But if they succeed, the client feels herself open to a bigger region; he feels addressed by a larger encompassing reality to which connection and conversation must be sustained. The repetitious compulsions that break our spirit and lead us into analysis, must give way to rituals of acknowledgment and confirmation of that other presence that has come to the analysand through their own unconscious. Without some ritual, the other remains anonymous to us. It needs to be named if we are to go on in relationship with it.

We need, then also, in addition to the feminine processing of experience in the flesh, in the small, in the deep downward inhabiting, the masculine process as well, to name, to find words for, to abstract and communicate. We need to stand forth and relate to it and describe its tremendous impact upon us. We need to say such things as, yes a specific way, a path exists for each one of us, objectively there, given, yet to find it we must create and construct, improvise our ways to it. We must articulate the tension between ego patterns we imposed on life and the fact that they are relative, invented, not final, but without which we never find our final path.

We need to speak about how our consciousness is struc-tured by forms outside consciousness which support and subvert it at once, that in fact we are dancing to a pattern going on in each session of therapy which is beyond the full control or comprehension of the participants. A living thing, or presence, inhabits the space and functions to push and prod and delicately touch us to open to its arrival. Sometimes the analysand thinks the analyst knows all about this pattern. I've been described by patients as the cattle prod in their transference. But I know from my side, that I too am responding to something that is right there, shaping and pushing me, flattening me and punching me down like so much bread dough to let the hot air escape. Only from the whole interaction of subject and subject does an objective meaning reveal itself.

If we hold onto our ego view, we refuse the larger pattern and eventually split into polarized versions of the dance pattern with its many conjunctions. Then we get the gender wars of masculine versus feminine, of adult versus child, of community versus individual, of theory versus praxis, analyst versus analysand, first world versus third world, and on and on. We degenerate into the know-it-all explanations of power relations. Even ethics is helper to helpee which is always power-minded, however muted.

We fall into a polarised differentiation of haves and have-nots, even with Winnicott, who helpfully translates the old dualities into psychological ones. For him, the "haves" possess a sense of self in a body that the "have-nots" lack. This description recommends itself to us because it cuts across the familiar lines of class, color, gender and wealth. Alice Miller also ably points out how we displace onto social injustices the rage and mourning we defend against by idealizing parents whom we protect saying, for example, "beating me for my own good; it made me strong." To become conscious of the rage at and mourning for what we missed does not keep us from joining causes against injustice. It makes us more effective because more flexible, no longer smuggling an unconscious personal agenda into the commonly suffered injustice. Wren-Lewis finds the same avoidance as Miller does when he traces economic injustice to our denial of the spontaneous, autonomous life bubbling up in everyone. Only by seeing this gift of life in the other and in ourselves do we join together to build a society that includes all equally.

Masud Khan says that when we deny dream space, we act out in society the rage and despair, often in criminal ways, that would plot our nighttime reveries (Khan 1974, 311, 314). Two Jungian analysts who investigated Mezoamerican myths find a meaning in the horrifying symptom of young adults, often women, cutting themselves ritually (Doughtery and West 1997). They cut their arms or face or other body parts because they cannot house archetypal forces, so they become obsessed and possessed by them, and act them out on their bodies. At the same time, such cutting is an effort to cut through conscious numbness, a cut-offness from the psyche. Cutting tries to cut through, to make contact. So like any symptom, it bespeaks the problem and the solution. Larger ritual placement of the symptom can help the analytical couple find how to cut open a portal between a too small consciousness and a deeper flow of life within such women's bodies and souls.

Ethics

If the product of going down into a different consciousness is living, and not products such as money, sermons, recipes, fame, lectures, degrees, job, and all the things of this life that we reify, prize, and make into idols, then our relationship with each other changes. Ethics changes from a giving of helper to helpee to a receiving and yielding of overflow. Living from a core that animates and feeds all of us we feel and know the spark of its presence between us, among us, that it keeps all of us in being and redeems us from sadness.

We become one of the animals in a tide of instinct that guides us, and that we consent to, making us human animals specifically marked, not by stripe or hoof or fur, but by consent, again and again. Something flows through us, out and back from a center beyond us, which contacts us also through a deeper consciousness and a consciousness of the depth. It generates us. It engenders us. Like the Sioux medicine man Fools Crow's "hollow bones," we become empty to accommodate its fullness. All together we share its presence; if one of us goes missing, we cannot proceed until we go out and look for the one who is missing. That may be a part of us or of a group of us. It deserves to be found. We also see that others carry things for us. The one suffering severe mental restriction carries the cross I do not carry, and evokes my gratitude and a willingness to carry the cross assigned to me.

We see that each of us does not, contra the advertising of psychological workshops, achieve wholeness, but we become part of a greater wholeness. We do not enter into congress with this presence flowing through us in the role of co-creators, but instead as co-respondents. The pun indicates both our capacity for betrayal as well as full-out risk-taking response. We enter into and are pulled into the currents of a thrumming, humming love that undergirds all reality, flowing ceaselessly out of its center into and round and among all of us, back and forth between us, then lunging down again into the depths. Only to pour out generously upon us.

An image of Saint Dorotheus pictures the way the ethics of overflow works. Each of us as a spoke of a wheel finds, as she draws closer and closer to the wheel's center, to the cog from which all the spokes turn and revolve, that we inevitably draw closer to each other. This is consciousness, so precious a gift to us, that we give back into its Giver.

8. The Gift of Consciousness

WICAM Lecture, Princeton Theological Seminary, Princeton, N.J., 1998. Published in The Princeton Seminary Bulletin, xix, 3, new series 1998, 242-259.

References

Doughtery, N. and West, J. 1997. Skin: boundaries, penetrations and power. Paper given at National Jungian Congress, Chicago.

Hadewijch. 1980. The Complete Works. trans. Mother Columba Hart. New York: Paulist.

Marion, J.-L. 1986. Prolégomène à la Charité. Szikra à Giromagny: Mobile Matière.

Jung, C. G. 1975. Letters. v. 2 of 2 vols. Princeton, N.J.: Princeton University Press.

Jung, C. G. 1988. Nietzsche's Zarathustra. ed. James L. Jarrett. 2 vols. Princeton, N.J.: Princeton University Press.

Khan, M. M. R. 1974. The Privacy of the Self. New York: International Universities Press.

Ulanov, A. and B. 1975. Religion and the Unconscious. Louisville, Ky.: John Knox/Westminster Press.

Ulanov, A. and B. 1987. The Witch and the Clown: Two Archetypes of Human Sexuality. Wilmette, Il.: Chiron.

Ulanov, A. B. 1986/2002. Picturing God. Einsiedeln, Switzerland: Daimon.

Winnicott, D. W. 1960. The theory of the parent-infant relationship. Winnicott, D. W. 1965. Maturational Processes and the Facilitating Environment. New York: International Universities Press.

III. Spiritual Issues

Chapter 9

Unseen Boundaries, Dangerous Crossings

Psyche and Spirit

The cutting edge of clinical work circles around perceiving the work of the Spirit in and through the flesh of the psyche. For the clergy, too, in church, temple, and mosque, the thriving of faith in the twenty-first century depends on seeing afresh the connection of the Spirit of God with the psychological experience of ordinary persons. "Spirit" and "spirituality" are words we often hear in this last decade of our twentieth century and of the whole millennium, in contrast to "religion" or "faith." People feel nervous, I believe, about being trapped into a dead denominationalism, or a lifeless rationalism, or a coercive dogmatism, or a wishy-washy liberalism. Spirit feels like wind, breath of life, the uncontainable that comes from the Holy and can never be captured by the human. Thus it can always revive our contact with itself, even in ruthless ways, blowing through our conventions, knocking them down, kindling a fresh flame of ardent love for the divine.

225

Clergy need to know this fact: the reality of the psyche. Otherwise, the religion they preach from the pulpit will not reach to the heart of people in their congregations. Religion will remain an intellectual content, or formula, full of words, but lacking the living word that changes lives. Clergy need not reinvent religion, but must reconnect the visible to the invisible, linking the eternal sacred symbols to people's experience of their own psyches as well as of their own world. When Christ says, for example, leave mother and father and follow me, we can hear the liberation from all those parental complexes that have freighted our connection to being. When Buddhist wisdom commands us to drop body and mind, we can see that obeying means freedom from the hamperings of conventional ways of thought. We grasp, for example, that giving up the self does not mean endorsement of masochistic denial, but rather seeing clearly into the elusive nature of self that harbors at its core a mystery as unfathomable as the mystery at the heart of God. That is what the Buddha nature sees and lives (Døgen 1985; Jung 1932; Ulanov, A. and B. 1975; Winnicott 1963b). The clergy need to know about the living psyche in order to see afresh how ancient symbols of their religious tradition speak to our souls beneath words, and how to bring that forward to their congregations at worship so that tradition comes alive.

Clinicians cannot adequately do their work in therapy without considering the subtle but decisive effects of Spirit on the problems of compulsion to suicide, of the tangle of perversions, of the sense of futility in the schizoid condition and of the loss of hope in depression, let alone what smashes into a person receiving news of terminal illness. From the psyche's point of view, when we take an interest in religious experience, we ask how religion functions for illness or for health in ourselves, in our group, in our world. Does it breed fanaticism, scapegoating, persecution? Does it inspire peace-making, compassion to neighbor, to self?

From the spiritual perspective, we ask different questions about religious experience. We want to know, "It is real?" From the psyche's perspective, when we feel summoned by God, we ask, "What was this experience like?" "How am I to integrate it?" But the soul questions are less to do with ourselves and more to do with the "object," the one who calls us. We ask, "Who calls me?" "How must I change my life because of Thee?" In actual life, in the worship service, in the consulting room, psyche and spirit are intertwined. But it helps to have these two angles of vision in mind when confronted with tough life problems and taxing clinical complexes.

Clergy in the religious institutions of our society carry a great burden. They stand publically for the existence of this mysterious heart of Being and its interest in us, its reaching out to us, to bring us home, no matter how long we have been away, or how far we have fallen into disarray and negligence. Just as mental health professionals must acknowledge the existence of Spirit and their own relation or non-relation to it to do their clinical work responsibly, so clergy must acknowledge psychic reality to which their function of symbolising the mercy of God must connect if they are to fulfill their ministry.

Clergy represent the connection to Spirit; the connection must include people's psychological life along with our political and social life, our ethical conduct, how we manage money, deal with citizens different from ourselves and receive their dealings with us. Psyche means intimacy – the wolf hour in the night when our anxiety eats away at our confidence, at our dreams both nightly and imaginary, at our trust that we belong to the heart of life, and are never cast out. Without spiritual connection through these aspects of psyche, the clergy's more public work will not take root. Ego-functioning, a priceless value, will not endure if the spiritual connection is omitted. If we do not already know this, clients of every description will tell us so by their fierce resistance to recovery when spiritual connection is omitted. All the sheep cannot function if we do not go out and look for the one lost.

Pastoral Counselors, unlike other mental health professionals, make a conscious and explicit acknowledgment of the sacred as part of the suffering and healing process of clinical work. We do not proselytise, use God-talk. But we are trained to develop an alert eye to see and an attending ear to hear the blowing and listing of the Spirit in the most unlikely of places – in the compulsion of perversions, the prison of rigid defenses, the lowly stable of complexes. Here the sacred enters and makes all things new.

The joy and privilege of clinical work spring from the time we spend at the center of human achievement where we see the capacity of people to make meaning, to find it and create it out of unspeakable suffering, which they then not only survive but use to augment the priceless treasure of a human self. Without a self we go mad and drive others mad. We discover that to be a self means to give and receive it in shared existence with others, and to enter a mysterious exchange with the transcendent. So we speak of psyche and spirit and connecting to the Spirit at the heart of life. In this territory of psyche and spirit, self and other, human and divine, we find our livelihood and our life. In our work year after year, decade after decade, working through what obstructs a person's or a family's life, we behold that mysterious ignition that enables all of us not just to endure and resolve, but to thrive, and to fill up with gratitude.

Dangerous Crossings, Unseen Boundaries

The borders that join psyche and spirit, self and other, human and divine confront us with dangerous crossings. Boundaries exist. They are part of life. They are not necessarily good or bad; they just are. Our first necessity in doing clinical work with the special consciousness of spiritual aspects of the work, is to see the unseen boundaries. This sounds simple. But most of the ethical problems we face in clinical work, and many of the social problems that face us in our society, arise from not seeing the unseen boundaries.

Take, for example, the problem of sexual acting-out. It is the unseen boundary here that causes trouble. For unless the clergy or clinicians involved are just depraved – which cannot be ruled out, but which is rarely the case – we have to ask ourselves an antecedent question. What happens here that allows decent people – good clinicians, or good clergy, trying to do their work with integrity – to cross the line to abuse their clients, betray their parishioners? Abuse occurs from two directions. We try to avoid the experience of the sexual and spiritual fires aflame in transference and countertransference by talking them out of existence. But with that excess verbiage we only seduce the other into a mental collusion that is deeply frustrating to body and soul. We are supposedly acknowledging these fiery emotions, but in fact we are doing so only to make them go away. We indulge in denial while talking as if we were confronting these emotions.

From the opposite direction, we may not only acknowledge the emotions but go on to act them out in literal sexual encounters and spiritual dallying. Sexual intimacy substitutes for the therapeutic one; sexual acting-out steals the spiritual fire. An unseen boundary is unwittingly crossed, to the detriment of the human relationship, the clinical work, and relation to spirit.

Only the way that houses as much passion and power as the sexual, but which is not in itself sexual, permits us to make this dangerous crossing. Rules alone will not prevent acting-out in an analytical relationship or that of spiritual direction (any more than we stop acting-out against the environment only with rules). In my experience with this issue, only a spiritual sensibility can make this crossing possible (Ulanov 1996, chapters 6, 7, 8). Everything else is too pale, too reasonable, without enough fire.

An example comes from a man suffering masochistic "perversions," as he called them, for over six decades. He developed an intense transference, as fiery and compelling as his complexes. Out of this fire emerged what had hidden in the shadows of his masochism: his need and capacity for veneration. Spirit often hides in sex. To find those unseen boundaries between himself and me, between our actual analytical intimacy and an imaginary sexual one, between psychological work and spiritual experience, inevitably required hard, slogging work, and also an awareness of Spirit in the room, in his complexes, in my response (ibid., chapter 3).

The sexual is not the only unseen boundary in clinical work. Persons who are unexpectedly struck down by terminal illness, either swift moving or painfully slow, lead us, before we even realize it, into deep spiritual waters where questions about the nature of evil or the meaning of life jump at us. One man, whose therapy focused on suicidal feelings because a hidden sexual life threatened his job and standing in the community, found that an unseen boundary confronted him with the most dangerous crossing of all. Without warning he was afflicted with a terminal illness that was always characterised by an accompanying psychosis before death occurred. He projected onto this derangement all his fears that his secret behavior would leap out and ruin his life's work, and, then, through a damaged reputation, hurt his children. Once again, he considered suicide. Our work located these projections, and brought them out to be seen. He was still afraid, but now he faced and took on the dangerous crossing: he offered up all his life in prayer – all his successes, hidden dramas, and above all his fear of exposure through psychosis. He gave it all back to the source of life, every bit of it. Of the few recorded cases of his rare disease, he was at his death the only one who did not go psychotic (ibid., chapter 9).

With a woman whose terminal diagnosis cut short her life, the clinical container needed to be made tough enough to house her terror and sorrow, and to bring into the light all her outraged questions – "Why me?" "Why now?" "What for?" When she looked at the boundaries these feelings and questions revealed, she almost miraculously, and with persistent grit, found the way to make her dangerous crossing from this life into the next. Having lost the ability to use language, she could no longer gather her dreams into words and thus lost the avenue of crossing from the here and now world of consciousness to the beyond that the unconscious prefigured. She faced that great loss and discovered she could draw pictures to replace the missing words. She produced a remarkable set of paintings that show not only her terror at going into the dark, but also her discovery that something waited there that "did not want to hurt you." She drew on spiritual resources she did not know she possessed and before losing her voice, articulated a particularly important spiritual component. She needed to tell me about what she experienced; otherwise, she said, she could not face it. Spirit means recognising dependency and the need to contribute to others (Ulanov, 1994a).

Borderlines and Homelessness

These unseen boundaries exist all through our society. We must see them, for a vital link exists between the homeless persons living on the borders of our society in every major city of our country and the clients in our office suffering from a borderline condition. Homeless persons have crossed over the boundaries of our society into a no-man's land where they are unable, for example, to choose when to take a bath or fix a cup of coffee, or use a toilet. They live uncontained, not housed, not held in being. The boundary between having a life and suffering it, between maintaining a living and being maintained in the catch-basin of our social welfare bureaucracy, is not sufficiently reckoned with. Hence no crossing back into a job, a home, a community is easily made possible. Instead, the so-called underclass swells to ever larger proportions.

We ask how this can happen in our country, with its tremendous endowments of nature, democracy, and the good-will of so many. It can be understood as a pathologizing of the boundaries, making them invisible. If we do not recognise signs of the unseen boundaries, they will manifest themselves in sociopathic ways. What we do not meet within will address us from without like an impersonal fate we cannot alter. Psychic reality is not just there inside us. It also exists outside and between us. But, we must remember, the boundary between psychic and social reality is not impassable, but actually permeable.

The concrete sufferings of the homeless on our streets mirror the sufferings of those in clinical treatment for a borderline condition, who are dispossessed of a psychic home much like those without physical homes. To see this psychic-community connection is part of the spiritual aspects of clinical work. Clergy helping the homeless often leave out the psyche; clinicians dealing with the borderline psyche, often omit its manifestations in society. For the homeless and for those suffering from a borderline psychic condition, there is no stable ego-house to hold in being the needs, feelings, instinctual experiences and potentialities of the personality. The borderline person is all over the place, uncontained and apparently resistant to any containment that may be offered by interpretation and a stable analytic relationship. The person maddens the counselor by seeming to posit a "Yes" for every "No," and a "No" to every "Yes," hopping from one perch to the next, never knitting a single whole identity.

Clinical work with such persons has brought me to a new vision of the borderline condition, which encompasses in its breadth the homeless who live on the borders of our society, and who give us insight into the Spirit as well. The ego of the person with a borderline affliction is different from the usual therapeutic goal of ego-constancy, of cohesion, stability, and groundedness, yielding a continuing sense of identity. The borderline ego is better seen, I believe, as an archipelago – a string of islands that look separate on the surface but are joined under water. Such persons appear and experience themselves to be more fragmented than in fact they need be. What is usually called ego-strength describes one kind of ego, the one that is stably rooted, on land. The borderline ego lives on both land and water, on land hidden by a wash of the unconscious flowing between and over its islands of consciousness. Borderline persons see psychologically and spiritually what we do not see; they possess an uncanny ability to put their fingers exactly on the spot in us where the waters of the unconscious wash over us, where a chink exists in our self-interpretation, or in a bit of complex not worked out in our selves, or in an unvoiced spiritual longing. Such clients have got our number; they touch us right where we are undefended, unhoused, resourceless, not unlike our homeless sister or brother.

The goal in working with a person with a borderline condition is not to achieve a grounded ego, solid in continuity, stable, and enduring. That is not a real possibility nor even a virtue to look toward. The goal, I suggest, is to get a big enough vision to include all the islands of the archipelago-ego, so that the maddening "yes-but" style of work with such a person transforms into "yes and no," "both-and." The ego organization, if looser now, is also larger and more inclusive of opposite forces in the psyche. The contradictoriness that bedevils the beginning phases of work with such clients, expands to a large embrace of all the opposing facts. The treatment creates a broad synthesis of ego-personality now, instead of the more customary ego-organization around a hierarchy of priorities. This synthetic-ego loosely assembles all the islands of consciousness, accepting their connecting links and that those links are unconscious much of the time, under the water that washes between the islands. Instead of an instrumental ego that plans chores and goals in sequence, illustrated well in the model of developmental tasks that proceed *ad seriatum*, the synthetic-ego that emerges from an archipelago condition circles around goals and chores, sometimes several simultaneously, seeming to get nothing done, only to arrive at a later point when several goals reach simultaneous completion. An encompassing wholeness is envisioned, rather than progress in moving from stage to stage.

To see this kind of ego-strengthening as a central goal of clinical treatment, we have to think big, and to include the spiritual aspect. For the borderline person brings us glimpses of the transcendent as present here and now, available at any time, ready to pour into us if we can stand up to its powerful presence. The gaps in ego-organization of the borderline client, viewed negatively, appear as lack of continuity, and a vulnerability to the fragmentation which is a typical defense of the borderline person. Viewed positively, these gaps constantly remind us that there is also in us something that is always open to the force of a bigger reality that surrounds our little islands of consciousness and washes over them.

Precisely because of the looser ego-organization the clinical work brings, we cannot take our ego-perspective as ultimate or even rely upon it as enduring. Borderline persons, like the homeless, know in the very pores of their body and intimate facts of their lives that at any moment reality can vastly change for better or worse. They feel themselves closely in touch with forces beyond ego-control that can evict them from their adamant assumptions, tried and true beliefs, customary life-styles. They show us that any one of us can be overwhelmed at any time, thrown out of our house or our conventional mind set, lose our job or our usual capacity to function, but also that we can be addressed at any moment by something that transcends consciousness. The borderline person knows the negative of this positive possibility. Clinical treatment alert to the role of spirit can bring about an acknowledgment of the positive that comes with the negative. For this openness to the forces beyond ego-control can itself be a medium through which the transcendent makes itself known to us.

We know that the unconscious cannot be equated with the transcendent God, but it may become for us one of the most direct routes through which we feel God – who transcends the whole psyche, conscious and unconscious – addressing us. Homeless and borderline persons show us that all our human monuments and fortresses of defense cannot keep the transcendent out, for it, like them, will reach right through to the exact chink in our defenses, the loop-hole in our interpretation, the secret longing that rises in our throats. The borderline person, with an ego open to the unconscious links among the islands of consciousness, shows us that no structure of society's establishment is fixed, everlasting. The borderline ego is permeable to what moves underwater, to the unconscious and to what moves through it toward us. The borderline ego is provisional to what could confound it or transcend it. It tells us through a narrative of its troubles, as well as through visions of a reality viewed through fragments, that no human system of values or projects can be precisely identified with the transcendent.

Thus the borderline and the homeless person on the street make us look at our own wound differently – not only as a hurt to be healed, but also as a point of access to reality. The transcendent addresses us, for example, through the problems that our training analysis did not heal, or may even have made more grave. The point of access may be the wound we have worked on for years that still bleeds. As in the parable of the fig tree, there are no seasons with God. It may be that these wounds serve the purpose of reminding us that with God there is only a yes, and a yes, and a yes. We cannot rescue everything into ego-functioning. Some parts of us must remain homeless. We are reminded that our final home is not here on earth, but only in what our restlessness drives us toward, what Augustine calls our ultimate "rest" in God. Our first move, then, is from boundaries that are unseen to crossings which are dangerous but not impossible, and which lead us to new life.

Too Tight, Too Loose

We are familiar with the opposing dangers of boundaries that are too rigid or too lax. Boundaries that we define too tightly result in our repressing or splitting off the unaccept-able from the acceptable, a move which translates into social prejudice, exclusion, scapegoating, persecution. In short, all the ills of social oppression find a root in our inability to house a more ample ego, with generous boundaries that can include the different (Ulanov 1990/1999).

In psychological terms, boundaries that are too tight constrict the space in which symbols are born. Our transitional play is foreshortened by our striving to meet inflexible super-ego standards, and by our insatiable need for acceptance which transmutes into a compulsion to meet others' expectations. Winnicott describes these twin ills as impingement and false-self compliance (Winnicott 1963a, 86-87). Lacking any elbow room, we lose the capacity to play and thus to find and create original solutions to difficult problems. Like the king of familiar fairy tales who lacks a wife and grows weak and worn out, we too must go on a far journey to find the missing feminine element that will hold us in a large enough space of being to be once again and to become whole persons.

There is a fitting example in a man born during a war-time air-raid of a young mother, with his father away at war, who grew up never feeling backed up, never supported by a reality any bigger than himself. Instead he felt held fast to his mother's belief that if only there were more money, they could be safe. Now grown up and himself a father, he still feels caught in the overly tight boundaries of his mother's complex – a literalism that only more cash would ensure survival. He succumbs to a plodding spirit that discounts his otherwise creative work. Work ceases to be vocation and becomes simply a burden, a taskmaster, a means to acquire the money that assures safety. Money moves into the center of life, his God-image. What Jung calls the Self, equates with dollars for him. He finds himself obsessing about bills, awaking at four in the morning anxious that his bank account should not run dry, fearing his blood pressure will mount under the stress of chronic worries, feeling, like Sisyphus, eternally bound to labor with no prospect of ever staying at the top of the mountain.

Untangling this man's complex in treatment proves most difficult, for he does need more cash. Whenever I go after the symbolic meaning of money, he feels abandoned, and worse, furious, because I seem not to empathize with him and what he faces financially. Nonetheless, we persevere. Slowly the boundaries begin to loosen and space grows where we can play around with the money-God. The play surprises us both. When we differentiate the God hiding in the money fixation and he speaks to it directly, of all things, his income begins to rise! When he tightens up again and equates the center with the cash, his income regularly falls. We had done a lot of work with his ego-management of his accounts and his budget. But it was his courageous crossing over to money as symbol of a greater reality addressing him through the lesser one of actual cash that made change possible.

On the opposite end, when boundaries grow too loose, we feel we are not even held in being. Then we fall out or through and cannot even find where or whether the boundaries exist. They remain unseen. For example, a woman addicted to barbiturates because she wants, she says, "oblivion," knew from her dreams as well as our work that major life problems demanded her attention. Chief among them was all the valuable aggressive energy tied up in a crippling rage that defeated any effort she imagined being able to make to get a toe-hold in her work or relationship to others. It all seemed too much. She could not find any boundary line of any territory where she could conceive of a series of small steps ahead. She had crossed a major boundary from suicidal impulses into life, but had not been able to go any further, to tackle the big life-problems that awaited her. The psyche, however, was relentless in its energy: it pressed for release. If she could not go forward to take these steps, then the energy flowed backward and regressed to a sur-rogate suicide of barbiturate-addiction. Here the task clearly was the opposite of the problem of boundaries that were too tight. Here the task was to tighten the boundaries to make a safe circle within which she could find or create little bits at a time of true-self-living.

Our social problems carry the same tensions. Too confining boundaries restrict us to a literalism that claims the only solution to any social problem is to throw money at it. A man who has worked over twenty years to provide housing for homeless citizens in New York City tells me that making apartments available at $75,000 per unit does not solve the problem. Such apartments are often wrecked within a day or a week at most, sometimes by persons mentally ill who need care and containment, sometimes by criminals or crack-addicts. But even on those rare occasions when the apartment remains intact, the newly housed cannot survive unless a community forms around the housing. That means schools, stores, churches, mosques, synagogues, in short a viable neighborhood. Being held in being is more effective than money.

A similar literalism infects our relation to nature. When we reduce the environment in our minds to a series of problems to be solved, we restrict it to a soulless surrounding. We need to expand our literalism to ensoul again the places of earth, sky, air, and water. When we see a tree as only an obstacle to a new highway, and ignore a century-old presence that has collected around itself the dreams and musings of generations of citizens, we lose its power as a symbol of the life of the community spirit. Abt, a Jungian analyst and Zurich professor of city and agricultural planning, gives the remarkable example of even the Swiss, the thriftiest of people, giving money to save such a tree by changing the highway route to go around it, to break boundaries in order to declare boundaries (Abt 1988, 144-145).

All over eastern Europe and throughout the former Soviet Socialist Republic, we witness the determination of peoples to define their boundaries more distinctly. Citizens want their own languages, religious identities, and cultural pasts identified with narratives of their own distinct history, in songs, poetry, dialects. These citizens' insistence on being held within defined boundaries of distinct nations and cultures follows the break-up of monolithic totalitarian governments where we all belong to some impersonal state. Yet our need for boundaries can take exaggerated forms of tribalism or spiritual fanaticism, as we see in some parts of eastern Europe. Such sectarianism, whether political, ethnic or religious, threatens the smooth evolution of a European Commonwealth. We must be careful not to gloss over our need for boundaries that hold us distinctly in being, nor our extreme exaggeration of that need. Winnicott made one of his wise cryptic remarks cautioning against too much boundarilessness, when he pointed out that the other side of the global village is annihilation. Because of finitude we need clear and precise boundaries.

Madness and Encounter with the Transcendent

If we can see the twin dangers of too tight boundaries that kill life and of too lax boundaries where nothing holds us in being, we are free to move to cross the boundaries that deliver us into the presence of what is beyond our limited existence. This should prompt us to ask new questions. How do we live in the presence of what is greater than we are and survive its overwhelming intense energies? How do we go where these energies lead within the frame of clinical work? How does such a presence relate, for example, to the annihilating rage of the woman addicted to barbiturates? How do we go on living with the unknown God who hovers in money images when we finally realize that God is not money? How do we go on living right up to the end of our days, so we can join in Winnicott's prayer when he knew his lung disease would kill him: "O God, let me be alive when I die!" Or echo the poet Rilke's prayer, "O Lord, give each person his own personal death" (Winnicott, C. 1978, 8; Rilke 1981, 21)? What is this presence? What happens there? What does the boundary bind? What is this territory we are about to enter?

We cross to a place of paradox, liminality, and in-betweenness. This territory exposes the wound at our core and what may heal it. This is the space between Jung's ego and archetype; it is Winnicott's transitional space between subjectivity and the objective world, which is the birthplace for our symbols, our art, our religion, as well as of our addictions, fetishism, and madness. It is the space of the split-off grandiose self and of the idealized-object of Kohut, of the "basic fault" of Balint, of what Freud calls the archaic mind as it subverts the ego. There are many maps of this territory. We all know them. Each of us can find the map that works best for our own clients and for our own psyches. I could go on listing them – the patterns of relationship in family systems theory, the space where the paranoid-schizoid and the depressive positions of Melanie Klein meet, where dwell the libidinal and anti-libidinal forces of Fairbairn. Whatever the map we turn to, we see that all theorists note this meeting place of the archaic and discriminating levels of our human mind, where the depths of the unconscious confront the values and differentiations of consciousness. Can we not also say that this territory opens onto the Vast, the All, the totally "Other" that confronts the world of human identity?

If our boundaries are too confining, we will never arrive at this juncture place. For then we live far away from the water, dried up, full of words, but never baptised in the living Spirit. If our boundaries are too open, we are simply dropped into an abyss, a void, a devouring chaos. We feel without foundations, falling, falling forever. It is here, in this gap between conscious

241

and unconscious, sexual acting-out poses such a danger. For when a client falls into this place of undefended openness, the counselor must see that a dangerous crossing is at hand and in no way and at no time take advantage of it. The client's descent to basic fault gives him or her an uncanny intuitive knowledge of the counselor's wounds. In this unconscious communication, a premythic unitary transference-countertransference field is engendered. Both analyst and analysand feel gripped by the field's powerful energy. The boundaries between the two persons disappear from sight. The risk of violation intensifies.

Clinical work – when it works – takes place in this gap, potentially so dangerous or so fruitful. We move from the concrete into a liminal space that permits symbolic discourse. When treatment goes well, we cross back and forth from the ego-world to the unconscious archetypal world, from the energies of instinct to their integration into energies for living.

Most of our clinical work is located in between the worlds of consciousness and the unconscious, because we have been drawn into a neurotic hang-up, fetish, even chronic rage. With luck, the gap, the potentially mad place, will keep being transformed into a space of vitality and reality, where we can humanise outsized desires and connect them to real live relationship to others, where our spiritual yearnings and intimations of a transcendent meaning can incarnate in our unique, concrete identity and contribute to our life together on this planet. But to integrate such spiritual aspects of clinical work is hard, slogging labor. We go in and out of the abyss of madness, in and out of the agonies of mental confusion, in and out of terror we cannot hold to the center and the center will let go of its hold on us. Spirit can attach to any complex and whisk us off our feet. To the danger of burning out in our job and routine life for lack of spirit, the danger of burning up from being unable to house the Spirit that comes into us threatens as well.

When we finally move into our symbolic space, creative living begins, flowing in and through us to others, back to us, down to the earth, up to the sky and back to us again, on and on, like the largest of circulations. We inhabit an alchemical mystery, as if part of the great beating heart of life itself. We arrive in a conversation that has been going on all the time. Or, reach it again after a period of madness in which we had gone out of existence and all conversation had broken off. This notion of conversation going on in our depths reveals the power of Ricoeur's insight that when we offer up to God our substitutions for God, our versions of the golden idol, we receive back the God who speaks, and speaks to us (Ricoeur 1967, 321). The clinical process may be likened to a crossing and recrossing over into this conversation and away from its meditative powers into madness and back again to its positive supports.

A woman client of mine suffering from a borderline condition often dreamt in the first years of our work, of living in houses without walls or roof, sometimes even without floors. There was a hole in her. She felt she might fall right through into nothingness. She knew that plunge as depression of a most dangerous sort, characterized by a lack of any hope that she could ever change. She described this sense of a hole in herself in different ways, saying, "There is something missing in me that should be there;" or saying, "I had no father. I lost my father as a little girl, so there is no place inside me in which to order or carry out living" (see Kohut 1984, 77-78).

Gradually our work filled this hole, this gap, through the transference-countertransference stretching between us. The threatened depressions found some housing and began to move more firmly into what Klein calls the depressive position (Klein 1952, 71-78). My client faced the reality of the people who had been both good to her and bad, and faced that she herself also had been bad as well as good to those she loved.

243

She felt sad realizing that her mother had not mothered her in the most important ways, but had in fact used her to raise her other children and then to support them financially when she achieved some business success. But she also saw now that her mother was a child not fully grown up, and that she had suffered bouts of nothing less than psychosis. She felt rage at her mother but also pity and compassion. She had felt rage all along at her stepfather who had beaten and raped her. But she also knew she had to reckon with all the good he had given her, for which she felt deep gratitude. He had taught her about the woods, how not to be afraid of the dark or the world itself. "He gave me animal courage," she said. Once again, she saw and felt the bad and the good and found both in herself, remembering how, when feeling enraged and sad and with that hole in her, she would go out and "trash money, just blow off a thousand here, three hundred there, on nothing, just junk." It was not as if she was spoiled. She had been born dirt poor and had worked all her life to make her money. But she did not know how to house her wealth, or her inner self to order her spending.

In this period of mourning and knitting together the opposites of bad and good in her experience of her parents and of herself, a new dream arrived that moved us both. In it she was in a new house possessed of all of its walls, floors, and roof intact. The house combined opposites. It was old, solid, with thick walls, and yet with big modern windows that let in much light. It was made of old wood and new steel. It was firmly on the land, but also near the sea. It was beautiful, stylish, secure. "This is my house," she said. But when she went up to a second-floor room, it turned out to be unfinished and she found herself standing precariously in wobbly high heels on a sloping roof suddenly in the outside air with no walls or ceiling to protect her, and in immediate danger of falling.

Here was our dangerous crossing, but with a big difference

244

now. This unhoused place, this hole, this place of gap without structure, was now housed in something bigger than itself. It was part of a larger solid house. The place of madness was now held, housed in a strong structure. It could continue to be worked on. Even the room exposed to the elements could be finished, could be brought within the house.

Lest we think it is only our clients who sound mad, let us remember how we sound when we talk about crossing over into the places of paradox. We sound as if it is we who are mad! In an effort, for example, to describe one of the deepest mysteries of being human, through anima-animus language, we speak of a woman arriving at sureness of living from her own sexual center with a clear hold of the penis in her (Klein 1975, chapter 12). Winnicott goes one better, saying Jung's notion of anima is "the part of me that has always known I was a woman" (Winnicott 1964, 485). We talk of allowing the witch or the wolf in us to live, or we refer to our crocodile rage. What would people outside our consulting rooms think? These crazy mental health professionals! They are making answers out of their problems. And what about our discourse as pastoral counselors, speaking of a person's wound unfolding the suffering of God, or our saying that the neurosis we suffer mirrors God's constriction of infiniteness coming into small human form to enter history?

Conversation and the Transcendent

When we make the dangerous crossing into conversation with something much bigger than our ego-perspective, the two levels of the human mind, conscious and unconscious, become real in us. In their interchange we know moments of real congress with the transcendent, a conjunction, an adumbration of union, a deeply mysterious sacred moment in which we feel whole, joined inside in a marriage of instinct and spirit, of past object-relations and present subject-relations, seeing others as persons, united with life on earth, with the world, with the cosmos.

The dialogue we enter between the archaic and the conscious mind, leads to the momentous discovery that the conversation we thought was two-way is in fact three-way. Another factor enters. It is presence. It greets us from the other side of the dangerous crossing, a presence that transcends the dialogue in our psyche, even though it may speak to us through the psyche.

We may experience presence through conversation with the nature inside ourselves — our sexual and aggressive instincts, for example. When a girl begins menstruation, she experiences the nature which had been outside her, now immediately inside her as she enters decades of conversation with its blood-tides flowing in monthly rhythms. When we seek to converse with our repressed sexual desires, rather than just to control them, we find ourselves entering into relationship with nature as it exists in the most intimate places in ourselves, thus ensouling once more the landscape around us. What we embrace inside, we see with new eyes outside. To respect the animals that turn up in our moods — our dragon-like anger breathing fire at our opponent, the spider web of our anxiety — is to know again the truth of Jung's insistence that as long as animals appear in our religion (specifically involving ox, eagle, and lion in the mandala round Christ, for example), then our religion will be healthy. When the animals leave, our religion is dead (Jung 1976, 284). We might learn to become, as Heidegger puts it, "shepherds of Being." Respecting matter within us and in the world, we come to care for what matters.

What matters seems to issue from a source, a true center.

This is what is present in the conversation we thought was two-way, that actually is three-way. The three ways are those of our ego position, our unconscious position, and the center that transcends both. There are many crossing points into this presence, but for each of us one way appears as our own. Working out what this way is, is to discover our vocation. Each of us is called. Each of us must find how to answer the summons.

I am always amazed how varied and specific the crossing points are. I see it in my Ph.D. students, all of whom must meet the same requirements, but each of whom must find his or her particular way to do so. Part of a teacher's job is to observe and meditate upon each student's style. One student, it turns out, cannot go at material systematically, but must gather it around separate numinous sparks, to enlarge the sparks into different fires of concentration and then link them up into a whole blazing dissertation. Another student must work from a reductive method, because for him it does not minimize but rather liberates meaning in a text or a client. Still another student finds that rage blocks progress and may defeat the whole project if not faced and worked through. Still another, possessed of an original mind, could be misunderstood as a woolly thinker if one did not realize that she perceives things mythically in great, all-encompassing patterns that throw them together into novel and revelatory combinations. For her, a teacher must play the part of the ego, complete with a red pencil, to check the main points of her argument so that she can string them together as a thesis. Another student, caught up in causes and parroting their slogans, needs to dig for her own particular voice and trust it to be enough. Another turns out to have a delicate psychosomatic balance as bodily support for his work and with it a physical rhythm that must be respected if he is to finish any work at all.

We all could give examples of the multifarious paths we see our clients, or our students, or our parishioners taking. In clinical work three ingredients contribute to finding and creating that path. There is the person with his or her special style of communicating; there is the material narrated or exhibited in the person's story, behavior, symptoms, transference, dreams; and finally, there is the counselor with all his or her quirks of style, specific training, skill, and spiritual psychic depth. All three engage with each other. If things go well enough, a buzzing conversation acts to cross and recross the gap between conscious and unconscious, self and other, present and past. Insights, symbols, resolutions of conflicts, and, above all, new ways of experiencing occur. But the shock of this conversation – the danger of its crossing – is a realisation that another party also takes part in the discussion. This one arrives before we do, and can even be said to have awaited us, and continues to abide with us, and will be there as we are gathered to our final rest.

Alone among mental-health professionals, pastoral counselors can allow themselves to speak explicitly of this other party to the conversation, to acknowledge its presence, to witness its unfolding. We speak of it as the sacred, the God who seeks to reach us in and through our complexes, transferences, and counter-transferences. Pastoral counselors, just by electing this profession, choose to be positioned toward the center to dare acknowledgment of the sacred, risk invoking the eternal, confess to seeing it crossing and recrossing the boundaries, and establishing itself as the containing boundary. In such positioning, we take the risk of meeting the center. Words cannot account for this completely. Most people think of the center as a geographical locus. That is a true way to imagine, but it is not all of the truth, perhaps part of Lacan's "mid-dire" where he says truth can be spoken, but only part or half truth, never the whole because we are not whole, never finished, never summed up (Clément 1983, 63). The center moving into us radiates a numinous energy. Here and everywhere, the center concentrates all things, and releases their circumference. Our dangerous crossing leads us into conversation with this ubiquitous presence.

Then What?

Is everything all tidy then? Is God, as Robert Browning wrote, in his heaven, and all right with the world? Can we sum it up, close it, never need to see the gap again? Hardly. Such jubilation happens only in epiphanies, those moments we call sacred, where we unite with a ceaseless play of giving. Such moments come in nature when we look into the eyes of a fox and see its impersonal gaze as if for an instant answer ours. It comes in those moments between mother and child when each recognizes the soul of the other. It arrives in moments of unbelievable coordination of improbables as in the 1982 Olympic victory of a US team of amateurs over Soviet professionals in ice hockey. It comes in a flash when we know we begin a mystic itinerary.

But for the most part, there is nothing to suggest utopia, terminus, neat solution, unambivalent conclusion. Even in clinical work, we cannot say a particular treatment brought a specific success. We all know the studies that say a third of our clients will get better anyway, with or without treatment. But clinical work, especially with a spiritual perspective is not a science; it is life, and thus messy. We know about our own treatment. We ourselves can say, "I was dead and now I am alive," as sometimes our clients say. But the dangerous crossing remains always before us into the central conversation, into the buzzing energy that we awaken to, to bring us to the *arche* – to absolute beginnings, to the originating point.

We enter there into indeterminacy, into all the different ways of picturing reality. Even its rules are changeable, capable of being looked at in all sorts of ways. This does not mean randomness reigns. For the *arche* addresses us, each one of us, and each of the left-out parts of our communities, our land, our psyches. This is the center to which all boundaries lead and all crossings deliver us.

What is this space like? Each of us will tell it her or his own way. Each religion speaks of this unspeakable center in different images – the kingdom, the city, the wedding feast, the Holy of Holies, the imageless All, the illuminating light, the fruitive dark. It is home. This place of absolute beginnings, this root-spring of freedom, is what poets lay bare in their images. They tell us that this space includes opposites that we in our tiny ego-conscious ways always separate. But here everything thrives – Freud's goal of love and work, and Jung's of the conjunction of the feminine and masculine. Two poets write of opposite paths into the same center. A woman who had a long battle with suicide said this poem helped her find her crossing into a restful, life-bringing dark (Ulanov 1996, chapter 10):

> You darkness, that I come from,
> I love you more than all the fires
> that fence in the world,
> for fire makes
> a circle of light for everyone,
> and then no one outside learns of you.

> But the darkness pulls in everything:
> shapes and fires, animal and myself,
> how easily it gathers them! –
> powers and people –
> and it is possible a great energy is moving near me.
> I have faith in nights. (Rilke 1981, 21)

A second poem, that celebrates the center in a shimmer of light, was brought by another woman who had come through an authentic Dark Night of the Soul. Her faith, her job, her home, even her health and her analysis had been stripped from her (see Ulanov 1992/1999). She doubted God and yet felt compelled to continue to pray. As she looked back on what had happened to her during this dark period and how she came through it, she brought this poem into her session as one expression of what had transpired. In it, Denise Levertov (1989) writes of Thomas's doubt of the risen Christ. His eyes alone cannot bring him faith, only direct touch, his finger placed right in the wound, on the body, of the risen Christ:

> But when my hand
>   led by his hand's firm clasp
> entered the unhealed wound,
>   my fingers encountering
> rib-bone and pulsating heat,
>   what I felt was not
> scalding pain, shame for my
>   obstinate need,
> but light, light streaming
>   into me, over me, filling the room
> as if I had lived till then
>   in a cold cave, and now
> coming forth for the first time,
>   the knot that bound me unraveling,
> I witnessed
>   all things quicken to color, to form,
> my question
>   not answered but given its part
> in a vast unfolding design lit
>   by a risen sun.

The questions that face us now are similarly direct. How do we house this light? How do we contain this dark? For all the boundaries, seen and unseen, will be turned inside out and turn us too. Seen now from the point of view of the *arche*, the beginning-point, this eternal conversation is the endless streaming forth of light and it is the deep unfathomable dark. We can see now that all our boundaries are efforts to mark out its light and dark presence.

Coming to this perception may involve the most perilous of all crossings, for it is bound to give us a threatening perspective from which to view the work we do. We dare not look at spiritual aspects of clinical work unless we can look out at it from within this central conversation. For otherwise we must distort things into combative either-or oppositions again and accuse each other of leaving out the essential half. What do I mean? Examples will reveal it.

In clinical work, we find everywhere the latent assumption that the mutative agent, the source of cure lies in the counselor providing a better object for introjection than the client's original mother or father (see chapters 1, 11, 14, 16). This idea carries some truth, but it also supports great arrogance. How do we know we are any better? Winnicott once asked a little girl suffering from abuse if she wanted a new Mummy. No, she replied, I want my old Mummy back (Guntrip 1975). From our usual ego-vantage point, we see many better things given a child, or the child-part of the adult in treatment through the clinician. But in this view we leave out the threads of a mysterious fate that may weave a much better fabric still, one which finally may disclose a destiny. We split into good and bad objects, preferring one opposite and omitting the other. What would it look like to include both? I am not advocating a do-nothing approach, or a denial of abuse and its consequences, which we must make every effort to correct, ameliorate, and even heal. I am asking how we are to understand as part of a whole life, our own and others', the searings, wounds, and scars that come upon us.

When we look at this issue from the perspective of the central conversation, we see that human tragedies, personal catastrophes, the sufferings of countries, can also be seen as the woundings of the infinite God who comes into our history. The All comes to dwell with the small. The streaming light enters the dark. The velvet dark opens to a harsh glare. It is wounded. It suffers. It bleeds and splits into fragments. At the center of the Judeo-Christian tradition hangs a bleeding, suffering God who has taken our suffering into his own body. Perhaps it is not only true that God is with us in our suffering, but that through our suffering, we become part of God's suffering.

This angle of vision offers us new insights into the conduct of our work. In hearing the family tragedy that produces so much suffering in our clients, in hearing of the tragedies of our clients' bodies breaking down into lethal illness, we must connect two sets of questions. Why does this happen? and What will heal it? must be joined by another view at the same time. Instead of simply looking for the cause in the past object-relations of the client, we must stand alongside Jesus' disciples in that arresting parable reported in the Gospel of John. They want to know, Was this man born blind because he sinned? Or because his parents sinned? Jesus answers No, to both questions, and pushes us to face the purpose toward which the affliction may be tending, not simply backward to find its cause. The affliction takes us, here and now, to the *arche*, to the absolute beginning, the originating point of eternal conversation. Jesus says that the man has been born blind so that God's work and glory may be made manifest. Jesus tells us, in effect, that no matter where we are, or how badly off we may be, God is there, ready to pour light into us, to make visible the restful dark that wants to inhabit us, to shine forth in presence and glory. This is the "I am" God, whom our little self mirrors, the God "who is with us."

We all should know these truths from our experience of the dangerous crossing of sexual attraction in therapeutic treatment, where our alternative is neither to suppress awareness of sexual fires nor to act them out, but to serve the fires as part of the center. Each person, client and clinician, finds his or her path of service to house the fire and let it feed the separate lives, always back into renewed life, without sacrificing true analytical intimacy by substituting an ersatz sexuality (Ulanov 1996, chapter 8). St. Teresa of Avila and Freud reached the same conclusion about this fire. For Freud, the goal of analysis was love and work. For Teresa, the fruit of union with God, as she told her nuns, was work, work, work in the world, showing forth God's glory (Freud 1949; St. Teresa of Avila 1957, vol. III). Service to a manifesting glory is the alternative to rigid rules or a licentious permissiveness.

To enter this originating conversation brings the sword as well as peace. We are summoned to our own true selves as well as to the bounty of being. Looking to see the unseen boundaries, and to make the dangerous crossings, we align ourselves with the center – to plant it, to dig it up, to eat it, to house it, to share it, to pass it back and forth, to become part of its endless conversing. We enjoy it, knowing Glory here made manifest. We echo in our boundary-crossing work what Irenaeus said, "The glory of God is human beings fully alive."

Address to National Conference American Association of Pastoral Counselors, Virginia, 1992.

254

References

Abt, T. 1988. *Progress Without Loss of Soul.* Wilmette Illinois: Chiron.

Avila, St. Teresa 1957. *The Complete Works of Teresa.* 3 vols. trans. E. Allison Peers. New York: Sheed and Ward.

Clément, C. 1983. *The Lives and Legends of Jacques Lacan.* trans. Arthur Goldhammer. New York: Columbia University Press.

Døgen. 1985. *Moon In a Dewdrop, The Writings of Zen Master Døgen.* ed. Kazuaki Tanahashi. San Francisco, Ca.: North Point Press, Farrar, Straus and Giroux.

Freud, S. 1949. *An Outline of Psychoanalysis.* New York: W. W. Norton.

Guntrip, H. 1975. My experience of analysis with Fairbairn and Winnicott. *International Review of Psycho-Analysis.* 2:145-156; also found in Goldman, D. 1993. ed. *One's Bones, The Clinical Genius of Winnicott.* Northvale, N.J.: Jason Aronson, 139-158.

Jung, C. G. 1932. Psychotherapists or the clergy. CW 11, *Psychology and Religion: West and East.* 1958. trans. R. F. C. Hull. New York Pantheon, pp. 327-347, pars. 488-538.

Jung, C. G. 1916/1958. The transcendent function. CW 8, *The Structure and Dynamics of the Psyche.* 67-91, pars. 131-193.

Jung, C. G. 1976. *The Visions Seminars.* vol. 2 of two volumes. Zurich, Switzerland: Spring Publications.

Klein, M. 1952. The Emotional Life of the Infant. Klein, M. 1975. *Envy and Gratitude and Other Words 1946-1963.* New York: Delacorte Press/Seymour Lawrence.

Klein, M. 1975. *Psycho-Analysis of Children.* New York: Seymour Lawrence/ Delacorte Press.

Kohut, H. 1984. *How Does Analysis Cure?* Chicago: University of Chicago Press.

Levertov, D. 1989. *A Door in the Hive.* New York: New Directions.

Loewald, H. 1978. *Psychoanalysis and the History of the Individual.* New Haven, Ct.: Yale University Press.

Ricoeur, P. 1967. *The Symbolism of Evil.* trans. Emerson Buchanan. New York: Harper and Row.

Rilke, R. M. 1981. *Selected Poems of Rainer Maria Rilke.* trans. Robert Bly. San Francisco: Harper.

Ulanov, A. B. 1990/1999. The double cross: scapegoating. *Lingering Shadows. Freud, Jung and Antisemitism.* 1990. ed. A. Maidenbaum. Boston: Shambala, 223-240; also in Ulanov, A. B. 1999. *Religion and the Spiritual in Carl Jung.* Mahweh, N.J.: Paulist, chapter 2.

Ulanov, A. B. 1992. The holding self: Jung and the desire for being. *The Fires of Desire, Erotic Energies and the Spiritual Quest*. 1992. eds. Frederica R. Halligan and John J. Shea. New York: Crossroad, 146-170; also in Ulanov, A. B. 1999. *Religion and the Spiritual in Carl Jung*, Mahweh, N.J.: Paulist, chapter 4.

Ulanov, A. B. 1994a. *The Wizard's Gate, Picturing Consciousness*. Einsiedeln: Daimon Verlag.

Ulanov, A. B. 1994b. Mending the mind and minding the soul: explorations towards the care of the whole person. *Journal of Religion and Disability and Rehabilitation*. eds. Sally K. Severino and Richard Liew, vol. 1, no. 2:107-110. Binghamton, N.Y.: The Haworth Pastoral Press (see chapter 1).

Ulanov, A. B. 1996. *The Functioning Transcendent*. Wilmette, Ill.: Chiron.

Ulanov, A. and B. 1975. *Religion and the Unconscious*. Louisville, Ky.: John Knox/Westminster Press.

Winnicott, C. 1978. D. W. W.: A reflection. *Between Fantasy and Reality, Transitional Objects and Phenomena*. eds. S. Grolnick, L. Barkin in collaboration with W. Muensterberger. New York: Jason Aronson.

Winnicott, D. W. 1950. Some thoughts on the meaning of the word 'democracy.' Winnicott, D. W. 1986. *Home Is Where We Start From*. eds. Clare Winnicott, Ray Shepherd, Madeleine Davis. New York: Norton, 239-259.

Winnicott, D. W. 1960. Ego Distortion in Terms of True and False Self. Winnicott, D. W. 1965. *The Maturational Processes and the Facilitating Environment*. New York: International Universities Press, 140-152.

Winnicott, D. W. 1963a. From Dependence Towards Independence in the Development of the Infant. Winnicott, D. W. 1965. *The Maturational Processes and the Facilitating Environment*. New York: International Universities Press, 83-92.

Winnicott, D. W. 1963b. Communicating and not communicating leading to a study of certain opposites. Winnicott, D. W. 1965. *The Maturational Processes and the Facilitating Environment*. New York: International Universities Press, 179-192.

Winnicott, D. W. 1964. C. G. Jung, Review of *Memories, Dreams, Reflections*. *International Journal of Psychoanalysis*. Vol. 45, 2-3; also found in Winnicott, D. W. 1989. *Psycho-Analytic Explorations*. eds. Clare Winnicott, Ray Shepherd, Madeleine Davis. London: Karnac, 482-492.

Chapter 10

Violence

Danger

As a group, you set before yourselves a vision to reject violence and to cherish life. You thus summon yourselves not to solve an issue but to enter a depth, to ground your identity. You thus put yourselves in danger. For you, for any of us, to say openly that we reject violence in ourselves and in society attracts violence in the forms of hubris, taunt, test, and defiance. Not only do demonic powers marshal to defeat you but other people too will want to challenge your vision, say it cannot be done, that you are fools. And of course, you are, standing as you do in the great tradition of fools for Christ.

The temptation to undo your vision will arise from within yourselves as well. Whenever we try to integrate our individual personality and here, in your vision statement, your corporate personality as womanly presence and the force of the feminine as sisters together, we can expect attack from all those parts of ourselves and those forces of society that now stand outside our aim, all the parts that remain unintegrated or even opposed to integration. We repudiate them as not-me, not-us. Indeed, in your words, it is the violent parts left out of the vision of non-violence that will direct attack at you and your vision. This places you on the frontier of evil, near to that mystery from which flows violence in the first place.

Some depth psychologists say Christ did not know evil the way we do, because, unlike us, he was without sin, and therefore he cannot know all we suffer. They are mistaken, I believe. Jesus chooses differently from us. He chooses the tree of life instead of the know-it-all tree of good and evil that we choose, and thus he experiences evil as always assaulting him from the moment of his birth to the moment of his death. This assault is symbolized liturgically: three days after the beneficent images of Christ as a baby at his mother's breasts, the Church marks the Slaughter of the Innocents, all those other babies murdered, whose mothers could not be consoled. Where we try to flee evil, protect ourselves from its ravages, fight against it, Jesus voluntarily places himself on its frontier. And you, in your vision, are doing the same.

Thus I feel, speaking with you today, danger around us. It is even a potentially violent situation to have a psychoanalyst speak with you on this subject. Maybe we will come to blows, because I am going to say we cannot hop over violence, but only get beyond it by going through it. As Augustine puts it pithily: We can't give what we don't have; *non quod dabet non quod habet.* So if we are going to put life and growth in the world in place of violence, we must know this life and growth, come to this clearing, and go on living in this creative place in ourselves. Dangers lurk everywhere – that we cannot find this creative place, that we can grow tired in our search for it, that we can be attacked because we have found it, and that we can think we have arrived there whereas in fact we go in the opposite direction. In the name of non-violence we can perpetrate violence, detouring aggressive energy into masochistic self-attack because we feel rage at another or at the system, and we think we should not feel this rage. Or we can fall into sadistic bullying of others who are afraid to seek non-violence because the world does not work that way and they need self-protection to survive.

On top of it all, whenever we discover that God is here, now, we undergo violent change. This season of Advent heralds the one who comes to judge as well as to offer the new, the one who brings the sword, as Simeon tells us, to pierce our soul as well as to bring salvation. Even when God's presence announces itself through a still small voice, it changes our house from the ground up, shaking all our foundations.

Aggression and Violence and the Core Self

Taking up the task of rejecting violence in ourselves and in society means we must look at aggression. We arrive in this life with aggressive energy which initially feels like a root impulse in our bodies (see also chapter 11). This energy initiates movement, gesture, reaching out, reaching in, becoming. We need this energy to live, to assert, to take, to thrust out into the world, to survive and recover, and especially to respond to and create the new. Violence is a perversion of this energy; it turns against what is expected or desired, turns away from the good. Violence springs out of three sources: damage to our core self which contains and channels our aggression; lack of something to push against and denial of parts of ourselves; and refusal to feel our own hate along with our love.

In the beginning of our development, our core self exists as wobbly and unformed. And any time we begin something new – like your new vision – we exist in a wobbly state. But we grow if supported and cared for by others and by ourselves.

Our core self develops slowly, like little islands in the ocean, that, when held and cherished by another, slowly join up to make a bit of earth arising out of the sea. We become a little territory. Because someone else has held us in being, we can take over the task of holding ourselves in being and stand on ground supporting us beneath our feet (Winnicott 1965, 56ff.; Bollas 1987, 10, 13-29).

If that core self is endangered, lost, or shattered, no container exists for our instinctual aggressive energy and violence will jump out in its place. Aggression not employed can detour into violence. Outer joblessness mirrors this inner unemployed aggression. Our core self resembles a wobbly bowl in the beginning, its rim and edges only sketchily defined, with permeable outline. Like jello not yet set or firm, its circumference is forming but takes no definite shape yet and can be destroyed.

If we lose that containing self or feel it to be at risk, we can switch all our aggressive energy to one part of what the bowl contains and concentrate on that as our defining characteristic. Kohut calls this part that substitutes for the whole self, a disintegration product (Kohut 1977, 120-121, 262). All of our aggressive energy goes into exploiting and living through that one part. We see ourselves fastening, for example, onto our sexuality, or onto our eating as the root impulse of our being and to express our whole being. Food is our God-image which both supports us and plagues us. Or we find our core self only in violence, as a teenage boy said to his mother, "I only feel alive when I am in danger." Our aggression which belongs to our whole self and should be moving throughout the whole container, pours into this one part which obsesses us, compels us, troubles us and makes our life difficult and makes us difficult to other people. But this one part holds our life. All of ourself harbors in this one part so we dare not give it up, lest we become totally unalive.

To avoid this catastrophe of addiction to one part of the whole self, we need from each other and from ourselves caring for this wobbly self until, like jello, it sets and shows a lustrous color of deep ruby, or flashing green. This caring depends on dependence – that someone lends their being to us temporarily and woos us into living our whole self by their holding us, and presenting the real objects of the world to us. This other, often a female or the female part of the male, we treat as what Winnicott calls a subjective-object (1971, 38-39, 52, 100); that is, an other who we first believe lives for us, in fact composes a part of us, who transforms the world into graspable bits for us. For example, a new mother can sleep her exhausted sleep through all the noises of New York City and awaken only at the sound of the cheep of her newborn baby. She supports the baby's illusion that this mother exists as part of the baby's self.

When we give a present to welcome a newborn baby, for example, it is best to give a tiny toy for little fingers, not a huge panda bigger than the child herself. That outsized toy cannot be grasped or imagined. A tiny toy that can accompany an infant in a crib and offer itself to a small mouth to gum and then to chew, and later to little fingers to be put into a small pocket, that toy becomes part of the self. Perhaps we can each remember this favorite companion of childhood – a bear, a lamb, a bit of blanket we loved with all our heart and mind and soul and which was alive to us and through which we came alive.

We call such a toy a subjective-object (a transitional one too) because its whole being refers back to us, the subject; it lives for us; it is part of us, and although it exists as a distinct object, we have created it. The toy symbolizes our being held and cherished by an other, usually our mother. When we play with this toy, we play with being separate from this one with whom we have been united. Religious relics function in a similar way. They symbolize God cherishing us and our playing with being united with and separate from this divine other. Initially we see our parent and even God as a subjective-object, and God permits it as St. John of the Cross reminds us: in the beginning of spiritual life we are taken on God's lap as a nursling, given sweet signs of presence and encouragement, and only later are we put down to the ground to learn to crawl and to walk, with fewer signs, so we do not substitute the signs for the lap. That would be to stop at the idol and never arrive at the real thing.

Dependence marks the beginning and the sustaining of our lives, as any baby's helplessness impresses upon us (see also chapter 13). But we need these subjective-objects all our life long, and especially when we begin something new to reflect back to us that we matter, that we exist as part of what matters. In your Order you are launching a new and a renewed vision, hence you are living in a vulnerable state. You need to depend on being held and cherished as this new island of creative energy that replaces violence rises up from the sea to join your already established territory.

Let us not fool ourselves, as religion in established forms often tries to do. We never grow out of our need to depend on others to support us, see us, cherish us, feed our core self. That comes with being human; we do not get some sort of mature religion that excludes this basic need for each other. We need times with each other, and with specific others who see us, and want to reflect back to us what they see. This feeds our core self. This is love in action.

We need this mirroring back of our core self, the unique self of who we each are. We register immediately in our gut instinct when someone does that for us. We feel possible; we expand down into our full self. Seeing the specific ruby or emerald or brilliant yellow color of our own or the other's unique self, is also, I suggest, a central part of religious devotion. When we pray the prayer "Veni Creator, Come Holy Spirit Come," are we not eliciting from the anonymous surround of our lives that generating presence who begets us, sees us, sustains us in being, that energy who wants to fill us and manifest through us? This is mirroring of the unique authority of our core self. And when we pray for that presence to come, we are summoning, opening to the silent witness to our truest self. We depend on this. We need it. God promises it as always available to us. That is why Jesus went away, he told his disciples, so that this ever-present loving could be accessible to us forever.

Mirroring, however, works both ways. Not only does God's spirit stand looking into us, but part of our religious devotion may be to mirror God. I think always of the woman with the ointment (Mk 14:3-14; Mt. 26: 7-13, John 12: 1-8). She pours costly ointment on Jesus's feet and then his head. The disciples, and principally Judas, protest she should have sold this ointment for all the money it would bring to be given to the poor! They repudiate her devotion as good for nothing, asserting that giving to the poor is better. But Jesus says no, and that all of us will remember her for her lavish loving. She, and only she, of all the people in all the Gospels, anoints him for living and dying. We will always have, and always be, the poor, Jesus says. The disciples are in danger of reversing the two commandments: serving the neighbor before loving God with our whole heart and soul and mind and strength, and then loving our neighbor as we love ourselves.

You too have elected to mirror the giving going on all the time. So you are electing to stand with the goodness that is good for nothing, to pour out in a feminine spiritual and sexual way a prodigal loving, praising, thanking. This means a conception of the church not as an agent of change, a food pantry, or a social action committee, but something else. Does that mean the church should no longer perform these services? No. The church will do them, but not as solution to a problem which can be solved, but instead as an anointing of the one we love, as acts of extravagant loving. That is what distinguishes the church's social caring from that of social agencies. It is the loving and the stepping into the current of love that ceaselessly goes out from the Giver mirroring our core self and back from us to the Giver, and whizzing between us as we give this mirroring to each other and take it in from each other and it flows back to the Giver. We live in the endless currents of the sea, all our little terrains supported, touching, mirroring. When this happens between us, we almost hear faint buzzing of energy, and feel a bodily relaxation of breath that brings the simultaneous knowledge that our breath had not been so free the moment before.

Losing hold of the core self and its need for mirroring detours aggression from sustaining the whole self in acts of lavish loving into the violence of fastening on one part of the self. If you are to succeed with your vision, you need to reserve times to conserve the core self of each of you and of your specific group, time to see and reflect back the unique living of each other and of all of you together. How do you do this?

Violence, Aggression and External Reality

If the first way we exchange natural aggression for violence springs from a deficit of support for our core self, the second way that fatal substitution happens springs from a lack of something to push against and denial of owning that we want to push. Life is not all support and pastel feelings. Bold reds, yellows, blues, the primary colors, flash from us and toward us! We cannot always be mirroring each other, nor do we always want to be reflected back to ourselves. We want also to push out, cut away, grab, chew, spit out, take, charge, jump, leap upon with a low growl. Life means spirit, and spirit means electricity, intensity, combat, raucous laughter, hearty appetite, lusty loving. Love that lasts is love tough enough to survive.

Aggression as energy pushes against the other and needs to know the other pushing back, who will not crumple but stay in relationship (Winnicott 1971, chapter 6). Otherwise we never climb down or get put down from our mother's lap, or from God's lap. We want to go on forever with sweet signs of God's presence, a coddling. Yet something in us, named aggression, wants more – to explore, to stand, to venture, to achieve, to connect and make something happen. So naturally out of our core selves grows strength to add to love, grows mind to add to feeling, grows feeling perception to add to thoughts.

We perceive where the other does not match our need. Reality intervenes between its fact and our expectation. Our projected image of the other falls short of who the other is. And we get mad – that discrepancy surprises us, even shocks us or wounds us. Why isn't my mother here when I need her instead of going to the bathroom! Why isn't my friend capable of owning up to her denial that her feelings have changed toward me, instead of pretending they remain the same? Why doesn't life afford me the opportunity to fulfill my hopes instead of landing me in the middle of a world war which throws all hope into confusion? Why does God let my mother die, or my father abuse me, or my child suffer a lingering illness? What kind of God is this anyway?

These gaps between wish and fact, desire and otherness, need and reality open our aggression and our aggression opens them. For we destroy our image of the other who fails to match our image and reality destroys our image. Aggression, whether from us or to us, wipes the other out as who we thought they were. We push against the other as the other pushed their reality against our image of them. That clash, that difference introduces a gap, a space between us and them, where aggressively we destroy our picture of them which their reality destroys.

265

If we both survive this destruction, which is not always the case, our relationship grows more real. We know the other really exists and is bigger than we thought. My mother now is the one who mirrors and supports me and, in addition, the one who goes off to the bathroom even when I need her. She becomes an objective-object in addition to being my subjec-tive-object (Winnicott 1971, chapter 6). She brings a personal-ity of her own, in addition to the one I endowed her with. God now is the one who takes me on the lap and, in addition, the one who puts me down and leaves me in the dark and does not answer my rededication of my vows in the way I expected. God disappears instead and leaves me hopeless. But after this destruction, I am surprised by the discovery that my rededica-tion fulfills itself but in a way I could never have expected, showing me I did learn how to keep hope alive in a hopeless situation. My friend is no longer defined by who I thought she was, but shows me a different side of her, as one who denies, and the question now is, will I accept that fact about her? If not, the friendship dies or confines itself to a superficial level. If so, the friendship deepens to include my seeing parts of her that she pretends are not there.

We need the objective reality of others to push against in order to claim our aggression for living in the real world. When we bump up against an other whose otherness defeats our image of them, our response is also to defeat, to destroy our image as defining the other. If both people survive this destruction, two amazing results occur. First, we enter into reality as real, external to us, there, relating to us from its own otherness. Aggression, says Winnicott, functions to establish the externality of reality (1989, chapter 34). We gain access to real objects who can show, bring, feed, display things to us out of themselves that we cannot find on our own. We come then to experience reality as a source of life. We see others doing and being things that we are not able to do, nor choose or lack time to do. Hence a community of interdependence grows up. Instead of envy and competitiveness with our neighbor for displaying what we lack, we feel grateful that our neighbor brings something we can partake of, because, by ourselves, we would never arrive there.

Second, our destruction of our image of the other changes into unconscious imagination (Winnicott 1971, chapter 6; Ulanov 1995). Aggression as destructiveness now operates like a windshield wiper to wipe the slate clean so we look at the other with fresh eyes. We still make images of the other, because we are created to be image-making creatures. But, as if on Jacob's ladder, we climb step by step toward the reality of the other, like the *via negativa* of theology. Our God-images, for example, keep pushing us up against the real God whose reality breaks them. One woman said, when her image of God collapsed, it was too tame, too small, something bigger burst through it. But we do not despise our old God-images for they act like our gropings in the dark as the light beckons us. Our aggression sustains us in our seeing the new coming over the horizon because the destruction of our images keeps wiping the slate clean of our projections onto God.

For the two people, or for us and God, or for groups to survive the destruction of our projection of our subjective-object image onto the other, we need to risk all-out aggressive loving, not to hold back, not to pull our punches. And we need to risk feeling that push coming out of us, or, if we are in the position of the other, of a pushing into us. (Think how often Christ receives our blows.) We need to survive the push out of ourself and not fear we will crumple. And we depend on the other to survive it out of themselves and not withdraw in hurt or reproach us with guilt. If both persons can survive the intensity of this aggressive energy, then aggression becomes connection, not violence, and destructiveness transforms unconsciously into imagination. Aggressive energy joins loving and we get love with teeth. With God, we do the absolute worst and God still comes to us, resurrecting in love toward us.

What we push against in each other is not only the other's reality, but also parts of us we deny. We all possess parts of us we do not like that we pretend are not there. They follow us around, like our shadows. We cannot get rid of them, even though we do not see them. Our neighbor sees them more clearly than we do. Standing here before you, I do not see what is behind me, but is nonetheless present in shadow, outside my ego's view. But you might see the swish of an alligator tail at the hem of my skirt, or hear a hyena laugh just at the edge of my voice. Jung calls these parts of us that belong to us but which we do not see our shadow (Jung 1959, paras. 13ff.). Do any of you remember that five o'clock Sunday afternoon program, with Lamont Cranston playing "The shadow knows the evil that lurks in the hearts of men, hahahaha?"

An image for the reality of the shadow comes from people who when returning from Florida vacations would buy in the airport on the way home cute tiny alligators just hatched. In Manhattan, they kept them in their bathtub. But then the alligators grew! What to do? Flush them down the toilet! All over Manhattan live alligators descended into the sewer systems, not to die, but to keep on growing. Our shadow consists of all our little alligators pushed into the unconscious, not to die, but to go on growing, and in addition, meeting each other. So under our civilised consciousness, underneath the city's pavements, amasses all our disowned life. Inside and outside connect. The amassing of unconscious life can cause choking of our body's arteries, or the choking of roads by thousands of unwanted refugees, erupting in coronary, or in the deadening of our society's heart to the plight of the homeless. The amassing of life in the unconscious mirrors the amassing of weapons to fight the alligators we spy in our neighbors' camps.

We cannot escape the shadow. If we try, by pushing its contents into the unconscious, they, like alligators, grow bigger and bigger because out of reach of any ego modification or control. These contents merge with everybody else's shadow, and with whatever else lives in our individual unconscious. So, for example, the sincerity of your vision consciously to renounce violence may repress your violent emotions into your unconscious where they grow bigger and contaminate your vision, by erupting as fury against those who do not share your vision, or as subtle manipulation of those you genuinely seek to serve. On the collective level, for example, our genuine wish to negotiate peace may be thwarted by our unconscious need to have an enemy who carries the shadow we do not want to own. What goes across the peace table gets sabotaged by what goes on under the table.

The shadow contents are not inert. We must use a lot of aggressive energy to keep them out of awareness. Hence again we detour aggression from supporting life into pushing these contents out of consciousness. But we have to keep pushing. Like holding a big beach ball under water, we must keep exerting energy to keep it under. Our arms grow tired and then the ball vavooms upward to hit us, and usually someone else, in the face.

All these examples make this point: contents we repress into the unconscious remain alive and amass life by regressing to more primitive forms because no ego reality modifies or limits them. These contents contaminate everything else that is in the unconscious, our own and everyone else's too. Thus a kind of pollution of our psychic air and water goes on in us personally and in our group life, so even what is good gets slowly poisoned. Anything unconscious requires energy to keep it so and that

269

drains our creative life energy, our aggression for life purposes. In the Protestant world in which I live, this suppression and repression of aggression accounts for the boring face we give religious life. Goodness turns into goody-goodness, a life of endless tuna fish suppers. The daring of a Ruth, the revolutionary impact of a Mary, the frank sizing-up ability of a Rahab gets pushed out as bad. But these female ancestors of Christ held the line of descent to the Messiah until it bloomed in the birth of Christ (Ulanov 1993/1998). She among us who catches hold of the shadow speaks and acts with authority.

Anything unconscious seeks to become conscious; we first find in our neighbor the shadow parts we are just becoming conscious of in ourselves. We project our shadows onto each other. We find over there, outside ourselves, what we do not claim as our own inside ourselves. Socially and politically a direct line extends from personal repression of shadow material, through its regression and contamination to projection onto our neighbors. From that projection of what we find bad in ourselves issues violence in the forms of prejudice, discrimination, persecution, oppression, genocide against others.

Working on our shadows takes aggression and comprises a worthy use of aggressive energy. To uncover, not to fight nor flee nor flinch, but to see, to contemplate the alligators, hyenas, scorpions in our own house and try to negotiate some sort of relationship with them withdraws from the world a great deal of violence. We deal with our own noxious fumes and do not pollute our neighbor. We try to find a leash for our own jumping dog and do not just let it loose on our neighbor's lawn.

Will recalling our projections settle all the strife and violence in the world? No, it will not. But it will subtract that tiny portion we contribute to the world's violence. And it will build up a community feeling of being fellow and sisterly sufferers of the same kind of inner wars. We can encourage each other, as

270

well as confront each other. We can take aggression to work through our battles. Where that proves impossible, we can use aggression to choose how peaceably to sustain or courteously to break connection with each other.

We use our aggression to see what personal bits of shadow we put on each other (the personal layer of our shadow complex); this is the particular sister I really dislike who is my roommate for life. I remember an analysand who dreamt that while she stayed in her place on an airplane, her sister went up and down, stabbing everyone in an aisle seat with an icepick. We use our aggression to see what cultural bits we project onto groups other than our own (the collective layer of our shadow complex). For example, the television show "Archie Bunker" made millions out of exposing shadow material in a humorous way, as does the Roseann program now. This shadow concept is not esoteric theory, but fact. We can be sure the authors of these shows did not read depth psychology! Finally, we use our aggression to glimpse the archetypal image of shadow (the archetypal core of the shadow complex), for example, in religious symbols, the devil himself, or in popular symbols, Darth Vader of Star Wars fame (Ulanov 1986, 127-145). Thus if we use our aggression to struggle with our shadow, it does not have to detour into violence; it is fully used, occupied. This is not a cure-all for violence of the world, but it is a significant contribution to others.

Remember Jesus's story about the sheep and goats and the surprise of those Jesus reveals to be sheep? When did we ever do these services to you that you say we did, they ask. Jesus answers that inasmuch as you did them to the least among you, you did them to me. We usually interpret this powerful parable to mean service to others. But we cannot give others what we do not have, so we need to understand the story as also pointing to parts of our own selves and our own group. Do we

271

visit the part of us that languishes in the prison of our defenses, cut off from the rest of our life? What about the hungry parts inside us, that we only feed vicariously through food for our neighbors in the world? One protestant pastor who suffered from great overweight felt herself to be starving spiritually, not because she had no spiritual life. Her ministry showed great success. But the spiritual food always went to her flock, never to herself. Or what about the part of us we have left naked of any protection, as vulnerable to abuse and neglect as the unwanted children in our world? What about the mad parts of us, suffering abysmal confusion, unable to join life? Are those parts of us out on the street corner yelling at passersby along with the mentally ill homeless? The inner parts of ourselves do not substitute for the outer neighbor. The poor we always have with us, but our poverty makes us part of that population. Inner does not substitute for outer, but neither does outer replace inner (Ulanov 1987, 119-120, 121-123, 235, 245). Augustine's words are never more true: we can't give what we do not have. Giving to the inner part helps us give more simply and directly to the outer neighbor.

What provisions are being made for you individually and together as a group to recognize the shadow at its personal, collective, archetypal levels? What ways exist that allow pushing against each other and surviving that, without withdrawing or reproaching? How do you recognize the reality of others who bring gifts you cannot find in yourselves?

Aggression and Ambiguity

Aggression can turn into violence if we lose hold of our core self, or if we fail to discover the reality of the other and of our shadow. Aggression can also turn into violence if we cannot join our hate to our love (Klein 1952). Most of us shrink at the thought of our hate. That is the other person's problem, not our own! We do not want to see where we hate, and we push it into our shadow. But unlike the computer where we can empty the bulging trash basket by the push of a button, the hate that we stuff away causes violence to explode into the world and against ourselves.

We need the intercession of consciousness (Ulanov and Ulanov 1975, chapter 11). We need to acknowledge the sorrowful fact that yes, we know times when we hate, and hate even those we love. We know times when we want to destroy what we cherish. We know moments when we want to hurt those whose very selves we want to conserve. For example, a woman in analysis reaches a good insight or feeling in a session. When she comes the next time, she does not remember it at all. It is as if it never happened; it is gone, obliterated. If I recall the good insight or feeling, she tears it to bits. It took me a while to catch on that in this behavior (not yet in her consciousness) she was communicating her effort and inability to connect destructiveness with the good. How to link them, instead of substitute one for the other? How to survive that we feel both?

We need also to acknowledge that we see in those who love us the same impulse to strike out, to obliterate, to ignore, to envy or steal or just neglect what they love, even if it is us. We need to grow tough enough to see that hate does not mean the other does not also love us and go on loving us, and that we go on loving them. Good and bad do not split into comfortably separate categories, but ambiguously mix together. Moral ambiguity exists in ourselves and in others, in the world. This is a sorrowful fact.

If our aggression lies at our disposal, we can accept this mixture of good and bad, love and hate, and the sorrow it brings. We participate in the sorrow of the world that goodness does not conquer all badness. We even draw near to behold the sorrowing Christ, who suffers our rejection of the good and takes it into himself (Marion 1991).

I am thinking here of an example I heard years ago from one of my Seminary students. She was working for the summer in hot New York City in a tumultuous city hospital, one that receives most of the poor, and most of the crazies off the street (see also chapter 2). She was enrolled in a program of Clinical Pastoral Education, training as a chaplain in the emergency room and in the obstetrics ward. It was hot. Patients seemed to flood into the emergency room in an endless flow. People shouting, people violent, people resisting treatment, refusing to tell their symptoms, shoving, suffering, numbed out on drugs, angry, resentful, sick. On the maternity ward, she said, cots of tiny babies shocked her because they lay there silent and trembling, withered, suffering withdrawal from the drug addiction passed on from their mothers who seemed indifferent to their infants, interested in getting back to a supply of crack. The student said she felt overwhelmed and increasingly shaky.

One Friday morning, she awoke and got ready to go to the subway to return to work at the hospital but she started to cry and could not stop. This frightened her. She had the wit to call a friend who had the wit to intervene. This friend called in turn her friend who headed up an inpatient hospital out of town and got my student into it for the weekend. My student went, still crying. Remembering it, she exclaimed, "It was like therapy camp!" She went from psychiatrist to psychologist, to group therapy telling of her work in the hospital and the stress it caused her. It broke open in psychodrama.

The drama therapist asked her to imagine talking to God. What would she say? To her shock she shouted, "I hate the poor! I chose this hospital to work with the poor. I wanted to serve them in your name. I want to love them. I know I should love them. But their refusal to take hold, the mothers who turn their backs on their babies, the men who jump on the nurses trying to help them, the anger they spew all over me when I've done nothing to deserve it, their stealing and tuning out, I hate it! I know I should sacrifice myself for them, but I'm afraid their violence will kill me. I can't make it better. I can't stop crying." Then the drama therapist said, "Now be God, and answer you." To her great surprise, she heard herself say, "I too weep for the poor, but I made the sacrifice. I made the last sacrifice. You do not have to do it. I have already done it. It has been done. You do not have to sacrifice your life. I too weep for those who do not take it."

My student felt stunned. She felt a psychological and theological revolution rising up in her; that hate could be part of love and not defeat it. She saw that her stress stemmed more from fearing her hate than the rigors of her job. As a Christian, she believed she shouldn't hate; she must love the poor, and what she actually experienced was that she hated them. Trying to suppress her violent feelings tore her up. She saw that she feared attack and retaliation for being hateful. She had been defending against her hate, and losing the battle. It just jumped out of her mouth like a frog. Accepting it, she felt a huge rush of new energy, aggressive energy, that gave her staying power and power to discriminate between her projections and other people's actual actions. Acknowledging her hate did not mean she abandoned her love of the poor and wish to help. Her hate made her want to repair, make amends, make reparation (Klein 1935, 265-266; 1952, 74).

Theologically, her aggression helped her differentiate between herself and God. For God had made the gesture even unto death. Remember former president Truman who put a sign on his desk saying the buck stops here? In Christ, all evil comes to stop in him, on the cross (Marion 1991). She needed to receive that, not identify with it. God had given God's own self, God's own blood, in the figure of Christ, there for the taking. If it was not taken it did not mean God did not care. God is weeping.

Grace is offered; wrath is the experience of not taking what is offered; we stay outside it. The student saw that she could feel hate along with love and the one did not defeat the other. In fact, acknowledging hate made her love more. She wanted to make amends. What did the student do then? She went back to work with the poor in the city hospital, able to do it now because she could use her aggression to make a difference where she could and entrust the rest to God.

These are not honeyed words. People actually experience this transformation and we need it to strike home in us so that we can meet and speak to victims after someone close to them has been murdered, so we can make come alive the reality of God's gift to us which makes us see clearly the reality of violence. This is not for saintly people, but for us here and now, living, changing each day.

If we can allow ourselves consciousness of this mixture of love and hate in ourselves, we can survive seeing the same mixture in others and in the world around us. This seeing protects our core self because we accept our aggression; it finds a place to flow along with our loving and love's capacity to resurrect in the unlikeliest of places. Seeing shadows in ourselves, in our society, and in others leads us deeper toward the mystery of the light that comes into the world where the darkness comprehends it not (John 1). We descend to the archetypal level and beyond it to a reality we glimpse with our ego but never finally comprehend.

At the ego level, loving and goodness exist in us, in others and in the world around us on a par with other powers and principalities. It does not put out the bad or remove the hate or make everything better. God does not perform the miracle of changing this world into the kingdom of heaven. We believe that revolution will arrive in the future, as God's coming into the world a second time, but it is not here, now, rescuing the women in Bosnia from rape-camps, or the refugees of Rwanda from genocide, or the children after the Chernoble nuclear plant accident from living their lives maimed, or the homeless people on Broadway from never being able to take a shower when they choose.

On the ego level this light that enters the world from God fights as one of the world powers. It is not put out, and it is not triumphant. It empties itself into the world, and takes on worldly size, the real flesh of the actual world. Nor are we individually ever without the ambiguous mixture of our own love and hate. We can rescue personal bits of our shadow and integrate them into wider, more vigorous ego living. And we can make inroads to integrate parts of our group shadow. But at the archetypal level, that heart of darkness from which evil flows, or, as a client of mine sees evil, that glaring parching brightness that extinguishes any refreshing deep pool of blackness, what a little boy patient of Marian Milner calls "lovely shiny black," we cannot conquer evil at the ego level (Milner 1947-48, 63). No miracles end all suffering. Instead we get glimpses of light, glowing and fighting, and not being overcome by all the dark. We do small errands of good which actually change people's lives, but do not remove all the suffering life will bring them. At the ego level, hate and love remain ambiguously mixed together and shadowing each other. At the ego level, life is tragic in the precise meaning of the word tragic: two powers battle, of light and dark, love and hate, goodness and evil in mortal combat.

But at the deeper level, in us at the soul level, and at the deep soul that extends underneath all our social life, so that praying here for a woman there in Bosnia does make a difference to her, maybe not the difference we intended, but a real difference that none of us expected. At this deeper level, the light already shines eternally and cannot be put out. There we are planted, granted soil by the blood and body of God, living deep in the shining light which is given us as our homeland. We are no longer homeless. A home is given to each of us and when we pray we turn toward it.

On the ego level, each of us in our core self is one of millions, a cog in the big wheel, a speck of dust, a blip on the screen of time, countless and insignificant to which the forces of the world are indifferent. On the deeper level, each of us, in our core self, is irreplaceable, and for God each of us is a unique person, and the person is the only form in which revelation of this truth of the already conquering light can be given (Frank 1989, 137, 149, 155, 190). At that level we need all the aggression we have gathered from supporting our core self, from looking into the shadow, from accepting the moral ambiguity of life, for here the light shines out, radiates, communicating itself to us and through us to each other. We need all our aggression to receive this, depend on it, let it expand us and make us joyful. Otherwise we burn up.

At this level, we use our aggression to go on differentiating between ourselves and God. We need not identify with God, only receive God, make a house for God. One woman, for example, dreamt of having to choose in which color to take on bodily the outlining shape of the manger to house the Christ child and the Holy Family. We, like this dreamer, need to expand to house this inrushing current of light and its radiating outward to others and then back to us again and then back to the Giver. Here we depend our full weight, we lean into God. We fall back into God's supporting arms, with the burden of our full shadow, our full confusion of love and hate, and let the light rush through us into the world. Here the root impulse in our body of love and aggression join into one: we make glad and merry and go out to meet the One who advances into visibility.

For Congregation of the Holy Cross, Sisters of St. Dominic, Amityville, N.Y. 12/8/96.

References

Bollas, C. 1987. *The Shadow of the Object and the Unthought Known.* London: Free Association Press.

Frank, S. L. 1989. *The Light That Shineth in Darkness.* trans. Boris Jakim. Athens, Ohio: Ohio University Press.

Jung, C. G. 1959. *Aion. Collected Works,* vol. 9:2. trans. R. F. C. Hull. New York: Pantheon.

Klein, M. 1935. A contribution to the psychogenesis of the manic depressive state. Klein, M. 1975. *Love, Guilt, and Reparation & Other Works, 1921-1945.* New York: Seymour Lawrence/Delacorte Press, pp. 262-289.

Klein, M. 1952. Some theoretical conclusions regarding the emotional life of the infant. In Klein, M. 1975. *Envy and Gratitude & Other Works 1946-1963.* New York: Seymour Lawrence/Delacorte Press, pp. 61-93.

Kohut, H. 1977. *The Restoration of the Self.* New York: International Universities Press.

Marion, J.-L. 1991. Le mal en personne. *Prolégomène à la Charité.* Szikra à Giromagny: Mobile Matière, pp. 7-41.

Milner, M. 1947-48. Some signposts – blackness, joy, mind. Milner, M. 1987. *The Suppressed Madness of Sane Men.* London: Tavistock.

Ulanov, A. B. 1986/2002. The Christian fear of the psyche. And, The psychological reality of the demonic. *Picturing God.* Einsiedeln, Switzerland, pp. 5-23, 127-145.

Ulanov, A. B. 1987. The God you touch. *Christ and the Bodhisattva.* eds. D. Lopez and S. Rockefeller. Albany, N.Y.: Suny Press, pp. 117-140. Also in Ulanov, A. B. 1999. *Religion and the Spiritual in Carl Jung.* Mahwah, N.J.: Paulist.

Ulanov, A. B. 1993/1998. *The Female Ancestors of Christ.* Einsiedeln, Switzerland: Daimon.

Ulanov, A. B. and Ulanov, B. 1975. *Religion and the Unconscious*. Louisville, Ky.: John Knox/Westminster Press.

Ulanov, A. B. 1995. Destructiveness and the spiritual life. Cheney Lecture on tape. New Haven, Ct.: Yale Divinity School. See also Ulanov, A. B. 2002. *Finding Space: Winnicott, God, and Psychic Reality*. Louisville, Ky.: John Knox/Westminster Press, chapter 5.

Winnicott, D. W. 1965. *The Maturational Processes and the Facilitating Environment*. New York: International Universities Press.

Winnicott, D. W. 1971. *Playing and Reality*. London: Tavistock.

Winnicott, D. W. 1989. *Psycho-Analytic Explorations*. eds. C. Winnicott, R. Shepherd, M. Davis. London: Karnac.

Chapter 11

Dreams: Passages to a New Spirituality

Jung distinguishes his approach to dreams from all other schools of depth psychology by linking them to spirituality. Dreams act, he says, as "organs of information," as a Spiritus Rector that calls us back to our proper way. Dreams compensate our conscious view which tips, like a see-saw, to an extreme on one side and needs the balance of the other side which the dreams bring, thus restoring the self-regulating capacity of our psyche-soma (Jung 1934/1954, 153, para. 332; Jung 1948/1960, 250, 252, paras. 482, 487). But even more striking, Jung says, "A dream walks in like an animal" (Jung 1984, 94). It is not a facade or a disguise, but "a living thing ... like an animal with feelers, or many umbilical cords. We are moved by dreams, they express us and we express them, and there are coincidences connected with them" (ibid., 44; see also Jung 1961/1968, 248, para. 569).

Jung would definitely include in his view of dreams the insights of Masud Khan that there is such a thing as a "good dream" where we have a real experience in contrast to what one of my analysands calls her "dresser drawer dreams" that just dump the contents of the day, not unlike our disposing of junk mail in the waste basket, or, God help us, the space junk we unload to orbit around our planet. In the good dream we integrate into a coherent narrative what has so far been split-off or denied aspects of the self (Khan 1983, 44). A good dream occurs in what Khan calls the "dream space" which we enter when we construct a dream. This space is part of us, "an area where new experiences are initiated, to be affirmed or negated." The dream in this space holds potential "towards self-experience" (ibid., 45, 47). For example, here we experience rage, and it might lead us somewhere important. One woman dreamt of intensely yelling out at her sister, "I HATE YOU!" which felt mad to the dreamer, in both meanings of the word. But owning that feeling was rewarded by the next dream where her sister drove them into a primordial woods, into a bigger, elemental space of nature which holds both of them going together. If we are undertaking real experiences in dream space, we are much less likely to act out that rage into social space. We know the horrors of shooting innocent victims when there is no space to dream our rage, like Mr. Ferguson shooting passengers on the Long Island railroad, or the two little boys in Arkansas shooting their schoolmates. We act out in social space what we do not metabolise in dream space into our ongoing living.

Jung would agree with Khan that the "dreaming experience" is what counts, what rectifies, what guides the psyche-soma into the right path, and it is different from remembering a dream text. Khan says, "The dreaming experience is an entirety that actualises the self in an unknowable way. The dream text gets hold of some aspect of this dreaming experience and works into it the conflictual data from the *vécu* (remembered or repressed) of the person, to make a narrative that can be communicated, shared and interpreted. Dreaming itself is beyond interpretation" (ibid., 47).

Animal Root Impulse and Spirit

It is to this experience beyond interpretation that dreams conduct us. Jung calls it nature, the irrational, the animal soul. He says of a woman, she "has looked into the eyes of the animal, and so the animal soul has gone into her; she has been united with the animal, with the deepest part of the collective unconscious, and that, of course, is an unforgettable experience which will cling to her and which will inevitably cause a tremendous conflict in her life" (Jung 1976, 65). This nameless experience that is nature in us is the locus of Spirit at the end of our century and millennium.

For us, Spirit is "down," in contrast to earlier centuries when Spirit was "up" – rising above the chaos of clamouring instincts into an airy dimension where truth is distilled into pure reason, abstract and unmuddied by the vicissitudes of living (see also chapters 4 and 7). Then we had to sacrifice our animal impulses to discern a bigger order and a higher way above the compulsions of instinct. But now, we need to go down, to find the earth in us, the animal root-impulse of all our being, that which spontaneously with all the force of instinct reconnects us to our path in this life, and through it to the heart of being itself. The dreaming experience, hinted at in the dream text, becomes, in the good dream, this nameless otherness walking in calmly, boldly, occupying the dream space, like an animal appearing from the woods. (I looked up one day from working at my desk, and saw through the window a coyote looking back at me.)

Wild animals, for Jung, are the original appearances of the gods. Jung says, "A wild animal is a pious, law-abiding being who fulfills the will of God in the most perfect way" (Jung 1984, 37). These "doctor-animals" remain central to lively spiritual life, for the animal is the only devout creature that lives its own patterns to reach self-fulfillment (see Jung 1988, vol. 1, 529; see also von Franz 1970/1992, 57, 64). Indeed, Jung goes so far as to say, "When animals are no longer included in the religious symbol or creed, it is the beginning of the dissociation between religion and nature. Then there is no mana in it. As long as the animals are there, there is life in the symbol ..." (Jung 1976, 284). Many of us at the end of our twentieth century have been living decades in this dissociation of religion from nature. We fear religion like a wild animal, that it will trap us and make us dead.

Dreams can restore us to this animal impulse of experience, the dreaming experience that the dream text hints at. From this instinctive source new life emerges, relaxed moments of mutuality, where we see afresh and surprise ourselves. One woman awoke with amazement that in her dream she was "Singing! Singing! Imaginative earthworm! O earthworm!"

The animal follows God's will because instinct guides and contains its life; it has no choice; it does what it is supposed to do. As human animals, we too belong to a way that is specific to each of us, that is our one way, our right path. But such a path does not unfold automatically with the clicking into place of instinct. We know a hiatus, a gap, a pause that demands our conscious reflection and response to instinct. Our choice. We cannot come directly from or to the mystery at the heart of life and at the heart of our selves. We need symbolic discourse to communicate experience of this mystery. This space of pause, of hiatus is essential to the human animal. We must create our way in order to find it. It is there but not fixed in place. Our searching and creating calls it into view. Our response makes us see that it awaits us. We cannot find it if we are not creating it. But when it finds us, we know that we did not invent it.

Bion describes the necessity of this response in his abstruse notion of beta elements needing the alpha function to transform emotional experience into something personal – a thought, or a dream, an activity that can be put to use in living. Beta elements are bits of undigested experience lying around in our psyches, so to speak, that we have not transformed into live moments. The evidence of their existence is found in our psychosomatic complaints, our sexual acting out, in proneness to accidents. In order to transform these disturbing bits into liveable energy, instead of just surviving them – like the effects of trauma over something terrible that happened to us, or something terrible that resulted from nothing happening to us when something should have – we must yield, choose, passionately desire to come into the lumination of truth: "O."

"The fundamental point" Bion says, "is, can you find what suits *you?*" (Bion 1978, 265). Can we find the way that is our path? That means resisting slapping in an answer that really is only a "space stopper" to "prevent the flood" of "the fact" of a "fundamental reality" through "the gap" which exists in that pause, that hiatus place between us and animal root-impulse (ibid., 266). If we can wait and not know, achieve what the Buddhists call the no-mind, the emptiness from which the wheel turns, an open-ended curiosity is revealed; it is ever-expanding.

Like Jung, Bion says we resist openness to our animal root-impulse: "you have to be open to impressions. Unfortunately the whole of our training seems to be at the sacrifice of our animal characteristics or our animal ability" (ibid., 274). For "the only thing that seems basic is not so much what we are to *do,* but what we are to *be.* That is why it is so important…" to be "capable of what I call passionate love" (ibid., 276). "We should get as near as possible to feeling it is the first time we have ever seen the patient" (ibid., 5). Or, I would add, the dream, and not know all about it ahead of time according to a theory. The theory gives a map; it cannot substitute for going to the territory.

Winnicott writes of the goal of seeing everything afresh: "Come at the world creatively, create the world; it is only what you create that has meaning for you" (Winnicott 1958, 101). Matisse echos this insight when he says of painting: "The effort needed to see things without distortion takes something very like courage; and this courage is essential to the artist, who has to look at everything as though he saw it for the first time: he has to look at life as he did when he was a child and, if he loses that faculty, he cannot express himself in an original, that is, a personal way" (Flamm 1978, 140).

For us, who do not possess Matisse's genius, his linking of the words original and personal directs us to see things afresh, for the first time; to perceive in an original way is to perceive in a personal way. For each of us is an original; we each possess an idiosyncratic way of looking at the world, derived from the particularities of our instinctual inheritance, our time in history, in culture, our particular family biographies, and what peculiar combination of archetypal images arise in our psyches (see also Bollas on "idiom" 1992, 30, 64). We must not perjure our originality by trying to be a carbon-copy of someone else, no matter how much we admire their superiority. That imitation amounts to defying the will of God, in religious language. We must risk going to the territory of original perception.

Going to that territory is going to the source, to the nameless level of living that does not yield easy translation into words. It touches us in that one spot Freud identified in every dream, as the "unplumable navel, as it were, that is its point of contact with the unknown" (Freud 1900/1958, 143). Here a different kind of knowing obtains, that is better called a kind of living that spirituality has known about for thousands of years. This knowing is Bion's "passionate loving," a pouring out of the soul, an overflowing, a *bouversé* of seeing, serving, sounding, honoring something transcendent to ourselves. This passionate loving springs from our animal root-impulse, and takes us into living, not a knowing about, not an explaining but a participating. No organised religion, whether mosque, temple, or church ,can survive if it does not include in its vision the seeing of this realm that dreams offer, that the arts display.

Dreams try to maneuver us into alignment with the fact of fundamental reality, by pushing us through compensation to see what we left out, and to locate our specific human situation at the time of dreaming in the archetypal surround so that the right instinctive attitude can again be evoked. That is what cures us if we consent to it. That is what issues in our response which contributes to the human family's wisdom of what to do in the face of this specific suffering. When reintroduced to the precincts of an archetypal motif, we see afresh that our suffering is not just our isolated failing or burden, but part of the human condition. That community of the large human family triggers our instinctive response to which we can then consent (or refuse). The dream brings us the archetypal motif, to convey, says Jung, that your "suffering was not only man's fate but God's fate" (Jung 1984, 130). By the dream putting us into the situation of the ordinary woman or man of all times, it releases "instinctive powers.. partly psychological, partly physiological, and ... the whole disposition of the body can be changed" (ibid.). We strengthen our animal courage to endure, to push through, to resolve conflict.

Ethics and Spirit

Our ethics and our sense of the Spirit and the transcendent change. By enlisting its archetypal depths, our notions of the ethical community expand. Community means others in our present life. It includes as well persons of the past whose representations may come to us symbolically, such as authors we love, teachers in history we admire – a Socrates, a Michelangelo, a Teresa of Avila, as well as our great grandmother whose covered wagon traveled south from Baltimore to Texas.

But community extends even further. Community includes archetypal "objects," that antiseptic word for other people invented by this crazy discipline of ours dedicated to improving human life. How odd to call subjects "objects." But here the word helps, because archetypal others take their places as part of our community. Not now the famous of human history, nor the personal ancestor, but the primordial – our ape-mother, our panther-soul, our bear-spirit, the primordial man, the ancient woman of days – these figures too come to make up our community, all the way back to even our animal ancestors. We know this. We just don't acknowledge it after childhood. What evidence do I offer? The favorite children's game: What animal are you? Your immediate association will tell you your own doctor-animal, the one into whose company your dreams may escort you to bring about healing. And the animal that must be present in your spiritual life if it is to carry mana.

Ethics changes then from obligation or duty to others in the here and now to participation in the human viewed *sub specie aeternitatis*. Our ethics includes perceiving and taking up our residence at the deepest possible layer of animal soul. It is this level of "common rhythm which allows the individual to communicate his feelings and strivings to mankind as a whole" (Jung 1950/1966, 105, para. 161). A woman dreams, "I look out my bedroom window and the pond is full of hippos, rhinos, seals and whales."

Spirit goes deeper than the cerebrospinal system which supports our intellect, to include the sympathetic nervous system where psychic contents "express themselves only in symbolic actions," ushering us into the company of the collective, of all living things, beyond ourselves, delivering us into emotional connection with what the Buddha expounds as compassion for all sentient beings (Jung 1984, 335).

Not only do dreams make our ethics change; dreams change our connection to Spirit from which ethics springs. As I said earlier, for us, now, Spirit is down "and just there the most primitive instincts come up" (Jung 1984, 324). By placing our specific human situation of the moment in the archetypal stream, dreams carry us down into another current. Dreams thus can release us from our repetition compulsion to usher us into creative repetition which reorganises our response in the present around the new fact of the unknown. Linking our ego power to an originating power, a conjunction of known and unknown, of now and eternally forever, of animal, human and divine, releases us into a state of promise (Jung 1984, 131).

Wound to Animal Root-Impulse

All very well and good. But if Spirit is down what happens if we are cut off from our animal root-impulse? Or if our connection to it is damaged? wounded? uprooted? all but severed? This problem illustrates that Spirit always desires the flesh: "if you love life, you want to live really, not as a mere promises hovering above things" (Jung 1988, 508). There is no individuation, no realisation of Spirit in life, without the body which is our animal root in the "definite facts which make you an individual, a self that is yourself and nobody else ... No individuation can take place ... without the animal, a very dark animal coming up from primordial slime ... is absolutely indispensable" (ibid., 63-64).

We feel the wound to our root-impulse in two opposite

ways. Traditional religions carry little mana for us; we fear being trapped in soulless rote behaviour. The mana power falls into our ego ideal and persecutes us with a fixed and false religiosity, dictating terms to be accomplished, or else damnation, excommunication, ostracism. Our symbol becomes an idol, rigid, lifeless, demanding compliance. Spirit dances out. Or, we feel wounded by an inability to land anywhere and plant roots; we float above every incarnation into a concrete spiritual devotion and practice, wafting to and fro on the eddies of new age spirituality, avoiding the tough fact of evil or just projecting it all into a lump in a predicted armageddon, or comet, or explosion of light on a certain day.

I find this uprootedness from the animal root-impulse, this wound to the spirit in the flesh, much more frequently now than in earlier decades of my clinical practice. Its manifestation is odd, for the people suffering this wound are often robust, talented, functional, or at least appear to be. But inside they experience themselves as falling apart, on the edge of tumbling into despair which they detour around by drinking benders or frantic clothes buying. They look normal but suffer from psychic impotence. If treatment succeeds, they reach the place where they can speak of not feeling individually alive, bereft of generative power.

People wounded in the root-impulse of their being feel adrift at the center of themselves and show it in ways that leave them poised between confusion and order. Their talk interrupts itself going off in different strands and direction. Their perception ranges wide, and shows attention to texture, slant of light, a pause in another's sentence. But it is as if they cannot assemble all their impressions into coherence. One woman's dream captures her sense of chaos: "I feel confusion about the math or orientation and see no North, South, East or West drawn out on a circle." She lacks a mental compass to orient herself in reality. Nonetheless, the picture her psyche gives her about her confusion begins to order her, locate her. The dream showed her a picture of herself before any ordering had occurred. The dream returns her to the original not-knowing place; she needs to see it, digest it, begin. I found myself saying, You have arrived; your core self is a plethora of plenty, a confusion of plenty. I mean that she had more than enough, a richness, not a lack, and needed to withstand her prosperity. Order would emerge in its way, not her way or my way, from the whole, a compass from the encompassing allness of every direction.

Another evidence of the wound to the root-impulse congregates around sleeping and waking. One woman dreamed repeatedly of her sleep being interrupted. Her mother, her sister, her husband, someone comes in, makes noise, disregards her sleeping and wakes her up, starts talking about what she should be doing that day. She awakes in the dream consumed with rage! "I don't exist! I am disregarded! I don't count! I can just be picked up or put down at the other's whim! They don't even think they are doing anything wrong!" She protests at this breaking of her natural rhythm that cuts her off from her true awakening. The dreams take her down to this wound to the rhythm of her being, which she also had overlooked, not seen, disregarded, much as the other persons did not respect her sleeping-waking cycle. The rage she felt overshadowed the wound and made her feel crazy. She feared her rage swamping her, so she dissociated it, put it away from her consciousness. For in her childhood, if she was not immediately cooperative with her mother's plans, for example, her mother got mad or hurt and called her selfish, dull. She felt cut off from vital connection to her mother. But if she complied with her mother's rhythms, she did so at the expense of her native body impulses. She could only rest in a withdrawn state, out of contact with others, but then felt denied any nutriment. When the dreams

showed her the picture of her being interfered with in her ordinary psyche-soma rhythm of waking and resting, her rage made
sense to her. Dreams returned her to feeling it and brought her
the origin of the rage: the spirit could not inhabit the body as
its thrumming pulse, its beat, its capacity to swing.

Some analysands bring the root-impulse problem through
sleep right into the session itself. One man sought treatment
because he felt divided up in his sexual orientation. When with
women as a sexual male, he felt driven to perform, to squeeze
his whole self into a persona. Exhausted, he found no rest
anywhere and soon petered out. He would dream of women
only as sound, like a horrific scream as a woman was thrown
out a high window, as if his animating connection to being was
murdered. When with men as a sexual male, he felt no place to
live what he called "the male part of me." He could relax and
meander around to see what spontaneously occurred to him,
but he could not use his force, or any ruthlessness. After some
months we began to get somewhere, I believed, when in sessions he would suddenly go to sleep. Forsaking both personae,
he broke a style of reporting, and a style of anguish in fearing he
was neither this nor that, for neither sexual gender alternative
really fit, by falling into sleep as if going back to a space before
the split. And we can see how close sexuality is to Spirit. For
he wanted to be in his life with all the energy sexual impulse
provides. Sex makes us exist as body, for the moment closing
that hiatus space, that "distance" between us and ourselves,
"in an experience of completeness exactly contrary," says the
philosopher Ricoeur, "to the incompleteness of perception and
spoken communication" (Ricoeur 1970, 382-383). This falling
asleep, I felt, was reaching to a beginning point, where he could
slowly find and create his own path. He however was dismayed
– what a waste of money and time to be sleeping in his analytical hour! – and broke off treatment. I had hoped in reaching

a formless place the root-impulse that fed his sexuality might re-mend.

Two other patients, both women, used sleep to signal to themselves, and then to me, that they were getting it right. Whatever insight they reached was striking into the core of them, all the way down to the root of their being. When one woman felt the stem of her chronic panic anxiety was reached, her eyes would roll up and she would almost sleep right there in the moment. The second woman would swoon when an insight hit her, all but faint away, as if something literally struck into her. Remaining quiet and bodily still, she would wait until she took the arrow right into her heart, so to speak. For both women, these sleep events were frightening and unnerving. But the unconsciousness they fled to as refuge served as entry point to the new. Each time, something took root and it bore fruit.

Another group of patients describe the wound to the animal root-impulse in words that convey they fall into an empty space, one without shelter or ignition. Instead, they stop dead. One woman says, "I feel there is nowhere to go and nowhere to come back to." Another woman voices her distress as, "I don't know what the next step is, or how to contribute." A man says, "I don't know how to start; I never have an idea or thought or desire to work from."

That place of animal root-impulse is the root we grow from, from which all our inherited potential flows and which must be engaged if we are to unfold into the real world as a real person. Root-impulse is the animal in us. It is the spine where kundalini energy mounts through successive body zones to bloom into the transcendent. It is the stem from which we flower or wither, for Spirit inhabits a body and must find roots in the body to thrive. The psyche needs a body and the Spirit needs a psyche-body to incarnate. Animal root-impulse is not elusive; it defines us, connects body and Spirit; we experience it as aliveness, readiness to be.

As human animals, at that place of root-impulse, a pause, a hiatus dwells, making space for our response. Unlike our animal friends, we bring something else into living in addition to instinctive spontaneity. We bring aggression and reflection. Part of our relation to the good object is our refusal of it. "This refusal of it is part of the process of creating it" according to Winnicott (Winnicott 1963, 182; also cited by Khan 1972, 302). We can say yes or no, and choose for or against, and do so many times over, over and over, given many chances, not just second chances but many, many chances. But not infinite chances. Instead of surmounting this root-impulse, going against it so as not to be compelled by it as in earlier centuries, at the end of our century we must consciously choose for or against this life in the body, in matter, in nature, this nudge of Spirit in our flesh toward what matters – a specific insight, change of attitude, embrace of action, another person. But, Jung says, "we would rather accept anything in the world, any devil or any hell, than accept ourselves in our particular concreteness. That is the thing of which we are most afraid" (Jung 1976, 86).

Our root-impulse can be blighted by lack of attentive loving it into being, by a failure to witness and welcome the unfolding of our unique person. Childhood traumas can inflict damage to this basic rhythm of being. The fast pace of our society, with its tremendous opposites of glamour and glitz on the one hand and utter misery and poverty on the other, encourage our not pausing, our failing to see, our choosing against the root-impulse of our being. We choose not to represent to ourselves what we experience. Instead we pop a pill or a drug, to wipe out the depression instead of hearing the message it brings; we hurry on, keep to the schedule, choose to remain in ignorance (see Kristeva 1995, 6, 9, 27).

We can refuse our animal impulse, or fasten on split-off parts of it, as struggles with food, alcohol, with any kind of addiction testify. Although our dreams generously return us time and again to the space where impulse and reflection may join, we can refuse their offering. At the one extreme, we obliterate the space of hiatus, where we stay silent and unknowable before the dream and it before us, like an animal stepping into a clearing. We refuse to pause until all our responses gather us up toward a self-experience. Instead, we hurl ourselves into language, shedding the fantasy, the mystery clinging to the dream and degrade our response to it by reductive interpretation. The dream that offers us potential space to be gathered into symbolic discourse, we violate by reducing to symbolic equation. A woman dreams, "A huge snake is interested in me. I fear it." Instead of pursuing conversation with this other, this big reptile with its slow blinking eye, we nail it into an equation: the snake means thus and thus. Language labels instead of translating (see Khan 1971; see also Hillman and McLean 1997).

At the other extreme, we so enlarge the space of the pause and reflection, that we sacrifice our animal impulse by never spontaneously responding. We must think it over, look at it this way and that, consider, reconsider, check with others' opinions, find out the right thing to do. Meanwhile, a crucial liveliness that touched us through the dream is lost. This endless hesitating wounds the animal root-impulse.

A Wound Within a Wound

A whole animal root-impulse contains both aggression and love. Within the wounds to our animal root-impulse, a vital other one lies hidden: the splitting away of our aggressiveness from love, and the aggression becomes destructiveness. That

295

ruthless energy does not fuse with our wish to connect, to join, to enjoy congress with others. Conjunction is not achieved, only dissociation, so that our aggression runs wild, does not get included as good ignition for the new, or as the durable energy to endure, as the staying power to persevere and make actual our vision of the good. Love falls into sentimentality. Soap operas substitute for life, gossip for genuine conversation, withdrawnness or power plays for jubilant communication. We do not feel quite real and the world and others do not feel real either. Dream and reality blur. We either pull our punches – fearing that if we let loose with all-out energy to go after what our animal root-impulse initiates, we would damage the other or ourselves. Or, we lose our concern for the other and for the consequences of our actions even to ourselves. Ruthlessness reigns. We roll over the other, and over what we cherish, in a fit of anger, or an urge to gratify, and afterwards say, "I don't know what got into me."

The wound to our root-impulse often results from our fear of our own ruthlessness, the animal in us who goes after what it wants in a simple instinctual way. The problem is the animal is not joined up to the human. We fear this impulse and separate ourselves from it and then lack the verve, the clinching emotion that makes us feel vibrantly alive, unable to meet that first of all great spiritual commandments – to love God with all our heart, soul, mind and strength. Only then can love for ourselves be given to our neighbor. Examples will help.

The man who said, I don't know how to start, elaborated on his emptiness through a powerful image that came to him from a childhood experience. A favorite way to play when he was a boy was to set up his room as if it were a store. But no one ever came in to buy anything. He felt then, and still does now as an adult artist, that he was expending all his energy on the stage set and not the living. He said, "Something is not right.

I'm surfing as if my life were T.V. channels. I set everything up but then I don't do it. I am not knowing what to do!" He felt all this despite successful work in his career and discharging his obligations to his large family. That was the problem. The life he was living felt to him as if it were all obligations. He felt unregenerated in our culture, seeing its problems and wearying of trying to transform them. He feared he would pass onto his daughter his prejudices. He felt broken down, without inner impetus. "I'm afraid where it would lead if I really let the other shoe drop."

He remembered this childhood room of the play store. It now seemed to him, "My life is like that empty room. In this dusty room I don't do anything. The tape has run out." "Stay there," I said. "See if something generates." He did. He stayed in that nothing place, empty, the boy doing nothing, the beginnings of contemplation. Several things bubbled up, but I will focus on the dream that came which showed him running through a huge, magnificent, but dirty old train station to change trains, to make a connection to a train leaving the station. He had arrived on one train and now was running through the station to catch another that was about to depart. As he runs more deeply into the station he sees more and more uninhabited rooms. But when he gets to the new departing train, he is told he does not have the right transfer ticket and must go back to get it. He had turned his ticket in when he arrived, but failed to get the receipt. He is furious.

The dream shows him this picture in response to his contemplating nothingness. We must ask who took the picture and what it means. What is the right receipt in order for him to get on his way? What does he need to hold onto in order to make the connection? And what does he need to go back for, what is unfinished and needs to be received before he can leave for the new? His fury at not having made the connection lets loose some of that ruthless destructiveness that is not yet bound up in his sense of where he wants to go. His willingness to stay in the empty, dusty room makes space for that destructive ruthless energy because he can let go of and even destroy the stage-set his ego is always manufacturing. He lets go of the ego fictions he has been imposing on his life. He goes into that space of wound to the root-impulse and spontaneously the psyche responds with a dream, begins the process of regenerating life. This feels like grace – if we can receive it, and know we have the receipt for it. He lets his ego be taken down to the empty place. Instead of being dragged there by his neurosis, he consents.

A second example is given in the dream of a woman who has had a lot of analysis who just that day was saying to some-one that dreams can give us missing pieces of ourselves, and dreaming them means that they are now accessible. She awoke quite shaken by what her psyche gave her (and thinking in the future she should keep her mouth shut). I will shorten her long dream.

"I am dreaming the gap in me," she said. "I can't do a dance movement. I'm trying and I can't. Then X, a man dancer who moves like an animal, whom I greatly admire and think is a heal-ing presence, says to me, 'Yes you can. It is that you won't.' I feel plunged into awful confusion. I feel annihilated. It feels like I can't, but X says I won't. I am so upset I do not protest. We walk together but he does not accept my inability. He changes it by his view that I am refusing, which means I must be capable and am not helpless.

"Then we are on the road of my childhood house. [She is middleaged.] X is driving and backs up the car very swiftly down the road, even with oncoming cars. Danger! A swift regression. I see right away in the dream that we have traveled away from my childhood home – the framework where I felt I can't – to the place where I won't, to the place before I feel I can't. In the dream it takes the utmost concentration to reach this place.

"Then I am alone in a hotel lobby and see a boyfriend ruthlessly, abruptly rejected, without feeling, by his girlfriend. He hauls off and punches her in the face with his fist. There is a loud CRACK. Maybe he has broken her jaw or her cheekbone. Her face immediately rises into a huge black and blue bruise the size of her whole cheek. I run to help her and yell 'Get a doctor!' She was too blunt and angry to her boyfriend and he hit her back. But he's still wrong to hit her.

"A little girl is forgotten. Her father likes boys best and her sister has an eating problem, but she, the little girl, is forgotten. I comfort her, hug her, and get ice for the girlfriend's face."

The dream takes the dreamer to her worst place, a gap of confusion and helplessness, and takes the place apart, getting under her inability to dance and shows why she refused. The dream takes her back before her defenses were organized into dissociation (helplessness and inability), to the root-impulse over which she can pause, reflect, and can choose to align with. X, the animal man, the healer, says, "Yes you can dance, you can be spontaneous, move with the rhythm, the beat; you are not stuck."

The dream shows two views coinciding: the dream-ego's which is confused and helpless, and X's who personifies the animal-root in her. Like a good animus figure, he makes a bridge for her to the Self (Ulanov and Ulanov 1994, 10-13). He tells her she can go back to where she can dance again, where she can respond to the native beat, and thus take responsibility for her dancing, or not dancing, no longer feeling she is unable. But to get there she must get out of the childhood mind, drive backwards, regress, to the time before her defenses were set. Once there, the dream shows her the trauma – the punching of the feminine in the face, breaking her cheek. She ruthlessly cut off her destructiveness and it breeds violence. The girlfriend ruthlessly dumps her boyfriend. The boyfriend ruthlessly retaliates by punching her with his fist.

Once the dream-ego sees that the gap in her confidence to dance mirrors the gap between the feminine and ruthless destructiveness, she is then shown an earlier trauma of what did not happen and should have. The little-girl feminine, who should have been included, has been left out. The father likes only boys, and the older sister – the older feminine – overeats to make up for this deficit, and the mother is nowhere to be found.

The Transcendent and Ethics

The dream occupied the dreamer for a long time, not only because it showed her the root of her woundedness, but also because it gathered to her the transcendent, in at least two ways, to help heal the wound. The first meaning of transcendence is that it always goes beyond our ego, reaching across to another starting-point. The dream presents another point of view that inhabits us, but which we do not originate. In this dream, it is the figure X who contradicts the dreamer's adamant conviction about her inability to dance. X is the kind of dream figure who represents some unknown that lives in us and has views about us, right there in our subjective interior, but which exists objectively beyond us and our power of invention.

Through X, the dream discloses another location from which to see our ego-stance, and thus dislocates us, in the best of ways, making us see how we impose our ego-fictions on life, patterns which we repeat and repeat and get stuck in. In my opening quotation from Jung he insists the dream is other, an animal, a live thing, that expresses us as we do it, "and there are coincidences connected with dreams." The coincidence here is the collision of the views of the dream-ego and the animal man, X. Usually we just identify with the dream-ego and think, "Oh yes, this is me, I know this place where I am unable to dance." But the psyche presents a picture to the ego that shows a view-point that transcends the ego's. The picture shows the world beyond the ego, the space behind the ego; we see that we could become conscious of our ego stance, rather than simply being identified with it.

The dream offers us a new kind of consciousness from the *coincidentia oppositorum* – the coinciding of two points of view. I am the subject with one view, and this object addresses me with another view, and both views belong to me. X is the subject with one view, and I am the object of his attention with another view. This converging of two views in the same person breeds a bigger, fatter, more supple consciousness which houses opposites and makes things more complex. The philosopher Husserl said something similar in his concept of the *époche*, the bracketing off of what we know in order to look at the phenomena before us, and in his conclusion that consciousness is always a partnership between subject and object. We are not conscious as a subject without simultaneously being linked to an object. The trauma was that the little girl was left out of this mutuality. She was the first gap. The second gap intervened between the dreamer's sense of her feminine self and her own ruthless energy. The third gap, the one she was conscious of, interfered between her wish to dance and her conviction she was unable to do it. To see from the dream all these gaps greatly enlarged the dreamer's consciousness and reconnected her to the animal root-impulse existing in her.

The advent of this enlarged consciousness changes our ethics. No longer can we conceive of ourselves as isolated subjects, separate, distanced from some object out there, separated and isolated. We are connected by virtue of our perceiving. Thus in this dream, the dreamer is also X, even though X's beliefs differ from hers (see Jung 1948/1960, 267-270, paras. 510-516). The view that transcends my view exists inside of me, alongside of my views. If I can get empty enough of my identification with my conscious perspective to receive the dream, it will change me. I can no longer act on the basis of one view, but must take into account other points of view, the neighbors whom I must love as myself, both the inner neighbor who lives with me and is not me and the outer neighbor with whom I live. I believe this is what Jung means when he writes, "In the deepest sense we all dream *not out of ourselves* but out of what lies *between us and the other*" (Jung 1973, 9/29/34, 171).

Ethically this change of consciousness places us in a network of interdependence. We see reality differently, and must act always keeping in mind the unknown other, the intimate neighbor who is part of our structure of consciousness. The dislocation of our ego delivers us into a territory that transcends the ego but which we can only perceive by seeing through the ego, seeing the space behind it, accepting its relocation as belonging to the whole. Jung says, "One cannot individuate without being with other human beings ... Being an individual is always being a link in a chain ..." (Jung 1988, 102; see also chapter 13).

This woman's dream shows a second meaning of transcendence as it pictures her taking action in the second half of the dream. Whatever spirituality is, we know from our glimpses along the frontier with the transcendent that it wants to step over into living. As Jung says, "the spiritual is just there [where] the most primitive instincts come up" (Jung 1984, 324). The spiritual needs a locale in space and time, a body in which to live, in the small, particular matter of our lives – the decisions, attitudes, actions, reflections that we make every day. The other in our dreams needs our small dislocated ego in order to become real in this life in this world. Dreams salute and solicit our answering consciousness. Without that, nothing changes. Jung writes: "Our dreams present an image, much in the same way as nature allows a plant to grow, and it is up to us to draw conclusions" (Jung 1950/1966, para. 161).

> And our dreams are like windows that allow us to look in ... to that psychological process which is continually going on in our unconscious. It is a process of continual transformation with no end if we do not interfere. It needs our conscious interference to bring it to a goal ... Otherwise, it is like the eternal change of the seasons in nature, a building up and a pulling down, integration and disintegration without end ... from which nothing comes unless a human consciousness interferes and realizes the result ... the revelations are without issue if consciousness doesn't ... grasp the treasure brought upon the wave of the unconscious (Jung 1988, 236-237).

If we pause, reflect, respond, try to understand, to stand under the dream and make something of it for our living in the world, we knit together again our animal root-impulse with the pause, the hiatus of consciousness where we reflect, respond, choose. In that joining the hidden wound between our love and destructiveness may also mend. Then we may each of us dream for the world, bring into the world the new, the missing connection, the energy that arises spontaneously out of being, the presence that enables.

Dreams meet us at the frontier of the seen and the unseen. Even in crazy dreams, the psyche reaches to us, bidding us see life from another point of view, while retaining our own. Right on that frontier we can feel all of life is a dream, and we are asked to make something substantial from it. Every night dreams offer us this space. Every morning we can live the spirit into our lives.

Collective Examples of the Wounds

Our animal root-impulse includes a ruthless instinctive energy which feels destructive to us unless joined to loving, to making unions, to binding in relationships one to another. When we are wounded in our root-impulse we fear this ruthless energy. It can run loose and endanger us or what we love. But without the component of ruthlessness that adds zest and excitement, we feel futile, unreal, going nowhere, with nowhere to return to. We experience the dissociation in collective life as random violence, even as evil. In the city where I live we suffered last year from an epidemic of slashings of strangers on the streets and on the subways. A sixty-year-old woman and a twenty-one-year-old pregnant woman were two of the victims. The slashings turned out to be initiation rites for a gang of teenagers called the Bloods. My fantasy of the meaning of this act was that these kids never knew a fusion of eros and ruthless destructive energy, never felt fully alive, so they needed an extreme act, a great sensation to feel real, one marked by actual blood that was linked to the eros of belonging to each other in a gang. No space existed between the real and the imaginal, so the blood had to be tangible. Further, the blood bound them in their guilt, together outside the law, making belonging to the inside of the group all the more binding.

A second example comes from a Rap and Rock concert, also on the East Coast, the audience mainly white teenagers and middle-class kids. In the first half of the concert the music connected and made the kids feel alive, excited, jumping up and down, thrilled, their juices running. This kind of primitive love – for being one of the crowd, for the liveliness the music represented at the heart of life, has destructiveness in it, too. We experience it as instinctive excitement, motility, having to move, to discharge energy, dance it, tap our feet, drum our fingers, nod in rhythm (Winnicott 1950). The concert set this energy flowing, but then came intermission and the resetting of the stage for the next musicians. So suddenly the energy had nowhere to go. The kids had been brought up to behave, but the energy got the best of them. With no channel to put the energy into while they sat around, they idly began to pull at the grass, then to pull it up and throw it around. Then they threw rocks. Then they tore up the fence, and finally the stage. There was no channel offered for all this hot stuff to flow into, and no training of the imagination to invent forms for it on the spot. What the music got going in the kids, kept going, in the ruthless fashion of no regard for consequences to themselves or to others. The second half of the concert never took place. The stage was destroyed. The concert was closed. No one took thought as to how to provide for this energy, to bind it in some social form, some collective channel that would join it with the love for music the kids felt.

How then are we to arrive at a point where the wounds to our animal root-impulse and to the wound within the wound of the splitting off of ruthless energy from our love can be healed? Here we focus on dreams returning us to this point. And they do. They return us to the point where the fusion of love and destructiveness can again happen. The man who sat in the image of his dusty room, empty of initiative, was given a subsequent dream that told him he needed to receive something that would allow him to leave the old station for the new. He needed to receive something to get on his way. He needed to have done something. The ball is tossed into his court for his response about what this could be. The woman who was told she could dance if only she would, was driven backwards to a place out of reach of childhood complexes, to discover that because the girl child had been forgotten and needed still to be loved for herself, the grown-up girlfriend had dissociated from her own

305

ruthlessness and acted it out against her boyfriend who ruthlessly punched her in return.

Return and Arrival

Dreams can return us to the empty space back before defenses are formed; there our ego is outstripped, made to empty itself. This place is fearful. We feel unhinged, asked to give up not just our fictions with which we make a world with images of directions of north, south, east and west, or maps of conscious and unconscious, but even more. We are asked to renounce the very thought forms which conceive of order in terms of this mental compass. It is impossible to go to this space without feeling one is losing one's mind. The therapeutic relationship helps but rarely cures, rarely heals to change the whole procedure of living. For that we must give up, renounce, let go, be taken down again to the animal, to the root, to receive the beat of life pulsing through us, there in the slime from which we once emerged. To do that – to concede, to bow one's head – is possible only if we cede our dependence on something greater. So just there where the primitive instincts come up is where Spirit dwells. We cover our mouth in the face of the greater, the beyond, the vast, that which encompasses all we know and do. Dreams can contain us as we make this fearful journey and thus offer us a chance of reconnection not only to the animal root-impulse with all its ruthlessness, but also to that space where we pause and respond to whomever, or whatever it is that made us as dreaming creatures, to that authoring presence which transcends even our dreaming.

Here is a vivid example of a woman reconnecting to a root animal impulse in a time of utmost crisis. Her large life earnings from decades of hard work had been stolen by the man she loved who managed her money and willed it to others when he died. Consumed by rage, her heart hurt, and she plotted to kill the people who were to inherit her money. She was unable to work, to think of anything else. Self-recriminations for leaving her money in his hands only added fuel to the fire. Planning to sue brought little relief. She was in a desperate state, bursting with outraged indignation and murderous impulses. The psyche responded with this image: she saw herself swallowing a huge sharp-footed steer, but its hooves still protruded from her mouth and she was staring down, she said, "looking right into its asshole!" The image gave her ways to contain and not act out her rage – she charted her days by where the steer was, farther down into her belly, or burping up again. The image allowed her not to be run over by her ferocity and lose all feeling, which she still possessed for the man she had loved. The image of the steer allowed her to process what she was experiencing without being dragged under. She was immensely impressed by the arrival of this image, and felt "it came from somewhere beyond me."

That "somewhere beyond" sounds the presence of the Spirit stealing in, or being there all the time, waiting for us to arrive. Whether or not we are religious in any defined denominational sense, we can only surrender the primacy of the ego, while still retaining its capacities, in relation to something beyond us that is also with us. From a therapeutic point of view, this sur-render feels like a drastic regression. We return to the point of rupture from our root-impulse, from the stalk of our true self from which we grow, from the ground-plan of what could have unfolded as our cohesive self, from the Self which Jung names as the center of the whole psyche. This is not just a pre-oedipal ego; it is pre-ego, a return to what Balint calls the basic fault (Balint 1968, 18-28).

This return, looked at from our ego point of view is losing our mind, losing the thought-forms, the ego functions, the structures which construct our personal and shared world, in order to get to the hurt which fixated our development and got covered over with rigid defenses. This return is very hard to do from the analytical point of view. It requires total dependence on the analyst which comes naturally when we are a child, but which is fraught with ambivalence when we are adults. As adults it feels to us like a dangerous regression from which we might never return. And every analyst has foibles, which as adults we see and fear and use to resist the downward-going road to the rupture place. For how could we depend on such a weak reed who will inevitably fail us, not out of intention or malice, but simply because of finitude, of limits, faults? Thus I question whether the mutative agent, that which cures, is the introjection of the object of the analyst (see also chapters 1, 9, 14, 16). Change comes with the help of the personal mediation of the analyst, but it is the new from the "somewhere beyond" that does the healing. But all that is mere talk, and not persuasive, when we stand before the fearful regression to the nothing place.

But from the point of view of Spirit, such a regression, such a drastic return, such a destabilization of the ego, is heralded as an advance, an arrival at zero-point, what Zen Buddhism calls breakthrough, and the 13th century Buddhist Døgen calls "dropping mind and body," what the New Testament calls becoming like a little child, which is necessary if we are to be amazed by grace. For we reach another order of mind. We have lost our old mind based on ego, and entered a new knowing which brings ego as offering. Emptiness is not empty, we discover, but a source place. Jung says of this arrival,

> "The 'taming of the beast' ... is indeed a long process and coincides with the dissolution of *egohood*. What you call 'deselving' I

call 'becoming a self': what previously seemed to be 'ego' is taken up into a greater dimension which dwarfs and surrounds me on all sides, and which I cannot grasp in its totality. In this connection ... [we] rightly quote Paul ... : 'For in [God] we live, and move, and have our being' (Acts 17:28). This experience ... is vouchsafed to us only if we give up the ego as supreme authority and put ourselves wholly under the will of God" (Jung 1975, 28/March/1955, 235).

On our way back to the source point, Jung says, "we integrate ... something of the brother animal, who is actually holier than us since he cannot deviate from the divine will implanted in him because his dark consciousness shows him no other paths" (ibid.). But for us, who do possess consciousness, and must go on possessing it, we can only risk our ruthlessness if we are responding to and feel held by the presence of this other greater than ourselves.

The Self

Jung calls this other in us the Self. Neither a fixed guiding personality nor an endless process, the Self here is the juncture of the known and the unknown, the congress of human and animal and divine, of a *coniunctio* of our tiny ego with an unnameable presence which the very concept Self makes a bridge to. The Self is not the Spirit, is not the abiding generous presence of reality that transcends us. For even the Self wants to deconstruct. That ruthless primitive energy works even here to keep ploughing under our icon that opens us to the eternal, lest it become fixed as an idol. Jung writes, "the Self wants its own destruction as a symbolic form" (Jung 1976, 473; see also chapter 16).

So the Self bequeaths to us a third meaning of transcendence. It is Spirit or Presence which exists beyond all our pictures of it, which transcends all our conceptions. It is what urges the Self to destroy itself as a symbolic form. Destructiveness joined to love works like a windshield wiper that keeps brushing off all the ways we see reality so that we can awake now in the moment, each moment, to see afresh, anew, with wonder, with gaiety and joy. The Self, like other symbolic forms, points to what lives beyond our grasp no matter how much we name it, integrate it, salute it. It is inexhaustible and unceasingly bounteous. For our mothers and fathers who fled to the wilderness in the second century, only the immense expanse of desert was big enough to contemplate the vastness of this plenitude. Our concepts and symbols approach its frontier. They deliver us to that border. Hence we need our ego and what it constructs. But our constructions do not take us into the living territory. For that we need to choose, consent, depend, and give thanks for the generosity of reality endlessly pouring itself out upon us, and into us. It wants to be received.

One place that transcending presence can catch us, find us, chase us, wake us up, and bid our response is in our own small, precious dreams. If we pay attention to our dreams, we will be ushered into that empty space where we give over our ego to something greater, where we are taken back and under and behind our wounds to mend the rupture from our animal root-impulse, and join the splitting of love and ruthlessness. I close with a woman's dream that returned her to a basic wounded state, unbearable to feel if not held within the dream imagery thus providing a sure sense she could depend on something beyond herself. The woman dreamt of herself and two other women, one older, one younger. All three of them had been wounded, in different ways, in their connection to their feminine nature. Each of them wanted to be whole and worked hard to repair where they had felt rejected, not good enough, unlovable. In the dream a fourth elderly woman, wise and securely rooted in her faith in love and her own value as a woman, is singing to the three the Countess's aria *Dove Sono* from the Mozart opera "The Marriage of Figaro." The dreamer went and looked up the lyrics: can love so ardent pass? No, he (the Count) will love again more truly. The dreamer, deeply moved by the *sound* of the dream, the beautiful melody, felt wounds, rejection, repair, the fact of love, its full reality that embraces all four women all fit together. Through their individual stories, she felt, the bright sound of love, its reality, is heard.

Address C. G. Jung Institute Chicago Conference on Dreams 1998.

References

Balint, M. 1968. *The Basic Fault*. London: Tavistock.

Bion, W. R. 1978. *Clinical Seminars and Other Works*. London: Karnac.

Bollas, C. 1992. *Being a Character*. New York: Hill & Wang.

Flamm, J. D. 1978. *Matisse on Art*. New York: J. P. Dutton.

Freud, S. 1900/1958. *The Interpretation of Dreams*. Standard Edition, vols. IV and V. London: Hogarth Press.

Hillman, J. and McLean, M. 1997. *Dream Animals*. San Francisco: Chronicle Books.

Jung, C. G. 1934/1954. The practical use of dream-analysis. *Collected Works*. v. 16. *The Practice of Psychotherapy*. New York: Pantheon, 139-162, paras. 294-352

Jung, C. G. 1948/1960. General aspects of dream psychology. *Collected Works*. v. 8. *The Structure and Dynamics of the Psyche*. New York: Pantheon, 237-281, paras. 443-529.

Jung, C. G. 1950/1966. Psychology and literature. *Collected Works*. v. 15. *The Spirit in Man, Art, and Literature*. New York: Pantheon, 84-105, paras. 133-162.

Jung, C. G. 1961/1968. Symbols and the interpretation of dreams. *Collected Works*, v. 18. *The Symbolic Life*. Princeton, N.J.: Princeton University Press. 185-266, paras. 416-607.

Jung, C. G. 1973 and 1975. *Letters*. 2 vols. Princeton, N.J.: Princeton University Press.

Jung, C. G. 1976. *The Vision Seminars*. 2 Books. Zürich: Spring.

Jung, C. G. 1984. *Dream Analysis*. Princeton, N.J.: Princeton University Press.

Jung, C. G. 1988. *Nietzsche's Zarathustra*. 2 vols. ed. James L. Jarrett. Princeton, N.J.: Princeton University Press.

Khan, M. M. R. 1971. The role of illusion in the analytic space and process. *The Privacy of the Self.* New York: International Universities Press, 251-269.

Khan, M. M. R. 1972. The finding and becoming of self. *The Privacy of the Self.* New York: International Universities Press, 294-305.

Khan, M. M. R. 1983. Beyond the dreaming ego. *Hidden Selves.* New York: International Universities Press, 42-50.

Kristeva, J. 1995. *New Maladies of the Soul*. New York: Columbia University Press.

Ricoeur, P. 1970. *Freud and Philosophy*. New Haven, Ct.: Yale University Press.

Ulanov, A. and Ulanov, B. 1994. *Transforming Sexuality, The Archetypal World of Anima and Animus*. Boston: Shambhala.

von Franz, M.-L. 1970/1992. *The Golden Ass of Apuleius*. Boston: Shambhala.

Winnicott, D. W. 1950. Aggression in relation to emotional development. *Through Paediatrics to Psycho-Analysis.* New York: Basic Books, 1975, 204-218.

Winnicott, D. W. 1958. *Babies and Their Mothers*. London: Free Association Books.

Winnicott, D. W. 1963. Communicating and not communicating leading to a study of certain opposites. *The Maturational Processes and the Facilitating Environment.* 1965. New York: International Universities Press, 179-192.

Chapter 12

When Religion Prompts Terrorism

In the wake of the catastrophe of terrorist attacks on New York City and the Pentagon, we can see how religion gets a bad name. Religious beliefs can inflate destructiveness to a cosmic dimension. Destroying innocent civilians gets conscripted into doing God's will.

In response, religious people are not without resource. As religious people we have a particular response and ability. For we know a center of reality exists, whatever names we give it. We know many spiritual practices which help us align with that center. Our job is to do so, to help channel its energy into personal and shared space, to help with lamentation, mind-numbing grief and exhaustion, and with impulses to revenge and violence. Because we know there is a center and prayer as a way of affiliating with it, our particular responsibility is to do this aligning work to make a different social place than the one we have been thrust into by fear, destruction, and sorrow.

This social space is not composed of one extreme position, such as, bomb the killers, nor its opposite, such as, let's ask them why they hate us. The social space does not take one opposite and exclude the other, nor even agree to disagree amicably. People are praying to God from opposite sides. To create a new social space is to dig down under the fence between the two sides, to dig down to God, to a new beginning which may embrace opposites and stand the tension of holding both in consciousness simultaneously until the new appears and both are changed. In this social space we do not want forms of debate that only express our point of view. We want a new emotional field where all sides are moved by charity to search out the truth, where all sides feel a self-restraint based on awareness that each of us can do harm.

To work for this social space and real solutions, we must draw on what we know about religion and its perversion, and also draw upon what we have learned about psychic reality. The religious impulse is ruthless. It is; it will express itself one way or the other. We all face the question what to do with the bad, what Jung calls the shadow, what Freud calls the instincts which include murderous impulses, cannibalism, hate, as well as sex and aggression. We all know that none of our images of God can be equated with the infinitely free, unoriginated transcendent. What we do not know as clearly is that we also have unconscious images for God, both personal and group gods, our subjective images for the Holy. These images vary greatly among us and are fascinating, deeply personal and meaningful. They make the transcendent God near, alive and real to us.

What is extremely dangerous, I believe, and religious people are particularly exposed to this danger, is to forget (to be unconscious of) the gap that exists between our private and group Gods and official names for God, the objective images of God which we receive from our various religious traditions. For example, a child sees God as Horse, not a horse, and not the horse, but Horse which is very different from traditional images of Yahweh in the Hebrew Bible as refuge, rock, or in the New Testament of Jesus as dinner party host, or God as woman looking for the lost coin. To fall into the gap between our subjective picture of God and objective images for God of religious tradition means psychologically we have equated the two. We have fallen into identification of our personal or group god with the God of religious tradition. That unconsciousness will act itself out on our neighbor. If I have identified my personal god with the God of my religion, I will require you to identify with it too. If you do not, you are out, infidel. I now speak for all of Islam; I speak for all of Christianity.

Subjective images for God can be anything – money, the market, a particular glimpse of the holy. Such images are not the danger. They are the stuff of feeling related to the transcendent unfathomable God. The danger is falling into unconscious identification with those powerful pictures and unconsciously insisting we possess the truth that everyone else must identify with too.

Even more perilous is the gap that exists between all human images for God, whether subjective from ourselves or our groups, or official from our religious traditions, and God who transcends them all. God is infinite freedom, unoriginated, immeasurable. When we fall into this gap, when this gap collapses, then our subjective picture of God, our group God, becomes not only what we publicize as what should be everyone else's religion, but now our truth becomes *the* truth for all time. We speak not only for Christianity, not only for all of Islam. We speak for God! We possess God. I am now identified with the living God in whose name I can kill myself and thousands of other people not related to my cause. Believe as I do or you are dead. Religion becomes a weapon, justified eternally. It lays upon us the duty to wipe out all who do not identify with this truth.

We learn from depth psychology that the unconscious exists. It is a psychic fact. It is a force full of lively energy that must express itself somewhere. This force is collective in the sense that we all share in it and all our individual consciousness arises out of it. Psyche is like the body. We share it in common and we each have our individual experiences of it. Freud talks of the unconscious as body-based instinct. Jung uses the word archetypal to indicate patterns in which psychic energy assembles and displays itself, patterns which can be discerned in all the world's religions and mythologies. It is objective energy in that it flows through us, among us, and can roll us in its waves. We do not originate it, nor invent it.

The unconscious is one medium for religious experience, others being scripture, the worshiping community, historical events, poetry, etc. Religious experience galvanises unconscious energy at a very deep level, at the primordial level that enlists our personal struggles and hopes, and also expresses those of humanity.

The danger that looms when we lose sight of the gaps between our religious imagery and the transcendent is that unconscious energy swooshes through us unchecked. Awareness of the gaps between our personal and group perspectives and humanity's as a whole, let alone the gap between our human perspective and the ultimate, affords us what Freud calls the procrastinating function of thought. We cannot be certain we have discerned God's will; we need hesitation, meditation, consultation with others. But unchecked, this unconscious energy invades and inflates and overcomes our little ego and our collective consciousness. It rushes through us; we are it and it is us, amassing force like the full fuel tanks of a jet airliner, bringing down towers over a hundred stories high. The lives of individuals, whether pilots or passengers, are totally eclipsed. This force grips us. We exist in a state of omnipotent merger,

grandiose in our identification with God, and we do not matter at all. Only it matters. Jim Jones of Jonestown Guyana is
another example of someone enthral to this force.

The response which religious people have to give the
community is knowing there is a center and aligning ourselves
with it which means knowing that our ego, both collective and
individual, is *not* the center. Consciousness of our limits helps
create the social space as the foundation for any conversation
between warring sides.

This knowing includes recognising simultaneously our
unknowing, that the center, the it, is beyond me, and beyond
us. This knowing means modesty in being sure we are not it. I
fear it, I serve it, but not blindly, not in a state of fusion where it
becomes my duty to engineer my death and that of many others
in the name of a living god. We are responsible to each other
to prevent a psychic epidemic, to know about the center and
that we are not it.

As people acquainted with religious faith, we also possess a
response and an ability for the big job of intercession for the
dead, the terrorized, those on the plane in shock, for those
bowed down by grief for their loved ones vapourised by tem-
peratures exceeding 1500 degrees.

We know that in prayer our usual ego-time does not obtain.
There is no past, present, future time in praying. So we can pray
backwards for the persons in the moment of seeing a building
coming at their plane, or in the building seeing a plane about to
crash into their office, for the persons caught between jumping
from fire into empty space to die far below. We can pray that
at those terrified moments they also felt a strong presence with
them, holding them, witnessing them, not leaving them alone.
We can pray that they felt something transcendent with them,
around them, welcoming them home in the hour of their death.
We can pray for the future life of those shocked into bereave-

ment, for the children whose parents have been stolen from them, for those shattered by their loss, for the rescue workers horrified by what they must uncover in the rubble, that they may know the power of loving resurrected in their lives, that the power of loving will accompany them and revive them in this dire hour of their need.

We can pray for the resurrection of loving in us, so that we see that each of us is cherished in the sight of God, and all of us together are called to be God's people, Yahweh's bride, that all of us may experience the community Ibn Arabi of Sufism describes in the opening sura of the Koran as the response of the Divine Presence when we pray: "Now there is sharing in common between myself and my faithful." Such prayer produces a space of community where each is responsible for the other.

Christian faith aims at making the power of loving adult in the face of hatred within us and outside us, a faith that the abyss of love is deeper than the abyss of death. For God places a living soul in each of us. God places a living psyche in each of us. Great is God's faith.

Remarks made September 19, 2001 to the Union Theological Seminary Community in Response to September 11, 2001; and expanded in a Public Forum: Why Did This Happen? When Religion Prompts Violence, sponsored by Auburn Theological Seminary with Saint James Episcopal Church and Temple Israel of the City of New York, 2001.

IV. Clinical Issues

Chapter 13

Transference, the Transcendent Function, and Transcendence

We need to take a fresh look at transference and transcendence which, I believe, are linked through what Jung calls the transcendent function. Clinical experience has taught me that through the transcendent function people in analysis come into direct contact with transcendence – that which surpasses not only our ego consciousness but our whole psyche – whether or not they give it a religious name.

Transference

Whatever theory of depth psychology we adhere to, we agree on the centrality of transference and countertransference in clinical work. There we reenact traumas that ruptured our original connection to self, or traumas that resulted from absence – what should have happened failed to and thus blighted our fledgling self from fully unfolding. We agree that in the field the analyst and analysand share the currents of transference and countertransference include ordinary human response to one another in our own idiosyncratic styles, activation of unconscious complexes that require analysis, and clues, through the impact of the other's unconscious on our own, to the specific unconscious dynamics constellated in the other and between us (see Racker 1968; Carotenuto 1986; Ulanov 1996, chapter 7).

Jung understands the transference as purposeful; it serves the individuation process by bringing up unconscious material to compensate for our one-sided conscious orientation (Steinberg 1990, 9ff). Jung analyzes psychic material with two methods – the reductive and synthetic – and on two levels – the objective and the subjective, but all of them serve to connect the ego as the center of consciousness with the Self as the center of the whole psyche, conscious and unconscious (Jung 1953a, paras. 121-140).

In reductive analysis, we ask where transference expectations directed toward the analyst come from, what role they position the analyst to play, and what the analyst is being used for. The analysand's psyche will press toward communicating what contents need to be admitted to consciousness and will use the analyst to carry them. Such projections cross the usual divisions of sex, age, race, or creed. For example, after our first meeting, a man sensitive and ambivalent about what he called his lower working-class origins, dreamt me swilling beer and smoking, much like his factory working father. All that was missing was the undershirt.

Using the reductive method, we analyze such an unconscious projection back to its historical antecedents. Interpreting on the objective level, we relate dream figures to the actual objects pictured – here, his father in the past and me in the present. The early object relation to his parent and the present object relation to his analyst combine in the dream to initiate in his ego a working free of the complex with his father and form a more adaptive relationship with me. This type of interpretation uncovers how the unconscious dream and transference material compensates for a one-sided conscious view. For this man consciously thought of me as opposite to his conscious orientation. He saw me as upper class and educated, about which he also felt ambivalent, suspecting I might be too refined, not tough enough to do the work he needed done. The dream yokes us together, as if to assure the dreamer he can find his father in me. From this reductive objective point of view, what starts out as symbolic, really turns out to be a sign, designating specific objects and psychic processes of wishing or striving that can be uncovered and recognized as belonging to one's own ego identity and assimilated to enlarge it (Jung 1971, para. 788).

An analysand's personal drama of transference, however, not only replays early object relations, but also announces a person's particular process of individuation as well. The transference anticipates the new. The same facts when interpreted on the subjective level, for example, direct conscious attention to what father represents in the dreamer's own psyche and between us in our field of interaction. The synthetic method tries to put together all the parts gathered in reductive and synthetic analyses and in objective and subjective levels of interpretation to open our consciousness to the wider vision of the psyche's whole enterprise. What is the psyche aiming at with this working-class father and analyst in this first dream? If the reductive method returns us to the ego's point of view, the synthetic method conducts us to the Self's perspective.

The dream told me, among other things, that a sturdy psychic field constellated between us because the analysand unconsciously linked with a fact unknown to him, that a similar fathering figure existed in my own background, as I was raised by Yugoslavian peasants, and the man did go around in an undershirt.

Archetype as Object

The synthetic method of interpretation introduces another type of transference object Jung calls archetypal which refers to contents that arise spontaneously from a deep layer of psyche Jung calls collective or objective. The synthetic method of interpretation tries to gather together archetypal and early object relations as they appear projected in the transference onto the analyst, so that the analysand grows conscious of where a complex around his relation to his actual father and now the analyst embroils him (the objective level), where that father attitude operates in himself and between us in the analysis (subjective level), and how the psyche employs this complex to further his development. This first dream gives inklings of the future self of the patient (Jung 1976, para. 549). The psyche puts him in relation to this father image as he embarks on analysis. If he corresponds with the psyche's aim, his individuation process will include finding his particular path, influenced by his personal history and by the culture he lives in, and by his particular analyst, to relate to the originating power of the father archetype (see Jung 1938, paras. 198-199; 1954, para. 400; 1959, para. 301; see also Ulanov 1996, chapter 5). How will he integrate what the father image symbolises – the invisible spiritual power to author and beget the new?

Instead of breaking the material down into its component bits, as in the reductive-analytic method, the synthetic-prospective approach seeks to find how the bits go together toward constructing a new reality. The symbol does not collapse into a sign of contents the ego can now assimilate, but points toward the unknown which is just coming into view.

The reductive method returns us to ego-knowing. We know what an unconscious content means because we know where it came from and why; it disguises itself because its intent opposes the ego's conception of itself; it deconstructs ego reality. The synthetic method leads the ego into unknowing. It builds up, elaborates and follows the lead of the symbol that aims toward an unknown or even unknowable purpose (Jung 1971, para. 820). We ask of the dream symbol or the transference-countertransference blockage or even of the neurosis itself: What is the Self engineering? Here our ego does not assimilate contents to itself, but instead is pulled across its borders toward a Self that paradoxically confronts and receives our ego with a coincidence and complexity of opposites, which it is our task to bring into a union.

The Self

This Self that addresses our ego is collective, a process of centering we share. We experience it as a push toward others and otherness: "We only become ourselves with people and for people ... the self is like a crowd, therefore being oneself, one is also many ... one can only individuate with or against something or somebody. Being an individual is always a link in a chain; it is not an absolutely detached situation, in itself only, with no connection outside" (Jung 1988, 102). Yet, in the opposite direction, the Self "by definition is the most individual thing, the essence of individuality. It is *the* uniqueness ... It knows you" (Jung 1988, 105; see also chapter 10).

In the history of depth psychology, we can hazard that the present problems people bring to analysts figure around the Self, whereas the early ones Freud outlined (hysteria, obsessional neurosis, paranoia, dementia praecox) focused on how the psyche looked from the ego's point of view (Fine 1962, 108; Freud 1894; 1895a; 1895b; 1896). Today we speak of narcissistic and borderline disorders that affect our whole character and demand for their resolution that we find new orientations in which we can put together inner and outer reality, chaos and complexity.

We feel pulled into this journey, or even dragged there by our neurosis (Jung 1920, para. 518). But to be whole means including all our parts – the loony ones, the mad bits, all that lies undeveloped alongside our most developed skills, talents, and desires. Our ambivalence about this task mirrors the outer chaos we find in our societies. The disorder of our societies results in part from our avoidance of the Self that addresses each of us. Jung says: "You see, the Self is such a disagreeable thing in a way, so realistic, because it is what you really are, not what you want to be or imagine you ought to be; and that reality is so poor, sometimes dangerous, and even disgusting, that you will quite naturally make every effort not to be yourself" (Jung 1988, 99). "We would rather accept anything in the world, any devil or any hell, than accept ourselves in our particular concreteness. That is the thing of which we are most afraid … But only when we accept the thing which is loathsome to us, have we a real will to change, not before" (Jung 1988, 86, 87).

Jungians must ask what advantage accrues to clinical work from using the symbolic concept Self and seeing it working from the beginning in the transference-countertransference field. What difference does it make?

Many. For example, we all know that analysis, if successful, recreates in the transference original injuries to our core self so that it went into hiding, or split into warring opposites, or dissociated into unconnected chunks, or fragmented into bits. Jungians see as well injury at the archetypal level so that the archetype presses its claims on the ego in damaged form. The ego is not in right relation to the archetype. In addition to relations to objects which originate outside us and from our internalised creations of them, Jungians recognize archetypal objects that arise from the psyche to speak to us about itself. It addresses us from territory different from the ego but needing our ego response to be lived here and now. The analyst must give attention to both sets of objects, charting the personal history of the analysand and the archetypal history as well.

Healing includes setting the archetype free from inflating the ego in compensation for missing pieces of ego reality, or deflating the wounded ego by driving it into masochistic substitute satisfactions. The archetype is set free for its function of making a bridge for the ego to the objective reality of the psyche, to what the Self is engineering, much as we might see setting our liver free from the pollutant of alcohol so it can perform its proper function in the body's economy.

Jungians agree with the object relations school that therapy aims to consolidate our ego and object constancy, but also see healing as linking our ego to the inner world of psychic reality whose center is the Self. A damaged relation to an archetype can kill us just as surely as a damaged relation to our liver, and not just us, but others too, as Hitler's identification with the savior archetype tragically illustrates. The Self brings us bulletins of what transcends our ego – the archetypal psyche. I would add, that the Self's archetypal reality acts like a bridge to what transcends our whole psyche – to what we symbolise by the name God, or It, or Isness. Hence, when we engage through the transcendent function in ego-Self conversation, we move ever further toward what the Self witnesses to: reality which transcends the whole psyche. That transcendent reality affects us here and now, our ego, our body, our world.

The Self concept helps analyst and analysand verbalise that impulse toward another kind of consciousness than our usual ego functional one. Here our knowing gives way to unknowing; we enter into a surround of energy that inhabits all life and annuls our ego separations into subject-object, inner-outer,

self-other, us-them. In those moments we feel part of something larger that we may rebel against or accept. But it feels
bigger and shifts our center of gravity. We feel addressed,
shocked into wonder that there is something and not nothing.
To recover this field of relatedness gives us entry into what Paul
Ricoeur calls "second naiveté," where our childlike gladness in
being finds itself tempered by life's suffering, but also strengthened like steel on stone (Ricoeur 1970, 543). Momentarily, we
are granted new vision that sees through the tragic sufferings
of human life to the objective presence of the center of life that
knows us. Jung uses the word Self to designate that presence.

The ego-Self relationship is a process that assembles meaning
whose referent is the transcendent. Living with this knowledge
affects not just psyche and spirit but releases physical events
in the world, in our sexuality, in our metabolism, in cures of
illness, in social epidemics and epiphanies. The Self acts as
bridge to this transcendent presence, points to it, witnesses to
it. Through symbols of the Self we find names for the presence
and our process of living toward it. We need the concept of Self,
or one like it, to express our experience that something lives in
each of us and among us that mirrors the mysterious process
of the origin and goal of life. Its mirroring process underlies the
mirroring that occurs in the transference-countertransference
relationship.

It is the mysterious factor the Self points to that urged a
man, for example, to persist in analysis over two decades, first
with one analyst and then with me. He sought not only to find
what failed to be given in childhood, with a father overwhelmed
by rage and a mother caught in narcissistic wounds, but to
reach durable connection to the creativity of being as it lived
inside him and to know it existed outside him, external to his
efforts. The transference to me broke open to this other level

of relatedness, a level that is not the analyst's to give or with-hold, for it holds both analyst and analysand in its unfolding.

The Self concept matters because it gives us a way to describe the shift that happens when treatment succeeds. The analysand comes to dwell in a bigger field than the transference-countertransference one. The ego-Self couple within, and also shared with the analyst, comes to replace the analyst-analysand couple; and then the analysand can leave analysis. Transference-countertransference skirmishes give way to moments of tangible evanescent presence which generously endorse life in each of us. We see that we are parts of a larger whole. We shift from asking, Who am I? to, What am I? meaning, What am I, and what are we together, part of? What larger purposes work themselves through me, and through this analysis, and summon our cooperation?

The body experience which accompanies transference and which we must always look into, brings home to both analyst and analysand the here and now reality of the transcendent. The man with two decades of analysis, for example, knew in the intimacies of the pressure of his blood when he was aligned to the center and when he missed it. Risky, elevated blood pressure signaled his off-course direction; lowered pressure ratified his correspondence.

Take a much less finished example of the bidding presence through the Self. A woman, also in a long analysis, suffering from borderline affliction that she manifests in still forgetting days or times of her sessions even five years into treatment, employs as her major defense a fragmenting of herself into bits. She can tolerate one bit of pain at a time, not all of them together, so she scatters herself into confetti. This defense protects her from massive pain, but dissipates her integrity. Slowly she has grown into an ego that can house all the bits together. In those moments, she feels aligned with a center that exists deep inside her and far outside her which she finds best in relation to her dreams, she says, "because they speak truth that doesn't come from me, or you, or textbooks, but from some other place." She illustrates the metaphoric speech we all utter when joined with this center: "It gives me sovereignty of the self" (see also chapter 14).

The Transcendent Function

Transference inevitably introduces the transcendent function. Transference makes the analytic couple consciously recognize and converse about the process already going on. With luck and success in the treatment, the analytic couple will be replaced by the ego-Self couple in each person.

The transcendent function is not a theoretical speculation but raises a concrete and practical issue: how to come to terms with "the Unknown as it immediately affects us" (Jung 1959a, 68). The transcendent function is part of the compensatory function of the transference. Like dreams and symptoms, the transference also brings up unconscious contents to offset the one-sidedness of our conscious viewpoint. The transcendent function is Jung's name for the process by which the psyche slowly moves our ego out of its fiction of being captain of the ship, say, or queen of the May, and builds up a bigger center for the whole psyche, conscious and unconscious.

Analysands come to treatment because they already know this process going on in their psyches, but usually in a negative form, of feeling opposite emotions in themselves colliding or violently alternating so that they can find no peace and no way forward in their lives. One young woman I saw for consultation and referral said she had "come for help because my life is completely stalemated." Yet she feared that help because if "I let go to all my feelings, I might not get myself back." She felt some other self looming on the horizon which threatened the narrow, but familiar, self she presently housed.

The analyst and analysand take up consciously what the psyche does naturally. We participate in the opposite points of view the psyche presents to reach its goal of building up a bigger center. We engage in imaginative conversation with both the conscious position and its opposite that presently has fallen into the unconscious.[1] We listen, we look, we try to give form to this counterposition while holding on to our ego view. One woman, for example, danced into being a current of energy she could not capture into words. When she attended closely to it, it moved her to arch her back and lift her legs and arms up and down. She drew this impulse as well, forming what eventually amounted to a closing circle of her pelvis lifting backwards to touch her head. She formed the opposite of the ouroboros symbol where our tender underbelly is tucked within the circle and protected. Here, the inner side of her body opened outward to the energetic beat. The meaning of this idiosyncratic symbol did not reveal itself to her until much later in her recovery in sexual intercourse of the rhythmic movement of her hips backward and forward toward her mate, which delivered her to long-sought orgasm.

This odd symbol communicated through her body impulse addresses her consciousness as a picture the psyche gives of itself. We could ask, Who took this picture? For the angle of vision differs from our conscious one; it supercedes the analysand's conscious and unconscious categories, and links her personal efforts to reach her sexual potential to an ancient symbol of wholeness, but now turned inside out. The symbol arrives as an additional object for her to take into consideration. It does not substitute for her personal efforts but moves through them. Both contexts are needed – the ego's and the symbol's. We cannot take the archetypal symbol in place of

331

her ego's effort to connect with her body in the context of all the object relations that served to disconnect her. Nor can we so emphasize her object relation history and its repetitions in transference to defend against the spontaneous thrust of the archetypal into her consciousness. Only with all these parts taken together does the psyche transcend the conflict with the arrival of the new.

The New

The transcendent function inaugurates transition to arrival of the new. The new initiates a third point of view that includes and surpasses the former two conflicting ones; it creates a third space combining conscious and unconscious from which symbols arise that address the ego like a bigger encompassing other which is what Jung calls the Self.

A new symbol comes on the scene, bringing some new attitude in us that permits us to feel greeted and to house the full impact of this novel presence and perception. It announces itself in symbolic form which possesses its own life; we see we could not have invented it. Hence we experience it as transcending our ego. It feels like a creative solution which is not the product of our will or thought, but is "in accord with the deepest foundation of the personality, as well as its whole-ness" (Jung 1958, para. 856). We feel addressed by something that "possesses compelling authority not unjustly characterized as the voice of God" (ibid.). Through this solution that arrives from the bigger Self territory, we glimpse a unitary field that holds all of us in being. Thus does the process of transcendent function within us act as a bridge to what transcends the whole psyche.

But the transcendent function also involves a descent away from ego reality, "to the *deus absconditus*, which possesses qualities very different from those of the God who shines by day" (Jung 1971, para. 427). Hence the initiation of this process of moving from a smaller to a large container begins with our sense of dis-ease, disorientation, even falling into a gap or a void. We feel threat, a breaking down of accepted categories, even a sense of our cracking up (Aimé 1994). We go down before anything appears which could be said to go up to transcend the opposites. Like the woman in the consultation who feared she would plunge into emotions and not get herself back, we feel the deconstruction of our known world, our known meanings.

Yet this downgoing road also leads us to the fault lines, the seams, the points of distress in our world view, and thus exposes us to what lies beyond, that our very valuable world view obscures from our vision. This presence cannot be rep resented in language or other human forms, for its infinitude outruns the uttermost boundary of our finiteness. We regress from the ego to the Self world which grants us new perception and perception of the new. What arrives as solution bespeaks a different order of consciousness. Although the process of the transcendent function begins with destruction of any system of meaning we create, it does not destroy the implication of presence. In this way, depth psychology overlaps with negative theology. There, the advance of the infinite strips away any equation we make of it with the finite.

In the process of the transcendent function we not only struggle with opposites in ourselves, we also inhabit the opposites of our historical time. Here is spirit in the body, not in the head alone or in some distant stratosphere, but right in the midst of people's specific lives, affected by their society and historical era. Our unconscious mirrors conflicts which seek resolution in our society. For example, a life-long communist who dismissed analysis as navel-gazing because true change could only originate from without, through society, found his personal world crack-up along with the collapse of Soviet Russia. His marriage, his job, his relation to his child, crumbled along with his former beliefs. He found himself driven into analysis as into an unknown country where he looked within himself for help.

In the struggle to go into ourselves and enter this unknowing state, we are not embarked on a hygiene project as one analysand insisted by hissing at me that she was not in my office "to get mental health!" We are participating in uniting our world. From what arrives as creative solutions, we contribute something new to others. In arriving at the space where the new arrives, we aerate the earth on which we all stand and from which we all grow. This insight lends dignity to analytical work. Working on personal problems feeds the psyche in all of us. The humiliation we suffer from being caught in complexes shifts to humble participation in the shared burdens of humanity. Every analysis is original research into the reality of the psyche.

The transcendent function and the transference that facilitates it are serious business, with concrete consequences and grave dangers. We enter with all our knowing and civilized ego values into dialogue with unknowing. We do not stand outside the circle in intellectual or aesthetic appreciation of "psychic process." We step in; it grips us. When, for example, a woman imaginatively confronts a huge man with iron teeth from her dream in which he trashed a whole restaurant, smashing the furniture and throwing the dishes, she faces violence in the raw about which we read in the newspapers every day. The violence inspires such terror in her that at first only her dream can bring it into the transference field. Then she feels it in response to my interpretations. When I stay quiet, which allows the destructive energy to live between us, we descend into not knowing whose violence this is, and explore how it feels when coming from the analyst, when coming from the analysand, when coming from the field between us. Only then does the analysand imaginatively face this terrifying man. Slowly, she and he become a couple whose conflict makes a third space within the analysis. She no longer experiences me as smashing all her psychic furniture nor herself as trashing mine, and she now possesses enough space to keep him from invading her in violent self-attack. But what was she to do with this guy? And with his TEETH!

She engaged him directly, imaginatively. This was not cordial conversation but a slanging match. She yells at him, "Never do that to me again, that shouting banging, bashing, violently intruding!" He yells back: "Then wake up and use me! If you don't, I'm using you!" Imagine our last explosive fight, where we really meant what we said, and said it top volume, in high emotional pitch. To do this sort of active imagination is to sweat, turn pale, tremble. We feel it in the body. Our pulse races. Our glands secrete. And all this conflict and urge to solve it, falls into the transference field and onto the analyst.

The analysand depends on the analyst to be really there, in it too. Hence danger lurks everywhere – of inflation, seduction, power plays, defensive intellectualising. Body means definite form. Spirit housed in body means bodily consequences – sexual arousal, explosive bowels, white nights of sleeplessness, as well as ecstasy, a thrumming of joy throughout ordinary days. Bumping around in the psyche and the spirit it witnesses to will suddenly release physical experiences.

Dependence

The antidote to danger, the pharmakon for both analyst and analysand, and on both the personal and archetypal levels, remains the same – acknowledging dependence on each other and on the advance into consciousness, through the transcendent function, of the mysterious presence of what lies beyond and undergirds the whole analytical enterprise.

As analysts we acknowledge dependence on a source of wisdom greater than our own and on all those who mediate it to us (see also chapter 9). When we feel our need, our poverty, even at times our bankruptcy, we disidentify from the power or whatever else the analysand would transfer to us. We see the power, do not deny its presence in the intersubjective field, but we do not claim it as our personal possession (see Atwood and Stolorow 1984; Atwood, Brandschaft, Stolorow 1987). This contemplative action takes us into a whole realm of countertransference which is the subject of another paper.

As analysands we acknowledge dependence on various central figures in our life and also the effects of their lack of mediation. We feel the gaps in the development of ourselves from others not loving or seeing us, from our experiences of abandonment because of war, or a parent's illness, death or divorce, from being used as a substitute for a parent's lack. Some of the darkest work in analysis occupies itself with these gaps in ourselves. Mourning and rage swirl because we were looked at as objects to be annexed, not subjects to be greeted and enjoyed. All these dependencies, met and unmet, fall onto the analyst and into the treatment to be relived, filled out, corrected, or felt for the first time.

Where no object has mediated, say, mothering, the archetypal presence of Mother looms large. It threatens to swallow up the client precisely because no human being brought maternal presence down to life size. I have known negative transferences directed at me because I did not fulfill the archetypal role by providing as a result of the analysis admission into programs for professional advancement, a loving mate, success in money ventures, all things that to the client conveyed unqualified acceptance by life. It falls to the analytical couple to bring the mythic down to life-size while still communicating validation by meeting dependency.

On the other hand, the gap left by failed object relations also offers direct access to archetypal presence, less cluttered by the intricate web of projected and introjected mediating objects. If we can stand the force and remain rooted in finitude, such direct access to an archetypal realm breeds unusual gifts for the individual and the world. My clinical experience has taught me that this insight comforts clients who suffer a serious lack of appropriate objects in their upbringing whether through parental madness or abandonment, or as a result of illness, poverty, war, or ghetto violence. Artists, witches, people of original insight and intensity fall into this category.

Transcendence, Transference and the Transcendent Function

This example comes from a small bit of a long analysis. It shows the radical effects of the transcendent function on transference and how, through the transcendent function, we experience firsthand the presence of the Transcendent, whether or not we call it by religious names. The first dream that began the analysis of a middle-aged woman I will call Grace, announced the first transference theme. Subsequent material comes from a six-month period of the second year of our work.

She dreamt she was summoned to help a little girl whose parents thought she was seriously ill. On her way there, she passes a prison which contains only one man, a war criminal, who is allowed only one visitor every ten years of his sentence. She feels the lonely pain of his punishment. On arrival, the dreamer sees that the little girl is not ill but simply has been left alone too long and needs someone to play with her, which the dreamer does.

The dream announces the first transference theme: I was summoned to play with her; we were summoned in our work together to make space for this child-part left alone too long and thought to be ill. We noted that the criminal was locked up for some massive scheme of destructive aggression, but he was not yet at center stage. This dream responded to something that had occurred in our first session. In order to better look at some drawings Grace brought, I sat on the floor, which astonished her; in her dream she sits on the floor with the child.

Gradually our work revealed how a whole chunk of this woman had been left alone too long as a child and continued split-off from her adult life. As she identified with the little girl, she found herself needing to bring into analysis and to me specifically "every piece of my life, all the work I've done, all the things I've hidden away that I love, memories, scenes, places, things I've created. Each piece needs to be valued, cared for, known about, and I cannot do that alone." The love inhabited her body and impelled her actually to bring things to our sessions. In this first transference theme, I was positioned to carry the good mother and she the little girl, and we worked as well on getting her aggression out of prison for use in facing various tests and burdens in her daily life.

At its most intense, her identification with the hidden little girl who needed to tell all her secrets compensated for her feeling outcast because she was fatally flawed. At those times of depression, self attack, and anxious sleeplessness, she played over a particular tape someone had given her of a public lecture I had delivered some years before in my work as a Seminary professor in which I had quoted Lady Julian of Norwich, the fourteenth-century mystic. She felt deeply humiliated by this practice and referred to it as a fetish. She said "I hate the part of me which longs for and needs to hear Ann's voice on that tape." What made the tape comforting, she said, was what she heard in the sound of my voice as a willingness to speak out of myself, to expose connection to a deep place from which I lived. She heard me speaking not from authorities or hearsay but from myself which she longed to do, but felt there was nothing there. Hearing the tape turned out to be important – hearing as opposed to seeing (an image). The sound as well as the content made her feel held from a deep place which counteracted her feeling something was deeply wrong with her, that, in a basic way, she existed outside of life.

She also felt ashamed to heap upon me all the materials of her life: what could I possibly do with them? But she made good use of analysis and endured this burgeoning child's longing that she housed as an adult sexual woman. Hence the longing carried with it unspecified sexual desire which made her feel exposed. Nonetheless, she risked bringing me copies of actual journal pages where she showed her innermost feelings, memories, thought (see also chapter 13). They seemed to her to be trivial meanderings, far distant from contact with any center. My reaction was the opposite; I remarked she was already in touch with a center; these were conversations with the Self. This struck lightning and she said she desired "to bring all of my life somewhere – to the Source of life, really to the God Julian of Norwich knows who treasures and knows us, who hides us in Himself." In these exchanges, I was positioned to carry the mother and the Self, but it was a mother she had never had and a Self she felt distant from, and she the little girl; the aggression she got out of prison to use in her life tasks, as she lived a busy, fruitful life with many demanding relationships and aspects of work. The aggression did not yet take center stage between us.

When we explored her feelings of being irredeemably flawed, the second transference theme announced itself. Here she carried the negative mother she experienced in childhood, and I carried the link to the little girl who wanted to be seen. She described her mother as "always rehearsing me, even at lunch I had to recite lessons, and thus invalidating me. I was part of mother's project." From the point of view of one who ought to accomplish lessons in school, in music, dance, art and athletics, she viewed this hidden little girl side of herself as "a shameful, formless place in me, damaged, something wrong." It filled her with humiliation. "Like a birthmark?" I ask. "That's too superficial" she answered. I saw that she felt the wrongness came with her; it was not even a wound inflicted from the outside. I said this part, different from her view, wanted to be seen because it left clues like bread crumbs in the forest, like forgetting her pen or her eyeglasses after sessions when the little girl had been around and having to return to fetch them, or like giving me the journal pages. She said she was lugging the transference around like Linus with his security blanket and it was mortifying.

Two views occupied our transference space. Her ego wanted to avoid and reject this little girl in herself whose needy longing and passionate desire to be in touch she saw as formless shameful wrongness. "I can't live from this place," she said, "because it is not viable." The little girl got transferred to me to deal with. It was speaking to me and I to it and Grace was listening in. The little girl's longing was just at the seam of her ego consciousness, its fault line, and, when followed, disrupted her ego stance, deconstructed it and took her down to a dreadful place of invalidity. For the little girl introduced an opposite view: She, shameful or not, wanted to be found; she longed to be seen and played with. She desired and wanted to be desired, a preview of adult sexual responses. She was not daunted by the invalidity that threatened Grace's ego. She talked to me and I listened to her and at times we ganged up on Grace. The analysand acknowledged this when she said, "this part is not ashamed of neediness; she wants to eat and run after the analyst." Increasingly, she felt our sessions contained dialogue between these two parts of herself – the wrongness, and the needy, passionate appetite. We made room for both.

The dreadful place in her psyche where she felt invalid also attacked her work, making her feel there was something she ought to know but did not and she did not know what it was. Therefore her reasoning spun on, "There must be something terribly wrong with me; this is a danger place: I could easily go into panic." I said, "Stay with the not-knowing place and look around and see what goes on." After this session she dreamt she is driving her car and comes to a construction site. She discovers where the earth has been dug up by big "earthmovers," shards and arrowheads of amethyst and stone; the construction work has uncovered American Indian relics. "It is a treasure hunt!"

The psyche began in this dream to dig up what was to become a new transference object; the Indian. But first we took another tack. When she held in consciousness both her self-rejection and her longing for connection, her aggression burst out of prison. I was the bad mother, or she was, aggressively repudiating her, finding her a burden, hopeless, tiresome, outside the pale. She dug up a lot of memories of feeling banished by her mother who could "withdraw behind an iron curtain if you disagreed with her and she felt affronted. She would take care of me and fulfill her duty and let me go off if I chose something different from her way. But she would have nothing to do with me." As a child, Grace saw her mother cut off contact with her own sisters and her few friends when they offended her. She never saw them again. Only her father kept contact with her mother, but "he never pressed too close." The client experienced him as a benign gentle refuge but never a help with her mother. I said a non-negotiable space existed around her mother and Grace had taken it as belonging to herself and that kept her a pariah.

When Grace held together the opposites of the aggressive mother and the child who was outside the pale, she dreamt of coming to her session and her mother came too. Grace feels awkward, stupid, a mess, isolated from me. The same night she also dreams that a young woman is put to death; "the front of her head blows off; it's ghastly. No one deserves to be treated this way."

Once out, the psyche started playing around with her aggression in relation to her desirous longing. The transcendent function of going back and forth between opposite points of view was operating. She dreamt of me lecturing in a public forum; she longs to speak with me afterwards but I am surrounded by "Harvard types," so she feels "utterly humiliated" and scorns herself for feeling a schoolgirl crush. Leaving, she sees a "herd of alligators" nearby in a wildlife refuge where animals can return to their natural state. On waking she remembered an earlier dream of a woman she took to be me with an alligator on a leash, telling her she must learn to lead it and take its temperature. Working imaginatively with the alligators, walking unconstrained in their mud, Grace came to appreciate them: "My alligators like their mud. Their huge jaws take big strong bites of life lived adventurously." I noticed aggression moving into service of living.

She also engaged her longing imaginatively and it changed too. She talked to it, received it and surprised herself. Such desire no longer seemed shameful and degrading but evidence of connection to what she called "this other level," to which she associated God. She said, "The longing is God coming to us. I received it, whereas usually I am ashamed of it or outside it." From this crossing back and forth between opposites of desire and aggression, and their influencing each other, the transference began to change. The analyst she longed for seemed now to her more a "mythic person who lived life with passion, not in fantasy, but with others." A dream took this further and announced the third theme of the transference: I was now the red Indian. The transference object changed.

Change of Object

Again she dreamt of me lecturing in public but this time does not know me personally though she feels I am terribly important to her. She says, "I want to see who she is, for apparently I have never seen her before. Again Harvard types are around her. When I finally make out who the person Ann is, I see that she is actually an American Indian. Though the center of a large group, she herself is very inconspicuous, plain looking, a traditional long braid down her back. Her appearance greatly surprises me."

This change of the transference object that the psyche initiated, strengthened her acceptance of the little girl longing. She began to see it heading somewhere and it felt less humiliating. But that meant the humiliation got dug up again. When suffering it palpably one session, I asked what sort of image does this affect of shameful invalidity give of itself. She answered, "It is like a deformed child ... no one wants around, something dwarfed, ugly, grotesque." When I asked where she felt this in her body, she suddenly remembered a dream of ten years before when she entered analysis for the first time: "I gave birth to a premature fetus, shriveled, deformed and thought this is awful, my husband will be horrified. I felt I needed to kill it because he would not stand for this sort of disaster. But as its mother I couldn't.... As I held it, it turned into a red Indian and became red liquid."

We both felt amazed. Here was the red Indian at the very inauguration of her analytic process a decade ago with the first analyst. She said it was like jello liquid, not yet set, and she thought the dream had depicted her initial fear beginning analysis that she would be too frightened to take on what it opened up, hence it would never get born. It would not reach bodily form. The analysis did open her but she could not keep it alive after her first analyst's death. Remembering this old dream in our session joined up the work of the two analyses and returned her to a loving connection with that first analyst. She felt a continuity. I was struck by the red Indian making its appearance even then.

Right after this session she dreamt again of construction, now done by giant cockroaches tunneling under the dirt floor. She says "They will not harm me, but I know I can't live here anymore." I say that the unconscious has reframed the issue from, What is wrong with me? to, I can't live here anymore. The psyche unites the feeling of being a deformed fetus changing into red Indian liquid with recognition she must change the place she lives, the location of her identity. This led to a change in the transference field between us. Not only did the transference object change – me carrying the red Indian temporarily – but she, the subject, her own ego consciousness – changed as well.

Her ego descended to an unknowing place where she just had to look around and see what is there. In contrast to the growing up process that Winnicott describes so well (1971, chapter 6), when we move from subjective-objects to objective-objects in the external world, here we grow down to the archetypal realm where the objective-object again becomes subjectively real. We move from subjective-object to objective-object to objective-subject. This happened to the analyst as the transference object, who became in this woman's psyche a stand-in for the eventual disclosure of a new part of herself.

Change of Ego

First, however, her ego needed to change, to house the new. Boundaries enlarge in this down-going road; our ego is not lost in regression to a pre-ego or splintered-ego state, but finds itself in relation to the surround, the whole that centers and circumferences. Grace said on a personal level that she knew she must let the analyst in which went against her life long stance of maintaining relation only by keeping distance, namely keeping the other from the deformed part of herself. She knew that admitting me meant pain. She said she knew I would fail her; it was inevitable. "I know I will get hurt. This is mother stuff. I will disappoint or offend you or you will just lose interest, or you'll make a mistake or just be getting on with your life and I will feel let go. That's how deeply I resist letting you in on a deep level because I will get hurt, whether I or you wanted to or not."

Yet she also felt me as connected to some deep place, some transcendence, that the Self witnessed to and that would hold her. Reaching this place is not the result of some technique the analyst can employ. Rather, both analyst and analysand arrive there as a return to sentient being, to Self as unconscious ordering factor that works in collaboration with the ego, anchoring it, feeding it, generating it, and linking it to what lies beyond the psyche.

In this new space we are directed to new attitudes toward living, with new objects. It is not quiescent or removed from life. We are pressed instead toward specific tasks. Grace found her task in response to a dream which connected her to her own analyst within. She dreamed she was rushing off to a lecture leaving her house "a mess and too small to hold all my things and all the boxes are around needing to be unpacked. The analyst drops in for a visit. I think horrible! No place even to sit and what will she think of the mess! But she just pushes the boxes out of the way, willing to keep me company."

Grace said this dream-analyst is like a friend who just hangs out with you; she is not there to be entertained or to do, but just to be, taking time, which is very different from my expectation she will be horrified by the mess. She summed it up by saying, "This is my Ann." The real Ann and the "my Ann" do not substitute for each other or cancel each other. Both exist distinctly. And weave in and out, expanding the ego's vision in two directions: the analyst who is the red Indian who wants to be with her even in the dreadful invalid mess place, and the analyst, me, linked with doing the analytical work with her.

The work, we discovered, was to unpack the boxes which meant something very specific. In the company of this inner Ann, who is not me, but her own, and working together with me, we discovered where her dreadful feeling that she ought to know something and does not really belonged. In Jungian vocabulary, we were asking, Where does the negative animus voice really belong? It belongs in the task of unpacking her own boxes. Not going out to hear a lecture of how someone else thinks or feels, but how did she? She needed to unpack her own way of thinking and feeling, both personally and in her business life, for there was something which she should know and did not: how her own mind and heart worked. In this new place she could and did find out, and found herself delivered into a long period of successful work.

Jung says that when something crosses over from the unconscious to consciousness, it imposes an ethical obligation on us to realise its concrete form in life. This is the second stage

346

of alchemy in Dorn's scheme, of joining up the *unio mentalis* to the body (Jung 1963a, paras. 686-687, 690, 694-695; Jung 1963b, 193). Body means definite, finite form in this life. We are directed to discover the specific thing we need to do to make real our new perception in relation to reality tasks and real people with whom we live. In this way each individual analysis contributes to society as a whole. Living from this deep place breeds kinship. Spirit exists in the body. Body houses spirit.

Naming Transcendence

This analysand described her change in transference terms: "This Ann, in the dream of the boxes, which is my Ann who just came to be with me, is like the goodness of God," she said, "something that comes of its own accord and wants to be with you. In the dream I change from rushing out to hear what someone else says to unpacking my way of being." She said, "The harmonics have changed. On a personal level, some way or another we would hurt each other." That was the lens of what she called her "mother stuff," what I called the mother complex. "But on this other level where someone comes to greet you and be with you," she said, "there is an absolute relation which does hold and is holding you and it doesn't matter if mistakes are made. This is not about mistakes or even about analysis. This is long term, a level where none of us is forgotten. It is primary commitment. It isn't that you couldn't hurt me. You could. But at that level, you won't ... I know I am important at another level that you are committed to and there you won't let go. Your absolute commitment to that level means I'm never let go of."

The culmination to this particular phase of our work came a month later, again with the red Indian now directly relating to her. She dreamt, "I am with others and an Indian in full head-dress of feathers and silver appears in our midst and shows us where to go. Then I am alone with him and know that with him I shall learn to be completely myself. It is some kind of initiation and I need not be frightened ... so I am ready to open myself to him (including sexually). It is almost impersonal yet intensely personal. The climax becomes so powerful that I am awakened from my sleep. I remember that as part of his lovemaking to me, he first put his penis in my ear and semen on my head."

In associating to the dream, she remembered listening to the tape and saw now it previewed penetration of her through her ear in this dream. She heard something new about herself through the transference and the transcendent function working between us in our making space for the opposite points of view in herself that produced such conflict. The ear was her way of getting into a deep space of unknowing and out of the ego which knew all about herself as "wrong."

In her ego, Grace had been captured by her experience of her mother's negative attitude. And it was that premise – that something was basically lacking in her and had to be rehearsed and given lessons to fix it – that comprised what was wrong with her. She was living from her mother's premise, not her own. What she needed to know, and did not know, was her own way of being.

In the new unknowing space where she was penetrated by a new object that aroused her spirit and her body, she heard "new harmonics." Her thoughts were fertilised. Her old "knowing" something is wrong with her changed to her new relation to the Indian. And she remembered her mother saying sharply to her, "Stop being a wild Indian!" Through that personal association to the Indian, we explored some of its power as an archetypal symbol. The redness in the American Indian tradition bespeaks joy, passion, ardor, energy, festivity, renewal of life. And the Indian himself stood forth as masculine aggression for living. In alchemy, the *rubedo* stage marks our getting into life what has been refined in the retort of analysis. The red unset jello liquid takes on red-blooded living. The Indian animus presence bridges to the Self, and the Self bridges to reality beyond the psyche.

In this phase of analysis, Grace named the transcendent as it broke in upon her and as she experienced herself arriving there through the crossing back and forth between the opposites of the transcendent function operating within her psyche. She brings home to us, with her names of the "new harmonics" and the "American Indian" that transcendence brings with it a name, or, we arrive at a name for our personal experience of its collective reality. It is just such idiosyncratic images of the Self that make a bridge for us to the unknown that intimately touches us.

Transcendence is not something up in the sky, far away from us, abstract; it is a change of place here and now – in the ego, in the object, in the body, in the world. Spirit and body go together. Transcendence always effects a striking conjunction of the particular and the universal, the awe-inspiring and the humdrum, the vast and the concrete. To live toward it we must name it. Analysands will find their own names and they must utter them, I believe, to realise and ritualise their relation to the reality to which the Self points. Otherwise, transcendence hangs in the air, or we wrap it up as precious and keep it in the back of the drawer, or in a locked safe. The transcendent is much too alive for such treatment. It wants to be lived, housed in our body, in our society, in different forms. We can all think of various names our analysands have created to speak of their unspeakable experience – now not the agony of being lost, but the joy of having been found, known, created.

Jung sums it up as the goal of treatment: "Analysis should release an experience that grips or falls upon us as from above, an experience that has substance and body such as those things which occurred to the ancients ... then it is convincing. It must be organically true, that is, in and of our own being. If I were to symbolise it, I would choose the Annunciation (Jung 1925, 80).

Address to American Conference 'Jungians at the Crossroads: The Interface with Psychoanalysis.' Maine, 1996; published in The Journal of Analytical Psychology, *1997, 42, 1, 119-138.*

Note

1. The opposites, Jung discovered, exist in and comprise the nature of the unconscious (Jung 1967; see also Thibaudier 1995). As our consciousness grows, we experience the opposites at first as spanning a conflict between the ego and the unconscious, that is, we will house one opposite in consciousness, and the other will oppose us from the unconscious, performing a compensatory role to our one-sided consciousness. As the transcendent function operates and our ego grows big enough to hold both opposites in consciousness simultaneously, it is as if the ego now mirrors the unconscious: both contain pairs of opposites. The construction of the Self and of the ego's conversation with it is not identified with either pole of the opposites but includes both. The opposites may still conflict, but the ego takes up its position outside this opposition, being preoccupied with its relation to the Self.

References

Aimé, A. 1994. An added degree of complexity. *Journal of Analytical Psychology* 39/1, 5-21.
Atwood, G. E. and Stolorow, R. 1984. *Structures of Subjectivity.* Hillsdale, N.J.: The Analytic Press.

13. Transference, the Transcendent Function, and Transcendence

Atwood, G. E., Brandschaft, B. and Stolorow, R. D. 1987. *Psychoanalytic Treatment: An Intersubjective Approach.* Hillsdale, N.J.: The Analytic Press.

Caratenuto, A. 1986. *Kant's Dove, The History of Transference in Psychoanalysis.* trans. Joan Tambureno. Wilmette, Ill.: Chiron.

Fine, R. 1962. *Freud: A Critical Re-evaluation of His Theories.* New York: David MacKay.

Freud, S. 1984. The neuroses of defense. *SE* III, 43-71.

Freud, S. 1985a. Obsessions and phobias: their psychical mechanisms and their aetiology. *SE* III, 71-87.

Freud, S. 1895b. On the grounds for detaching a particular syndrome from neurasthenia under the description "anxiety neurosis." *SE* III, 87 – 121.

Freud, S. 1896. Further remarks on the neuro-psychoses of defense. *SE* III, 159-189.

Jung, C. G. 1920. General aspects of dream psychology. *CW* 8. *The Structure and Dynamics of the Psyche.* New York: Pantheon, 1960.

Jung, C. G. 1925. *Analytical Psychology, Notes of the Seminar.* ed. William McGuire. Princeton, N.J.: Princeton University Press, 1989.

Jung, C. G. 1938. Psychology and religion. *CW* 11. *Psychology and Religion: West and East.* New York: Pantheon, 1958.

Jung, C. G. 1945. On the nature of dreams. *CW* 8. *The Structure and Dynamics of the Psyche.* New York: Pantheon, 1960.

Jung, C. G. 1953a. *Two Essays on Analytical Psychology. CW* 7. New York: Pantheon.

Jung, C. G. 1953b. *Psychology and Alchemy. CW* 12. New York: Pantheon.

Jung, C. G. 1954. Transformation symbolism in the mass. *CW* 11. *Psychology and Religion: West and East.* New York: Pantheon, 1950.

Jung, C. G. 1958. A psychological view of conscience. *CW* 10. *Civilisation in Transition.* New York: Pantheon, 1964.

Jung, C. G. 1959a. The transcendent function. *CW* 8. *The Structure and Dynamics of the Psyche.* New York: Pantheon, 1960.

Jung, C. G. 1959b. *Aion. CW* 9:2. New York: Pantheon.

Jung, C. G. 1961. Symbols and the interpretation of dreams. *CW* 18. *The Symbolic Life.* Princeton, N.J.: Princeton University Press.

Jung, C. G. 1963a. *Mysterium Coniunctiones. CW* 14. New York: Pantheon.

Jung, C. G. 1963b. *Memories, Dreams, Reflections.* ed. Aniela Jaffé. trans. Richard and Clara Winston. New York: Pantheon.

Jung, C. G. 1967. *VII Sermones Ad Mortuos.* Somerset, England: Watkins.

Jung, C. G. 1971. *Psychological Types. CW* 6. Princeton, N.J.: Princeton University Press.

351

Clinical Issues

Jung, C. G. 1976. The Visions Seminars. 2 Books. Zürich, Switzerland: Spring Publications.

Jung, C. G. 1988. *Nietzsche's Zarathustra*. vol. I of 2 vols. ed. James L. Jarrett. Princeton, N.J.: Princeton University Press.

Racker, H. 1968. *Transference and Countertransference*. London: Hogarth.

Ricoeur, P. 1970. *Freud and Philosophy: An Essay on Interpretation*. trans. Denis Savage. New Haven: Yale University Press.

Rilke, R. M. 1923/1992. *Duino Elegies*. The second elegy. trans. David Oswald. Einsiedeln, Switzerland: Daimon.

Rilke, R. M. 1988. *Selected Letters 1902-1926*. trans. R. F. C. Hull. London: Quartet Encounters.

Steinberg, W. 1990. *Circle of Care, Clinical Essays in Jungian Therapy*. Toronto: Inner City Books.

Thibaudier, V. 1995. Seven sermons for bringing the dead father back to life. *Journal of Analytical Psychology* 40/3, 365-383.

Ulanov, A. B. 1996. *The Functioning Transcendent: Studies in Analytical Psychology*. Wilmette, Ill.: Chiron.

Winnicott, D. W. 1971. *Playing and Reality*. London: Tavistock.

Chapter 14

Countertransference and the Self

Jung's notion of the Self adds a major dimension to the therapeutic enterprise, both in theory and in practice. If we know
the Self-dimension, we live our lives differently, fundamentally
changed. It is awkward to be speaking in public about something
which operates silently, and maybe sounding as if it is something
we do as analysts which is so important when it is this other
presence we name the Self which does it and is in the doing of
it. But it is the analyst's witnessing to the silent workings of the
Self that makes its eloquent presence audible to both analyst
and analysand.

We all share amazement, for example, at the psyche's
particularity in reaching us. We feel that frisson of recognition
of the new when we hear of a youth in his twenties still locked
into fantasy who sees for himself how his aggression stalls
when the psyche gives him an image of a particular Civil War
general whose campaigns he had memorised and modeled with
toy soldiers. This general waited too long for reenforcements
instead of attacking, and hence lost the battle.

When a person comes for a consultation to discover if he or
she will begin analysis, I usually say at the end of this first meeting that the goal of analysis, as I understand it, is to establish an

ongoing, vital conversation between you and the unconscious, and that the analyst's role is to act as translator and maybe even mediator. When you establish that conversation, you can be done with the analyst. This is all I say about the process of analysis, but I am after what happens in a successful treatment: to experience the reality the Self makes a bridge to.

The Self

The Self, as we know, manifests as both process and content, as ordering principle in the midst of chaos, and as disordering force that defeats and breaks down our ego when we hold too tightly to our constructed schemes. Any of us working in analysis knows that the Self feels like the sacred that can break into the humdrum at any time. We hope that the rituals of analysis we construct with each analysand contains these break-ins and transform them into break-throughs.

Jung's word Self offers a vocabulary to speak about a fact of the psyche, not just my psyche, or yours, but what the psyche shows and speaks of itself. An objective, given path or way exists for each of us. But to reach this objectivity, we must go into intimacies of our subjective history, not just what we claim and know, but also what we have buried, hidden, put into another room, what terrifies us and makes us ashamed. We cannot find our path without creating it.

The Self makes a bridge to a reality that exists far outside our psyche and yet also deep within it. We contact this objective reality pointed to by this odd word Self (which is not a very good term to refer to something beyond ourselves) only if we subjectively construct relationship to it. Paradox looms. Operations go on in the psyche (to which dreams, religious visions, alchemical imagery attest), not just when our ego initiates them or participates in them, but they do not exist for us unless we help make them, assemble them, pay homage to them.

The Self and the reality it points to need to be felt, received, and known by us for us to participate in it. This reality which deconstructs every human form we invent to receive it, calls for our human welcome and gathering of forms to respond to it. Thus our relationship to this reality always begins in a muddle, a formlessness, a meandering around until the new germinates, incubates, gestates, slouching toward Bethlehem to be born. (As analysts we often experience this blankness in a session when we realise we haven't a clue what is going on, what the analysand's dream means, or what the transference dynamics are, and wonder if we should give the patient's money back.)

The psyche tells us about itself and about the reality it witnesses to. It grips us with inner intensity, so that a poet like Rilke dedicates his whole life to speaking this first thing, this paramount presence which forces itself with "unremitting vibrations" into his being, changing, he said, his body into soul, so that even a near-by flower fills "with boundless meaning" and a bird-call transforms into "an event of ... deepest conscious-ness ... inexplicably uniting outer and inner worlds into one uninterrupted space by not stopping   at the confines of his body" (Rilke 1912/1923, 118-119). Jung too marks the moment when he consented to this other closer than his heartbeat and it changed his life: "It was then I ceased to belong to myself alone, ceased to have the right to do so.... It was then I dedi-cated myself to the service of the psyche. I loved it and I hated it, but it was my greatest wealth" (Jung 1963, 192).

As analysts we know such moments that quicken our blood, or make our breathing hasten as if we are running to greet some ineffable presence. This is what got us into analysis in the first place and enabled us to survive training. This sense of the other addressing us particularly (like the youth with the image of the General) sustains our going on being analysts, keeping us alive and excited in the work, for me now thirty years. Each of us may describe those moments with Self somewhat differently and including different body experiences of energy or excitement, a watchful stillness, or feeling plugged in, or even ignited, but we share the sense of something there, pushing, pulling, or absorbing us, requiring our response. For without our response, it remains anonymous and a defeat for the ego, instead of a greeting, such as Rilke described as "a feeling that the infinite was gently penetrating him from all sides and that the stars were resting in his breast" (Rilke 1912/1923, 120).

Countertransference covers vast areas. I want to focus specifically on the analyst's countertransference to the Self as it constellates in analysands' material, in the transference-countertransference field, and in our own experiences of the Self and what we make of them in living our lives, for that brings a background into the treatment from the analyst's side which influences the field and our vision of the analysand's material.

I. Theory: Jung and Others

Most theorists assert that the transformative agent in therapy invariably comes down to the analysand's new introject of the analyst. Jung anticipates this insight into the crucial importance of the personal object relation: "The psychotherapist ... must be absolutely clear that the treatment of the soul of a patient is a *relationship* in which the doctor is just as much involved as the patient...." and, "The personality of the patient demands the personality of the doctor ..." (Jung 1934/1964, pars. 338, 352). But other schools of depth psychology stop there, with the new object relation as the fulcrum for transformation of the analysand.

Although other theorists notice something bigger going on in clinical treatment and even employ religious language to describe it, they deny its referent. Words like ontological (Laing 1969, 39ff.), sacred (Winnicott 1971a, 5), prayer (Bollas 1987, 17, 31), faith (Bion 1970, 32), resurrection of the body (Milner 1960, 238), are increasingly used to describe psyche while jettisoning the reality of God or of a transcendent realm of Isness, All, Source, and Goal to which the psyche belongs. This exclusion is proper insofar as psychodynamic theorists do not see themselves as investigating what used to be called metaphysics. Furthermore, the displacement of passion in official religious bodies from the bedazzlements of the divine to the administration of doctrine, ethics, and politics that flow from such a vision has invested religion with such a hortatory tone that analysts want to eschew it altogether. But in clinical terms, this means emphasis falls on the personal as the agent of change, to the exclusion of what Jungians call the archetypal and all that it mediates of reality beyond the psyche.

We find, then, the transcendent hiding in analysts' vocabularies and the relationship between analyst and analysand carrying all the weight of transformation (Ulanov 1986/2002). The open rejection of religion by Freud shifts transformation to his illusion of a future effected by psychoanalysis instead, where, for all his impassive neutrality, the analyst lends out his ego, and sometimes money as well, to his patients, as a source of greater vision and freedom (Freud 1927; Roazen 1975, 310, 329, 422, 423, 425, 435). Even in Hans Loewald's application of Freudian ideas to religion where primary and secondary process mentation balance in a sense of living time in eternity, it is our relation to our analyst in the present which shows us how to reorder and respond anew to our past (Loewald 1978a, 51; 1957, 224-225; 1977, 379; 1978b, 387-398). We cannot interpret what Lacan calls *le mot* from the other language of unconscious drives and biology, without our analyst as the mediator of reconnecting desire and word, what Kristeva calls bonding, that makes a place again for the soul in our world of opulence and misery (Lacan 1966, 111ff.; Lacan 1968, xxvii, 102 n33, 104 n41; Kristeva 1995, 4, 9, 27, 29, 33, 44). Even with Klein repudiating religion as squashing intellectual freedom and personal authority, we reach our most intense knowledge of good and evil and the moral ambiguity of life and death in accepting the good and bad breast operating in ourselves and the analyst (Klein 1946, 2, 5, 6; 1952, 62, 63, 66, 72).

When we agree with R. D. Laing, quoting Heidegger, that "the dreadful has already happened" in the loss of our soul by a divorce of our behavior from our experience which empties life of all meaning (Laing 1967, 12), only the therapeutic relationship blasts through this void to restore self to self, and with it a sense of purpose. Being thrown into existence rouses us to a vision of our own creativity, that Edith Weigert says we forge with the therapist by authentic choices to become active guardians of our own existence (Weigert 1970, 239-248).

With emphasis on the environment to reach the creative living that Winnicott counts as more valuable than health, we need playful freedom with an analyst who lends us her being as a subjective-object by holding us and reflecting back to us our sense of I-am that links up with the I-am of monotheism (Winnicott 1971b, chapter 4; Winnicott 1968, 243; see also Ulanov 1996, chapter 1). If the curative effect of treatment comes down to the personal relationship of the therapeutic couple, as Guntrip concludes, then transcendence locates in the human person (Guntrip 1973, 180-184). The analyst recreates the role of what Bollas calls the transformational object which our mother once played, so we can unfold our true self idiom that was foreclosed by trauma or neglect and restore our inalienable human right to ecstasy (Bollas 1991, 21, 44, 111).

Whatever school of depth psychology, the weight of psychoanalytic cure falls on the analyst functioning as Kohut's notion of the selfobject for the analysand who then can recover narcissistic energy which, through phase-appropriate optimal frustrations with the analyst, transmutes into worthy ideals supported by sturdy self-esteem and, as well, blooms in qualities of wisdom, compassion, humor (Kohut 1971, 50, 64, 172, 197; 1984, 81ff.). The analytical couple operating within the inter-subjective system, as emphasised by Stolorow, et al. (Stolorow, Brandschaft, Atwood 1987, 9), acts as the agent of change in the analysand. Working successfully with clients whose distress displays nonverbal, somatic forms of communication and often requires hospitalisation, depends, many authors agree, on the analysts' registering countertransference reactions in their own bodies and minds, which locates the source of relief in the analyst as a new object within the client's psyche, like a new planet whose beneficent gravity rearranges the whole orbit of suffering (Alexandris and Vaslamatzis 1993).

Jung and Jungians do not quibble with these excellent points made by many analysts. Yet, if we take the Self seriously, we must also take seriously the difference its presence makes in the clinical work of analysis. This is not theory, but experience, and one I understand to be the source of transformation for the client in analysis. Just as anima or animus forge a bridge to the Self, the Self functions as a bridge to what transcends the psyche and from which healing flows (Ulanov and Ulanov 1994, chapter 1; Ulanov 1996, chapter 3; see also chapters 7, 13, 16). Thus to experience the Self, means a process of what an analysand, recovering from three suicidal attempts, calls "really living, not just surviving." She did use me as the new introject the psychoanalysts describe, often ruthlessly. But she used this introjected me to reach through to something else. That something else is Self country and the reality it witnesses to. Her dream sums it up: she awakes in the dark but is not afraid because she now possesses on her bedside table a small, delicate, feminine, silver flashlight which she can turn on to look around in the dark. Associating to the dream, she said to me, "That's you. You are the flashlight. The flashlight is you in me; it's mine, to use as I need."

When I say to a person the goal of analysis aims to establish a sturdy conversation between you and your psyche, I am meaning an experience will happen if we succeed in our work, that will change your whole life. It may relieve us utterly of symptoms; or we may retain symptoms but the carrying of them acquires a different meaning that makes the whole venture worth it.[1] For this woman, the flashlight, however valuable, was not the point or the goal, but rather what it illuminated was the goal. She could now see into the dark that three times before nearly killed her. The image of the flashlight making light in the dark made a bridge for her to what she felt was central, her picture of God, though she eschewed any religious belief. She called the central territory "a dappled world," neither the glaring light that left her parched and isolated and drove her to suicidal attempts, nor the thick dark of her depression, but a play of light and shadow, of good and bad, of others and self, of sorrow and sweetness (Ulanov 1996, chapter 10).

Absolute Knowing

The added dimension Jung brings, and calls archetypal, reaches to the facts of the psyche, already there before we create them, but which become real to us only as we create and find them. When we connect to this archetypal world and especially to the archetype of the Self which orders and centers the archetypal world of the unconscious, we come into another kind of knowing which Jung calls absolute. There we just know something, or something in us does. The knowing goes on outside the ego. Jung calls it a knowing that is a '"perceiving which ... seems to consist of images, of subjectless 'simulacra'" (Jung 1952, 493, para. 931; see also Neumann 1956; see also von Franz 1972, 212-214; see also, Aziz 1990, 110-115, 119-122). It delivers itself to us. We do not invent it, think it up, create it out of wish or will. Fact arrives and bestows authority.

When we experience this absolute knowing, like the poet Rilke, our usual ego dualities of inner and outer, subjective and objective, body and spirit, time and space dissolve. The stars take up residence in our breast too. A self-subsistent meaning shows itself to us; through the impact of synchronistic events, we know the *coniunctio* of the large and the small, the macro-cosm in the microcosm of our particular limited individuality, our body shimmering into spirit and the spirit luminating into body.

To arrive here extends the transformative effects of analysis. Transformation does not arise only from the analysand's new introject of the analyst. For who is to say the analyst is so much better an object than the original parent, an assumption that amounts to a shadow of hubris in our analytical profession, and which also disregards the value of relating to one's destiny. Transformation occurs as the analysand comes into relation to the Self which yields moments of absolute knowledge about reality well beyond as well as lodged deep within the depths of the psyche. The isolated patient, the one, becomes the many; the lowly individual coextends with the totality. We need each other to reach this depth. We depend on personal relationship to reach relationship to the transpersonal. But we do not create the transpersonal out of a new introject or object relation.

To arrive here reverses the aim of analysis. Jung says, "Thus you can not only analyse your unconscious but you also give your unconscious a chance to analyse yourself, and therewith you gradually create the unity of conscious and unconscious without which there is no individuation at all. If you apply this method, then I can come in as an occasional adviser, but if you don't apply it, then my existence is of no use for you" (Jung 1973, 460; 2 May 1947).

This perceiving of facts of the psyche, this absolute knowing that goes on in us is not connected to our ego. But we cannot know about its presence in us unless our ego connects to it (Ulanov 1987/2000, chapter 1). Jung's method of approach helps. We submit our ego to the chaos of emotions. We find the images that express those emotions, images whose resonance inhabits our body as well as our soul. Then we translate those images into the language of analytical psychology which grants us sufficient distance from them so that we can collect and compare them and thus map the objective psyche as it intersects with our personal experience (Jung 1963, 181, 186ff.). We achieve then, a many layered experience of our own self in relation to the Self. We acquire aid for our problems at the same time we are ushered into a bigger space of the objective psyche and the reality of which it too is a part. Psychology includes ontology.

Three Levels of Countertransference

When we examine our reactions to the Self, we must keep in mind the three levels of countertransference. On the normal level, we are referring to our personal style, to the natural rhythm of our responses crafted out of our own history of object relationships and experience with the numinous. For example, some of us always register the animal level of Self. I found myself spontaneously greeting an analysand whose sessions for the previous month were conducted on the phone because he was recovering from a traumatic illness that left his vision impaired. I put my face next to his, kissing his cheek hello, which I had never done in all the years of analysis beforehand. Uncertain whether he could see me, I wanted him to smell my nearness, much as an animal does, to scent our glad and durable connection to each other which survived intact despite his being pitched onto the borders of life and death. Later, I brought up my behavior for his analysis.

Abnormal countertransference hits our own complexes which need more analysis, the ones that send us back to GO without collecting an extra two hundred dollars. The complex monopolises our freedom to see clearly by reintroducing old wounds into the present relationship with the analysand. For example, if a patient adorns me with the idealization that bespeaks the Self, I must wrestle with dogged wounds to self-esteem and try to tolerate the transference without changing the subject, or prematurely interpreting this splendor as belonging to the patient or the Self. Analysands often see us as so much better than we are, as more whole, more faithful to the center, more vitally living. But if our personal complex of inferiority intervenes, we detour the analysand's process. Part of our burden consists in carrying this numinous figure, much like the ass on which Christ sits. On the other hand, no comfort comes from being seen as much worse than we are. I remember perceiving in a first interview that if treatment were to succeed, the person's entire constructed world-view was going to be dismantled in order to reach the original traumatic rupture from the Self for which the world-view compensated. And the agency of destruction was going to be transferred to me. I was going to be the target. I fought against the negative transference and countertransference, trying to explain what was happening and going to happen. My naiveté and cowardly wish to duck out were firmly punished by months of icy control of me under a facade of niceness, all of which made me suffer the deadness within myself that communicated the repressed deadness in the patient.

Objective countertransference, so named because induced in us by the unconscious in the analysand, gives us valuable information about what is making its way to consciousness in the client. Again, we may be asked to carry intimations of the Self the analysand has yet to realise. This can be a positive, or a negative experience. For the Self leaves clues for us to find, much as the breadcrumbs in the forest lead to the witch or to the healing fountain. What stands out as important is the analyst's capacity to spy the Self beckoning to the analysand. It may be buried in the client's personal complex, or lying around in full view like the generosity of *prima materia*. For the analyst to point to the Self changes the client's capacity to see it.

For example, one woman suffering from grave self-doubt and loathing, felt compelled nonetheless to show me pages of her journals while dismissing them as mindless meanderings (see also chapter 13). What I read there, however, amounted to her conversations with the Self which she had carried on for a long time. I said as much, which galvanised a tremendous reaction. What she thought was worthless, in fact gave evidence of connection to something deep within her that also transcended her. Some of her aggression then sprang loose from being frozen into repetitious self-attacks to use for the task of seeing the Self and not superimposing her personal complex between it and her. I said consciously what was making its way from her unconscious. The psyche, through my remark, reframed the issue confronting her. Her focus shifted from how meager her efforts proved, to what did she make of this other she had been conversing with all these years, and what did this other make of her?

We must keep these levels of countertransference in mind when we look to see Self events in our analysand's material, to see Self dynamics in the transference-countertransference field between us, and to see how the work with an analysand touches our own living toward the Self.

Countertransference to the Self in Analysands' Material

To spy Self dynamics in material analysands bring to a session of course reflects our personal style of doing analysis. To be alert to countertransference means we explore our physical responses, our conceptual framework, and the sigh of our souls too deep for words. Does our body temperature rise? Do our whiskers twitch? Do we descend to a place of spacious calm? Do tears come to our eyes? Are we moved into a response beyond words? For me, I register a quickening, an excitement, a sense of pulsating energy that focuses my attention acutely. On the negative side, I must watch not to get carried away by excitement and pounce or pronounce about the Self material. What the client is saying gives information, but it is something through what is said that seems to signal an added presence. I see or hear something through the material, often grim material.

For example, a woman of fifty was describing her activity as a six-year-old child: "I was a serial doll-killer. I took off their heads and then their arms would come undone and then their legs." The dismembered parts left around the house alerted the adults to her wanton destruction. They warned her off other children's dolls, forbidding her to touch them. While listening to her, I was remembering her receiving letters from the serial killer Ted Bundy when he waited in prison on death row, and her willingness to answer them. She also had dreamt some years before of a Ted Bundy figure jumping on her back, threatening to break it. At the same time she said of the dream, yes, he is sadistic but also he embodies a terrific force of energy which, in the dream, she imagined she could harness for creative living. Listening to her story about beheading dolls, I heard myself asking, "What were you looking for?" She surprised herself when she answered: "I wanted to see what made the eyes see, or not see. My mother had beautiful blue eyes, like the dolls, but she never saw me when she looked at me. This was important scientific research I was doing. But when I snapped that one central rubber band back of the eyes, the whole doll fell apart, and I could not figure out how to put it together again."

The two of us, then, in our session saw through her sadism to a steadfast persistence to understand the cause of her mother's inability to see her. Beheading dolls, which looked like horrendous behavior, in fact harbored a hidden task of self-repair. For her mother succumbed to psychotic fits and beat her little daughter. It helped the daughter immensely in surviving those beatings to speculate that her mother could not see you, even though her mother appeared, like the dolls, to be looking right at you, and that she did not intend to kill you when she beat you but instead fell apart like the dolls, and could not put herself back together again.

What was it that made me see she was looking for something and spy in her sadism the compassionate effort to understand her mother's absence of seeing? Something was silently nosing into my mind; it elicited an answering activity from the analysand who then uncovered a deep intent in herself. Self dynamics arose between us and communicated to us from the shared field but was triggered by my angle of vision which changed her view. Spying Self activity keeps us young in our profession, excited and amazed, for its presence enlivens the work. We do not know what is going to happen. The session may turn into an adventure, into primary research, as the six-year-old girl conducted with her dolls.

When that something comes into a session, or when we discover its presence there all along, it frees us from burdens of overconscientious responsibility. We see that we do not have to be doing all the work – the understanding, the uncovering, the putting together, even the interpreting. Something else is rustling, fluttering, scouting, advancing into visibility. *It* does the work. We need to be alert to this *it*, to find the ego-attitudes that allow us to perceive its begetting. Usually, we think three of us exist in a session – the analysand, the analyst, and the psychic objects communicated back and forth arising out of the field between us. To our astonishment, a fourth resides here as well, in which the whole work takes place but which also does the work. But we only see this presence initiating and synthesizing the work if our egos are involved, actively alert, working as hard as we can, yet capable of being surprised and gladdened.

This seeing unearths our collective context as well, bringing to the surface what sort of heremeutic shapes what we find and construct. In the case of our Jungian clan, the existence of the Self comprises one of our basic ontological premises. Among our different Jungian tribes, we debate what we mean by Self. We must be mindful of our own assumptions, the premises of our method, for they shape not just our interpretations, but our angle of vision. We accept our moments of non-knowing blankness, for example, if we acknowledge the existence of objective, invisible, psychic forces doing their work. Our ego moves over for the Self. Yet if we hold that the Self constitutes a process as well as content, and does not drop ready-made into our awareness like a guiding parent, but rather that we construct conversation with it, then we see our ego also must contribute something to our moment of perceiving it.

For example, with the serial doll-killer, the concept of

completeness as distinguished from perfection shaped my see-ing, so that the goal was not for her to put aside her sadism in dismembering the dolls, her mother, and, in the transference, me, but instead to include all the parts, bad and good. Listening to her, I discovered I was gathering bits and pieces – as if drifting on the ocean floor to see what swam by. Ted Bundy swam into my view, and the threat of a broken back in her dream, and her seeing that violent jumping as energy crammed into too small a package of sadism. Those bits assembled and rose up in me as enthusiasm for her six-year-old child-self embarked on scientific research into the origin of perception.

Countertransference to the Self in the Transference-Countertransference Field

In the clinical field of interaction between client and analyst, Self dynamics arrange both parties to see the unseeable. Synchronistic events occur which startle both parties. For example, an analyst I was supervising brought to our session a painting his patient brought to him which depicted the patient's gripping experience of the Self. The painting amazed the analyst because it presented an image that the analyst himself had been working on, unknown to the patient, which embodied the Self for the analyst. The patient's painting looked like the alchemical pictures of the *Sol Terrenus*, the sun in the depths of the earth, a fiery bright disk blazing out behind a blackest dark center (Jung 1953, 94, 99-100, pars. 113, 120-121).[2] At the center of the earth, this solar light illuminates the unconscious, bespeak-ing an earthy masculine arising from the depths in contrast to the heights of the heavenly solar Apollo. The patient's painting emerged from his work helping AIDS victims in a residence for homosexual men, hence bearing on the chthonic masculine.

He painted a huge, densely black circle from which emitted hundreds of tiny bright rays almost sperm-like with their energetic, whipping tails. I gasped when I saw the picture and heard what the analyst made of it in terms of his own image of the Self, because both pictures portrayed a vision of dark and light that had imploded into my consciousness when a little girl and stayed with me over many decades since. The image of deepest dark with brightest light coming from behind it presents the ambiguity of light and dark, of good and bad, each being either and both, and neither one overcoming the other. Here were we three – the analyst, the patient, and the supervisor – unbeknownst to each other, each in our own lives, beholding a shared image of the fourth. This fourth was a Self-image conveying the numinous nature of reality, its mixture of opposites, which had emerged in this particular form in our separate lives and joined us in this synchronistic moment in the here and now.

Such synchronicity carries authority to say the unsayable. We are given an image of what belongs not just to this trio of analyst, patient, and supervisor, nor even to all of us here at a conference, but to everyone. This Self-image points to reality to which we all belong, and ushers us into its precincts, moving us to feel its presence infiltrating each of us, binding us together. To glimpse what objectively holds us in our work as analysts buoys our strength, gladdens our hearts.

Countertransference and Absolute Knowing

Penetrating to archetypal layers of the psyche, and especially to the centering archetype of the Self, arranges a field between analyst and analysand that can prompt spontaneous behavior that surprises both people. Legal dangers of malpractice and ethical transgressions of another's integrity, if they threaten at all, usually lurk here, I believe, because we cannot always tell whether this behavior speaks more of our countertransference complex needing additional analysis, or of our genuine risk to respond to the Self with the new, with what colors outside the lines. Usually, alas, a mixture of the two prevails. Thus rules for analysts prove invaluable aids, like a home base in a game of tag, or delineated boundaries in a swimming hole. We know on paper what not to do. Do we know what to do, when to say yes to an impulse which nonetheless breaks the rules? (Jung 1963, 192-193).3

What helps us is familiarity with the ontological premises of our method. Our hermeuneutic makes a container for the shining presence of reality. Part of our theory derives from Jung's discovery in his descent into psyche that opposites comprise the unconscious (Jung 1925/1963, 11-14). When neurosis unbalances us, consciousness carries some of these opposites in conflict with their counterparts in the unconscious. Treatment amounts to gathering into consciousness the opposites split between conscious and unconscious so that we suffer consciously what before warred interminably between our conscious reason and our unconsciously derived symptom, our conscious resolve and our unconscious compulsion. To gather all the tension of opposing forces into consciousness, to suffer unappeased desire consciously, to survive the devastating intimacy of exuberant affect versus steely refusal ignites the transcendent function, which, *Deo concedente*, yields a creative solution that houses the whole.

On the way to such expanded consciousness, moments arise in the field between analyst and analysand that illumine the reality that holds us in being. We are transplanted to a depth where we see the radical congress this reality conducts with us. We still keep mindful of the tasks of analysis and the inequities of power in the relationship (see Guggenbuhl-Craig 1971; see also Ross and Roy 1995) as that is our ego working along like a good donkey. But alighting it, making an entry through this ego work is a spark of the divine come into the human, a tiny fish eye in the vast dark of the cosmos, that yields glimpses of unending light existing there in the depths and in the heights all the time. One is moved to act in surprising ways.

Such surprising events happened in the analysis of a woman I will call Kate, who maintained relation to her aggression at the expense of splitting off her dependence, when she confided a trauma from her earliest two years of life. Her distress over the trauma compounded because she did not know entirely what had happened, only something hurtful and horrible which left her standing in the hospital crib, holding onto the top bar of its railing looking out into the dark, feeling utterly alone. This event occurred before her ego existed intact, so she never metabolised it, suffered it and integrated it. Nor had she words to capture and represent to herself what had happened (Kristeva 1995, 7, 29) but only body feelings, disparate images and odd behavior expressing injury and her response to it. The event stood dissociated from her sense of self, always existing apart, threatening to invade her with feelings of madness as well as acute pain. In that split-off space existed emotions of desolation, utter aloneness in a vast world, and more frighten-ingly still, a sense that intense destructiveness threatened to kill her.

She remembers waking up crying out for help in the dark. She cried out, needy, hurt, afraid. Someone finally came, she said, but "the one who came hurt me. So I knew then it was dangerous to cry out for help. Don't call out! They'll hurt you. I remember standing there feeling utterly alone, no one to depend on, so I'd better depend on myself, I'd better take care of myself." She remembers a big face disconnected from a body looming over her and blotting her out and everything else too. Behind the face, just thickest blackness. The face seemed to lack a mouth, or a hand was held over her own mouth. She couldn't breathe and thought the words she later crafted of, "I am going to die," described her suffocation. Hearing this, I commented that for an instant, and hence carried in her body forever after, she experienced a blotting out of self, an annihilation, "a psychic state of 'notness'" (Olney 1993, 56).

Was she touched? she remembers wearing a hospital coat, open, with no pants. Was she invaded in her tiny most private womb of femininity? Yes and no. Before ego, without consolidated language, only terrifying wisps of ghost-like memories remained and odd behavior which took her several years into analysis to confide: she slept all her life, single and married, mother of four grown children, a woman with some experience of sexual affairs, in soft white cotton underwear, like a child's underpants. She slept with her hands folded between her legs, the left in a fist which expressed fury and fear of the energy that might annihilate her, and the right protectively over her vagina.

We worked on this trauma bit by bit over the years, not all at once, but with steadiness as we made our way down to its core. The day after the trauma, she went home from the hospital. "The first effect," she said, "was I cut myself off from my mother. I would not let her mother me." Her mother had not mothered her much before her trip to the hospital, or after. Being too nervous to take her daughter for the operation, she enlisted the aunt to do so. Also, when the next year she took the client's older sister to first grade and discovered that the school provided a kindergarten as well, even though my client was only three, she was very bright, and her mother convinced the school to admit her, which made my client feel her mother had gotten rid of her. Kate said she became her mother's mother after the hospital: "I went round to her side; I became empathetic to the other's need." For with keen empathic skill she developed exceptional gifts to aid adolescent psychotic patients in her first adult career as a psychiatric nurse, and later as hospital chaplain, and finally as spiritual director. But her own dependency needs went into hiding, to be relieved only vicariously through helping those of others. She knew this and said that we must watch not to repeat this pattern in our relationship.

With her dependency needs split-off, what stood in front of them was ruthless aggressive energy which she used to shield the undefended hurt child within and to size up safe places without. She went to a rough city school and made it clear to schoolmates that they could not mess with her. In her church, which enraged her with its rejection of women, she spoke up against injustice in the world. She developed a masculine tough-ness that would not let her, as she put it, "sacrifice myself for relationship," but which was not strident, but full of life, humor and sexual passion. She baptised this energy Arnot, and dreamt of it as a big thug who threw "suburban Mommies" out of her car. But she refused to let this Arnot energy destroy her, so in the dream, she jumps in the driver's seat and runs him over!

Arnot stood in front of her dependency needs, protected her, and allowed her to create with other men what she could not find in her own marriage. The sexual and emotional intimacy with her partner, in relationships that lasted as lifelong friends and existed as lovers only one at a time, held her split-off child part. Her husband was absolutely bound to her — hence she projected her dependency into his own and could not leave him without leaving behind her own unlived soul piece of emotional need. But he did not want emotional closeness, did not want to know about the possible combination she yearned for, of the Arnot energy and her dependency that she and her mother abandoned, of sexual excitement along with spiritual surrender.

Other men found in her their own link between sex and spirit, acceptance of dependency and passionate excitement. But she did not find it in herself, though perceptive men could see it in her. One of her hospital patients whom she helped through a disabling disease, said to her with surprise, "Why, you're a sheep in wolf's clothing!"

The image of the clenched fist she felt in her solar plexis (the power chakra) gradually melted into energy that went all through her body and broke down the compartments she made of her life – job, home, children, friends, lovers. Her dreams early on in the analysis represented this compartmentalization through images of her living in big buildings with many separate apartments. But the melting of the fist also brought to the surface that dense blackness behind the looming hospital face and she suffered terror that it would annihilate her, dreaming herself crawling in the subway, weak and helpless, with her husband standing by, not helping. She said, "I am the Ayotollah toward the needy me." In that gap between her aggression and loving dependency she felt congealed, immobilized, she said: "It's a place of suicide and overwhelming energy. When I gave up on someone being there, I became everything – subject and object, all-powerful. When I went home from the hospital, I thought I must take care of myself and I started having tantrums to get my way. That was Arnot."

As she gave up the protection of the Arnot thug energy, she said she felt that renunciation tossed her into the darkness, to be shot like Anwar Sadat. The gap of unorganised energy and swirling neediness opened. Panicked, frozen, powerless, she also felt something more lurking in the black energy behind the looming hospital face. For the energy had a scent to it that she linked to Christ who, in her religious belief, meant less to her than God. Her dependency shifted more overtly onto me but she feared I would not want to go there into that black energy, to be in it with her.

It was then she confided that she had worn the child-type underpants at night for over forty years. She felt tremendous shame that she had needed to do so, felt shame for sounding full of whiney self-pity, and shame that somehow she had deserved what happened in the hospital, that she was being punished for being different from her mother and sister who appeared as a nervous symbiotic unity whereas she thrummed with all this aggressive energy.

In the midst of our interaction in this field of despair and shame, energy and terror, sorrow and rage, I spontaneously offered to her a catalogue picture and order-form of an adult woman's soft white cotton underpants that I found wonderful. I surprised myself as well as her. I did not know or plan to do this and later worried over my impulsiveness. It just felt right to do and I hoped I had caused no harm.[4] Something sure in me knew and carried me along with its knowing, but not my own will or thought-out strategy. I went with it, trusted it.

When we analysed it, she said, "I knew you broke a rule. I've broken rules all my life. It was that someone broke them for *me*. You felt like a mother to me. I never had anyone to tell the truth of the underpants to or to receive it myself. It's when you broke the rules that broke it open for me. I did not believe it (that someone exists I can depend upon) until then." Clearly we dwelt in the archetypal field of the Mother. But it broke open something else that led to the experience of absolute knowing that Jung writes about. For following my action, the gap between her aggressive energy and loving dependence fell into her consciousness, instead of one opposite staying conscious, striving against the other in the unconscious. She suffered the whole tension consciously. We shared it between us as a field of circulating energy that rearranged her personal conflict and revealed through it a decisive God-image.

She had dreamt almost a year before of a Self-image as a huge whale swimming toward the ship where she stood at the railing with her daughter. It was clear the whale would severely cut itself on the ship's propellers and wreck the ship. The whale was the abysmal dark that carried Jonah, or swallowed Christ. In the dream, she hands a baby to her daughter and goes to rescue the women and children. The ship and its crew sink, to which she associated that her usual way of running things, "business as usual, is finished." She said standing at the ship's railing was like standing in the hospital crib.

She felt so much concern for the cut-up whale she engaged it in active imagination and felt it saying to her it sacrificed itself so she could discover compassion, that even though it will get hurt in the process, it never dies, only gets scarred, and that she too will bear scars for helping the whale. She wanted then to live hidden in the whale, in her own cut-up wounded place of unmet dependency. The whale lets her stay for a while and even return there occasionally, for it will always be there if she needs it. But the whale insists she return to live in the world. Unexpectedly, some months after this active imagination, she found herself in a town whose name meant Whale. There she accepted a gift of a body-work session where, through her body being touched, she felt all of herself held, and the energy and her dependency, heretofore separated into compartments, bridged the gap. She said, "The whale brought me to an experience of external holding." But what was left out was the murderous aspect of the energy that also inhabited the wound.

After the underpants incident, she and I lived out in our relationship her dependency, and, when I failed to match it with attunement, her fury. For example, she got up the courage to call me once when in need between sessions, something she hotly resisted until now, and I did not immediately recognise her voice on the phone. I was as surprised as she was, because I usually do hear voices accurately. She sounded so different to me on the phone that I registered shock when she said who it was. We surmised that maybe it was the voice of her dependency that I did not know well yet. In another session, when we reached the little girl, I was so engrossed that I let the time run over five minutes and it was she who had to notice and call us to conclude. Because she had to assume a management role to contain the vulnerability, the role she usually took for others, it impeded her from really leaning on me. Though expressing murderous feelings toward me, she was less interested in prosecuting my limitations than she was in exploring her experience of dependency and being let down. Hence we endured a fruitful process of what Kohut would call optimal frustrations which allowed her to build structure inside herself, a structure that she bemoaned lacking when she said, "I have no way to keep connected, alive. I am missing something inside" (Kohut 1971, 50, 64). Slowly, she built up in herself what she felt was missing. I was amazed and grateful, on top of being sorry for failing her, that my limits proved so profitable to her, that she made so much out of them to her own benefit.

A few months later she returned to the underpants incident and said, "I don't need you anymore in the mother spot. That finished with the underwear." Right after this an odd synchronicity occurred that clinched her full experience of dependency. Although objectively unrelated to Kate, this event touched her most vulnerable spot. A medical emergency blew up in my family which necessitated rearranging the times or places of clients' sessions for a few weeks. I did not explain to Kate any details of the emergency which turned out to be pivotal because it strengthened her efforts to resist falling into the temptation of her usual role of taking care of the other person and retreating into self-holding of her own dependency needs (Winnicott 1962, 58). This was the old pattern she had warned against our repeating in the beginning of the analysis. She would exercise her well-developed compassion to give to the other person while holding herself up until the emergency passed. She would withdraw her own dependency on the other person, not to overburden them in their crisis. She could not do this with me, because she knew no details, nor even whose emergency it was. And she wanted to bear the strain and avoid repeating her old pattern.

Her dependency intensified because, though she knew I was flapped as my emergency persisted, our relationship went on as usual with my presence to her in our sessions. She leaned her full weight upon me to keep in touch with her out of myself, regardless of what else was happening to me. That whole spring of sessions she was aware of this – that our continuity endured because of me, not because she could use objective information about my situation to withdraw into self-holding and minister to me and hence vicariously to her own need. She recognised I went on being there with her even though something urgent and demanding called my energies elsewhere.

The combination of these transference-countertransference dynamics around the mother archetype and the underpants incident breaking the rules, made Kate feel the gap closed in herself between dependence-denied and ruthless energy exploited as armor. Proof of that mending was her dream of me on our summer recess: a bubbling spring of healing energy arises between my right toe and the one next to it. I had told her I would be briefly inaccessible because of foot surgery that summer, but not the precise nature of it or which foot. Her dream pictured the precise toe that was to be operated upon. She said she saw through the dream that there was an objective connection through the psyche, that she did not have to befriend me to make it happen.

Because of the safety the whale image of the Self offered her a year and a half before, she could bear with a new frightening image that arrived that summer. The image was a vortex of violent churning energy which threatened to pull her down and under, to kill her by moving her to kill herself to escape its power. This spot was acutely painful because she felt so helpless and felt murderous impulses toward herself to escape from the pain. She felt the utter defeat of her ego to control this energy, and she was terrified to submit to it.

This phase of her analysis put her into what we might call the dark side of the Self – knowing no way out, not wanting to escape, but not knowing how to stay faithful, all markers gone. The strategies her ego had perfected of vicariously getting her dependency needs met through meeting those of others, while holding her self up and refusing to lean on others, all went by the wayside. These ego-crafted containers were too small for all this energy. The Self defeated them. They either crashed, or something in her moved her to renounce them.

It was at this time she gave up the possibility of lovers; she wanted to face this murderous energy in the gap directly and not detour it through helping a man mend gaps in himself. She made use of an interpretation I made of her distressing symptom of vomiting after sexual intercourse with her lover. I said the little girl in her wanted someone to depend upon; she was too young for sex. She said it was fraudulent: the man thought he was getting a woman and he got a little girl. But she had no replacement yet for this defense, and in giving it up, felt menaced by immediate energy which she might not survive because she could not house it in herself. She felt in danger. As Jung says, in such darkness there is nothing we can do but wait, "with a certain trust in God, until, out of a conflict borne with patience and courage, there emerges a solution destined – although I cannot foresee it – for that particular person" (Jung 1953, 31, para. 37). Kate did trust in God, but she still felt I did not get what a struggle it was to survive because she, Kate, made it look easy. She said she was doing her best not to do anything and see what happened to this self-destructive energy.

When we try to live toward the Self, unexpected, unique creativeness happens (von Franz 1959/1980, 159). For Kate a dream inaugurated the new. A new image of the Self appeared that ushered her into the reality to which the Self makes a bridge. She dreamt she finally gets quit of her mother, and then, at the beach, a female photographer appears who dismisses a piece of jewelry Kate's lover had given her, and instructs Kate instead to lie down. Kate obeys. A female deer appears and at first licks her toes; then the deer lunges onto Kate, as if for sexual intercourse, even though the deer is female and Kate is terrified the deer will suffocate her with its weight.

To the female photographer, Kate associated the capacity to take a picture, to get an image of tumultuous emotions, to reflect on immediate experience. To the deer, she said it is the abandoned Bambi, and my urge to reunite carried by sexuality. The deer image would not let Kate alone, so she engaged it imaginatively. Its mixture of sexuality, femaleness, and suffocating energy united all the bits of her previous work in analysis. Imaginatively she climbed down a deep canyon to the river beneath and though terrified, she lay down and submitted to the deer which covered her. The smell of the deer permeated her whole body with "a heavy, rich, earthy, scent," she said. "The deer's eyes are the same as mine," she reported, "and the deer understands, gets it all." The scent of the deer flows into Kate's body, everywhere, like a current, like an essence, "like feeling a smell," she said. The deer gives her the gift of its presence to reside now in her. Then the deer gets up and is gone.

Kate rests and then sees that she has changed the location from which she lives. She had climbed down to the river to meet the deer and she sees now she can live next to the river and need not climb back up the high canyon to where everyone else lives; she can live from this new depth.

After admitting the deer, Kate said its scent stayed with her every day like a tremendous energy in her body. Her manner of living changed as well as the location from which she lived. She felt inwardly directed to resign her hospital job and singly pursue her career in spiritual direction without guarantee of salary. She felt opened to receive from others, not just to give to them. She received her own gifts and people's acknowledgment of them without flinching which she had done regularly before. She now felt able to name these gifts which before she avoided, seeing this naming as a use of masculine energy rising out of the indwelling female deer scent. She communed with the deer and felt its gentleness as a presence in her body, pulling her into a process which told her to wait, trust, not act out sexually again. She felt, finally, with both these masculine and feminine energies, she could survive.

The female deer, what we might call an image of the Self, connected Kate with the reality that transcends the psyche. In this way a Self-image functions like a God-image,[5] for the female deer carried all the force of the holy for Kate, filling in as well the missing feminine lost with her mother. The Mother archetype led to the Self-image of the deer which functioned like a God-image. She said the deer was the part she could not receive in the past, "the soft, feminine part which I switched off and received by giving." To give up the sexual part, which Kate felt she did in renouncing the possibility of a lover, was handing over something very precious which she had fought to preserve. She neither wanted to give up the sexual part nor to act it out. "So what am I to be doing with it?" she asked. The deer always answered her, wait, trust, the scent will transform it, let it be, fear is part of the process.

Archetypally, the deer symbolises a big range of meanings, stretching all the way from the Paleolithic cave drawings of a revered animal to representing through its horns, the tree of life and the eternal waxing and waning of life; the deer symbolises the role of true psychopomp, an intermediary between earth and heaven. The deer also represents sexual passion and the power to trample on Satan. Sometimes Christ is pictured as a deer. That Kate's deer is female accents the mythology of Lapland where the doe embodies the sturdy feminine spirit that can traverse thousands of miles of snow-covered land always uncovering food. In the Siberian Sami's creation myth, the creator creates the world from the body of the female deer, selected as the favorite because of her loving heart. How was Kate to live this energy, this spirit that uncovers nourishment and makes a passage between earth and heaven?

One place she felt most able to stand all the energy was in participating in celebration of the mass. There she felt safe, she said, present in a sacred encounter with ordinary others as well as with Christ. "That enables me," she said, "to be in the scent process." A synchronistic event strengthened this impression of living this energy in the midst of life. The newspaper reported that a live deer turned up in her old city neighborhood, wandering around the park she played in as a child. She felt the deer related to a goddess part of the divine that you found in the midst of everybody celebrating the mass together, or as turning up unexpectedly where you lived, or like the scent of energy running throughout your body, as a part of the spirit. She connected the scent to the energy of Christ that she had intimated several years before.

Because Kate submitted to and embraced this new God-image, I could go after the last bit of the trauma that had split love from power, and dependency from aggression. Now we could look at her previous refusal of the other because now she had accepted otherness in the deer who was so remarkably unexpected, so surprising in its behavior towards her, and so different from her conscious religion. The hospital trauma happened to her; injury was done to her. She was one of the innocents who suffered what Ricoeur calls the scandal of sin which can never be reduced to the sin of fault (Ricoeur 1967, 341). But in any trauma, each of us must also ask, how did I respond to what injured me? (Symington 1993, 35-37, 47-49, 65-71, 74-77, 81-82). Kate responded by resorting to self-holding, and to receiving only vicariously through generous giving to others because her dependency went into hiding. Now, by receiving and naming the deer goddess-image, she faced all her prior refusals of receiving for fear of the gap of swirling energy that would consume her when she gave up the Arnot protection or the sexual detour. That battle was over.

Kate said, "The work now is how to go away and come back. I never came back to my home. In accepting my energy, so different from my mother's, and accepting my talents, the question expands from, Will the other stay in relation to me when I own all that is mine, to, Will I stay in relation to the other? And what is the ethical obligation after I get what I want?"

We see here that our most personal receiving of the Self means simultaneously sharing it with others (Jung 1958, 452, para. 852; 1963, 192-194). The personal conducts the collective into consciousness. Like the spokes of a wheel as St. Dorotheus said so many centuries ago, the closer each of us proceeds to the center, the closer we live to each other (Every 1984, 80). For Kate, closing the gap that separated her loving from her aggression and her dependency from her power, meant housing energy in her body. Receiving the gift of the deer meant receiving the power of her own gifts which propelled her to devote her energy to others looking for their way to the center. Consenting to our personal fate allows us to feel we have a place in the universe (O'Kane 1994, 55). Kate said she knew the pain of the gap from the hospital bred her skill in empathy: "I feel gratitude for the pain; it was my fate and gave me my place in the cosmos."

Countertransference to the Self in Our Own Lives

We come round to the last question: what sort of ego attitude do we as analysts need in order to see what the Self is engineering in our analysands' material, and in the transference-countertransference field between us, and in our own lives which bears upon our work with clients?

We need a consciousness of consent. This means several distinct attitudes. Humility before the Vast that the Self brings into sight results from our being rubbed down to our bones by suffering the opposite now in consciousness, and no longer split between conscious and unconscious. We experience defeat and unknowingness in response to some big presence that increasingly takes on the tones of a central I-am, and I am with you. We do not know whether this presence mirrors us or we mirror it, or both processes go on simultaneously because this type of consciousness ushers in a steady sense of circulating energy all the time, from little to big and big to little, from outer to inner and inner to outer, from self to others and others to self.

Willingness characterises our proper ego attitude, willingness to see, engage, smell, open up to, fight with, put our case before, listen into silence, envision an answering procession of the new into our horizon. We go on being willing to ask in our life and in our work, What is the Self engineering? When I say at the beginning of each person's analysis, that the goal is to establish vital conversation between you and the psyche and the reality the psyche opens onto, I experience the Self as the fourth in the session that already is made up of the three – the analysand, the analyst and the psychic material between us. The fourth, the Self, must enter the analytical encounter if it is to work. But at the end of the analysis, I see the fourth as our consenting consciousness, as our creaturehood that is willing to provide a residence for the transcendent to manifest under the limits of time and space.

That humble willingness leads us to gain a new discourse which falls between the logic of directed conscious thinking and the prelogic of nondirected unconscious fantasy. Our new language partakes of both, for we need to converse with the Self and the reality it bequeaths us, images as well as words, affects as well as reason, smell and touch, as well as sight and hearing. Who knows how the unknown will choose to greet us, and in what form?

Consenting brings double vision. We step outside and observe we are slung back and forth between clashing opposites while we endure it. We live paradoxically. We remain nonattached while at the same time devoted to life here and now. Planted in our own particular identity, our roots touch the All that shines through our identity. Capable of commitment to methods of analysing, we also can be called out onto long voyages into unknown territory requiring unknown methods to make intercession for the lost sheep of the shameful perverse habit, the imprisoned mad bit, the part that has never yet been found and loved.

If I am correct in believing that the Self functions like a bridge to reality that transcends the psyche as well as dwells in it, then consciousness of consent summons a religious dimension, what Jung called that decisive question we each must answer: Are we related to the infinite or not? (Jung 1963, 325). For whom are we consenting to? We must name that other who advances into our consciousness.

As a tribe of Jungians with our shared language we speak of the bridge to that reality as Self. Good enough. But for each of us in the living of our lives, we must go further and name it concretely, personally. Otherwise, we do not go across that bridge to the other side, nor know when the other side crosses to greet us. As von Franz pithily puts it, You can't talk to a ball of fire (von Franz 1980, 29). If the ball of fire symbolises what lies beyond the Self, it must come into more conversational form.

Kate, for example, persisted in seeing the unseeable. She uncovered the hospital trauma, the underpants, the whale, the vortex of energy, and finally the deer which stands in for the unknown which offers her this image of itself. Kate consents to the particular way the reality makes itself known to her, even to lying down and submitting to the deer scent entering her body. What she gets in return is the generosity of spirit she gave to everyone else, now for herself. And not entirely for herself. For touched by the transcendent, she devotes herself to helping others go deep down and look, not to obliterate what is threatening, but to make a residence for its transformation. And Kate must go on traveling the gap back and forth between this deer-goddess and the traditional mass. Just as the patient with the silver flashlight that enabled her to see the dappled world, must go on stepping into that dappledness to find out how, for her, light and dark dwell together. Such efforts on the part of people build up what we might call a metaphysics of psychology.

We each must find the names of our personal God-images the Self opens us to for they conduct us to the reality beyond the psyche. If we do not, our relationship to the transcendent remains impersonal, unhoused in the limits of our body which means in the here and now of time and space. We may have known a thrilling experience of the immediacy of the transcendent in our analysis or our training, but if we do not go on relating to it, speaking to it, naming it and hearing its answer, then the relationship becomes an artifact, a relic of splendid happening in the past. Or, it fades. We may even come to doubt the importance of what so transfixed our gaze when it occurred. The relationship to the Self and to what the Self opens to then remains a time limited event that happened once, or twice, operating in the well-developed short-term limits of analysis itself.

If we do struggle to name what addresses us, what transcendent presence advances into visibility, our names fall far short of its reality. We know that, and we know that the fanaticisms of the political left and right stem from trying to foreclose the gap between our tiny subjective names for objective reality to which they point. We make symbolic equations and lose both reality as real and our own subjective footing. We drift into the archetypal world and realise too little in this life from its advent into our consciousness. Or, we try to dragoon that huge energy of transcendent reality into our ego plans. Insisting our view is the only one, we foist it onto others, sometimes at the end of a gun. The huge power of the transcendent when piped only through our little voltage wires either blows up our whole world or captures us in a power-complex we act out upon our neighbors.

How do we speak in public of this transcendent reality that our countertransference to the Self points to, especially when so much of our witness of it goes on in silence? Because we live in a body which means concrete form, we live committed to what our particular images of the Self reveal of reality. Our personal images of the transcendent makes it really real to us. This is what we bring to the end of our lives as the stone which we dug out of our complexes and that endured the fire. This is the love we really have loved, the truth we have served. These are our little glimpses of the long range, the real that outlasts time out of time, long after we finish with analysis. This view, whatever it is, this exposure to the territory the Self shows us, that our rituals of analysis witness to, imposes upon us the ethical obligation to live differently, to live with the door open to this transcendent reality.

We live in a specific space with the door open to the far-flung immensity; we live in this body with its mortality with the door open to multiple bodies; we live with the sequence of events in our lifetime with the door open to the simultaneity of all events. The ego attitude that allows us to see what the Self is engineering springs from unending appreciation, a glad gratitude, for the generosity of reality that pours out on each of us as much of the other as we grow equipped to permit and survive.

Address National Conference of Jungian Analysts, New York City, 1996; published in Journal of Jungian Theory and Practice, *Fall 1999, 1, 5-26.*

Notes

1. Jungian analyst Marion Woodman writes of her gratitude for a food disorder: "I have had an eating disorder all my life, but I have reached the point where I thank God for it because it brought me into such close connection with Sophia. I would never have known anything about the feminine principle if I had not been forced to my knees.... I rely on the dreams to guide us to the real trauma, the place where the soul went underground" (excerpts from an interview by Dorothy Reichardt in *The Round Table Interview* May/June 1995, Part Two).
2. Geological research confirms the alchemists' intuitions of a fiery sun at the center of the earth. See "Under Our Skin, Hot Theories on the Center

of the Earth" by Kay Davidson and A. R. Williams, National Geographic Senior Staff. *National Geographic* Jan. 1996, 100-111.

3. Jung writes of the collision of the yea and nay of conscience, when we must choose between two goods (Jung 1958, pars. 839-843, 854, 856).

4. Other examples of this spontaneous knowing are these. Another patient also slept all her adult life in underpants but for a different reason, not to protect but to reject the body area her mother called "down there," that harbored gushy and ghastly fluids which left her wet and would not get wiped away if she got up at night to pee. I found myself spontaneously getting soft Kleenex tissue from the box on the table and showing her how to fold it to wipe herself dry. A third example is taken from my book *The Wizards' Gate: Picturing Consciousness* (Einsiedeln, Switzerland: Daimon, 1994). There my analysand was dying from a terminal brain tumor. Near the end, a spontaneous idea came to me, to spend our last few sessions reading over to her the notes of our work since her tumor was diagnosed that recorded what she had done to face into her coming death.

5. Jung says, "This 'self' never at any time takes the place of God, though It may perhaps be a vessel for divine grace" (Jung 1959, para. 874).

References

Alexandris, A. and Vaslamatzis, G. eds. 1993. *Countertransference Theory, Technique, Teaching.* London: Karnac.

Aziz, R. 1990. *C. G. Jung's Psychology of Religion and Synchronicity.* Albany, N.Y.: Suny.

Bion, W. F. 1970. *Attention and Interpretation.* London: Tavistock.

Bollas, C. 1987. *The Shadow of the Object: The Unthought Known.* London: Free Association Press.

Bollas, C. 1991. *Forces of Destiny, Psychoanalysis and the Human Idiom.* London: Free Association Press.

Davidson, K. and Williams, A. R. 1996. Under our skin, hot theories on the center of the earth. *National Geographic.* January, 100-111.

Every, G., Harries, R., Ware, K. 1984. *The Time of the Spirit.* Crestwood, N.J.: St. Vladimir's Press.

Freud, S. 1927. *The Future of an Illusion.* SE XXI, 3-58.

Guggenbühl-Craig, A. 1971. *Power in the Helping Professions.* New York: Spring. Subsequent editions: Putnam: Spring.

Guntrip, H. 1973. *Psychoanalytic Theory, Therapy and the Self.* New York: Basic Books.

Jung, C. G. 1925/1963. *VII Sermones ad Mortuos.* trans. H. G. Baynes. Dulverton, Somerset, England: Watkins.

Clinical Issues

Jung, C. G. 1934/1964. The state of psychotherapy today. *Civilisation in Transition. CW.* 10. trans. R. F. C. Hull. New York: Pantheon, 1964.
Jung, C. G. 1952. Synchronicity: an acausal connecting principle. *Collected Works* 8. *The Structure and Dynamics of the Psyche.* trans. R. F. C. Hull. New York: Pantheon, 1960, 417-532.
Jung, C. G. 1953. *Psychology and Alchemy. CW* 13. New York: Pantheon.
Jung, C. G. 1958. A psychological view of conscience. *Civilisation in Transition. CW.* 10. New York: Pantheon, 1964, 437-455.
Jung, C. G. 1959. Good and evil in analytical psychology. *Civilisation in Transition. CW* 10. New York: Pantheon, 1964, 456-466.
Jung, C. G. 1963. *Memories, Dreams, Reflections.* ed. A. Jaffé. trans. Richard and Clara Winston. New York: Pantheon.
Jung, C. G. 1973. *Letters I: 1905-1950.* vol. 1 of 2. trans. R. F. C. Hull. eds. G. Adler and A. Jaffé. Princeton, N.J.: Princeton University Press.
Klein, M. 1946. Notes on some schizoid mechanisms. Klein, M. 1975. *Envy and Gratitude & Other Works 1946-1963.* New York: Seymour Lawrence/Delacorte Press, 1-24.
Klein, M. 1952. Some theoretical conclusions regarding the emotional life of the infant. Klein, M. 1975. *Envy and Gratitude & Other Works 1946-1963.* New York: Seymour Lawrence/ Delacorte Press, 62-93.
Kohut, H. 1971. *The Analysis of the Self.* New York: International Universities Press.
Kohut, H. 1984. *How Does Analysis Cure?* ed. A. Goldberg with P. E. Stepansky. Chicago: University of Chicago Press.
Kristeva, J. 1995. *The New Maladies of the Soul.* trans. R. Guberman. New York: Columbia University Press.
Lacan, J. 1966. *Ècrits I.* Paris. Èditions du Seuil.
Lacan, J. 1968. *The Language of the Self, The Function of Language in Psychoanalysis.* trans. A. Wilden. Baltimore, Md.: Johns Hopkins Press.
Laing, R. D. 1967. *The Politics of Experience.* Baltimore, Md.: Penguin.
Laing, R. D. 1969. *The Divided Self.* Baltimore, Md.: Penguin.
Little, M. The positive contribution of countertransference. Little, M. 1986. *Toward Basic Unity, Transference Neurosis and Transference Psychosis.* London: Free Association Press, 129-134.
Loewald, H. W. 1977. Reflections on the psychoanalytic process and its therapeutic potential. Loewald, H. W. 1980. *Papers on Psychoanalysis.* New Haven, Ct.: Yale University Press, 372-383.
Loewald, H. W. 1978a. The waning of the oedipus complex. Loewald, H. W. 1980. *Papers on Psychoanalysis.* New Haven, Ct.: Yale University Press, 384-404.
Loewald, H. W. 1978b. *Psychoanalysis and the History of the Individual.* New Haven, Ct.: Yale University Press.
Milner, M. 1960. The concentration of the body. Milner, M. 1987. *The Suppressed Madness of Sane Men.* London: Tavistock, 234 – 240.

Neumann, E. 1956. The psyche and the transformation of the reality planes. Neumann, E. 1989. *The Place of Creation.* Princeton, N.J.: Princeton University Press, 3-62. Also found in *Spring.* trans. H. Nagel. New York: Analytical Psychology Club, 1959.

O'Kane, F. 1994. *Sacred Chaos, Reflections on God's Shadow and the Dark Self.* Toronto, Ca.: Inner City Books.

Olney, J. 1993. *The Language of Poetry, Walt Whitman, Emily Dickinson, Gerard Manley Hopkins.* Athens, Ga.: University of Georgia Press.

Ricoeur, P. 1967. *The Symbolism of Evil.* trans. E. Buchanan. New York: Harper and Row.

Roazen, P. 1975. *Freud and His Followers.* New York: Knopf.

Rilke, R. M. 1912/1923/1992. Erlebnis. Rilke, R. M. *Duino Elegies.* trans. D. Oswald. Einsiedeln, Switzerland: Daimon.

Ross, L. and Roy, M. 1995. *Cast the First Stone, Ethics in Analytic Practice.* Wilmette, Ill.: Chiron.

Sedgewick, D. 1994. *The Wounded Healer, Countertransference from a Jungian Perspective.* New York: Routledge.

Stein, M. ed. 1995. *The Interactive Field in Analysis.* Wilmette, Ill.: Chiron.

Stolorow, R. D., Brandschaft, B., Atwood, G. E. 1987. *Psychoanalytic Treatment, An Intersubjective Approach.* Hillsdale, N. J.: The Analytic Press.

Symington, N. 1993. *Narcissism, A New Theory.* London: Karnac.

Ulanov, A. B. 1986/2002. Needs, wishes, transcendence. *Picturing God.* Einsiedeln, Switzerland: Daimon, 47-61.

Ulanov, A. B. 1987/2000. *The Wisdom of the Psyche.* Einsiedeln, Switzerland: Daimon.

Ulanov, A. B. 1996. *The Functioning Transcendent.* Wilmette, Ill.: Chiron.

von Franz, M.-L. 1972. *Creation myths.* Zurich, Switzerland: Spring.

von Franz, M.-L. 1980. *Alchemy, An Introduction to the Symbolism and Psychology.* Toronto, Ca.: Inner City Books.

von Franz, M.-L. 1993. *Psychotherapy.* Boston: Shambhala.

Weigert, E. 1970. The goal of creativity in psychotherapy. *The Courage to Love.* New Haven, Ct.: Yale University Press.

Winnicott, D. W. 1962. Ego integration in child development. Winnicott, D. W. 1965. *The Maturational Processes and the Facilitating Environment.* New York: International Universities Press.

Winnicott, D. W. 1968. Clinical illustration of "the use of an object." *Psycho-Analytic Explorations.* eds. Clara Winnicott, Ray Shepherd, Madeleine Davis. London: Karnac, 1989.

Winnicott, D. W. 1971a. *Therapeutic Consultations in Child Psychiatry.* New York: Basic Books.

Winnicott, D. W. 1971b. *Playing and Reality.* London: Tavistock.

Chapter 15

Ritual, Repetition, and Psychic Reality

Ritual of Treatment

We have all spent many years in treatment rooms, as patients ourselves, and in our offices where others come to us. What is it to be talking to persons who give us their whole attention? What is it we do and want to do when we listen to the unfolding of a person in front of us? And what is doing us, so to speak? Such listening jump-starts a patient into listening to the psyche. Our close attention brings the patient's psyche into focus.

It is the listening of the analyst to parts of the analysand which have never been heard before or may never have spoken which is so moving to the analysand, and to the analyst. Conversation thus generated with all parts of the person is what makes this work so exciting. Such speaking – such giving – happens when matched by an equal receiving, not to explain or fix or make different, but just to hear, to take in and let other persons explore their experiences in your giving and receiving company.

The ritual of treatment – of analysis, therapy, psychiatry – sets off space and time, daily, weekly, monthly, marking out both a territory and a listening hour for a patient's being. Within the ritual of treatment, each of us says, "This is who I have become; here I want to know what I know. I know I cannot hear myself speaking until I tune in to what is talking within me."

This directed focus on the self cannot be accomplished alone. To take me in, to accept all those parts I did not hear before, I need you, an other. As patients, we are not looking for the object of the analyst. We look for what can really be relied upon. Only we do not know this.

We come to know it by what goes on between us, doctor and patient, in the ritual of treatment. Though we vary in our articulations of what this ritual is according to the methods we use, we can agree that it brings psychic reality into view. This is what patients want to know about and live out of. For until this new reality links up with our daily living, it remains too abstract, and the analysis which made it present to us is just something out of our past, a ritual we are done with.

An ancient religious mystery symbolised by the relation of the numbers three and four complemented the Christian Trinitarian picture of God. By uniting the three of the Godhead and four whose symbolism included evil, matter, and the feminine, scholars could gain inclusion and thus a true wholeness could be represented. Jung notes that this problem of three and four that turns up in Plato's *Timaeus* and in Goethe's *Faust* Part II and all the years in between is summed up in the alchemical axiom of Maria: "'Out of the Third comes the One as the Fourth'" (Jung 1952, 513, para. 962; see also Jung 1948, 121, 196, pars. 184, 290; see also Jung 1953, 23, 25-26, pars. 26, 31). For us today, in the rituals of treating the psyche, the combining of these numbers symbolises the task of realising in actual life what we experience in analysis. In other words, here we confront the practical problem of mysticism in everyday life, the ethical issue of how we put our money where our mouth is: how do we live what we believe? How do we take what rituals of treatment open to us into daily life?

This practical task turns up in every analysis. The symbolism of converting three into four describes how we take with us into our life the psychic reality we experience between ourselves and the doctor. The analysand and the analyst comprise the one and the two. Psychic reality composes the third that comes into focus in the ritual of treatment in the space in between ourselves (as one) and the doctor (as two). But only if we take psychic reality with us into our daily living and change our life, do we complete the ritual of treatment. That realisation in life of the effects of treatment comprise the transformation of three into four. Failing that, then we repeat the ritual of analysis and the journey to psychic reality once again, or many times. We embark on more analysis with a new analyst or a different school of analysis. Or we repeat the process of medication, now with a different drug. Or we redo the same business ventures, or engage in reruns of relationships, or duplicate our previous efforts to vanquish our depression or anxiety. Like the fateful Monday we once again begin the diet, sure we will succeed. But each time we repeat the same ending, the same old record. Such repetition breaks our spirit, disheartens our soul and conquers the ritual of treatment.

To put the point in the clear words of a young patient trying to hold his life together: "I want to feel real and in the flow of life, glad for it, not as if it intrudes on me or foils me." What is it to feel real, alive, to know our fullest selves, with all the parts included? Where in us does this occur? Is it the soul? But then what is the soul and do we concern ourselves with it in our work with the psyche? How do the repetitions of psyche connect with the rituals of soul?

With our perception of the reality of the psyche, we witness something of the greatest importance. That something stands behind our theories. That may be what the patient sees when looking into the face of the doctor, seeing his or her self witnessed to, because the analyst is being witnessed to.

It is an extraordinary experience to sit with someone at an appointed time for weeks, months, years, whom one gives a whole-hearted hearing. We are witnessing the human need for support, which extends from birth with all its dependencies to death with all its dependencies. Our patients constantly remind us of this fact, as they bring us experiences of crossing from deadness to aliveness, from being to non-being and back again. This adventure touches analyst as well as analysand, and opens up the field of psychic reality between them, where the much sought-after wholeness reveals itself not as a container that wraps around the two, but as a ritual exchange between them.

As analysts, we know the value of ritual, both negative and positive. This is how we stay alive year after year, decade after decade, learning from each new client, living, witnessing to the reality of the psyche. We remember in this awareness of reality, that the deaccessing of religion from the psychiatric code for diagnosing pathology began in one such psychiatrist's registering of his own primordial experience. He knew that what he knew and what knew him was not an experience of illness but a witnessing to a significant part of reality that had witnessed to him (Dr. Francis Lu of University of California Medical School at San Francisco, New York Times 2/10/94, A16).

The answer, then, to my initial question – what are we doing and what is doing us in our treatment rooms – is a multiplying of instances of conversation. We listen in on the conversation within the self of the analysand, obsessed perhaps, foreclosed, or not even participated in. To hear that conversation we must ourselves receive the bulletins directed to us by the self within us. So it is that the analysand heeds, or tries to, one set of conversations and the analyst another. A third set discloses itself as the conversation between the analyst and analysand deepens. Through all the vicissitudes of transference and countertransference, the two find themselves talked to and through themselves by this third dialogue, conscious and unconscious, going on between analyst and analysand.

There is more, a fourth dimension, where causality gives way to synchronicity, where uncausally related events simultaneously coincide and break in upon our subjectivity. When we correspond to such events, we find ourselves in a world where time and space coalesce and convey an immediate sense of the unity of the whole in a world of endless interdependencies. Jung says: "The soul cannot exist without its other side, which is always found in a 'You.' Wholeness is a combination of I and You, and these show themselves to be parts of a transcendent unity whose nature can only be grasped symbolically ..." (Jung 1946, 243-244, para. 454).

In the treatment room, we experience this unity of the "other side" as the fourth aspect of reality that puts together the other three (Jung 1952, 512-513, pars. 961-962). Analysand, analyst, and the field between them all speak of the It, the There, the Center, the God, the Isness, the Vastness, the All that religions make it their business to point to and to reach to in their defining rituals. We experience this fourth dimension in our work as that which clients are after in their dependency upon us. They are looking around for what will help them look into themselves, not just *at* themselves. When they look into themselves they find some other presence greeting them.

Dreams often appear as a good guide to this presence, for they give the dreamer immediate knowledge of a dynamic process that will bring out what needs to be said. I find this particularly helpful with people suffering a borderline condition. One such client said she reached trust in psychic reality because of her dreams. She did not make them up, she said, nor did I, nor did they issue from a textbook: "The real work goes on in me at night."[1]

The mirroring we seek in our transferences is of our experience when we find our dependencies met, recognized, and received not just by a person but also by some indefinable but unmistakable presence at the heart of things. This does not mean we don't need each other as persons or do not find it through each other as persons. Surely we know that we depend on each other and the objects reality so generously offers us with which to unfold our truest selves. What would we do without friends, without being made into a mother by our children, teachers by our students, into lovers by the one who loves us in our bodies and souls? In exactly the same way, we are turned into analysts by the patience and perseverance of our analysands.

Through such intertwining of subject and object we are made to feel something inexorably mixing in us and through us to others. Here we meet the energy necessary for our thriving. Here, if we lack connection to it, we feel not merely deprived, but broken into pieces, falling into the gap of nothingness, present only to an absence. This is the absence the Judeo-Christian tradition calls sin, the emptiness from which boils up envy, resentment, grief, anger, and the deadly refusal to receive anything.

When we live connected to this energy, we feel plugged in. We take life in, we give it out. We live to the fullest, risking and cherishing by turns, everywhere drawn to the conversation of psyche and soul.

Analysts of different schools of depth psychology strain to express this experience as the goal of treatment – what Winnicott calls living creatively, and Masud Khan the self-experience that "depends on when and from where we live, how and with whom ... then [it is] we either thrive from *jouissance* à la Lacan, shared with the *other*, or suffer from the lack of its spontaneous reciprocity" (Winnicott 1970; Khan 1985, 20). Bion seeks what he terms "O" to come into every session. That advent of the infinite, that emotional truth of the session, whatever we choose to call it, is ultimately what cannot be known directly, but can only enter once removed as an item in our domain of knowledge (Bion 1970, chapter 3). Klein puts the aim of treatment more simply, as gratitude, a way of bringing ourselves to live with gladness and industry, another way of expressing Freud's goal of analysis as love and work (Klein 1957; Hale 1980, 29-42). Hans Loewald, speaking in the Freudian tradition, and Jung from a far opposite point of view, both invoke the presence of love as the essential fourth in the ritual of treatment that unites and surpasses the three. Loewald says of psychoanalytic process:

> It is impossible to love the truth of psychic reality ... and not to love and care for the object whose truth we want to discover.... Our object is the other in ourselves and ourself in the other. To discover truth about the patient is always discovering it with him and for him as well as for ourselves and about ourselves. And it is discovering truth between each other, as the truth of human beings in their interrelatedness (Loewald 1970, 297-298).

Jung speaks of the process right out of the process:

> I falter before the task of finding language which might adequately express the incalculable paradoxes of love.... In my medical experience as well as my own life I have again and again been faced with the mystery of love, and have never been able to explain what it is.... [It is] something superior to the individual, a unified and undivided whole. Being a part, man cannot grasp the whole.... He may assent to it, or rebel against it; but he is always caught up by

it and enclosed within it. Love is his light and his darkness, whose end he cannot see (Jung 1963a, 354-355).

We rarely mention love as the dimension in which the ritual of treatment occurs, and that is correct. As the poet Rilke reminds us, echoing Kant, this grasp of love within the experience of the reality of love, and the accompanying effort to honor its presence in our work is the purposiveness without purpose of all authentic work. Rilke writes of the painter Cézanne, "The incarnation of the world *as a thing carrying conviction*, the portrayal of reality become imperishable through his experiencing of the object – this appeared the purpose of his inmost labors" (Rilke 1988, 146). Cézanne discovered that reality possessed "no contours at all, only countless vibrating planes merging into one another" (ibid., 147). The quivering, undulating energy Cézanne captured in his colors Rilke felt in himself as he beheld the paintings in the museum, as "gathering into a colossal reality. It is as if these colours took away all your indecisions for ever and ever. The good conscience of these reds, these blues – their simple truthfulness teaches you ... how necessary it was to get beyond even love ... if you show it, you make them less well; you judge them instead of *saying* them ... and love, the best thing of all, remains outside your work, does not enter into it, is left over unresolved beside it" (ibid., 151-152).

How does love, the best thing of all, enter into our work? Just as a good parent gives love which the child takes in and uses as part of his or her own personality, and just as we find our reward as parents in seeing our child living well out of a vibrant self, and not from thank-you notes or a labeling of part of the child as indebted to Mom or owed to Dad, so this mysterious fourth dimension which holds the ritual of treatment between us and our patient, goes into both of us individually and circulates between us in the psychic reality we share. This love does not label itself either, as owed to God, or as indebted to the transcendent. It gives itself in abandon to be lived by us and between us.

In the same way we must give into the ritual of our work, rather than the talking about it in a way that leaves this energy, this love, outside it. When we listen to our analysands, we listen in on the conversation inside them between the surface mind, the ego, and the deeper self that centers the whole psyche, conscious and unconscious. That conversation energizes our own inner conversation and the ensuing conversation between analyst and analysand, brings home to both the fact that the mystery at the heart of our shared being mirrors the mystery at the heart of being itself. Being speaks in all these conversations.

Religious moments, like Dr. Lu's, what my husband and I have called primordial experiences, register this depth and surround us with it (Ulanov 1975, chapter 1). We know ourselves gripped by something that shatters our ego complacency and conducts us to a space where we know we are known as the subject of a greater subject. These moments mark us; we may not understand them, but we never forget them.

If we fail to change our lives in accord with what these moments bring, we are doomed to repeat them until we finally get it, even when the repeating holds us in an apparently unshakable compulsion. When we are released into psychic reality again and the love it witnesses to, all our suffering is rearranged and restructured.

I have heard two patients struck down by terminal illness both say that the gigantic grief and rage they bore for a life lost, was "all worth it," when that rearranged space opened to them. They meant, I believe, not that good was coming out of evil, redeeming it, so to speak, but rather that evil did not snuff out the good. The good was firmly there, real, to be laid hold of even in these most dire circumstances. For each, that meant the rage and grief went on, but did not capture them in a senseless repetition. They were planted instead in a fruitful zone, a space where life somehow thrived even in their days' dying. The man described it as a blue fog holding onto what his self was until the last, despite a crumbling of all his faculties (Ulanov 1996, chapters 7 and 9). The woman painted what she saw in colors, purple, gold, silver and blue, calling the paintings "icons of eternity" (Ulanov 1994). Fate transformed into destiny.

Repeating Repetition

But we now come back to the small and familiar, the mixing up of repetition and ritual in analysis. We know from countless hours in our treatment rooms that the psyche stages rituals of its own, which it repeats tirelessly until they accomplish their unconscious task. The task consists of restaging the original trauma which we suffered but could not metabolise, so we are compelled to repeat it until we digest and make it our own.[2]

We experience such rounds of repetition almost altogether negatively, replaying thoughts, projections and projective identifications, entrapping behavior and an intellectual rehearsing that break us down. We lose heart. We lose hope. We live under a spell of humiliation so profound that we must repeat our repeatings in order to find a way out. I speak here of repetitions all of us suffer, by no means confined to our patients alone. The repetitions that besiege us present themselves as compulsive workaholic schedules; enthralment to drink, to prescription drugs, or to substances like cocaine; as fixation to food or its absence; as monotonous patterns of relationship, or its lack; as recurrent bouts of elation and disillusionment.

We all know our secret prisons and the humiliation they inflict on us. How we wince when someone innocently touches the place we feel most exposed! A woman unable to seek a job, despite superior qualifications, suffers agonies of shame at any social gathering when asked, What do you do? We feel mortified to be so captured by something we do not understand, to be helpless in the face of something we cannot control. We feel especially ashamed because our compulsion seems so trivial in the face of what so many citizens of the world suffer from famine, disease, war and death that the four horsemen of the Apocalypse let loose in our world.

Nonetheless, such entrapment in repetition can take up our whole life. A man sought analysis in the eighth decade of his life, seeking liberation from what he called his "perversions." We saw together how repetition compulsions repeat, not only to master our persecutions and defend against them, but to get it all right finally and be done with it. This man worked in analysis and found in the masochism that had embroiled him all his life a breakthrough to its concealed drive to venerate something quite beyond himself and serve it (Ulanov 1996, chapter 3).

My point is this. Repetition and ritual mix with each other. Each can be positive or negative. Although we usually see repetition as negative, my clinical experience has taught me it plays a secret positive role. It can lead, if held within the ritual of treatment, to a different kind of consciousness, both in mode and location; to a missing piece of self hiding in the repetition; to a rerouting of aggression from rigid defense to support connection to the presence of this fourth dimension of love which gives itself to our living, and which we must name if we continue to relate to it.

Religious ritual, too, we know, can be destructive, used to ward off, encapsulate, control, constrict, imprison, with all the obsessive features that led Freud to insist upon similarities between religion and neurosis. However, the philosopher Paul Ricoeur says somewhat wryly in response, similarity does not equal identity (Ricoeur 1927; Ricoeur 1970, 533). In its positive role ritual marks off the necessary space and time to acknowledge our relationship to an essential otherness, to coordinate our response to the address of the transcendent. Such ritualized awareness of the power and meaning of being happily occurs at the expense of denial, linking the here and now to the eternal Now. A surprising sense of mutual enhancement grows between our finitude and the infinite. Awareness of this otherness, this transcendent mutuality distinguishes ritual from mere repetition.

To state it as simply as possible, to break free of negative repetition, we must find a new ritual to permit us to go on relating to the integrating and transcending forces bound up in the old compulsion. We must name what we find and bring into clear consciousness what we make of what we find. Otherwise, we may be stuck in analysis forever, or relapse, or lose the compulsion with age, but never profit from its underlying strengths and truths.

Something precious in the unconscious has been seeking to break through into our consciousness. The repetition that compels us hides something we need to know if we are to live all of ourselves rather than being always held in a constricting little space, like a horse with one of its feet hobbled. In the process of connecting with that lost bit of ourself, as we come to know it, we see that we are known by something both far outside us and deep inside us. This igniting energy brings us to a new way of living.

Religion, when it channels and contains instead of merely defending, knows about this awakening and calls it *kairos*, the eternal in the now. It offers us its own images and rites and symbols of understanding. One such image is Creation as

403

Michelangelo allegorized it on the ceiling of the Sistine Chapel. When the outstretched hand of the Creator reaches to touch the hand of Adam, a very small gap remains between them. We can sense that when that gap is traversed and the touch completed, energy will blaze across the meeting to be lived, elaborated, expanded, circulated in the living of human life. Feeding is another such image bound up with ritual. In the Christian narrative it appears as the Madonna with the child at her breast, and in the Eucharist rite where an exchange of energy demands from the human side an offering of all the things we have fallen into and identified with and put in the place of the holy (for example our repetition compulsion), and from the divine side the offering of the All to feed the particular, bestowed in the bread and the wine.

A Case

A middle-aged woman winning through her long-standing addiction to sweets illustrates how one works through the perils of repetition. This is not just an interesting example but exemplary of the whole species – the ridiculous conceals profundity. Again, think of our own secret repetitions that show up in workaholic schedules, dogged habits of procrastination, set sexual procedures that we fear to vary lest impotence appear, fixed prayer routines we fear to change lest we lose hold on God. It is always the other person's repetitious compulsions that appear to us as absurd, or exaggerated. Just get over it, we say; use your will; here is a plan. But will and power and plan all crumble under repeated compulsive behavior. We each know our specific area of repeated compulsion – often as ridiculous as this woman's compulsion for sweets – where we feel helpless and suffer humiliation at being entrapped in something beyond our control. Precisely in that weakness lies concealed our deep desire to be connected to the center of being.

This woman, accomplished in her business and a hard worker in analysis, knew all about her obsession, but it did not change her behavior. Even while understanding that she displaced onto sweet food the love she did not receive from her mother, she still could not control her gobbling, nor her dependence on knowing her favorite sweet waited for her at the end of every dinner.

She understood that through the sweets she held herself up, did not need to risk the fathomless falling which was her great fear, what Winnicott calls the agony of falling forever, when she depended on someone else to give the love the sweets represented (Winnicott 1962, 58). She tried to control her habit and sometimes succeeded for a short time, only to be flung back in the opposite direction on the rebound, repeatedly stuffing herself with sweets. Binges brought on self-attack, pictured in her dreams as savage underground muggings by a subway maniac. She saw that her plentiful aggression was first employed to control her compulsion and then to assail her for failing to do so, sounding a basso ostinato of the humiliation of helplessness, in her subjugation to endless need.

Change in the Mode of Consciousness

She knew all about this, but it made little difference, except as an intellectual map. What changed it was a new ritual of successive lookings into instead of merely at the repetition compulsion, to converse now with the side that so propelled her to eat and then with its opposite that forbade the sweets and lectured her about thinness. In these conversations her consciousness changed modes from standing back looking at her compulsion abstractly, to entering into it to make space for all the points of view it condensed. Being flung back and forth between the opposites of control and gorging, drew her into an alternation between opposite shores of what, to her amazement, turned out to be the same river.

When she sided with her appetite for sweets it took the imaginative form of an exuberant little child taking great bites of life: "Sweets are an early form of loving!" she declared. Her pleasure in the taste, texture, and chewing was a lavish expression of her loving appetite for the world. She saw that child part of her "just opening up and going right out to others. I am eating love," she said. Her wish to eat was her wish to give and receive love. Food was love's substitute and its signature.

Why food? Because of the particularity of her object relations, for each member of her family was a superb cook. Food, at least, was generously offered in her family; it was delicious and a natural emblem for love.

When she sided with the opposite point of view – that such appetite must be controlled – the ensuing conversation surprised her. She had known already that she wanted to stop eating sweets in order to become thin. But what was thinness? Thinness revealed itself as desire to shed feeling stuffed up, congested, full of obstacles such as thinking about food all the time. Thinness expressed her desire to open to the circulating currents of life, what she called living near the fire, not in any metaphysical sense, but directly, in her body. And body meant here and now, the living of each day. To her surprise, she found herself conducted to the same space to which her appetite led. From different angles all the parts of her converged on full engagement with life, refusing either to be deprived or to be stuffed but instead living with her whole heart, mind, and strength.

Aggression and the Lost Bit of Self

As the opposites joined together, her aggression broke out. Analytic sessions focused on her dreams of being assaulted, her feelings of being invalid and her helplessness to do anything about it. One dream image defines them all. She sees herself in the subway where a mutilated female dancer is raging at her. One of the dancer's arms is a mere stump, cut off at the elbow; the other ends at the forearm. "How can she dance? She can't balance," my patient wailed, "she is helpless!" The dreamer saw personified in this dream figure her own helplessness which she had denied by substituting food for the missing love. That displacement left the dreamer dosing her own dependency needs with sweets, so she did not need to risk leaning on others, but also, then, she was never really fed. In her lovelessness, she was the mutilated dream figure who could not balance herself. The dream exposed the folly of the defense. There were no arms to hold the woman up. The murderous aggression surrounding the unmet dependency attacked her, left her disarmed, not at all in control, everything crammed into the food compulsion, all her resolves to end it vanquished.

The defense of food both guarded her against lack of emotional food by feeding herself actual food, and constricted and controlled her instinctive appetite for love and life thus perpetuating her problem of emotional deprivation. This ploy of substituting food for love, with its rigidity and monotonous repetition, shows the characteristics typical of our defenses when we build them in reaction to fear instead of in response to impulse (Winnicott 1988, 63-64, 120-121, 136-137). When we build up defenses in response to instinct, they show a supple quality, a capacity to adjust in response to the energy they channel.

The repetition ritual did not end; it kept breaking open. Her ego now made space for the dependent, unloved, little girl in her. She was part of the dreamer's self, hiding in repetitious obsession with sweets, telling her story the only way she could, not in words but in her behavior, wanting to gobble up the missing love. She depended on food as mother and father – and love. The mode of her consciousness changed from abstract knowing about to direct making space for the bits of her true self hiding in her repetition compulsion. The aggression she had needed to keep this helpless child out of sight she now needed to sustain receiving her.

The little girl was the part of her which had looked into the void of the missing love. When she looked, she saw nothing. Her mother accepted her collectively, she said, as one of the children, but not in or for herself. Her mother used to run through all her siblings' names before finding her own. Her father did the same, providing material support but no real attention, remaining a benign distant figure. She knew she could not depend on those around her, knew in her bones she would fall forever if she tried to do so. To protect against this agony she shifted her need onto food, which was plentifully given, and with the special sweets that came with holidays. She needed the aggressive energy contained in her rage at being denied love and deformed, so that she could look once again into the nothing and sustain herself.

For her, the gap between the Creator and creature that Michelangelo painted was unbridgeable. She fell into nothingness. To haul herself out of the danger of losing herself forever, and to secure some kind of foothold on one or the other sides of the gap, she built an ersatz bridge of sweetmeats. To sustain herself she repeatedly had to locate herself inside the repetitious compulsion. Like those around her whom she had experienced as a child as denying that anything was wrong, now as an adult she found herself denying that anything was missing, denying the pernicious absence of love by gobbling sweets. Sweets meant love, affection, and a reliable dependency to her though in fact none of them existed. All of this was linked to her body-feeling at the end of every gobbling that she still needed more, still felt unfulfilled even when her stomach ached from all the sweet food.

Her perception, however, of her repetition compulsion changed. Though still humiliated by it, now she saw it had protected a split-off piece of her self, her appetite for life and love. Her repetition compulsion provided refuge for this part of herself against being invaded and coopted. While still expressing her helplessness, she also saw this vexing attachment to sweets played a positive role. It protected her spontaneous capacity to take big bites of life. She saw her shameful repetition compulsion told her something existed in her psyche beyond her ego that looked out for her, that promoted her transformation into a bigger self by preserving a precious part of her until it could be better lived.

Aggression that she used to separate, close off and defend, she now used to bond with this missing part. Her connection to food moved out of the pre-oedipal incestuous-object stage into life as a complete object in itself (Loewald 1978). No longer a subjective-object (Winnicott 1971, 130) that she omnipotently controlled, or a selfobject which soothed her depleted self (Kohut 1971, xiv), food separated itself from her projections as an objective object, to be used and enjoyed, to be picked up or put down. Her aggression, which remained in its omnipotent form to defend her split-off, unmet dependency, was transformed into imaginative, vigorous energy to sustain conversations with her "nothing-place" and the little girl who nearly plunged into it (Winnicott 1968; Jung 1963b, 495-496, 528-531, pars. 706, 753-755). The readiness of her aggressive energy for the tasks of her imagination gave her a new range. She could try now this, now that, facing what had so long ter-rified her and remaking it as something fully alive for her. She moved out of the embattled us-them position, where she could only annihilate what she feared would annihilate her, into a big-ger space to welcome and repair even this part of herself, weak as it was, frightened, hungry for true love, not empty sweets. To recognize and live all this made her sad but also on the way to becoming whole (Klein 1952, 71-80).

Presence Glimpsed

Freed from encapsulation in the repetition complex, she felt keenly energy pressing her to complete herself, like a chord changes in music looking to find the resolving key. Living through the dependency in her transference and emerging from it, did not exhaust her sense of energy wanting, waiting to be released. She did suffer in the process, what most of us do, relapses into the old war of opposites, where ego is assimilated to unconscious instinct and we are driven to act out the rising energy or its very opposite, the depletion that brings about a sense of humiliation (Jung 1966, 163-168, pars. 254-259).

In this brief summary I do not mean to minimize the enor-mous labor that went into this woman's analytical work. What rescued her from her relapses was a new, if slow, growth issuing from the breaking open of her complex into the ritual field. Ritual always emerges from our weak spots, where spiritual power can break through. For this woman it was the gradual discovery of new meaning in the feeding process, and with it, through directed reading, the central place of feeding in countless rituals. The symptom that had vexed her was transposed now into a symbol of reality, a nourishing procedure of exchanges that quite exceeded her personal problems.

Food had acted as the sign of her repetition compulsion. Now it transmuted into a symbol of a barely graspable life process; and not only in the food-chains of evolution. Food had been her way of bridging the gap and sheltering her appetite for life. She saw even her fixation upon sweets, trivial and humiliating as it was, as related to the problem that faces all of us of how to get into right alignment with the center of life, to be fed by it and to feed it. This perspective set her personal problem in the larger context of the human need to find oneself part of a continuous process of creation and transformation.

Transformation – of psyche to soul, of repetition to ritual, of sign to symbol – must be fed to keep it alive. She saw her work in analysis as a kind of continual feeding by her ego of an unconscious process going on in her psyche. Set in this wider context, the transference-countertransference skirmishes between us yielded to a matching rapport (Kuras 1992). Together, we beheld the psyche working through its use of our interactions to close the gap in the feeding of her true self, and to promote nourishment for human life lived in depth. We must remember that it is from disorders of this kind that famine arises even when the world produces more than enough food for its billions of people. We cannot give what we do not have, even if literally we do possess it. We cannot share what we feel deprived of, and cannot receive what we fear.

In dealing with her particular personal problem, she penetrated to the processes of transformation in the depth psyche, which always must be fed by human efforts. Rituals of food exchange symbolize this connection of surface and depth minds, as, for example, in the opus of *cibatio* in alchemy, or the eucharist in Christianity where we feed God what is most precious to us and God feeds us with the body and blood of

the divine (Edinger 1995, 193, 199). It is not only that our consciousness changes its mode from knowing about a repetition
compulsion abstractly to become a spacemaker for the lost bit
of true self hiding in our repetition compulsion, and reroutes
the aggression needed to sustain connection to the self from
which we have suffered rupture. In addition, our consciousness changes by being linked to the transpersonal reality to
which our repetition compulsion tries to direct us. Yes, it is its
very repetitions that look to bridge the gap produced by our
original deprivation. The object we fixate on in our repetition
complex – our food, our overwork, our inability to apply for a
job, our procrastination, that ridiculous shameful object – and
the routine we tiresomely repeat and repeat in our behavior
constitutes our effort to bridge the gap, the rupture from our
self and between ourself and what it venerates. The intent of
our repetition, the drive of it, the repeated instinctual urge
hiding in it, seeks to complete connection to the large objective
presence to which our psyches belong.

Change of Location of Consciousness

To put it more simply, the autonomous drive at the root of
any repetition compulsion is a thirsting for the eternal, and the
repetition will not finally resolve itself until we achieve a satisfac-
tory link with the eternal. That means the ego must change its
location to a humbler place. Not mastery but submission brings
relief. The ego must submit itself to intimate relationship with
the unconscious processes of the psyche and through them to
the mysterious presence beyond the psyche that is making itself
known to us. The ego's role becomes one of witness to this
objective presence, just as the doctor witnesses to all parts of
the patient's psyche.

The resultant change of location and mode places the ego outside identification with either of the opposites caught up in our repetition complex. In this woman's case, for example, she no longer fell so often into identification first with the one opposite of extravagant eating, and then with the other of stringent denial in the guise of a beckoning thinness. Those impulses continued to war in her, but her ego was less vulnerable now because it was otherwise occupied, with relation not only to the larger center that opened in herself, but through it to a center outside herself. What fed her now was the profound insight that her efforts were contributing to a continuous process of crossing the gap between Creator and creature. She felt release from her hungry desires as she was being fed by this connection with eternity.

Ritual

Our sense of a greater context, and an objective presence that addresses us so specifically, is brought home to us by experiences that reach across space and time. Jung called them synchronistic events (Jung 1952). Here a brief example features a man of middle age, and veteran of several analyses before we worked together. He had tried to bring his private ritual into his job as a company's executive officer. He had elaborated over the years a series of symbols for the different quadrants of life and his own personality. He had painted the whole picture, and even walked it into the sand at the beach as a meditative exercise to show how all the parts and functions cohered. He was making space to contain all the parts of himself – memories, relationships, earlier jobs – and through them what they symbolized for him – feeling, thinking, inner and outer life, politics, spirituality, the immediate community, the world community.

413

When he tried to implement this overall design in his current job, it did not succeed. Other people felt imposed upon, as if he were playing a solo hand. They felt controlled, and fought back, trying to limit him. He felt hurt because in trying to give his best vision of the wholeness of life, they refused him. It ended badly.

I sensed some element of overdetermination in his gift, something too tight. When a private secret ritual, an unmistakable repetition compulsion came to light in our analytical work, the source of his rigidity broke open; he moved to a new job where his insights were welcomed and supported with time and money and he was able to give them with an open hand, without controlling others. A synchronistic event burst into his private repetition ritual. The collision of this outer event in no way causally related to his inner event deeply impressed him. It jolted him out of his repetition ritual by allowing him to perceive matter and psyche as two aspects of the same reality, the same wholeness.

We had been working hard on a repetition compulsion that featured a sexual fetish: obsessive attraction to a woman's nylon stocking. It aroused him to awe as well as excitement; a kind of reverence stirred his body and soul. This dissociated obeisance clearly dwelt alongside his long, fruitful partnership with his wife. He felt himself thrown back and forth between fascination with the fetish object on the one side and his conscious humiliation and wish to rid himself of the enthralment to it on the other. He had imaginatively engaged both of these opposites in conversation for some time in the analysis. On the particular session when the repetition broke open, we were speaking again of an early traumatic event when his father – with his mother also present – in exasperation at his repeated calling out from his room at night, ousted him from bed, flung him into the dark attic, and locked the door. He shook in terror. Within a few moments, thankfully, his father released him again.

I hazarded the comment that for a few seconds in the attic he had felt himself gone, annihilated. He had been out of existence momentarily and ever after had carried inside himself a great gap, a place where he did not exist. He housed in himself an interruption of his life. At that moment he saw the stocking as what he had created to bridge the gap. The stocking linked the two sides together, being and non-being, existence and its annihilation. The stocking also bridged the gap between adult comprehension of his father's exasperation and his own abject childhood terror. His awe rose before the stocking that had moved his whole being to life, including sexual erection and his humiliation at being bound to it. Our subsequent sessions continued moving through and working over these insights. But before the next session, he sent me through priority mail a newspaper clipping and photograph he had just received from an out-of-touch distant neighbor that arrived right after our decisive session. The photo showed that his original childhood house had been struck by lightning, but it only burned and destroyed the old attic room, nothing else. He felt pictured there the obliteration of his repetition complex built around the fetish object, leaving the rest of himself intact. The stocking had accomplished a transformation into a blazing perception, and here, remarkably enough, outer reality confirmed his inner work.

A Glimpse of the Whole

Such experiences, when ordinary categories of space, time, and causality seem to dissolve and show the unitary nature of reality, give us an unconscious knowledge not connected to the ego. Jung calls this an unconscious knowing or absolute knowledge (Jung 1952, 493, par. 931; Aziz, 110). It is associated with "self-subsistent meaning." In analytical work we know that such meaning strikes when we hear our analysand say, "Yes, that clicks," in response to an insight they have arrived at, one which opens a field of psychic reality between us to which we both have access.

In this interactive field we expand to acquire non-sensory knowledge of events that transgress the usual subject-object dualism as well as any outer-inner dichotomy. Instead we experience continuum, a linking of parts into whole, or more accurately, we glimpse a whole of which we compose the parts. We enter a realm where our inner eye and ear pierce to the heart of things (Jung 1952, 489, par. 923; Aziz, 111). This glimpse perceives the fourth unitary orientation which expresses the identity of all that divided into world and psyche, ego and unconscious. Instead of ego knowledge of the object, we see the "formless preeminence of that which infinitely surpasses all ego cognition" (Neumann 1956, 110; see also, Neumann 1976).

To live connected to this unitary field is to become sensitive to repeated synchronistic experiences, both small and large. This is what the religions mean by "signs," where indications of providential intervention assure us of the interdependence of all life. When distorted, we seek signs as substitutes for necessary ego choices, saying to ourselves "God made me do it." Such substitutes mean deprivation of both a functional ego and its connection to its surroundings. A symbol means connection.

The experience of connection to this larger containing unity shifts our lifelong dependency on self-objects into this field. We depend on the field – the space between us and others, between subjectivity and objectivity – to sustain and support us in our dependency upon each other. It supports our dependency by showing us the interdependent nature of all of reality. We can tell when we are living in relation to it – what the Chinese call living in Tao – by synchronistic events, large and small, that happen all around us and in us.

Our dependency takes on a rhythm, an ebb and flow of emptiness and fullness. Our creativity springs from recognition of the larger whole; its invocation calls us to our vocations; we offer humble ego-witness to the center of which we are a part. We circle back to a pre-eminent presence of love. Simone Weil, the activist and mystic that she was, said only desire will bring God down to the soul (Weil 1951, 111). Lady Julian of Norwich, the fourteenth century Christian mystic, insisted that only love lasts, only what we love will survive beyond the grave (Julian of Norwich 1961). This is the begging-bowl attitude of Buddhism, or what Fools Crow, the Teton Sioux medicine man, calls achieving hollow bones (Fools Crow 1991, 35ff.).

In all these humble but passionate attitudes of witness, desire, emptiness, loving, poverty of spirit, we respond to the giving forth of the transcendent dimension that waits patiently to attract us to take due notice of its abandon (Marion 1982, 3, 48, 98-99). In divine life this operation is symbolized by God's pouring out "good tidings" on Jerusalem, where the "glory of the Lord shall be revealed" (Isaiah 40:5, 9); by the Bodhisattva of Tibetan Buddhism who renounces bliss in order to help all of us receive it; by what Phillipians 2 in the New Testament describes as the operation of *kenosis*: the divine plenitude empties itself to take on human form, to become servant of all.

Our dependency on each other, which we both meet and fail to meet, rests on this larger rhythm of giving and receiving. In alternations of emptiness and fullness we receive and give from what we have first received. We begin to perceive that such sharing is the whole point. For sharing does not lessen what is given or even empty it, but rather protects it, by making space to receive more and more. The change in our small ego-consciousness that comes from spacemaking mirrors that rhythm in the large. What we experience as dependence on each other turns out to be in fact a circulation of life energies to weld us into a whole. Our giving to our patients is in itself a flow of energy, a bountiful reaching back into the humming of life's source. Our patients' giving to us creates in the small space of our offices what can be found, if we look for it, in all of life, a sharing that creates organic cohesion and coherence.

Naming

What then can we call this unitary field, this homeland of the gods? My clinical experiences have brought me to the conviction we must name this great presence in order to go on relating to it. If it remains anonymous, our clarity of perception of it fades. We know it exists, there is a there there, but it ceases as a personal connection. We behave like the patient's mother who called her daughter by all her siblings' names before recalling and using the daughter's right name. Similarly, if we call this transcendent dimension now this, now that, as we fail to find the name that speaks to us out of our finite personal connection to it, our experience remains collective, not personal; general, not specific; abstract, not embodied. It is as if we had relation to the opposite sex as generalized woman or man, and not to a specific person in an unfolding intimacy. Nameless, our relationship to this transcendent dimension does not grow; it does not incarnate, but regresses into words. We talk about it instead of directly to it.

This transcendent presence does not go away, however. Instead it falls in displacement onto other values, chiefly our repetition complex, with all that represents. We may make a religion out of our psychoanalytic theories: Freud becomes the source of all, or Jung, or whoever. We regress to symbolic equations, where we close the gap between the Creator's and the creature's hands. Our theory masquerades as the truth; it no longer points to the truth. This caricatures depth psychology whose function is to unshackle us and deliver us into living, not to substitute itself for life.

In the same way, religion falls into idolatry when it misuses its symbolic treasures. Like all those figures in medieval and renaissance religious paintings who stand to one side of their canvases, pointing to a central divine presence, religion, when it functions rightly, points to the unknowable God who knows us. It does not substitute its rules, doctrines, liturgies for God (Marion 1982, 163-167, 224 n.5, 226 n.6, 228, n. 14). At its best, religion simply reminds us of the gap between finite and infinite because nothing finite can equate with the infinite. We can even say our personal experience of the gaps in our development that subject us to repetition compulsions, mirror the same existential gap between the human and divine. Just as we depend on another person to help us recover and fill in the gap which convicts us of our dependence on each other to live and to thrive, so the gap between the human and divine convicts us of our dependence upon God to cross the gap and to annul it. In the gift of Torah, the gift of the Son, the gift of Satori, the gift of Bodhisattva, the gift of the Koran, God enters into our particular life and we come to feel an overflowing gratitude for the overflowing gift that matches our dependence.

In all enduring beliefs, we live in and across the gap, creating out of it a faith that the psyche will press for wholeness. In our treatment rituals, for example, we trust the analysand's psyche to communicate the problem and intimations of its solution. But each of us, patients and doctors, needs to name this transcendent presence communicated through the psyche that we trust, and open a conversation with it that continues through all our time, all our life.

Naming this presence, wedding ourselves to the truths we cherish, we are made constantly mindful of the gap between our images and our names for the truth and the truth itself. We see that gap between the theories we cherish and the presence they point to. We need to find our own names for this presence that undergirds the ritual of treatment and enables us to do our work.

We know our names never define this presence, but they do focus our meditative gaze where we can look upon it with what Lao-tzu calls the long hard stare. This rhythm of filling up with our names and emptying out of them, of contemplating and disidentifying, becomes for each of us our own ritual of acknowledgment of the reality that supports the work we do, from which our work must draw if it is to know any success.

Our continual naming and recognizing that our names do not define this presence becomes our repeated ritual that allows us to keep believing in the work we do, to be enlivened by it and grateful for it. Guntrip tells us that the healthy person is the loving person (Guntrip 1975). What, then, do we love? In Winnicott's words, what experiences make us feel alive and real? In Klein's words, What are we grateful for and to whom? In Freud's terms, what is the work we love? In Jung's terms, what is the infinite which summons us? In the terms I have used this morning, what ritual breaks us open as it bursts our repetitions?

Oskar Pfister Lecture, American Psychiatric Association, 1996, New York City.

Notes

1. Masud Khan cautions against capturing dreaming in the analyst's employ and against the temptation to make a fetish out of the dream text (Khan 1972, 307; see also Khan 1983, 42ff.). I would add as well that we need to resist the imperialistic claim that only we who interpret dreams can give them their proper understanding. The process of dreaming acts as healing; the dream experience heals, which is not to say interpretation does not add its own mending effect (see also chapter 11).

2. Freud originally coined the term Repetition-Compulsion. It refers to "active repetition of a passively experienced unpleasure ... [which] helps the individual master the anxiety involved in passively suffering some trauma (narcissistic mortification) ... in some cases aggressive pleasure was achieved; in others, at least unpleasure was eliminated." It operates "to bind tension and eliminate excitation ... an expression of the Nirvana Principle, and as a derivative of the ultimate aim of the aggressive (death) instincts, the return to an inorganic state." We see it clinically in children's play, traumatic neurosis, fate neuroses; in the transference we see the revival of repressed wishes of infantile neurosis, and in relation to the uncanny, we find ourselves in the same situation again (Eidelberg 1968, 374-375, #1821).

   Repetition compulsion "endeavors to make the psychic trauma real – to live once more through the repetition of it; if it was an early affective relationship it is revived in an analogous connection with another person" (Freud 1938/1957, Part III, Section I). We "postulate the principle of a *repetition-compulsion* in the unconscious mind, based upon instinctual activity and probably inherent in the very nature of the instincts – a principle powerful enough to overrule the pleasure-principle, lending to certain aspects of the mind their demonic character, and still very clearly expressed in the tendencies of small children; a principle, too, which is responsible for a part of the course taken by the analyses of neurotic patients. "We may assume that as soon as a given state of things is upset there arises an instinct to recreate it, and phenomena appear which we may call 'repetition-compulsion'" (Freud 1933, 106-108). (Fodor and Gaynor 1950, 157).

   Kierkegaard asserts that repetition "has an essentially different significance in the natural and in the spiritual sphere ..." (Kierkegaard 1941, xiv). Repetition sketches the several stages through which freedom must pass "in order to attain itself" (xvi). In the first stage we feel freedom as pleasure and fear repetition as dampening it and plunging us into despair. But despair ushers in the second stage where we feel freedom as the shrewdness "to see constantly a new side of repetition" (xvii). But we are still left in the world of finiteness, concerned with finite objects. This too ends in despair. Then freedom breaks out "in its highest form, in which it is defined in relation to itself ... Now the highest interest of freedom is to bring about repetition, and it fears only lest change might have the power to alter its eternal nature" (xvii). Freedom means repetition is possible and repetition means freedom is constant.

References

Aziz, R. 1990. *C. G. Jung's Psychology of Religion and Synchronicity*. Albany, N.Y.: State University of New York Press.

Bion, W. R. 1970. *Attention and Interpretation*. London: Tavistock.

Edinger, E. F. 1995. *The Mysterium Lectures*. transcribed and edited by Joan Dexter Blackmer. Toronto: Inner City Books.

Eidelberg, L. 1968. *Encyclopedia of Psychoanalysis*. Editor in Chief. New York: The Free Press; London: Collier-Macmillan Limited.

Fodor, N. and Gaynor, F. 1950. *Freud: Dictionary of Psychoanalysis*. eds. New York: Philosophical Library.

Fools Crow. 1991. *Fools Crow Wisdom and Power*. T. E. Mails. Tulsa, Okl.: Council Oak Books.

Freud, S. 1927. *The Future of an Illusion*. SE xxi: 5-59, 1973.

Freud, S. 1933. Anxiety and instinctual life. *New Introductory Lectures*, Lecture XXXII. *SE* xxii: 81-111.

Freud, S. 1938. Moses and monotheism. *SE*. xxiii. trans. James Strachey. London: Hogarth, 1957.

Guntrip, H. 1975. My experience of analysis with Fairbairn and Winnicott. *International Review of PsychoAnalysis*, vol. II: 145-156.

Hale, N. 1980. Freud's reflections on work and love. *Themes of Work and Love in Adulthood*. eds. N. J. Smelser and E. H. Erickson. Cambridge: Harvard University Press.

Jung, C. G. 1946. Psychology of the transference. *The Practice of Psychotherapy. Collected Works*, vol. 16. trans. R. F. C. Hull. New York: Pantheon 1954.

Jung, C. G. 1948. A psychological approach to the Trinity. *Psychology and Religion: West and East. Collected Works*, vol. 11, trans. R. F. C. Hull. New York: Pantheon 1968.

Jung, C. G. 1952. Synchronicity: an acausal connecting principle. *The Structure and Dynamics of the Psyche. Collected Works*, vol. 8, trans. R. F. C. Hull. New York: Pantheon 1960.

Jung, C. G. 1953. *Psychology and Alchemy. Collected Works*, vol. 12. trans. R. F. C. Hull. New York: Pantheon.

Jung, C. G. 1963a. *Memories, Dreams, Reflections.* ed. Aniela Jaffé. trans. Richard and Clara Winston. New York: Pantheon.

Jung, C. G. 1963b. *Mysterium Coniunctionis. Collected Works*, vol. 14. trans. R. F. C. Hull. New York: Pantheon.

Jung, C. G. 1966. *Two Essays on Analytical Psychology. Collected Works*, vo. 7, trans. R. F. C. Hull. New York: Pantheon.

Julian of Norwich. 1961. *The Revelations of Divine Love.* trans. James Walsh. New York: Harper & Brothers.

Khan, M. M. R. 1972. The use and abuse of dream in psychic experience. *The Privacy of the Self.* New York: International Universities Press, 1974, 306-316.

Khan, M. M. R. 1974. Beyond dreaming experience. *Hidden Selves, Between Theory and Practice in Psychoanalysis.* New York: International Universities Press, 1983, 47-51.

Khan, M. M. R. 19895. Fate-neurosis, false self and destiny. *Winnicott Studies* 1/Spring 1985: 5-26.

Kierkegaard, S. 1941. *Repetition, An Essay on Experimental Psychology.* trans. W. Lowrie. Princeton, N.J.: Princeton University Press.

Klein, M. 1952. Some theoretical conclusions regarding the emotional life of the infant. *Envy and Gratitude & Other Works 1946-1963.* New York: Delacorte Press/Seymour Lawrence, 1957, 61-93.

Klein, M. 1957. Envy and gratitude. *Envy and Gratitude and Other Works 1946-1963.* New York: Delacorte Press/Seymour Lawrence 1975, 176-235.

Kohut, H. 1971. *The Analysis of the Self.* New York: International Universities Press.

Kuras, M. 1992. Intimacies of the impersonal. *Journal of Analytical Psychology.* 37/4: 433-455.

Loewald, H. W. 1970. Psychoanalytic theory and the psychoanalytic process. *Papers on Psychoanalysis.* New Haven: Yale University Press 1980.

Loewald, H. W. 1978. The waning of the oedipus complex. *Papers on Psychoanalysis.* New Haven: Yale University Press 1980.

Marion, J.-L. 1982. *God Without Being.* trans. T. A. Carlson. Chicago: University of Chicago Press.

Neumann, E. 1953. The psyche and the transformation of the reality planes. *Spring* 1956: 81-111.

Neumann, E. 1976. The psychological meaning of ritual. *Quadrant.* Winter: 5-35.

Ricoeur, P. 1970. *Freud and Philosophy.* trans. New Haven, Ct.: Yale University Press.

Rilke, R. M. 1988. *Selected Letters 1902-1926.* trans. R. D. C. Hull. London: Quartet Encounters.

Ulanov, A. and B. 1975. *Religion and the Unconscious.* Louisville, Ky.: Westminster/John Knox Press.

Ulanov, A. B. 1994. *The Wizards' Gate, Picturing Consciousness.* Einsiedeln, Switzerland: Daimon.

Ulanov, A. B. 1996. *The Functioning Transcendent.* Wilmette, Ill: Chiron.

Weil, S. 1951. *Waiting on God.* trans. Emma Craufurd. New York: Capricorn.

Winnicott, D. W. 1971. *Playing and Reality.* London: Tavistock.

Winnicott, D. W. 1962. Ego integration in child development. *The Maturational Processes and the Facilitating Environment.* New York: International Universities Press. 1965.

Winnicott, D. W. 1968. On "The use of the object." *Psycho-analytic Explorations.* eds. C. Winnicott, R. Shepherd, M. Davis. London: Karnac 1989.

Winnicott, D. W. 1970. Living creatively. *Home Is Where We Start From.* New York: Norton, 1986.

Winnicott, D. W. 1988. *Human Nature.* London: Free Association Press.

Chapter 16

Hate in the Analyst

"Hate" is a hard word, one we want to avoid as too harsh, especially in relation to our work in analysis that we love. We prefer the word "aggression" as connoting energy, verve, even confrontation. Hate seems to spell only destructiveness. Yet we know from our theory about the opposites that we cannot know love without hate, and we know from the work of analysis over decades that often we must face hate – in the analysand, in the transference and countertransference field between us, and in ourselves, if the work is to get done.

If it is true, as Jung claims, that the basis of our personality is affectivity (Jung 1907/1960, para. 78; see also Jung 1963, 177, 187) and that affects are archetypal, then we are faced with the task of living and transforming our hate into personal and communal terms. If we do not, if hate is left unconscious, it burgeons, inflating personal relatedness, just as an ordinary stream becomes a torrent when flooded with surplus emotion. Then we become fanatic in the holding of our theories for they are overdetermined by the unmetabolised and unmediated emotion.

We experience hate both as a primitive force that instigates behavior and as an affect that seems to endure (see Rycroft

1968, 61). Unlike anger, for example, that is passing toward someone we love, hate persists, directing malice, a wish to injure, to harm, to destroy. And it is this nexus of hate and destructiveness that I want to focus upon, for the word 'hate' leads us to the underlying meaning of aggression, mixing it up with destructiveness.

It is the destructiveness that worries us in the debate about whether aggression is an instinct belonging to the core of our personality, pressing inevitably for release, actuating hateful behavior, or whether aggression is a defensive reaction to prior deprivation and that is the central character issue that should be our focus in analysis. Whichever view we hold bears significantly on our clinical work.

On the aggression-as-instinct side of the debate we find Adler, Freud, Klein, who urge us to analyze aggression in its hateful persecutory aspects so that it will not undermine our capacity to love, but instead act as a booster shot, setting loose our capacity to make reparation, and bolstering our belief in the force of eros to carry the aims of love and work (see Lear 1990, 12, 27-28, 169, 172, 177, 181). On the aggression-as-defense side of the debate, we find Sullivan, Fairbairn, Guntrip, Kohut, and even Fromm, all of whom see destructiveness as reaction to some prior deprivation or attack to the self, whether it be overwhelming anxiety, or not being loved unconditionally but instead frustrated in our intense dependence and object-seeking libido, or an ego weakness that retreats from object-seeking love, or failure of the selfobjects to respond appropriately to our developmental needs, or threat to our survival and vital interests (Mitchell 1993, 155-157). More recent relational psychoanalysts distinguish between healthy innate assertion as a biological potential within a relational context, and destructiveness when we feel endangered (Mitchell 1993, 166ff.). For theorists who see aggression as reactive defense against threat, the clinical focus is to discern under what conditions we respond with joyful healthy energy and what circumstances evoke destructive versions of our selves which remain intact lifelong, but which we learn to recognise and contain (Mitchell 1993, 160-161, 171).

In Jungian terms, hate is shadow stuff, the destructiveness that gets mixed in with aggression, compacting it into lethal passion toward the object of hate (see also Boss 1963, 125-126). Here the question is whether hate stems only from personal unconscious realms of shadow material, in reaction to wounds and deprivations, or whether it arises from the objective archetypal core of shadow and can be conscripted into the Self bearing down upon the ego. If destructiveness just is, as a principle of being, then we are led into debates about the dark and light sides of Self, and to theological issues of God as *summum bonum*, or God as containing, as Jung averred, unconscious destructive archetypal affect that is our task to protect against and to reform by our tiny, precious, conscious, ego response, following Job. These theoretical conversations are very important and cast the background of my focus upon destructiveness in the analyst and its transformation in the work of analysis.

I was surprised and deeply heartened to discover in the long months of nursing my husband towards death that hate plays a part which, if admitted, transforms into a light, humorous energy that fertilizes the temenos we were building for this journey to the end. Being ill, being bed-ridden, being in pain is truly awful. Hateful. Trying to care for one who is ill, in pain, bed-ridden also has awful, hateful aspects to it. We could feel ourselves pulled into an undertow. We decided to grant both of us fifteen minutes a day — to complain, scream, curse, yell, jump up and down, no holds barred, to express how we hated this suffering. Then the rest of the day we talked about everything else. Allowing hate a voice in its own key, freed us to enjoy all we could the rest of the time, for we could release this force of destructiveness building up within us, between us, around us from the relentless stress of pain of all kinds. So far, so good.

But, we came to blows over the bath. Sterner measures were needed. There, I suggested, we could hate each other, if needed, all-out. "Hate?" Barry protested, "Oh, no! Much too strong a word; I would never hate you." "Oh?" I replied, "Is there a third person with us in the bathroom emitting these toxic rays through your fiery eyes? Hate it is." So we risked feeling all-out, pulling no punches. To our astonishment, the bath gradually became fun. A student gave us water pistols. Barry's three inches long, mine eighteen. The pain was still there; my clumsiness did not vanish; his not helping enough persisted. But mixed in with all this, like a twining new tendril coming up from a compost heap, was laughter, even sexual play, both commodities in short supply when illness strikes. He and I had been composted by admitting our hate. It transformed from heavy, dense, suffocating material into gorgeously black, airy, spongy matter. We had been fertilized, made gay in our distress, brought closer in our night-sea journey.

In analysis, it is the same. Hate must be admitted in the analyst to herself, for the work to get done. We know this. We talk and write about it together in terms of examining all the levels of our countertransference (Ulanov 1999, and Ulanov 1982/ 1996). When I am struck dumb in the face of an analysand's dream – feeling what a client, herself a professional, calls an attack of "acute stupidity" – the questions arise: is this a normal idiosyncratic part of my style? Is this an activation of a complex of mine blanking out my brain that needs more analysis? Or is this dumbness in me induced, giving me objective information about what is unconsciously attacking the analysand? Or is this blankness not only an intersubjective creation between us, perhaps replaying an early relation between the analysand and a parent, but also a presentiment of the archetypal constellation between us, destroying the present clarity as it constructs a fresh way of perceiving? (Mitchell and Aron 1999, xiii; Bromberg 1993, 381-385).

We know our experiences of hate in analysis. The first step within the temenos in which it may be transformed, is to take its full force into ourselves. Our hate comes in all forms – of feeling clueless about what is going on in a session, under attack either from a patient who is communicating we are a dope, or from an inner accuser insisting we are a fraud. Even though we know the contempt an analysand shows us reflects the destruction of his inner world, we still feel blitzed by a comparable shame and humiliation. An analysand's scorn for our shoes, our voice, our vocabulary withers our initiative. Or we feel a blast of rage or malice which we can interpret as our own "defense of the Self" (Fordham 1974) as an attempt to ward off the hateful accusation that we are poisoning the analysand's sexuality, or causing the tumor to grow in her stomach.

We can sense our own answering hate in giving interpretations, especially if they are correct, about the rupture from the Self now being repeated in the transference, which invariably includes our attempt to avert the attack by blaming a distant parent and by offering our explanation to fix it. Alice Miller (1981, chapter 3) calls our attention to the subtle disdain conveyed in the assumption that our interpretations fix all problems, and to the contempt we may unwittingly dish out when we must fit a person to a DSM-IV diagnostic label for insurance payment.

Sometimes hate comes through the body, as when my weak hip starts aching in a session with a man denying his life-threatening disease. I can feel his illness galvanising illness in me and register I am sick of him. When an analysand threatens to kill off the good work done in the previous session by denying it happened or diminishing its importance, we know firsthand an answering volcanic lava that might erupt and smother all the carping, dodging, whinging and whining that covers up despair. And pulling a patient back from suicide brings not only floods of relief but sometimes also rage; we are so mad we could kill them!

What are we to do with such primordial destructive affects in analysis? How are we to deal with them in ourselves? The focus is now not the affect of hate in our analysands or even in the field between us, but our own hate and aggression. We much prefer aggression as a word because it means to approach, from the Latin *aggredi*, evoking our experience of spontaneous instinctual energy that goes out, goes into, charges up, asserts, goes to confront. When such energy becomes overladen with shadow material of hurt, insult, dismissal, then anger, envy, spoiling, vengefulness, sadism pile on this energy, conscripting it into hatefulness.

Surprisingly, hate etymologically can be traced to the Greek *kedos* as care, sorrow, affliction, akin to hate and related to *accidia* or *acedia*, the root of, or route to, sloth, a faulty shape. Thus destructiveness connects with not filling out one's shape fully, from not caring (Partridge 1959). What does analysis offer us for the transformation of such destructive emotion into useful aggression for the work of analysis? Where do we put the bad? How does it transform? What does our transformation of aggression offer to analysis? These are questions which occupy me.

Help comes from other theorists. I knew glad relief reading Harold Searles years ago when he felt the only thing he could do with a schizophrenic patient was to "fuck him or kill him" (Searles 1979, 431, 492, 528). Admitting into awareness such hateful affect liberated Searles from the inflated view that the therapist is responsible for everything that happens, and from the imprisoning "idealized self-image as an all-loving, omnipotent healer" (ibid., 80). Hate also, however, masks the grief and guilt we all feel for not rescuing our patient from suffering (ibid., 31).

By admitting our own hatefulness, analysands are better protected from analysts acting out negative feelings. And awareness of hatefulness helps equalise the power differential in the analytic couple because the analyst, when he knows how much bad he harbors, is less apt to hog the role of helper who provides the good. Opposites of love and hate belong to both persons, and both sit in a field where hate and love objectively push both of them around. Searles concludes that by facing who he actually is in the analytic session "one braves the threat of destruction both to the patient and oneself, in taking into one's hands to declare one's individuality come what may" (ibid., 372).

This willingness to risk finding one's way, what Jung calls individuation, goes on in the analyst in the consulting room as well as outside it. This "act of high courage flung in the face of life, the absolute affirmation of all that constitutes the individual ..." means including our hate too, our destructiveness as well as our loving (Jung 1934, para. 286). But what actually changes our hate into another form of energy?

Kohut asserts that suitable mirroring of the unrecognized idealised self and of our need for an idealized object will restart the client's interrupted developmental process and include optimal frustrations that will mutate aggression into appropriate ambition and sturdy values, thus harnessing destructive forces into creative living. Kernberg argues that nothing less than active dismantling of the pathological self will release hateful aggression to be modified in channels of self in relation to others. We are indebted to Melanie Klein for her bold recognition of aggression as a central component *de novo* of the personality.

She also asserted that only relentless interpretation of the death instinct will modify aggression into symbolic forms that can be taken up into play to stimulate reparation from which stems all our creativity. In my experience when witnessing is called for, relentless interpreting only inflames, and has more to do with the analyst's hatefulness than the client's benefit. Klein was criticised for translating her clients' phantasies into the vocabulary of her theories, leaving her patients, finally, with only a substitute instead of a transformation. Winnicott calls our attention to the role of destructiveness in establishing the externality of the object, though he himself was criticised for the failure of such transformation with Masud Khan, one of his most gifted analysands, who destructively wound down through alcohol and transgression of boundaries to a lonely end (Hopkins 1998).

Jung reminds us that the urge to become who we are is ruthless. The instinct toward individuation will have its way with us whether or not we consent: "the psyche, as an objective fact, hard as granite and heavy as lead, confronts [us] as an inner experience and addresses [us] in an audible voice, saying, 'This is what will and must be.'" (Jung 1934, para. 303). The work of analysis is fueled not just by repetition compulsion to bring into consciousness a past wound continually acted out, but also by the drive to realize our ownmost possibility, which includes other people, and indeed, even the world.

Ruthless aggression works against falling into sloth; experiencing this energy with which we reach for our own vocation, to respond to what calls us. For this inner voice speaks of a wider fuller life, a more comprehensive inclusion of all the parts and thus whispers something negative which is our particular danger that escorts us into consciousness of the evil from which our whole community suffers (Jung 1934, pars. 318-319; see also Jung 1988, 102-104).

Thus in our specific consulting room, small and insignificant in the large scheme of things, we face not only the unworked out wounds in ourselves where our hate still proves stronger than our power to love, but also the destructiveness threatening the community in our culture, in our historical era. We are ushered into the questions about evil itself. Where does it come from? Why do the unjust prosper and the innocent suffer? How can we survive the destructiveness threatening us?

I. Transformation of Aggression: Persona Level

What do we as analysts do in sessions with our own destructiveness that yields its transformation into energy that sustains the long labor of the work? Where do we put the bad? (see Redfearn 1977). By bad I mean responses which stymie us, in contrast to those we would wish to have to a client's material, and that the client needs us to have, for example, not feeling compassion for the other's suffering but an oddly cold unmovedness. I felt like a stone listening to one woman, and alternately berated and worried myself over this flinty response. Was I the right analyst for her? Was she touching off a complex in me? Was something in her inducing this reaction in me? Was I defending myself against what felt like too much suffering? Why couldn't I figure this out!

In time I discovered my countertransference included all these levels: it was induced in that I did echo her cold refusal to take up her own suffering. Instead she parceled it out among her many acquaintances, telling and retelling her plaints to various friends, supervisors, colleagues. My annoyance also carried my idiosyncratic response to look first for what one can oneself do about a trouble and only later turn to others. And my coldness did strike a complex in me that replayed my childhood defense of self-holding in the face of no one to depend upon. So my destructive stoney attitude rang the changes of countertransference: it was my personal style, my complex to be worked on, and objective feeling-state induced by the patient. My countertransference touched something archetypal as well, because through my destructive lack of empathy a larger deconstruction hove into sight.

What came clear was that she and I had to sit tight in the temenos we were given, and its destruction which led us to another container. This ego-consent is necessary to create a vessel in which the operations of analysis continue. She had to stop blabbing and I had to endure hating (destructive coldness). No symbolic space can constellate if either analyst or analysand is always taking the lid off the pot, either by this woman talking to everyone or by me not wanting to feel like a stone in response to her narrative. Nothing cooks.

With another person I made the mistake of not being ruthless enough when it seemed I was perceived as repeatedly, though kindly with a smile, knocking down the analysand as if to start again from the bottom. I questioned if I was being given an objective message and another analyst would be a better match. But in retrospect that just delayed what I saw from the very beginning must happen, and did happen, a dismantling of the analysand's worldview, not because it was necessarily wrong, but because it was conscripted into defense against hitting bottom where new growth could take root. The analysand's unconscious saw the necessary state of affairs. I was just too chicken to get on board immediately because it seemed so destructive.

Winnicott shows us that if the baby is allowed to have full experience of ruthless instinctive impulse – ruthless in the sense of not considering consequences to self or other – and the mother can survive the baby's aggressive impulse and not change her attitude to the baby but instead reflect the experience back to the baby, then that instinctive aggression will transform (Winnicott 1971, chapter 6; Winnicott 1947/1975). The mother will become to the baby an objective person in her own right, external to the baby's image of her because the baby has destroyed his projections upon her and she is still there, not retaliating, not crumpling in hurt, not going away, nor changing her attitude toward him. She survives his instinctual assault out of her own resources which he can now perceive as belonging to her irrespective of himself. Her reality external to him, coupled with her still dwelling with him, not retaliating for his biting her, for example, but reflecting back what it must feel like to be cutting teeth, establishes her as a real object with real food for him, that is, a resource in reality that nourishes and promotes his fullest experience of living. If instead the mother withdraws in hurt, or fails to reflect back to the baby the goodness of his instinctive impulses, the baby withdraws from his own instinctive energy in order to protect the mother, but thereby severs connection to his own "animal-root-impulse" (see chapter 11). That withdrawal may widen into a split for which therapy will be sought as an adult. Winnicott's theories change withdrawal into regression to dependence on a good enough object, usually the analyst.

Jung turns regression to dependence on the object into reconnection with archetypal source. He goes through the mother, so to speak, also to include what she symbolises – love and hate, support and aggression. We find in Jung, then, that healing stems not from the new introject of the analyst as with many schools of depth psychology, but from reconnection to archetypal source (see chapters 9, 11, 14). How does this happen to the analyst in relation to her own destructiveness?

On a personal level, we are required with hateful feelings, just as with any other responses, first to admit them, consent to them, suffer the full force within ourselves, not with the analysand. I agree with Masud Khan that the best counter-transference is the one that operates silently (Khan 1979, 214). Don't duck out; if we feel like a stone then accept that card dealt to us. That consent feels like submission when the affect runs counter to what we believe should be the case and what we would wish for the patient's benefit. Hateful affect destroys the temenos of our analytical container – what we believe an analyst should bring to the work. It runs counter to the view among most schools of depth psychology that the mutative agent therapy offers is the analysand's introjection of the new object of the analyst with whom to experience a new kind of object relation. To feel like a stone destroys that belief. I was not a better object than the client's original mother or father. I was worse.

Negative affect submits us to humiliation, self attack, soma-tisation, and, depending on the style of our conscious attitude, acceding to alchemical operations. We are the matter being worked on, just as is the analysand! We may have to bear the fire of *calcinatio* to dry out our too soggy view of analysis; we may be plunged into the bath of the unconscious, like Bion's non-knowing, a *solutio* to dissolve our treatment plan (which was a good one). We may be plunged into a *nigredo* of irritation, crankiness, repelling observations, infiltrating nullity, chilling scrutiny, and not know why.

Not only is our analytical persona destroyed in front of the other person – we are not the empathetic presence hoped for – but our persona is destroyed in front of ourselves. How we see ourselves in the world, how we see ourselves being seen by others, how we have known ourselves to be, gets destroyed. Jung reminds us, that persona is that "which oneself as well as others think one is" (Jung 1950, para. 222; see also Jung 1976, 333-334). What we have come to think of ourselves is destroyed by hate in the analyst. This is radical. We knew ourselves as introverted or extroverted, a thinking or feeling type and so on. These convictions about our nature, not to mention the accumulated conclusions we have drawn from our history of analyzing our own complexes, go by the board. We do not know. With Bion we have eschewed memory and desire. And our blankness, our stonelikeness, let alone more riotous negative affects, usher us into another realm.

The first analytical persona temenos is destroyed. This happened to me very quickly with an extremely poised and accomplished woman. I dropped my papers, I mixed up appointments, I was late for the hour. In short, I made and was a mess. Inferior functions took over, and I was pushed out of my usual way of beginning analysis and conducted into a nether realm. As Jung says, "the inferior function is practically identical with the dark side of the human personality. The darkness which clings to every personality is the door into the unconscious ..." (1950, para. 222). The personal level of persona gives way to the archetypal.

At the persona level the analyst-me I am used to and counted on crumbles under the invasion of destructive mess-making (which filled me with hateful affect toward myself and the situation). Just as from Winnicott we see how the external object becomes real because it was destroyed as a product of subjective projections, so we see with Jung that the subjective me also becomes more real because my projections on myself, so to speak, are destroyed. The analyst-me I counted on decomposes under the assault of my becoming a stone, or a scattered dodo who cannot master her schedule, or the one who wants to duck out of negative constellation. My own subjectivity becomes more objective to me and hence more real. A subtle link of identity with this ego inhabiting me dissolves or breaks and I can walk around my inner ego I-ness as an analyst as if it were a three-dimensional statue, no longer completely identified (combined) with it.

The first step toward transformation of our destructiveness is to allow it, to experience the affect that invades us, which destroys our persona in our own eyes as well as the analysand's so that we become disidentified with who we are. The second step is to observe what affect affects us and relate to it (Ulanov and Ulanov 1991/1999, chapter 2). How do I feel about it? What do I think in this new state? Am I appalled that I messed up my schedule or am I intrigued by this new unexpected event? Am I curious about what this means? Shifts in perception occur, from linear causal thinking – that the present problem comes from past wounds, and from prospective thinking – that the present problem leads to a telos, a purpose that is unfolding – into synchronistic thinking. In a synchronistic consciousness (Bright 1997) we perceive the whole surround of events simultaneously. We glimpse a unity, a whole holding us and the analysand, and itself.

In this shift we take a second step. Our first step was to allow destructiveness, to admit it, submit to it. Now we reflect on it. That allows time for consciousness in the ego to catch up with other sources of consciousness in the body and in the psyche (see Neumann 1953/1956). Other sources of consciousness turn up in dreams that personify points of view different from our ego's, or in experiences of the Self enforcing its view, defeating the ego, or in body symptoms that address the ego. Only in digesting all aspects of destructiveness can any decision arrive how and what and when to share in words with the analysand an interpretation, a communication of this larger surround. For example, with the woman of great poise, I eventually said I feel I am arranged to make a mess so a way will open for us into the unknown.

Making a symbolic space for the psychic contents of the client also means the analyst is stretched to make more space in herself for what comes up from the archetypal realm. In the example where I was like a stone, the properties of the stone turned out to be exactly what the client aimed for – containment, hardness, *coagulatio* into a discrete, defined object, not scattered all over in bits and pieces, nor subject to every wind of opinion. One can do the same sort of work on feeling like a dope, a scorned object, an erupting volcano, a contemptible dodo.

II. Transformation of Aggression, Archetypal Level

If in the face of hateful affect destroying the persona temenos of analysis, deconstructing the analyst we knew ourselves to be, we hold onto the ego's view, we then get identified with the wound dealt us, either by our analysand or ourselves. We collect a "grievance" (Lemaitre-Sillere 1998) and get stuck there. Aggressive energy goes to restoring the ego's view with its inward persona which usually amounts to bullying the patient. I devoted two arduous treatments (separated by twenty years) to one woman, with much short-term but no long-term success, because we could not dislodge her need to defeat her father by her own self-destruction. Conscripted almost from birth into carrying his anima, she dedicated herself to refusing to succeed at anything lest her parent appropriate it. She had suffered his theft of her early childhood successes; they became his boast as if he owned them. She could secure her existence external to him by her failure to thrive. Though in analysis she moved beyond her anorexia, and even suicide gestures and severe drug dependency, we were never able to advance toward aggression supporting joyous living, except in short bursts. Aggression always returned to armor the stubborn persona from which she adamantly refused abundant life. When I went after the rage consolidating this position, the lure of mind-numbing prescription drugs grabbed her again. I took a stand, insisting she seek drug detoxification because she was either sleeping through sessions in the office or not showing up. She left treatment. In retrospect I am ambivalent still whether I was not also bullying her out of hateful frustration as much as I was urging a correct course of action.

If, on the other hand, we consent to the destruction of the persona-level temenos and give up our identification with our ego-stance, we are thrust into archetypal depths. A new question arises: What is the Self engineering? Here another destruction takes place, a true cycle of death and rebirth, and our job is to discern what is the archetypal pattern living this analysand's life. What pattern is playing them and us? A destruction-creation cycle occurs. As Jung puts it, "at the climax of the illness, the destructive powers [are] converted into healing forces. This is brought about by the archetypes awaking to independent life and taking over the guidance of the psychic personality, thus supplanting the ego with its futile willing and striving. As a religious-minded person would say: guidance has come from God.... I must express myself in more modest terms and say that the psyche has awakened to spontaneous activity...." Something comes up "from the hidden depths of the psyche – something that is not his ego and is therefore beyond the reach of his personal will. He has regained access to the sources of psychic life, and this marks the beginning of his cure" (Jung 1932, para. 534).

How do we know this? By change in imagery which binds affect in new ways. For example, one man seeing a pattern of death and rebirth playing through him rescued himself from the magnetism of the ensnaring mother through wanton anonymous sexual attractions. For him rebirth came in forging an axis between his ego and a centering Self through the labor of working at his poetry. Instead of the siren song of the passing stranger which inevitably led to nothing, his articulation into image and word of the precious animating connection to being, rooted him. I was changed from being occupied with frustrating images of his diluting, losing him now here and now there in his various wanderings, to a concerted energy, strenuous exertion in the forging of a connecting link to a passionate center of life.

Another analysand sought treatment because her guilt for breaking her marriage vow with sexual affairs was so attacking she feared her depression would take her to suicide. She presented herself as so watery, undefined and unspoken, caught in a web of fantasies, that I felt myself arranged to speak out, give lecturettes on the role of aggression in life. I was appalled. But she responded by confessing that her previous attempts at therapy had ended when she disagreed with the therapist but never said so, instead over-adapting to what the analyst said while inwardly fleeing. To assert aggression for her was unthinkable, though she did so, I pointed out, by going out looking for her submerged sexuality which she could not find with her husband. She also, I said, asserted herself ruthlessly by insisting on her own life, even though she did not know what that was, by refusing "to get on the train," as she put it, of her husband's life-plan. She resisted his insistence she speed up the commercial aspect of her art and also that she get immediately pregnant. By all this talk we created a space to house her dreams where all the aggression had fallen and to include my hating my own talkativeness, which I eventually commented on. The usual way of conducting analysis was destroyed and a new temenos constructed itself of exchange back and forth. I knew something was transforming in her aggression when the dominant image in her paintings which she brought to show me changed. The old series pictured her father deep underground, knee-deep in water, and another series pictured her own face looking blankly unfocussed, though emitting despair. The new series depicted trees with roots reaching deep into the ground and branches full of light stretching into the sun. I changed into blessed silence, freed from the necessity to speak out.

Another woman grasped in an image of a huge cement block pressing on her chest the nameless sorrow that had haunted all her life. Her ego task was not to be crushed. I felt crushed by the sorrowful affect in the room and had to fight off my impulse to get out of it by coming up with remedies, or to get her to talk too soon *about* the block of sorrow – where it came from, what it meant, etc. Through the analysand's imaginative work, the stone lifted to allow her some movement underneath it. Then, next, the stone block showed itself as completely water-logged, sogged up with condensed sorrow. Her task changed, as did mine: holding my cranky impatience, it converted into sustained gazing on the stone. Her task was how to release the water, for the cement block was now a huge brick of wet yeast. How to get it to dissolve and be removed from over her chest? No imaginative solution worked. My aggression was now harnessed toward an alert attention. In response to her persistent efforts, and to the actively contemplating field between us which took all our energy to support, a dream appeared: Torrents of water were released from the heavens, a rain so hard it ran down the top of a hollow tree and gushed out the bottom. The waters so saturated the earth that trees upended, gullies swelled, rivers flooded as the overflowing water rushed back to the sea. The stone block of sorrow transformed into torrents of feeling. Our work now took all our energy to relate to this archetypal flood, some of which returned to the objective psyche, and the rest she needed to integrate into personal feeling in her life, which meant hard work in the transference field.

III. Transformation of Aggression, Primordial Level

Such an overflow at the archetypal level leads us to the psyche as objective, addressing us from outside as well as from inside ourselves. Here collective images from religion, art, culture address us in the task of transforming within the temenos of destructiveness. I think of the four women named in the New Testament as ancestors of Christ, and heralded in Judaism as heroines who secure the line to the coming Messiah (Ulanov 1993/1998). Each of them – Tamar, Rahab, Ruth, Bathsheba – are victims of destructiveness done to them. And each of them destroys the boundaries of tradition as she transforms destructiveness into fuller life for herself and her community. Tamar acts the prostitute, turning a trick on Judah who tricked her, verging on incest to forge a new temenos for Israel by giving birth to Perez, an ancestor of David's. Rahab, a whore, plays traitor to her city-state Jericho, to rescue the hundreds in her family from the invading army of Yahweh to whom she gives a whole, purifying devotion. Ruth connives with Naomi to seduce Boaz, thus releasing them from famine and exile into the safe home of Israel by bearing Obed, the grandfather of David. Bathsheba, taken in adultery and complicit in murder, figures centrally in David's transformation from ambitious king to penitent king, author of psalms.

If we endure hate in ourselves, as analysts, it takes down the persona level of being analyst and delivers us into the archetypal surround of a particular pattern of death and rebirth in each analysis. But this is still not the end. We are destroyed once again, for the temenos which holds us and enables us to discern archetypal patterns of destruction-creation, is our Jungian theory with its symbols of ego relating to Self. We need a theory to guide us in this underworld, but the theory is not immune to the force of archetypal tides. Even the temenos of our theory about the Self destroys itself.

Jung says, "The Self as the *Deus Absconditus* can undo its own symbolism for a certain purpose: When the great swing has taken an individual into the world of symbolic mysteries, nothing comes of it, nothing *can* come from it, unless it has been associated with the earth, unless it has happened when that individual was in the body.... The reason why the whole structure of symbolism is being pulled asunder is that the Self wants its own destruction as a symbolic form...." (Jung 1976, 473). We are delivered to the destruction of the temenos of our theory, of our Jungian tribe. The Self engineers its own destruction, and we are taken down still further, to a living encounter with primordial reality.

Winnicott says that destructiveness grants us not only perception of the externality of the object, but also that the excess aggression goes into unconscious imagination (1971, chapter 6). Thinking over this terse statement I understand it to mean this: our excess unconscious aggression operates like a windshield wiper, wiping away all previous accumulated perceptions, projections, ideas, so that we perceive freshly, with the eyes of a child (see Ulanov 2001, chapter 6). In Bion's terms, we do not know about but instead are one with what we experience (Bion 1965/1991, 31, 33, 162-163). Our imagination exercises bigger reign, fueled as it is by aggression to wipe aside the accumulated weight of traditions we cherish. We destroy tradition in order to find and create our own view, and we conserve tradition as the windshield against which we are pushing everything aside. Traditions hold us as we perceive the new afresh, with excitement.

Jung helps us here, because even the lynch-pin of our theory – the Self concept – desires its own destruction so that we will not escape into theorizing or drift off into the "stream

of life" becoming the "whole river" where "nothing has happened because nobody has realized it" (Jung 1976, 473). The
Self destroys itself so we will make something of reality which
addresses us, embodying it in living. In this scary place which we
hate going to because it exposes all our ego constructions as
merely that, we see with fierce clarity that no human construction, neither our own, our tribe's, our religion's, our analytical
theory's, is ultimate. All is finite, from dust, and to dust it shall
return. The clinical task now, which demands a lot of aggressive
energy to undertake, is how much lightning can we stand.

For what faces us is the radical freedom of who comes in.
Jung notes, "If you can train yourself to the point of being able
to experience psychical contents as objective, then you can
feel a psychical presence, for then you know that the psychical
contents are not things you have made ... you are not alone in
the psychical world." We can say, "'Here is the object. Here is
reality.'" We are in "... the presence of something which is not
I, yet is still psychical. Such an experience can reach a climax
where it becomes an experience of God. Even the smallest of
things of that kind has a mana quality, a divine quality" (Jung
1976, 72-73).

What I have learned from focusing on hate in the analyst
is that without it we cannot find its transformation and we
cannot arrive at the vision where even the smallest of things
participates in the largest life of the divine. This vision sustains
our analytical work over decades, because we can see in the
ridiculous complex that still plagues us the beseeching of the
divine to reach us. We can see how what appears trivial, and
therefore is hatefully scorned, in fact, is the secret doorway to
spiritual renewal (Ulanov 2002).

The theologian Paul Tillich saw Jung making room for changing symbolic interpretations of underlying archetypal structures
(Tillich 1961; see also Ulanov 1971, chapter 5). Here, I am going

even further, saying we can see changing archetypal structures (including the Self) revealing an enduring reality speaking through them. At this depth, transformation of our hate grants us double vision: to see into the unknown and to see our need to keep making it known, in picture, fable, myth, God-images, while simultaneously accepting that the beast always jumps out of the cage we have built, no matter how precious and valuable our construction.

In the depths of living encounter with reality, hate meets its opposite love, destructiveness meets its opposite creativeness, and their conjunction bequeaths certain gifts to us: focus, endurance, ruthless concentration, wonder, devotion, generosity. The ability to focus and endure seeing into the unknown translates in the humdrum work of analysis into the ability to go on with a case that appears hopeless. That endurance brings hope. That focus allows us to be ruthless in discarding the dodges, rationalizations and embroideries in a client's material to concentrate on the center, on what the Self is engineering in this person's psyche.

In the face of living encounter with archetypal patterns which we know we did not create but which arise spontaneously from the depths of the psyche, we are filled with wonder. Here we are put in touch with sources of healing beyond our invention, that instill in us attitudes of "extraordinary devotion to the work," of "serious meditation," "unusual concentration, indeed with religious fervour" (Jung 1953, para. 389).

By disidentifying with our own ego-stance, while we still hold it, we see our subjectivity more objectively, which grants the client elbow room to make a wedge between his identifications too. A certain generosity begins to circulate in the field between analysand and analyst, that springs from the analyst's own experience of being beheld as an object of attention of a greater subject (see Kradin 1999). That greater subject is the living reality encountered in fresh form. It can be terrifying; it can be amazing and exhilarating; it can be anything and everything, but for each individual analyst it will be specific and numinous and fuel the work of analysis as much as it fuels the analyst's individual life. Seeing that other source in the midst of an analysis enables a spirit of intercession to circulate in the field between analyst and analysand. We see the other in the client's self; we see the client's self in the other; and feel the other seeing both of our selves.

That living encounter with reality is what the Self is engineering us toward, I believe. How we express it amounts to the temenos we build (on the ego and archetypal levels) but no longer identify with. The image of Jazz is suggestive to me as a picture of wholeness with parts. In Jazz each part has its solo, and all together they make up the whole, including the listeners too with what they bring in response to the moment of hearing. The glorious music that can result is an audible *circulatio* of the conversation going on between ego(s) and Self in the saxophone, the piano, the horn, the listeners, in all of us all at once. Jazz is synchronistic consciousness made audible.

An example of this is a fight an analysand and I had. In a session I thought I was making a passing remark helpful to her, but instead it galvanised a series of questions to me and I began increasingly to feel dragooned into an agenda lurking under the surface. We struggled on thrusting and parrying to the end of the hour. I was stirred up and had to submit to the levels I've sketched here, exposing myself to the full heat of my affect and the destruction of the temenos of my ego position. I recognized again the archetypal pattern we had been swimming in, where she, instead of being frozen out by her well-intentioned but emotionally absent mother, had begun to squawk. We tossed the affect of anger to and fro between us, an exchange she had never had. She was braving the archetypal mother, manifest as me, who was getting dismembered, and I was squawking about it and humanising this awesome presence with my own foibles, hurts and emotional presence.

When we met again we rehearsed the whole scene. We each had our solo. And we entertained together this It between us that aroused so much aggression and hate in each of us. What makes it easier on the analytical couple is if both recognize this It pushing and shoving them, which empties out the personal complexes to see clear to the bottom of what the Self, and beyond, might be. We both had felt manoevred to the other's hidden agenda and hated being manipulated. What was this manipulating energy aiming toward, we wondered. It allowed my patient to experience fighting without annihilating or being annihilated but staying in relationship, something that never happened with her mother who would cut you off dead if you disagreed. This aggressive energy was busting up the *coniunctio* we had established in which the client had reclaimed much of her aggression for living, having chosen and succeeded in a new career. The hatefulness between us – for we were each steamed up – was aiming to unearth the piece yet to be healed to bring it within a yet-to-be-achieved temenos we were constructing.

Our destructiveness dug up the client's basic stance in reality. She believed she was destined to live in outer darkness, not needed or desired on a personal basis. She had built a much bigger life around this one piece of her new career, but the void still held her fast. The Self, so to speak, engineered us toward the archetypal patterns operating right there between us. I was reminded of the fairy tale of the two children abandoned by their mother on a cold night. The girl was so weary and felt so alone she lay down and put her head on a stone. The cold night froze her hair to the rock and she perished in the darkness. Our hatefulness could be warm affect to melt the frozen state. The analysand was reminded of the first dream in our analytical work of a man imprisoned for life, the only inmate, in utter solitary confinement, for guilt over aggression by association. Like Spier in Spandau prison, a creative architect who got caught in Hitler's machine, this dream man, contaminated by a larger aggressive field, was held in solitary loneliness, allowed to write only one letter to the outside world a year. In that first dream, the client passed by on her way to rescue a child (see chapter 13). Now, she and I entered that imprisoned aggression. Lively destructiveness, when sprung loose from hateful affect, goes on digging up what remains as obstacles.

Obstacles to what? To receiving the self-communicating reality, ever alive, new, lively, that wants to step over into concrete life and be lived by us. It wants to join with us in conversation, circulation, play. It wants to be transformed into livingness, to be incarnated into everyday terms where we know the All in the small, the Vast in the particular, the presence of the power of loving even in the face of losing the object of our love or our belief in the strength of love. This is the underground river that waters the community, and without which our *polis* runs dry and perishes through unresolved conflict.

Artists show us the most visible transformations of aggression into livingness. They take the most unimaginable horrors and make them bearable through, for example, sound. My first example is Penderecki's "Oratorio on Auschwitz." He wrote this piece in 1967; it was first performed on the grounds of the former death camp. We hear in the opening "Lamentation" how quarter tones, swelling sounds, sharp contrasts, sudden pauses and jarring bold blasts of sound transform our murderous acts into mourning that waits for the blessing of the comforter. Jung cites Spielrein who says "This tendency towards dissolution or transformation of every individual complex is the mainspring of ... every form of art" (Jung 1952, para. 201; cited by Dougherty 1998, 489).

449

The second example comes from the last symphony of Shostokovitch, the 15th, when he was dying. His music portrays the destruction of death because he did not let go when he knew he was dying. In the exuberant opening of the symphony, he humorously transforms destructive forces of the soviet military into toy soldiers come to playful life, and thumbs his nose at Stalin as well as at death. He includes briefly a Rossini melody that we will recognize from our American radio culture that signals the hero who rides to the rescue (the Lone Ranger!) to vanquish the powers of destructiveness.

My last example is from our greatest American artist, Duke Ellington. His sense of the incomplete which he understood, allowed him to suggest what goes far beyond the surface. Here he sounds the amazing harmony that results when the opposites unite instead of destroy each other. Love and hate, sensuality and spirit, make us glad to be alive just to hear "Something Sexual."

Address, National Conference Jungian Analysts, Santa Monica, California 2001; published in Journal of Jungian Theory and Practice, *Fall 2001, 3, 25-41.*

References

Bion, W. R. 1965/1991. *Transformations*. London: Karnac.

Boss, M. 1963. *Psychoanalysis and Daseinanalysis*. trans. Ludwig B. LeFebre. New York: Basic Books.

Bright, G. 1997. Synchronicity as a basic analytic attitude. *Journal of Analytical Psychology* 42, 4, 613-639.

Bromberg, P. M. 1993. Shadow and substance: a relational perspective on clinical process. *Relational Psychoanalysis, the Emergence of a Tradition*. eds. Stephen A. Mitchell and Lewis Aron. Guilford, Ct.: The Analytic Press, 1999.

Dougherty, M. 1998. Duccio's prayer. mediating destruction and creation with artists in analysis. *Journal of Analytical Psychology* 41, 4, 479-492.

Fordham, M. 1974. Defenses of the Self. *Journal of Analytical Psychology* 19, 2, 192-199.

Hopkins, L. B. 1998. D. W. Winnicott's analysis of Masud Khan: A preliminary study of failures in object usage. *Contemporary Psychoanalysis* 1998, 34, 1, 5-47; cited in *Journal of Analytical Psychology* 1999, 44, 3, 417-419.

Jung, C. G. 1907/1960. The psychology of Dementia Praecox. *Collected Works* 3. *Psychogenesis in Mental Disease*. trans. R. F. C. Hull. New York: Pantheon.

Jung, C. G. 1932. Psychotherapists or the clergy. *Collected Works* 11 *Psychology and Religion: West and East*. trans. R. F. C. Hull. New York: Pantheon 1958.

Jung, C. G. 1934. the development of the personality. *Collected Works* 17 *The Development of the Personality*. trans. R. F. C. Hull. New York: Pantheon 1954.

Jung, C. G. 1946. Psychology of the transference. *Collected Works* 16 *The Practice of Psychotherapy*. trans. R. F. C. Hull. New York· Pantheon 1954.

Jung, C. G. 1950. Concerning rebii th. *Collected Works* 9:1 *The Archetypes of the Collective Unconscious*. trans. R. F. C. Hull. New York: Pantheon 1959.

Jung, C. G. 1953. *Psychology and Alchemy*. trans. R. F. C. Hull. New York: Pantheon.

Jung, C. G. 1956. *Symbols of Transformation. Collected Works* 5. trans. R. F. C. Hull. Princeton, N.J.: Princeton University Press.

Jung, C. G. 1963. *Memories, Dreams, Reflections*. ed. Aniela Jaffé. trans. Richard and Clara Winston. New York: Pantheon.

Jung, C. G. 1976. *The Visions Seminars*. 2 books. Zurich: Spring.

Jung, C. G. 1988. *Nietzsche's Zarathustra*. 2 vols. Princeton, N.J.: Princeton University Press.

Khan, M. M. R. 1979. *Alienation in Perversions*. New York: International Universities Press.

Kradin, R. 1999. Generosity: a psychological and interpersonal motivational factor of therapeutic relevance. *Journal of Analytical Psychology* 44, 2, 221-236.

Lear, J. 1990. *Love and Its Place in Nature*. New York: Farrar, Strauss and Giroux.

Lemaitre-Sillere, L. 1998. The infant with a depressed mother: destruction and creation. *Journal of Analytical Psychology* 43, 4, 545-558.

Miller, A. 1981. *Prisoners of Childhood*. New York: Basic Books.

Mitchell, S. A. 1993. *Hope and Dread in Psychoanalysis*. New York: Basic Books.

Clinical Issues

Mitchell, S. A. and Aron, L. 1999. eds. Preface. *Relational Psychoanalysis, the Emergence of a Tradition*. Hillsdale, N.J.: The Analytic Press.

Neumann, E. 1953/1956. The psyche and the transformation of the reality planes. trans. Hildegard Nagel. *Eranos Jahrbuck XXI, Zurich: Rhein Verlag*. New York Analytical Psychology Club: *Spring*, 81-111.

Papadapoulos, R. K. 1998. Destructiveness, atrocities, and healing: epistemological and clinical reflections. *Journal of Analytical Psychology* 41, 4, 455-458.

Partridge, E. 1959. *Origins. A Short Etymological Dictionary of Modern English*. New York: MacMillan.

Redfearn, J. W. T. 1977. The Self and individuation. *Journal of Analytical Psychology* 22, 2, 125-142.

Rycroft, C. 1968. *A Critical Dictionary of Psychoanalysis*. New York: Basic Books.

Searles, H. F. 1965. *Collected Papers on Schizophrenia and Related Subjects*. New York: International Universities Press.

Searles, H. F. 1979. *Countertransference and Related Subjects*. New York: International Universities Press.

Tillich, P. 1961. Paul Tillich. *Carl Gustav Jung, A Memorial Meeting 1975-1961*. New York Association for Analytical Society.

Ulanov, A. B. 1971. *The Feminine in Jungian Psychology and in Christian Theology*. Evanston, Ill.: Northwestern University Press.

Ulanov, A. B. 1982/1996. Transference-countertransference: A Jungian perspective. Ulanov, A. B. 1996. *The Functioning Transcendent*. Wilmette, Ill.: Chiron.

Ulanov, A. B. 1993/1998. *The Female Ancestors of Christ*. Boston: Shambhala. 1998. New edition. Einsiedeln, Switzerland: Daimon.

Ulanov, A. B. 1999a. Countertransference and the Self. *Journal of Jungian Theory and Practice*. Fall, 1, 5-26 (chapter 14 of this volume).

Ulanov, A. B. 1999b. *Religion and Spirituality in Carl Jung*. Mahwah, N.J.: Paulist.

Ulanov, A. B. 2001. *Finding Space: Winnicott, God and Psychic Reality*. Louisville, Ky.: John Knox/Westminster.

Ulanov, A. B. 2002. *Attacked by Poison Ivy, A Psychological Understanding*. York Beach, Maine: Nicholas-Hayes.

Ulanov, A. B. & Ulanov, B. 1991/1999. *The Healing Imagination*. Einsiedeln, Switzerland: Daimon.

Wiener, J. 1998. Under the volcano: varieties of anger and their transformation. *Journal of Analytical Psychology* 41, 4, 493-508.

Winnicott, D. W. 1971. *Playing and Reality*. London: Tavistock.

Winnicott, D. W. 1947. Hate in the countertransference. Winnicott, D. W. 1975. *Through Paediatrics to Psycho-Analysis*. New York: Basic Books.

V. Coda

Chapter 17

After Analysis What?

I. The Question

I want to address the question, After analysis what? Not so much with our analysands; that is a separate and fascinating topic that goes off in another direction, and is of especial interest to those of us who have been practicing many decades. That topic includes such questions as, Does analysis last for the analysand? Does it affect their children? What do they value in retrospect? For example, I wrote a paper on the analyses of a father and a son (two different analyses, separated by twenty years) and the shared anima issue between them. Melanie Klein's two-and-a-half-year-old patient, now an adult, remembers her as "a dear old thing," but recalls nothing of her breast-penis vocabulary. Another of her toddler patients showed much interest in touch and texture; he grew up to work in the textile business. Then there is the terror of every analyst who is also a parent. Erikson reports a dinner conversation among friends, all of whom were analysts. A boy of six, son of one of the couples, when asked, what did he want to be when he grew up, said enthusiastically, "A patient!" Who could blame him? All the passionate fascinating talk at the table concerned these creatures called patients. And Kohut reports that the way he slowly devised his revolutionary Self Psychology, breaking with his Freudian tradition, grew from his experience of analysing young adults who were the children of his analyst colleagues and who were coming to him for their second or third analysis! The classical Freudian treatment had not reached their undernourished and hidden sense of self.

But tonight our focus falls on the analyst, a scarier topic, whether we are at the beginning of our profession, in the middle, or with many years of practice. Do we live the ego-Self axis we profess? Is our pudding containing the proof? Does our theory map a territory that really exists which we now inhabit? These are questions I hope we will discuss tonight.

I shall approach this topic gradually by mentioning first certain technical issues of great importance. Jung emphasizes the necessity of the analyst being analysed, for the good reasons with which we are all familiar:

"I stipulate that analysts ought to be analysed themselves ... If the analyst does not keep in touch with his unconscious objectively, there is no guarantee whatever that the patient will not fall into the unconscious of the analyst. You probably all know certain patients who possess a diabolical cunning in finding out the weak spot, the vulnerable place in the analyst's psyche. To that spot they attach the projections of their own unconscious ... exactly in that place where he is without defence. That is the place where he is unconscious himself and where he is apt to contamination through mutual unconsciousness" (Jung 1935/1976, para. 323; see also Jung 1948, 485, para. 1160; see also Jung 1955/1961, paras. 447, 449; see also Jung 1913/1961, para. 536; see also Jung 1914/1961, para. 586; see also Jung 1934/1964, para. 350).

Jung adds as well another necessity:

"I set it up as a self-evident requirement that a psychoanalyst must discharge his own duties to life in the proper way. If he does not, nothing can stop his unutilized libido from automatically descending on his patients and in .the end falsifying the whole analysis" (Jung 1955/1961, para. 450).

So two requirements are set before us: to be analysed and keep in touch with our unconscious objectively, and to live our own lives. It is these tasks I want to discuss in the work and life of the analyst herself and himself, ourselves.

II. Training

How we answer the questions about the ego/Self axis depends in part on our experience of training. Problems that I have seen over the years come to mind. Sometimes we conform our identity to that of the analyst we depend on, even if that analyst's typology is opposite to our own. We want, however, to find our own authentic style of being an analyst; otherwise our patients will suffer because they are getting a carbon copy, not the genuine goods. Sometimes the identification mix-up stems from idealization of the analyst and failure to analyze the persecutory underside of idealization and the fear of differentiating from the analyst on whom we depended. In effect, as trainees we want to do the work the way the admired analyst works, and fear not to do the work the way the admired analyst works. Then as trainees we fall into Cinderella's sisters' problem of trying to shoehorn our own nature into a size that does not fit and usually it is the patient who pays and then the analyst too. We are trying to be someone we are not and we fear our ownmost style is inferior. Our subsequent work in analysis must face head-on the embrace of this inferior way, or there will be no career, despite graduation into the profession.

Sometimes we discover in training that all our lives we have lived out of the wrong type or function; then we must claim our true typology or we will bear the strain of what Winnicott calls false self doing and miss true self being. We miss our own vocation.

Another example poses more grave issues. Sometimes we have been grievously wounded by the training and the wound must be healed, our confidence in our ability repaired, our zest for the work regained. Like any wound, this means working over again and again the bleeding place. It means mourning, finding one's part in it, and perceiving the part of others. One may arrive at the necessity to forgive the others and pray for the grace that will happen. One may be unable to work the wound through and get caught up in a grievance. Sometimes we hop over the wound and attack, rebelling against the theory in which we elected to be trained. Kohut remarks that trainees narcissistically wounded, whose wounds remain unaddressed, may become the revolutionaries who want to overturn the theory or the people teaching it by whom they feel betrayed. Rumor has it that Noll who published a book subverting and attacking Jung's theory was first rejected for Jungian training.

Sometimes we cannot let go of the shelter of analysis begun in training and it continues for many years after graduation. This particular analytical couple remains the locus of soul-life and replaces the real life of the graduate. Then Jung's second necessity of the analyst living her or his life fully is dodged. The soul should not have to pay for its discourse. Once found, it should be freely spent in the living of life.

The end of training does not necessarily mean the end of analysis nor of supervision, nor should it. What I want to bring out here is a possible negative effect of training on our ability to go on doing analysis (and supervision) with ourselves or with analysands. One criterion for a good outcome of training is being glad to be done with it, and really to be done. Aside from the feeling of "free at last" after years of expense, time, homework, commuting, and being evaluated, there is the deep satisfaction of having come through and being ready. A mark of being done is the gratitude for the dependence met by the training. This has been a privileged time in our lives when many people have taken deep interest in what we experience, write, think, do, in our work. They have tried to feed us food of all kinds.

The end of training also raises technical issues and it would be interesting to compare how we each solve them. How do we go on monitoring our cases when no longer in weekly supervision? Do we devise a system of our own? Do we seek periodic supervision? Do we form a group of colleagues for shared supervision? How do we go on with the Self when no longer in analysis? I am assuming for the moment that at some point analysis does end, though not necessarily when training does. Do we go back into analysis? Do we go to a different series of analysts over the years? Do we go to an analyst of another school of depth psychology? All these options I have seen done.

The elder statesmen of my time in training offered still another option which has been thoroughly challenged more recently, though it still shows some merit. They said the work with analysands offered them the process of analysis with themselves. They meant, I believe, their own complexes would get touched and necessitate working through them once again; they would learn new things, and the unconscious would be constellated for them as much as for their analysands. Surely that is true for all of us as the continuing concern with countertransference testifies, but it should not be overdone, I believe. It can lead to abuses of the analytic contract, such as sexual or power acting-out. It can stimulate overemphasis on countertransference revelations, or encourage just forgetting that the focus is the analysand's material; the analyst is drawn in by the analysand's material; it is the analysand's hour. Nonetheless, what remains of value in this point of view is the reminder that all these hours focusing on another person's psyche are hours of the analyst's life too. This is our history with each of our analysands, our life we are living too. Individuation goes on for us in the office as well as outside it.

We know soon enough we did not simply choose this profession, but landed there, as Jung puts it, "in accord with the instinctive dispositions of [our] own life" (Jung 1946, para. 365). So we recognise soon on in our training to become analysts that in addition to our conscious goals of seeking analysis for the sake of our living with proper due, and of seeking analysis as a requirement to become analysts, that we are also engaged in what Jung calls "the dialectical discussion with the unconscious [that] still continues ..." for "there is in the psyche a process that seeks its own goal independently of external factors ..." (Jung 1963, para. 4). He states that our labors

> "are directed towards that hidden as yet unmanifest 'whole' man, who is at once the greater and the future man. But the right way to wholeness is made up, unfortunately, of fateful detours and wrong turnings. It is the *longissima via*, not straight but snakelike, a path that unites opposites, reminding us of the guiding caduceus, a path whose labyrinthine twists and turns are not lacking in terrors. It is on this *longissima via* that we meet with those experiences which are said to be 'inaccessible.' Their inaccessibility really consists in the fact that they cost us an enormous amount of effort: they demand the very thing we most fear, namely the 'wholeness' we talk about so glibly and which lends itself to endless theorizing, though in actual life we give it the widest possible berth" (Jung 1963, para. 6; see also the goal the psyche seeks in analysis described in alchemical terms as Mercurius, Jung 1948/1967, para. 283).

For us, then, as persons who have become professional analysts, we are in for the long haul, indeed for the rest of our lives. The *longissima via* is our road, hence the pressing nature of the question, After Analysis What? How do we go on meeting the two requirements of giving our due to living and meeting our professional responsibility to keep our own analysis going for the decades of work before us, and behind us?

III. The Jungian Legacy

Jung stands out among other analysts by offering us two specific ways to continue the dialectical discussion between the "I" of consciousness and the "You" of the unconscious: through dreams and active imagination. These methods support in the most practical way Jung's belief in psychic reality. They provide concrete individual experience of this reality and, because the unconscious for Jung is collective and objective as well as personal, our access to the "You" connects us to our neighbor as well. Jung writes "One cannot individuate without being with other human beings ... how little you can exist without being related, without responsibilities and duties and the relation of other people to yourself." And, "Individuation is only possible with people, through people" (Jung 1988, 102, 104). And, "without the conscious acknowledgment and acceptance of our kinship with those around us there can be no synthesis of personality" (Jung 1946/1954, para. 444). Through continual dream work and active imagination, we go on processing our personal complexes and connecting with archetypal patterns that manifest through them, and experiencing the objective reality that communicates to us through the collective, arche-typal layers of the psyche.

While we go on struggling to see through the personal material of our complexes to the archetypal patterns informing them, complexes which do go on because that is a normal way the psyche operates, we also are moved out of our particular personal ego stance into living connection with other people and with what Jung calls objective psyche. With luck, we achieve a transparency of gaze or transparency of complex.

A complex can still harass us if it becomes "abnormal," overtaking the guidance of the personality by swamping the ego with undigested affect, shoving the ego out of its proper role as receptor and transmitter of Self communications (pun intended). When our ego functions in relation to Self engineering us through the complex, we arrive at that glorious discovery that our subjectivity can grow capable of becoming conscious of itself. Not only do we analyse the unconscious but we reach a place where we can tolerate, and indeed welcome as revelatory, the unconscious analysing us. There, of course, we still exist as our small subjective selves, full of our life plans, our griefs, our problems and possibilities. But we also have gained a standpoint outside this subjective sphere and can see how our subjectivity is positioned toward reality. Rightly or wrongly, this is who we are, our real self, so to speak, receiving reality that transcends us.

We suffer that larger reality as impersonal and unaware of us if we have not fashioned our own idiosyncratic ways, both individually, communally as groups, and as collective traditions we embrace, of apprehending its signals to us, its signs and wonders as the New Testament says, its communications of itself to us. Then we fear we will disappear into the Void and we experience reality as at least an insult, and at worst an assault, a betrayer, an abandoner.

If we go on improvising through our dreams and imaginings ways of communicating with this "You," we know that this reality personally addresses us through our dreams and imaginations. We know we have a connecting link to reality and that it connects to us – through a line of music, a rope bridge of thought, a tendril of green living thing, an intensity of red, or the mystical presence of primary numbers, a passionate personal relationship, or through ritual of worship, through Kabbalistic tradition or practices of meditation or prayer, through all the ways human beings fashion relationship to the transcendent. Then we experience the generosity of reality pouring out upon us, even in times of death, illness, poverty, national tragedy. Von Franz writes, "When we pay attention to our dreams, the impersonal world around us loses its meaningless arbitrariness and becomes a realm full of individual, significant, mysteriously ordered events" (von Franz 1997, 335). This is a kind of consciousness I have elsewhere called synchronistic (see chapters 13, 14).

Seeing our subjective stance toward reality changes it somewhat, though it does not wipe out our history, our body, our long years living or avoiding our gifts. But we get elbow room. We can walk around our subjectivity as if it were now a three-dimensional statue. We live in paradox, because this life is still our own, yet we are released from it somewhat – to see it, honor it, suffer it, be grateful for it. We gain this freedom often in experience of death of someone we love or know well. We honor the whole arc of their life, and see it more distinctly as it reaches now from an end back to a beginning. We honor its sum, its particularity and what has shined through of our shared human condition, and what the transcendent bequeaths to us through this our nearest neighbor. The other instructs us, even in their parting. Thus one can learn a lot from others we know and even from others in history whom we never meet in person. My husband, for example, had his life changed by loving and learning from Augustine even though he never met him in person, as much as he loved and learned from Duke Ellington with whom he traveled for a year.

Engaging our dreams and exercising active imagination offers us adjuncts to traditional spiritual practice and ground it in the body of actual personal and cultural experience. Psychic reality is also the flesh in which the Spirit incarnates. A somewhat humorous but pressing question arises here. What should we do with all the papers recording our dreams and active imagination work? Shred them? Foist them on our children, or libraries? Burn them? What if some future generation of students of the psyche decided to study these personal notes of Jungian analysts? Would it finish off Jungian depth psychology for good, as critics tried to do vis-à-vis Jung's autobiography, claiming, Ah, at last we have proof he was psychotic? In such work with the "Unknown as it intimately touches us" (Jung 1916/1958, 68) we are exerting tremendous effort to continue reconciling the opposites of animal impulse and spiritual aspiration, of individual and collective life. These routes of dreams and imagination Jung sees as ways for us to continue analysis after analysis is over.

Where do they lead us? Where do we end up? For this would be the answer to After Analysis What? The answer is more analysis now guided less (or not at all) by another analyst and more by the objective reality of the psyche addressing us through dream and active imagination. We are familiar with these methods and I need not rehearse them. Instead, I want to give examples of where they lead people in fact, not in theory, in the discharging of their duty both to live fully, and to engage in analysis of oneself, in order to go on doing analysis with and for our analysands.

They lead into ongoing conversation with this the other side, with the goal that the psyche seeks independently. And in that conversation, that other side needs to be named by us. Religions have known this necessity for centuries, but it needs to be reemphasized in depth psychology, I believe. If we are in a conversation, it cannot be with an anonymous other. We would not tolerate that in personal relationships, being called by someone with whom we are intimate, "Hey you!" or "Hey human being, or Hey Man, or Hey Woman." We would want to be addressed by name, and the more intimate the connection, the more endearing, even private, the name. We insist on something more intimate if the conversation is to continue.

With the transcendent it is the same. The other who communicates with us through the idiosyncracies of items in our dreams or active imagination sessions needs our reaching for a name, a style of acknowledgment that grows out of the ongoing exchange between us. Further, we seem to be given a name too. By the images that address us and the cumulative effect of their maneuvering us into change of mind and heart, we discover ourselves in new ways. We are not who we thought we were, or not only that.

For example, in a dream a dog is looking reproachfully at a woman the way dogs do when you are at table eating something. They come sit by your chair and look mournfully up at you, as if to say you have never fed me my whole life. You are neglecting me. In this dream, food was not the issue, so what was the reproachful look about? In the dream, the woman did not like this little dog, nor the guilt trip it laid upon her. But she distinctly felt that she was to follow the dog and as soon as the woman in active imagination got up and walked toward the dog, it lost its hangdog expression and briskly trotted off as if finally things were right; the woman was following it. The issues for this woman are not only what is this dog, and where it's leading her, but also, Who sent the dog? As yet she has no name for this invisible presence.

The names we give what addresses us anchor us in space and time. We then know we are in an exalted condition or a terror state or with mana flowing in. The names make us aware we are in conversation with our own subjectivity as well as with something objective. Otherwise, we are insane, caught in the flow of individuation, the most ruthless of our instincts (Jung 1976, v. 1, 74, v. 2, 321).

IV. Examples

The big issue after analysis, both for us in our professional groups as well as individually, is how to live simultaneously both in the here and now and the beyond of the objective psyche. I think we would agree that analysis is not problem-fixing so much as it is reorientation of attitude and stance toward psychic reality and what communicates itself through it. We often see that the problems that hounded us dissolve after they deliver us into this larger perspective. From this bigger world our complexes are redeemed. Instead of just vexatious impasses that stymie us, indeed torture us, so that we long to solve them and, failing that, to jump out of them, we see they are the *materia* through which we work out our salvation, so to speak, or through which we are worked until we glimpse the source there that heals us here. Furthermore, and I think this is the most extraordinary fact, when our complexes bring us to see what speaks through them, and we arrive at names for this presence, we will see that our very complexes figure in the naming. Our problems are truly part of our solution. I know this happens individually and will give examples of it. It is worth thinking about in terms of our professional groups because it is a distressing fact, that challenges the validity of the theory we endorse, that our Jungian groups all over the world (indeed most psychoanalytic groups) split apart. I can see how what I am saying might apply to that splitting.

In the last interview given in her life, Marie-Louise von Franz, already sick with Parkinson's disease but still able to speak about her experience of it and the meaning it laid upon her, said she thought it felled her because she got too close to a "secret of God" in her last book, *On Dreams and Death* (1986 and 1998-1999). Of course the interviewer asked her, Well! What was the secret? She laughed, refusing to tell, saying it got her into enough trouble the first time and she's not asking for more! Then, at the end of the interview she confided what preoccupied her in these her last days, who the "You" was she conversed with. A whole new archetype, she said: "Aphrodite."

Any of us who have read her books and learned from this woman know her brilliance and maidenly discipline, especially in researching fairy tales of many cultures and in researching different schools of alchemy. One imagines the great left-out piece of her life was precisely the lavish lusts and beauty, the sexual charms and urgencies of the sensual which the image of Aphrodite conjures. Thus the ending conversation with the unknown one arrives at, that confers an intimation of a final *coniunctio* of conscious and unconscious, reflects the whole arc of a person's life, still seeking to complete it.

Von Franz who analysed religious documents fashioned her own images of the transcendent in her belief that "every person has within the depth of his psyche that which he needs ... his own access to the ultimate primordial ground of his being ... to an experience of God. He has an opening at the deepest level of his psyche where something eternal can flow in ... always unpredictable and always deeply stirring whenever it happens" (von Franz 1997, 372). This encounter goes on into death, and maybe after. She thought so.

Our conversations with figures from our dreams and active imagination lead us to craft our own visions of reality which go on going on, so to speak. These intimations of reality are not fixed but they do take definite form because for reality to be real, it must enter concrete living. Take Jung, for example, or my interpretation of Jung. He struggled with the problem early on in life of where to put the bad, as evidenced in the fantasy of a giant turd smashing the cathedral. Redfearn credits both Jung's and Winnicott's lively communication of psychic reality to the fact they did not give too much of rage and love away; they both stood out as men who incorporated a lot of the Self into their ego living (Redfearn 1977). Jung came to put the bad in God, saying Yahweh was unconscious of his shadow and repented of it in his answer to Job by himself suffering in Christ on the cross. God was dark and light. Finally, at the end of his life, Jung puts the bad in us, by saying we continue God's transformation by incarnating in ourselves the *complexio oppositorum*. Through shouldering the opposites within us, and through much analysis draining our complexes of their overdetermined personal material to expose the archetypal structures giving rise to the complexes, we go on housing the opposites in ourselves which reflect the opposites in the divine, and thus serve our creator.

Jung's not sacrificing too much of Self by the ego granted him close body-felt experience of the ruthless timeless urgings of Self which will step over into concrete ego reality one way or the other. Thus Jung suffered the Self, and described it often as a defeat for the ego. Nearness of Self made him appear crazy to other clinicians, caught in the grip of the unconscious, rather than relaying it into consciousness. Jung himself complained of the same thing, saying he regretted his hurting of other people, his ruthless discarding of them. The "daimon in me" pressed him on. It brought him low with fever until he wrote out in a furious pace his response to Job, naming it as his subjective confession (Jung 1963, 194, 217, 222, 356-357).

We could say of Jung that this need for consciousness, and this reliance upon it, was both the area of his complex, and what he fashioned as the link to the transcendent, just as the passionate libido-saturated urgings of Aphrodite both eluded von Franz and yet infused her extraordinary output of work with liveliness and ardor, especially her lectures. Jung relentlessly stressed consciousness. Only with consciousness can we descend into the unconscious, repeating, as he did, the facts of our ego life like a raft to hold onto – I am a psychiatrist, I have five children, I live at etc. (Jung 1963, 181, 189).

Consciousness for Jung is first a receiving from the unconscious the full impact of tumultuous affects, then the images that bundle them into some form, and only then a knowing about what has arrived by translating affect and image into the terms of his psychological vocabulary. That is why his "system" seems so unsystematic to critics, indeed, even weird. What are we to make of his suggestion we sit down with our anima, even nail her down, to learn what her world is like in contrast to our own?

Consciousness was all in all to Jung – it saved him from his complexes, guided him through them and became his way of serving God. It was his God-image in a sense, for our spiritual practice or devotion, as he saw it, is to help God become more conscious by our carrying the struggles of opposites we spy there, in the transcendent, in the here of our own lives. The whole arc of Jung's life – his struggle with aggression, his fascination with religion, his discovery of the depth unconscious – is summed up in his vision of how to give our proper due to living. We serve God by wrestling with our own problems which in fact may be God's problems (Jung 1963, 333-334, 338).

Jung's vision of reality and how we are to serve it stir admiration and wonder in response, and embolden us to fashion our own visions. I do not think we can appropriate another person's discovery, because we have not trod his *longissima via*. We trod our own, and it is from our own that our vision of ultimate reality must grow. That is the wholeness we seek, and it includes our most private and humiliating complexes and transcends them. If we do not continue to work on our own inner creative task, but for example, try to substitute someone else's, even Jung's, we will deteriorate as analysts, at the expense of our patients, and not give our just due to life with others.

As a third small example of the work with dreams and active imaginations, moving from the sublime to the ridiculous, I would mention an experience of self-analysis which amazed me that I have written about elsewhere (see Ulanov 2001). For every year of my life from about the age of five onwards, I have succumbed to poison ivy, sometimes ferocious bouts, sometimes small ones. One of the worst attacks occurred in 1988 and I needed to warn my analysands, lest they were allergic, or, if not, and came for sessions, that my troll-like appearance was due only to this vexatious allergy. One analysand, who had worked in analysis some time and had seen my smaller attacks in previous years, voiced a question which changed my life dramatically: Had I ever asked why I got poison ivy every year? Stunned, I realized that No, I hadn't, nor had any analyst or doctor with whom I had worked.

I began then what resulted in a ten-year inquiry, treating this contact allergy as if it were psychosomatic. Very little is written about any cure for poison ivy. In effect, there are none because it is classified as a contact allergy; thus avoid contact if you do not want to catch it. Nothing is written about poison ivy as psychosomatic. Nonetheless, that was the tack I took in my brooding over it and imagining about it: what meaning was making itself, indeed repeating itself in this annual breakout, this blooming of the ivy? I began to dream of the affliction which I had not remembered ever doing before. Active imagination gradually engaged the suffering the body expressed through the allergy.

The truly amazing result, one that still inspires wonder, is once I searched for psyche in soma, I did not get poison ivy again. The attacks that recurred every year stopped! The conditions of exposure were the same, no extra precautions were taken, no new medicines. Nothing different happened except the inquiry into the psyche's role in the physical suffering. A complex had been enacted in and on my body; the psyche used a physical susceptibility for purposes of its own, for "its own goal independently of external factors" (Jung 1963, para. 4). When I dragged into conscious experience all that the ivy attacks symbolised through the soma, the body was relieved of carrying this burden. And though embarrassed by the disgusting nature of the affliction, I felt constrained to write about it to speak to the other members of the Ivy League. The publisher who finally took the manuscript said it was weird, but I mentioned that the American Academy of Dermatology reports that in the United States alone, ten to fifteen percent of the population, that is twenty to forty million people are felled by this allergy every year! (Ulanov 2001, 32). One's struggle with individuation affects other people too, and reminds us of our kinship with our neighbors. And theirs with us.

The author Jean Rhys gives another example. In a final interview in her life, she expresses clearly how each person's struggle to do their creative work contributes to the whole. We know that clearly about Jung, as here we all are, a group because of his theories, creating and finding our own professions because of the theories issuing from his own struggles. It is not always so obvious about the less famous. Jean Rhys said to her biographer, David Plaute:

> Listen to me, I want to tell you something very important. All of writing is a huge lake. There are great rivers that feed the lake, like Tolstoy and Dostoevsky. And there are trickles, like Jean Rhys. All that matters is feeding the lake. I don't matter. The lake matters. You must keep feeding the lake. It is very important (Rhys).

Coda

The answer, then, to the question After Analysis What? consists in going on through dreams and active imagination with the conversation between the "I" and the "You" in the very specific terms of each of our own visions of the greater whole of reality. We contribute to the whole by working out those visions, articulating them, naming them, and living out of them. Thus, I believe, it is not we who become individually whole, as a good many of our complexes keep us wrestling with them until the very end of our lives. Our wrestling becomes more supple, and we are caught less fully in the complexes and we know more about what catches us. But it is not we who become whole. There is wholeness and we become aware of how we are parts of this greater whole reality – of shared existence with others, with animate and inanimate life on our planet, with the cosmos. Our way to know about this greater wholeness proceeds through our particular and personal visions of reality, which could also be called God-images, and of which traditions we adhere to, in which communities and tribes we call home.

To do that fashioning of visions we need intense concentration, a kind of devotion to the conversation, and alert observation of the moments we are particularly conscious of the unconscious. We need what Jung calls *pistis*, a trustful confiding of self to the experience of the numinous (Jung 1937/1958, para. 9). Not only are we fed by the deep springs of the psyche, but, as Jean Rhys says, we feed them. Our attention to our personal struggles and whatever we come to believe engineers them also feeds the underground psyche. What the alchemists called the operation of *cibatio* goes in two directions; we are fed and we also do the feeding; we contribute in (see chapter 14). How do we do this? By continuing to project our libido and affect onto reality, onto the "You" who addresses us.

We are familiar with projection as a phenomenon of something unconscious making its way into consciousness by break-

472

ing up our state of archaic identity with the object who usually squawks at being so projected upon. We are familiar with projection as a defensive operation to get rid of an emotional conflict or content that is painful to our egos. We are familiar with the need to differentiate the object from our projection and withdraw the libido from the object back into our own psyche and to examine there our relation to this psychic content. Some piece of that projection can often be assimilated into our ego functioning. The rest of the energy contained in the projection falls back into the unconscious to stir up deeper levels of the constellated archetype.

It is this last function of projection – to stir up the depths and to make its way to consciousness – that gets enlisted into the visions of reality we put forth. These visions – Jung's of the incarnated conflicting opposites, von Franz's of Aphrodite, Jean Rhys of the little trickles into the big lake – are pictures of the greater whole to which the individual belongs. Except that after analysis, we know perfectly well these visions are inadequate to capture the whole. So we live paradoxically – both believing them and committed to them while simultaneously seeing through them as unable to capture the infinite.

We live in those two modes, which reflect the two participants in the conversation between "I" and "You." Our projections into the visions make the conversation possible for our tiny egos with the other side. And the other side seems to need our ego responses and pictures in order to be heard, received, touched by us, even if incompletely. It is as if we are trying to construct a bridge that reflects a bridge already complete. Magritte's painting "Heraclitus Bridge" depicts what I mean. Our constructions of reality, both individually and communally (including political, social, scientific and aesthetic and religious visions) show our best efforts and constantly undergo destruction and reconstruction.

473

Jung sums up the attitude needed from our side, as an "extraordinary devotion to the work ... 'serious meditation' ... 'unusual concentration, indeed with religious fervor'" (Jung 1963, para. 389). The theologian-philosopher Nicolas Berdyaev sums up the other side, in his particular vision of the core of reality: "freedom is more primary than being ... it is bottomless and without foundation ..." "Spirit is freedom ... a creative act which is effected in depth ..." (Berdyaev 1953, 68-69, 74).

The question facing us after analysis is how to encompass different individual and group ways, and be planted in our own, committed with heart as well as mind, yet receptive to those of others. The answer, I believe, has less to do with matching up parts of one's own theory to corresponding parts in another's theory, and more to do with noticing the direction of invitation,. We find unity in our looking to the same origin point, in our struggling to concentrate upon it, and not veer off. We share together the labor of forging a bridge to the origin point which is also the end point and to survive and sustain its bridges to us, really to recognize them. Mystical experience demands a lot of aggression.

Paper to New York Association of Analytical Psychology, 2001.

References

Jung, C. G. 1913/1961. General aspects of psychoanalysis. *Collected Works 4, Freud and Psychoanalysis*. New York: Pantheon.

Jung, C. G. 1914/1961. Some crucial points in psychoanalysis: a correspondence between Dr. Jung and Dr. Löy. *CW 4*.

Jung, C. G. 1916/1958/1960. The transcendent function. *Collected Works 8, The Structure and Dynamics of the Psyche*. trans. R. F. C. Hull. New York: Pantheon.

Jung, C. G. 1934/1964. The state of psychotherapy today. *Collected Works*. 10, *Civilisation in Transition*. trans. R. F. C. Hull. New York: Pantheon.

Jung, C. G. 1935/1976. The Tavistock lectures. *Collected Works* 18, *The Symbolic Life*. trans. R. F. C. Hull, Princeton, N.J.: Princeton University Press.

Jung, C. G. 1937/1958. Psychology and religion. *Collected Works*. 11, *Psychology and Religion: West and East*. trans. R. F. C. Hull. New York: Pantheon.

Jung, C. G. 1946/1954. Psychology of the transference. *The Practice of Psychotherapy*. *Collected Works* vol. 16. trans. R. F. C. Hull. New York: Pantheon.

Jung, C. G. 1948/1967. The Spirit Mercurius. *Collected Works* 13, *Alchemical Studies*. trans. R. F. C. Hull. Princeton, N.J.: Princeton University Press.

Jung, C. G. 1948/1976. Depth psychology. *Collected Works* 18.

Jung, C. G. 1955/1961. The theory of psychoanalysis. *Collected Works* 4.

Jung, C. G. 1963. *Psychology and Alchemy*. *Collected Works* 12. trans. R. F. C. Hull. New York: Pantheon.

Jung, C. G. 1963. *Memories, Dreams, Reflections*. ed. Aniela Jaffé. trans Richard and Clara Winston. New York: Pantheon.

Jung, C. G. 1973 and 1975. *Letters*. 2 vols. ed. G. Adler, A. Jaffé. trans,. R. F. C. Hull. Princeton, N.J.: Princeton University Press.

Jung, C. G. 1976. *The Vision Seminars*. 2 vols. New York: Spring Publications.

Jung, C. G. 1988. *Nietzsche's Zarathustra*. 2 vols. ed. James L. Jarrett. Princeton, N.J.: Princeton University Press.

Berdyaev, N. 1953. *Truth and Revelation*. trans. R. M. French. London: Geoffrey Bles.

Redfearn, J. W. T. 1977. The Self and individuation. *Journal of Analytical Psychology*, 22, 2, 125-142.

Rhys, J. 19?? New York Times Sunday Review of Books.

Ulanov, A. B. 2001. *Attacked by Poison Ivy: A Psychological Understanding*. York Beach, Maine: Nicholas-Hayes.

von Franz, M.-L. 1986. *On Dreams and Death*. Boston: Shambhala.

von Franz, M.-L. 1997. *Archetypal Patterns of the Psyche*. Boston: Shambhala.

von Franz, M.-L. 1998-99. Conversation between Marie-Louise von Franz and Suzanne Wagner, *Psychological Perspectives* 38, Winter, 12-39.

Picturing God

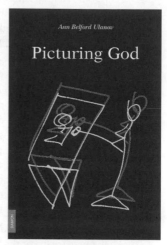

Ann Belford Ulanov submits that we have all painted our own pictures of God. Most were formed in early childhood and now lie buried in our unconscious selves. Even though we may be unaware of our images of God, they play an active, sometimes harmful role in our spiritual development.

Picturing God demonstrates the importance of confronting our unconscious selves and allowing our images of God – both positive and negative – to surface. Such inner exploration reveals not only relevant insights about ourselves, but also pulls us beyond our private pictures of God toward a truer view of the living God. *Picturing God* shows us how to explore our unconscious selves and how this spiritual exercise can change the whole of our lives: how we respond to God, how we relate to others, and how we view ourselves.
(208 pages, ISBN 3-85630-616-1)

Receiving Woman

We live in a time of unparalleled opportunity for women and a time, just because of that opportunity, of great stress. It is a time when every woman can find her own particular style, to develop her skills, to acknowledge her needs and failures, and to claim both her satisfactions and dissatisfactions. The old stereotypes are all but dead. But another danger threatens; of new stereotyped roles for women in the very range of choices and opportunities presented to the.

"*Receiving Woman* grew out of a decade of reflections on women's experiences – my own, my patients', and my students'," writes Professor Ulanov. "From all of them, a common voice emerged speaking about each woman's struggle to receive all of herself. Each was trying to find and put together different parts of herself into a whole that was personal, alive, and real to her and to others. I know that women want to be all of themselves and want to be their own selves, not examples of types. They want to work out their own individual combinations of what have been called the masculine and feminine parts of themselves. This book focuses on that possibility, on women receiving themselves, all of themselves, wisely and gladly."
(190 pages, ISBN 3-85630-606-4)

Sandplay Therapy:
Treatment of Psychopatologies

Eva Pattis Zoja (Ed.)

Ten Jungian sandplay therapists describe how severe psychopathologies can be treated in the 'free and protected space' of the sandbox.

The sandplay therapy cases in this book illustrate some of the most difficult, yet also most effective applications: psychoses, borderline syndromes, psychosomatic illnesses, drug addictions, or narcissistic character disorders.

Sandplay seems to access areas of human suffering which have otherwise always resisted psychotherapeutic treatment.

Recent research in neuroscience explains why this is possible: trauma is not remembered in verbal form – what has never been articulated in words nor ever 'shaped' cannot be outwardly expressed. In sandplay, however, 'it' manifests itself as a form, shaped by the hands.

The inexpressible can be seen and touched – therefore, it can be transformed. (272 pages, illustrated, ISBN 3-85630-622-6)

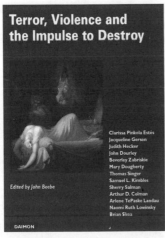

Terror, Violence and the Impulse to Destroy

John Beebe (Ed.)

Papers from the North American Conference of Jungian Analysts

These papers address the process of terror as it confronts us in international situations and in outbreaks of violence in homes and schools. The thirteen contributors, seasoned Jungian analysts and psychotherapists, have often faced the reality of undermining destructiveness in their work with clients. Here they offer their theoretical and therapeutic insights, drawing from their experience of the psyche's healing resources to identify the consciousness we need if we are to survive and reverse the contagion of hostility.

(410 pages, illustrated, ISBN 3-85630-628-5)